GW00382312

THE TRIUMPH OF IGNORANCE AND BLISS

THE **TRIUMPH** OF **IGNORANCE** AND **BLISS**

Pathologies Of Public America

James Polk

Montreal/New York/London

Black Rose Books No. LL362

National Library of Canada Cataloguing in Publication Data

Polk, James

The triumph of ignorance and bliss : pathologies of public America / James Polk

Includes bibliographical references and index.

ISBN 978-1-55164-315-1 (bound) ISBN 978-1-55164-314-4 (pbk.)

1. United States--Civilization--1970. 2. United States--Intellectual life--21st century. 3. Popular culture--United States--History--21st century. 4. United States--Social conditions--1980-. 5. United States--Politics and government--2001-. I. Title.

E895.P64 2008   973.931   C2008-902982-8

Cover images from Wikimedia Commons

C.P. 1258	2250 Military Road	99 Wallis Road
Succ. Place du Parc	Tonawanda, NY	London, E9 5LN
Montréal, H2X 4A7	14150	England
Canada	USA	UK

To order books:
In Canada: (phone) 1-800-565-9523 (fax) 1-800-221-9985
email: utpbooks@utpress.utoronto.ca

In the United States: (phone) 1-800-283-3572 (fax) 1-800-351-5073

In the UK & Europe: (phone) 44 (0)20 8986-4854 (fax) 44 (0)20 8533-5821
email: order@centralbooks.com

Our Web Site address: http://www.blackrosebooks.net

Printed in Canada

Contents

For my mother.

Preface

THERE IS SOMETHING PROFOUNDLY perverted about a mindset that throws collective fits at the sight of a woman's nipples while sheepishly accepting the mutilation and slaughter of its sons and daughters for reasons deliberately contrived. Adding insult to injury, where engaged public discourse should channel effective dissent, there is ignorance; where public outrage should ignite corrective action to oppose the status quo, there is bliss. *The Triumph of Ignorance and Bliss: Pathologies of Public America* examines the foundations of a culture that favors "bring-'em-on" firepower over diplomacy, passions from the pulpit over rational critique, and the star appeal of media idols over the struggle with real problems.

Under the banner of neo-liberal economic policies, America's conservative-corporate power apparatus has unleashed forces unprecedented in their ability to stymie dissent, thwart potential counteraction, and dismantle the public sphere. State-sponsored spins on reality not only dispel critique, but also rob potential opposition of even the appropriate language with which the instruments of dissent might be carried to and used by society's growing number of victims. While employees struggle to stave off the permanent effects of Wal-Mart practices and a seemingly inexhaustible supply of cheap labor in and from developing societies, those most affected by an unmitigated redistribution of wealth and by the destruction of the natural environment are blinded by the relentless pursuit of fun, games, and firmer abs.

Preoccupied with irresistibly snazzy marketing images, sports icons, and the sex appeal of the weekly *People* persona, few Americans care about the class war being lost around them, or about the disastrous long-term consequences of their actions. Instead of storming the Bastille in response to the most terrifying government/industry-induced changes in living memory, the people placidly continued with business and niceties as usual.

As we are largely ignorant of our Selves as specific moments within the history of ideas and the continuum of struggles for power and influence, the themes of the following chapters may at first appear disparate. We must not forget, however, as Marx reminded us in the *18th Brumaire of Louis Bonaparte*, that "the tradition of all dead generations weighs like a nightmare on the brains of the living." The symptoms highlighted in these mere slices of everyday American life find their unity in modernity's own promises and shortcomings. For those willing occasionally to step back, the historical structures and tendencies that have shaped our world become most visible in the mundane itself.

Peering beneath the surface is not easy. The deafening din of consumption-driven immediacy has filled our minds with grotesquely misplaced priorities held in unworthy reverence and blinded us to the most urgent cosmopolitan issues defining our era. Encrusted ruts of perception present a formidable barrier to those still seeking a better world. As Theodor W. Adorno so aptly put it in *Minima Moralia*, "the value of a thought is measured by its distance from the continuity of the familiar. It is objectively devalued as this distance is reduced; the more it approximates to the preexisting standard, the further its antithetical function is diminished, and only in this, in its manifest relation to its opposite, not in its isolated existence, are the claims of thought founded." With neither the appearance of completeness nor claims of methodological stringency, the following narratives may, it is hoped, help to break open the surface of our fossilized constructs and to widen the opening for greater opposition to the status quo.

Just as people are judged by the company they keep, civilizations and their eras are assessed in terms of the dominant motifs that shape public interest and the ideas that capture the essence of daily life. As an exploration of the quotidian, the present study takes to task a lifestyle that has catapulted the mundane and banal to undeserving levels of importance while acquiescing to policies inimical both to working people and to the only life-sustaining environment we have.

James Polk, June 2008

Chapter 1

Nowhere In Suburbia

IF YOU'VE EVER DOUBTED THE CAPACITY of places to affect your physical and emotional well-being, spend a couple of months in the intensive care unit of a major county hospital, preferably one stripped to barebones buckets and bedpans, courtesy of your local "compassionate" conservatives. Or get a job that binds you to ten winters straight in some godforsaken rain magnet north of the 50th parallel, where residents have to take pictures of the sun when it does come out, just to remember what it looks like when it doesn't (most of the time). Still not convinced? Join the bunks of the hardcore playmates at a high-security lockdown. You'll learn fast.

Once-inhabited places are never able to rid themselves entirely of the human events, joys, and sorrows that haunt them. For those of us blessed with wonderful childhoods cloaked in warmth and bathed in the security of our mother's love, an eventual return to the cradle may awaken a magical Peter-Pan wish that "the future" should never have happened. The less fortunate return to places that have hosted their experiences and witnessed the agony of their despair with déjà vu, as if the past, canned in place, were stealing away their hard-fought victories and denying them the reality of escape.

Humans share with a host of other living beings the pronounced need to find a suitable harbor of safety in which to rest, play, and nurture the families they acquire. For most of the non-nomadic among us, that place is home, one of the most precious and enduring concepts in the trove of ideas dear to our hearts. The very thought of being homeless in a cold, hostile world of indifferent strangers induces panic; being forcibly torn away from the nest of security created by the permanence of our loved ones is heart-wrenching. Just "Over the Rainbow" is the magical assurance indelibly etched into our minds by the immortal Judy Garland that *there's no place like home*. Most of us long for stable roots, for a home where the heart is, be it a fifty-room mansion or a one-room shack. In fact, so much of who we are and what we become depends on the places we come home to. Being spared the complete annihilation of place as a context for life is truly an immeasurable blessing rarely acknowledged. Rwanda and Darfur are thankfully the exceptions rather than the rule even among the impoverished nations of Africa.

The history of homes is a by-line in the narrative of civilization itself, with newer chronicles recording dwellings in a wide array of places, shapes, and sizes. Dating back to the Roman republic, the wealthy often had country estates as retreats for a summer *villeggiatura* on the outskirts of the city. In Rome itself, or *urbs* as the Latin speakers called the quintessential city, society's less fortunate typically inhabited the low-lying areas below the seven hills constituting the city proper, hence the subsequent medieval term *sub-urbs*. Roman nobles, in contrast, sought escape from the daily grind in the likes of the palatial settings of Tusculum, about fifteen miles southeast of the city, where Cicero had a home; Antium, a favorite resort to many of the city's upper class; or in Tivoli, home of emperor Hadrian's Villa Aelia Tiburtina and today's papal summer palace. Pliny the Younger maintained an elaborate villa at Laurentinum, replete with spectacular vistas, ornate gardens, and spa-like features to satisfy the physical pleasures.[1] In the Middle Ages, for land-bound serfs prohibited by possessive feudal lords from taking up residence within the fortified walls of the city lest they obtain their freedom ("Stadtluft macht frei!"—"city air liberates"), suburbs were often camps of barter that served as portals to a better life. Both as asylums of leisure for the wealthy and as marketplaces for the poor, suburbs are as old as the layers of material on which civilizations are built.[2]

Roots in Romanticism

The positive motives for the American mass movement into suburbia are rooted in Romanticism with its emphasis on a peaceful, idyllic environment in the midst of nature and an almost naïve notion of human love as a marriage of unwavering trust and undying attraction. Romanticism's early critique of the Enlightenment, itself an echo of Rousseau's insistence that city life had led to our collective undoing, laid the groundwork for such movements as transcendentalism, which stressed the human need to find the way back to a primordial unity with Nature. Anti-classicist at heart, Romanticism was in part a reaction against the dominance of rationalism and the implementation of the scientific method that had explained away the nature of the human psyche as a calculable response to the environment's impressions or input on an originally pristine slate or *tabula rasa*.

In late eighteenth-century Germany, authors and playwrights of the *Sturm und Drang* sought to liberate from the strictures of no-nonsense rationalism the forgotten other side of human nature by exposing the public to issues of human sensuality, passion, and the individual's role in controlling destiny. Creative curiosity was also aroused by the exploration of new frontiers and reports of the natural, untouched habitats of Dryden's noble savage, projected as the epitome of harmony and authentic content. Similar motifs form the foundation of William Blake's *Songs of Innocence* and *Songs of Experience*. Central to the romanticist rebellion was the shift in focus onto the Self, its alienation from Nature, and the inner conflict between the dictates of accepted behavioral systems and the forms of passion crying out for fulfillment in the bourgeois subject now at liberty to think and dream of untold forms of self-expression. Torn in the ontological difference between the facticity of developing bourgeois society and unfettered visions of what could be, the individual subject was trapped in what E.T.A. Hoffman defined as the essence of Romanticism: *infinite longing*.

The era interpreted nature itself in terms of this longing; the elements of the pastoral landscape portrayed in a complex dialectic of prose and lyrical reflection the spectrum of human emotions and the insatiable urge to find fulfillment. A deep sense of melancholy surrounds much of the poetry, prose, and art of the era. Writers and painters lamented the fading opportunities of time that vanished each day in the light of the evening sun; they mourned the loss of vigor and youth in the autumnal twilight of life. Such is the unspoken subtext in J. W. Waterhouse's *The Awakening of Adonis*. Prostrate in a lush idyllic garden, handsome Adonis is kissed awake by a scantly-clad, rosy-cheeked maiden of exceptional beauty as two children of cherubic innocence welcome the tacit promise of eternal youth. The sweeping vistas and warm pastels of John Robert Cozens's *Distant View of Windsor Castle from the South West* resemble the answer to all of Dorothy's problems when she first glimpses Emerald City before falling asleep in the poppy fields.

Sublimely reflected in the captivating light canvassed by Caspar David Friedrich are many of Romanticism's key components: a spiritual transcendence of the material realm (*The Cross on the Mountain* (1812?)); a quiet, enigmatic solitude in harmonious but mysterious unity with Nature (*Woman in the Morning Light*

(1818), *Wanderer above the Sea of Fog* (1818), *Owl on a Tombstone* (1836), *Coffin by Graveside* (unknown date)); and the benevolent serenity of Nature herself (*Meadows near Greifswald* (1820), *Landscape on the Rugen near Putbus* (1824)). Embodying in David d'Angers's words the "tragedy of landscape," these images haunt us through their engagement of our innermost longings. At their best, Friedrich's paintings incorporate a manifold of Protestant emotions—the lilting sorrow of the opening movement of Brahms's Fourth; the inescapable solitude and celestial transcendence of "Wir setzen uns mit Thränen nieder" in Bach's glorious *St. Matthew's Passion*; the bleeding pathos of mortality in *Tristan und Isolde*'s "Liebestod" ("Mild und Leise").

In the United States, the romantic content of ceaseless yearning was beautifully depicted in much of the work of the Hudson River School. Here, too, is the promise of fulfillment that evokes in the observer the conviction that *All would be well if I could just step into the panoramic tranquility* of Thomas Chambers's *Hudson Valley, Sunset* with its inviting village cradled in the warmth of alpenglow. Asher B. Durand's magically luminescent *Summer Afternoon* lures with the glimpses of a world at peace and the hope of a better tomorrow just beyond the golden hues. *The Beeches* (1845) leads the viewer into the simplistic friendliness of a winding country road behind a flock of sheep heading back home at sunset. Barely visible in the distance, a lone white church steeple beckons with the comfort of spiritual harmony and good will.

As if pre-ordained in an elaborate, divine interpretation scheme of perfect harmony, the varied patterns of landscape wait to fulfill their purpose of providing

> In winds, and trees, and streams,
> and all things common,
> In music, and the sweet unconscious tone
> Of animals, and voices which are human,
> Meant to express some feelings of their own... .
> —Percy Bysshe Shelley, *The Zucca*, 1882

The reflection on passion recurs in countless melancholic lines of the era's great poets and storytellers. Shelley's homage to love ("one word...too often profaned") in the metaphors of

> The desire of the moth for the star,
> Of the night for the morrow,
> The devotion to something afar
> From the sphere of our sorrow.
> —*The Desire of the Moth*

testifies to the same infinite longing for fulfillment in that which, in the words of Ernst Bloch, is forever *noch nicht* (not yet), just over the horizon, bathed in the promise of golden light and a long-awaited arrival at home, the ultimate metaphorical destination. Romanticism's obsessions fell on fertile ground in the United States in the work of such writers as William Cullen Bryant, Nathaniel Hawthorne, Emily Dickinson, Walt Whitman, Ralph Waldo Emerson, and Henry David Thoreau. Bryant's *Thanatopsis* (literally "view of death") provides the intended reader ("…to him who in the love of Nature holds communion with her visible forms …") with a description of death as transfiguration with the totality of life and the natural world, a "mighty sepulchre." Bryant's lyrics address the recurring themes of solitude, the human necessity of coming to terms with mortality, and an undying yearning for fulfillment in harmony with all that is embodied in the magnificence of Nature.

These themes became core concerns for writers of the transcendentalist movement. Eclectic in its choice of sources, the group embraced many of the same goals of those who would later become epithetically known as "Massachusetts liberals." Persistent among all members of the movement was the conviction that urbanization and the materialistic, business-oriented lifestyle had alienated human beings from Nature as the source and end of life. Once again, the seasons and the winds; trees and flowers; birds and bees; the sun, moon, stars, and planets; hills, streams, and the human individual, became pertinent themes permeating both prose and painted landscape. These issues were perhaps nowhere more poignantly addressed than in the work of Henry David Thoreau—critic of the alienation from Nature generated in the citified ideals of industrial society; rabble-rouser against narrow-minded conformism; prosecutor of materialism and the business class; defender of the universal *vita contemplationis*. Though not especially well received in its initial printing, Thoreau's *Walden* laid out in highly readable form the author's ideas of the good life, and in subsequent reprints succeeded in influencing generations of thinkers who listened to "a different drummer." True to his Rousseauist nature, Thoreau used the insights he gained during his extended camping trip tucked away in the woods at Walden Pond to hammer home his message "proclaiming culture the whore and nature the virgin,"[3] challenging received notions of the human condition and its disturbed relation to the natural world.

Throughout the romantic era, the virgin landscape promised unity with Otherness and resolution of discord in one final Hegelian/Wagnerian moment of the

Absolute. In art, literature, and music, Romanticism succeeded in bringing to life the magnificence of the natural world and in liberating a previously unrecognized pathos and will to power in the human psyche. Where there was neither life nor sentiment, Romanticism filled the void with projected human dreams. And the end of the line for ceaseless longing, the answer to all desiderata was that one place where permanent love, always requited, does not err, stray, or betray; where, as Ernst Bloch aptly put it, "no one has ever been"—*home*.

Little wonder then that those able to ultimately kissed the claustrophobic world of the inner cities good-bye and answered the siren's call to Arcadia.

Moving Out

Romanticism's influence in the United States has perhaps been deeper and more permanent than it has been in Europe. With leaves in the plentiful forests beckoning with rustic bliss and an expanse of sunlit glens offering up cool fresh water in its natural purity, the pull of the countryside became an overpowering hit among those who had known nothing but city sidewalks. Although France also shared much of the enthusiasm for forests and the natural landscape (one is reminded of the astonishing achievements of the Barbizon painters, and of the national status once enjoyed by the country's quintessential Wandervogel and first marketer of touristic getaways,[4] Claude Francois Denecourt, *le Sylvain*), it was the English and Americans who immediately saw pastoral sublimity as a place worthy of residence. Urban development and suburban expansion were mutually linked to innovations in public transportation. The first measurable wave beyond many traditional city boundaries was carried by the introduction of omnibus coaches in France in 1828. The success of this efficient and inexpensive means of public transport led to its expansion in many other cities in Europe and North America. When steam engines eventually replaced horses, steel rails soon stretched across the landscape to link once distant dots on the map in a smooth, effortless journey that required a couple of hours as opposed to days. The outward drive had begun, and by the mid-1850s an onslaught of country estates was rapidly replacing pastures and forests with sky-rocketing property values.[5] Although the original stigma attached to the suburbs as unsophisticated outposts of the uncouth had by no means vanished, the mere fact that regions in the wild, just hours away from urban centers of activity, had become attractive to society's upper classes quickly changed perceptions. For those of modest means—the vast majority of the population—the choices were clear: move into the country and become a farmer (what else was there to do?), or stay in the city and stick it out to the bitter end. Even with increased access between the city and local outback, the cost of a round-trip daily commute would have been prohibitively expensive, consuming a substantial portion of a working family's income.[6]

One notable exception was Brooklyn Heights. Consisting predominantly of farms until the early 1800s, the land across the river from Manhattan became accessible by daily steam ferry in 1814. According to an 1815 issue of the *Brooklyn Star*, the town was destined "to become a favorite residence for gentlemen of taste and fortune, for merchants and shopkeepers of every description, for artists, artisans, merchants, laborers, and persons of every trade in society."[7] The trip itself quickly became a mundane routine in which hordes of commuters lined up each morning for the ride over to Manhattan to begin their workday; evenings witnessed the procedure in reverse. The novelty of the daily spectacle prompted Walt Whitman in "Crossing Brooklyn Ferry" to comment on the beauty of the experience:

> Gorgeous clouds of the sunset! drench with your splendor me,
>   or the men or women generations after me!
> Cross from shore to shore, countless crowds of passengers!
> Stand up, tall masts of Manhattan! stand up,
>   beautiful hills of Brooklyn!

With affordable housing and room to expand, Brooklyn offered masses of commuters a viable alternative residence just a pleasant boat ride away from the centers of trade and finance. Accordingly, Brooklyn's population grew by more than 500,000 in just fifty years. Large numbers of these were newly arrived immigrants with limited English skills. As Kenneth T. Jackson has noted, the very things that had made Brooklyn attractive as a place of residence had vanished by the end of the nineteenth century as the city began to look more like Manhattan: noisy, grimy, and congested.[8]

Other suburban upstarts were much less heterogeneous in their socio-economic and ethnic makeup. Since most of these communities were strung out like "beads" on a necklace (to use Jackson's metaphor) along railway lines, the time and money involved in the commute automatically precluded all but the wealthiest members of society from putting down roots in rural sublimity. But money was there, and with the *zeitgeist* riding high in the saddle of Romanticism, the upper crust conquered the rural landscapes in safe smelling distance from America's larger cities. They erected vast villas with enormous lawns, golf courses, and the ever-trendy country club in dozens of tony regions: Lake Forest, outside Chicago;

Mount Vernon, New Rochelle, and Scarsdale in Westchester County (home to the famous big-shot hangout, the Westchester Country Club); Chestnut Hill, a suburb of Boston, to name only a few. In a number of such cozy gilded corners, socioeconomic stratification resembled the harsh realities one finds in many developing nations, with a distinctly dominant upper class pulling all the strings, a substantial population segment fulfilling the roles of paid slaves, and not much in between. As with the growing numbers of illegal immigrants today, the lower castes fulfilled important tasks determined by the silk-pajama crowd, but were basically stuck in a financial rut with few nice exits. In Europe, too, well-heeled nobles took to imitating classic architecture to create the appropriate ambience for the gardens surrounding their own villas. The same pattern was repeated in many other metropolises continent-wide with such prominent secludes as Saint Germain-en-Laye and the Bois de Boulogne outside Paris offering the landed classes a valued reprise from the congestion of city life.[9]

It wasn't until the end of the nineteenth century, however, that entire communities of peaceful little houses for everyone, surrounded by lush gardens and meadows, became a promoted public vision.[10] The idea was as charming as it was simple: take the conveniences and opportunities offered in the large cities; get rid of the congestion, pollution, poverty and filth; use a sensible design and solid, readily-available construction materials; pick a size of land big enough to accommodate thirty thousand, and you've got the basic starter kit for a garden city. This "perfect marriage" of rural serenity with the opportunities and technical niceties found in the cities was the leitmotiv that led to the construction of one of the first real garden cities, Letchworth, in Hertfordshire, England, as a prototype for future development.[11] Predating even Letchworth was the original "garden city" suburban community, Llewellyn Park, New Jersey, designed by Llewellyn S. Haskell and Alexander Jackson Davis. Founded on the spirit of individualism, the idyllically situated design featured winding roads in contrast to right-angled streets and blocks, as well as a hiking area in which residents could roam through the woods on designated pathways. Llewellyn Park was significant in that it set in motion plans that favored the integration of landscape architectural designs into larger residential construction projects of similar scales. These model suburban hybrids of natural settings in reasonable distance from urban hubs thus began to dominate in Anglo-American architectural residence planning schemes.[12] With signs posted to keep out lower-class intruders, Llewellyn Park also ranked among the first of America's many "gated communities," with access being restricted to the upper income brackets. But the planned Garden Cities Ebenezer Howard envisioned were to be accessible to a wide spectrum of people from diverse economic backgrounds. As Howard laid out in *Tomorrow: A Peaceful Path to Real Reform* (1898), the garden cities (which carried the planner moniker "town-country magnets") were to be situated on approximately 6,000 acres of agricultural land with the central hub of the garden city community taking up a circular area of 1,000 acres in the middle zones. Influenced by the work of James Buckingham, Peter Kropotkin, Edward Gibbon Wakefield, and Henry George, Howard envisioned "six magnificent boulevards—each 120 feet wide" crossing the community, thereby forming six separate areas of equal size. The focal point of each radius was to be a large and lavish central garden, skirted by municipal buildings and structures earmarked for art museums, concerts, libraries, exhibits, and hospitals. This inner zone was then to be flanked with a large circular park of 145 acres, beyond which lay the individual houses with their cute little gardens. Everything in this vision glowed in hues of friendly green, not surprising perhaps in rain-friendly England.

The planned garden cities were just large enough (30,000) to allow a sense of community to form in the minds of the residents, but small enough to offer cozy *Gemütlichkeit* and a sense of tranquility to pacify their hearts. In the Foreword to the 1965 edition of Howard's book, re-titled *Garden Cities of Tomorrow*, F. J. Osborn proudly reported that after the New Towns Act of 1946, twenty-five communities modeled on Howard's Garden City scheme had sprung up in various parts of Great Britain. Osborn emphasized the widespread attention the communities had received around the world as practical, humane solutions to overcrowded cities and noted that urban planning was finding its way into public policy handbooks worldwide.[13] In Lewis Mumford's assessment, Howard's *Garden Cities of Tomorrow* was more instrumental in shaping the concepts and goals of modern urban planning than had been any other comparable work.[14]

The Garden City Associations were careful to distinguish the intended communities from suburbs. Unlike the latter, garden cities were separated from larger metropolises by miles of countryside. Suburbs had grown as an outward expansion of central cities whereas garden cities were planned as distinctly separate communities, safely secluded from any larger urban concentration by miles of trees, streams, pastures, and grass.[15] In light of the concrete development of both the planned garden city community and the natural expansion of suburban bedroom communities, one would have to conclude that the difference was nominal at best.

The Garden City movement's influence on community planning in the United States did not proceed seamlessly, but rather grew indirectly as Progressive Era planners linked the need for improved housing for the nation's poor with the recognized need to provide quality affordable housing on the outskirts of major industrial hubs.[16] Whereas in England the movement had underscored popular socialist concepts of communal authority governing councils and the collective use of available land, the American counterpart looked to private enterprise as a driving force to propel much-needed construction—an approach that seemed to be more adaptable than the British version, which was already deeply influenced by models laid out by Unwin.[17] The American free-market, pro-investment direction in planning more attractive, friendlier communities also dominated the work of the Regional Planning Association of America, founded in 1923 as the trans-Atlantic counterpart of the Garden City Association[18] at a time when efficiency coupled with "organic ideology" (so Mumford) constituted a must-have element of regional planning.

Just after World War II, the Federal Housing Administration and the Veteran's Administration through the Veterans Emergency Housing Program (VEHP) actively supported construction of low-cost housing projects across the country in an effort to provide homes to all the young soldiers returning home from service. The GI Bill gave the young vets and their families greater access to mortgages at excellent borrowing rates. The government's program to house these young families in attractive and affordable homes was seen as both a reward for those who had risked their lives as well as a much-needed economic stimulus package. This was very much in keeping, as Barbara M. Kelly has argued, with the deeply ingrained American notion that owning one's own home is one further hallmark of solid republicanism.[19]

The American middle class finally came into its own suburban rights thanks to two distinct developments. The mass production of the automobile theoretically allowed for the expansion of suburban communities in all directions precisely because the car provided complete personal independence from public transportation. Secondly, beginning in the 1940s, changes in construction methods, coupled with state-sponsored programs benefiting both potential buyers and mortgage lenders suddenly made the American dream of home ownership a reality for hundreds of thousands.

It was the vision and entrepreneurial spirit of one family team that brought those dreams to fruition: Levitt and Sons, established in 1929 by attorney Abraham Levitt. What started out as a few hundred homes constructed for a project on Long Island in the 1930s grew to a couple of thousand in 1941 when the father and sons team successfully bid on a government project to construct military housing units in Norfolk, Virginia. Then in 1947, the first real "Levittown" was born in Island Trees, Long Island. By restricting the architectural design to two simple styles, Levitt and Sons created a community of affordable modern "little boxes" with enough green grass, blue skies, and space between neighbors to attract a wide following. *Time Magazine* reported in 1950 that one-eighth of all houses constructed in the United States at the time were Levitt productions. The family-owned business continued to dominate the housing construction sector until the 1960s.[20]

The concept took off, and when U.S. Steel opened in Fairless Works in Bucks County, Pennsylvania, in 1952, the surge in job openings drew in workers from the entire region in need of a place to live. Levitt and Sons was poised to meet the demand. The company had taken out two full-page ads in the *Philadelphia Inquirer* to announce its opening and on the first weekend attracted more than 20,000 prospective home buyers.[21] In the first year alone Levittown, PA, raked in an average of 1,600 house sales per month, and it became common to see four or five dozen families closing the deal on their dream homes all at the same time.[22] The houses, too, began to show variation in style and offered increased comfort. The svelte *Levittowner*, a California-style ranch house, became the trendsetter among young couples seeking bliss among the birds and bushes.[23] And with an asking price of just $9,999, it was affordable. Later, more upscale models such as the *Country Clubber*, the *Jubilee*, the *Pennsylvanian*, and the *Colonial* featured open- floor plans, picture windows, a Frank Lloyd Wright-style living room fireplace, split levels with room for attic expansion, and an enclosed garage. All models offered highly modern built-in kitchens with a variety of automation. Since city folk normally knew next to nothing about the proper care of trees, flowers, grass, and shrubs, Levitt provided instructional guides on cultivating the green thumb needed for the awe-inspiring lawns that surrounded the houses.

And there it was, the first real glimpse of the promised land; the answer to the endless search for *Pleasantville*; the American dream-come-true of Kinkade- cottage coziness, where husband, wife, Wally, and the Beaver live the perfect life of plenty and ready-made happiness. And right next door were Ozzie and Harriet Nelson with their two sons, Ricky and David.[24] With the most lethal and destructive military conflict in human history relegated *ad acta*, life in the 1950s was predicated on bountiful optimism in spite of what was perceived to be dangers from the East. It was *Morning in America* time, with Reagan still in Hollywood where he belonged. Apple pie was still the sweetest thing around; piping hot turkey and dressing (without cilantro) took center stage around the family Thanksgiving table, where the family actually sat together and conversed. Sock-hops and rock-'n'-roll set the stage for puppy-love affairs that rarely produced anything that might have slipped through a condom. *Amos and Andy* and *The Honeymooners* symbolized the entertainment innocence of an era.

And what could possibly be wrong with the wish for a nice home and garden surrounded by friendly neighbors? There was certainly no shortage of the like-minded. A 1957 cartoon in *Electrical Merchandising* depicted a city skyline in the background with an exit road snaking into the foreground past a road sign reading "Suburbia straight ahead." As far as the eye could see there were moving vans, cars, and trucks packed to the brim with family belongings, all headed in one direction.[25] In this instance, the grass really was greener. The American dream of shutting out the world and answering to no one but one's own inner drummer: to live a life of comfort and ease, peace and security, nestled into a beautiful house with a clean-cut lawn, trees, and flowers of one's own choosing, were the visions on which suburbia was founded.[26]

The idyllic image of familial harmony posing against a backdrop of serenity and convenience caught on like wildfire. From the 1950s on there was no stopping the trend. Cities across the country witnessed a decimation of their middle-class populations as like-minded couples took out a convenient mortgage and moved on up and out of sight of the inner cities.[27] From Main Street to Jefferson Street, downtowns everywhere gradually struggled with increasing numbers of closures as suburbanites sought out more conveniently located shopping facilities within driving distance of their new homes or neighborhood schools. Inner-city complexes, once hubs of activity, crumbled over the years or were razed. Left behind were the have-nots of society. No job. No savings. No bank account. No mortgage. No peace of mind in Sunny Oaks.

This was also an era in which many white American housewives sought out and found role models not only in Hollywood's leading ladies, but also in the figures beamed into the living rooms Monday through Friday in dramas like *As the World Turns*, *The Guiding Light*, *The Secret Storm*, and *The Edge of Night*. The series often challenged narrow-minded suburban morality by depicting highly sympathetic characters in what tradition considered "immoral" situations. "Ellen

Lowell" (played by Patricia Bruder) of *As the World Turns* had defied convention by engaging in sex out of wedlock and then giving birth to a male love child. Malice and petty gossip from the residents of Oakdale—ah, that everlasting connection to wood—eventually drove the mother to hand over the baby for adoption. Disheartened and suffering from depression, the young woman often sought solace in the busy streets of the city (to the tune of Petula Clark's *Downtown*), away from the psychological death traps of the alert and ready suburban family values police. Maternal attachment eventually led her to devise plans to be close to the young boy who had been adopted by a Dr. David Stewart. The young mother worked her way into a position of employment in the Stewart household as a nanny. At the death of Mrs. Stewart, Ellen and the good doctor became an item and eventually married. She had escaped the trappings of the petty-minded and managed to find happiness despite the obstacles.

Also of major importance among the female characters was "Lisa Hughes." Given to outright manipulation and deceit in order to get her way, Lisa (played by Eileen Fulton) aroused both shock and awe among America's bastions of stay-at-home suburban moms through very un-lady-like antics that many viewed as dishonest and extremely selfish. But this character, too, offered the nation a role model of welcome deviation from the stifling, straight-laced subordination that characterized many middle-class "ideal-type" *Pleasantville* households of the 1950s and early 1960s.

For nearly a century, the consistent move has been away from urban centers and into the burbs. According to the 2000 U.S. Government Census, the percentage of all housing units located in suburbia in the last decade of the twentieth century was 60.2 per cent, up from 29.1 percent in the 1920s. Surprisingly, a slight majority of American households nowadays consists of singles toughing it out alone. The house styles and sizes of suburbia have changed immensely, employing every architectural design feature known.[28] The inhabitants now derive from every walk of life, sexual orientation, economic status, ethnic heritage, and religion. No longer the domicile of unsophisticated hicks, suburbia is the expected norm—New Jerusalem with a mall.

But suburbia is suburbia is suburbia. Endless rows of houses, lawns, garages, and driveways, lining endless miles of Lanes, Circles, Places, Avenues, Streets, Squares, Views, and Vistas. Row after endless row; mile after endless mile. And then the next suburban project starts.

Class War Games

Just south of the San Fernando Valley, cozily nestled into the foothills of the Santa Monica Mountains, lie two of America's most impressive bastions of the *nouveaux riches*: Brentwood (of O.J., Nicole, and The Getty fame), and Westwood, home to the UCLA Bruins. (By the way, there's also a university attached to the football team, but let's stick to American essentials.) Here, Upscale comes home to roost. As fortresses of financial success, the two satellites are veritable role models of suburban life, avouching for the triumph of millennial American leitmotivs: plutocratic principles, an entrepreneurial spirit, Machiavellian ethics.

Anyone who drives through the more residential, chicer sections of these tree-studded *petites villes* is easily overwhelmed by the knowledge of "culture" which distinguishes the inhabitants of these pristinely white enclaves of West Coast *haute couture* from their rival counterparts in the American outback. Brentwood unquestionably boasts more wine experts per square mile than all Bordeaux chateaux combined. And God help the waiter whose misinformed recommendation clashes with the Brentwood VIP's studied plan for the clinching soup coup. (In the enclaves of the Lear-jet set, corporate Humvees tread with preference on society's financial fringe; evenings out at the local candle-lit pasta center in mock Greco-Roman ambiance are tried-and-tested proving grounds for the entertaining aggression games played against the help hired to tolerate the Pol Pot-style civility chuckled their way.)

But Woodies are exemplary upscale suburbanites not only at the dinner table. In many ways, Brentwood and Westwood are L. A.'s microcosmic versions of the hundreds of other predominately white, tree-lined suburbs that are home to the trend setting Charles Schwab crowd from the right sides of America's tracks. The confidence and gung-ho-ism of all that inhabit the nation's moneyed strongholds must be seen, or better felt, to be appreciated. The *enfants gates* of Reaganomics are so self-assured of their own immortality that normal traffic laws are routinely suspended per diktat. Impervious to the threats of head-on collisions or petty-change traffic citations that plague déclassé low-lifes, America's 18-hole set routinely adopts the British convention of left-side driving in an I-dare-you maneuver designed to assure its rightful place ahead of the competition. What might begin as an innocent drive to a convenience store can quickly escalate to obstacle-course difficulty as drivers strive to avoid hitting their virtuous Highnesses in their fleets of new BMWs and Bentleys. These people may not only get away with acts that would land a poor person behind bars, they also cleverly exploit to their best advantage the moral fortitude residual in others. And never look back.

Such was the case in one of America's most famous hideaways for the rich and famous, whose own exclusivity demands the definite article in its name: The Hamptons. It was here that another Brahmin caste local low-cal fuse went off in the wee hours of July 7, 2001. As reports at the time had it, the sleek blonde PR mogul had had another row with her ex, who just happened to be the owner of the Conscience Point Inn (what's in a name?). According to witness reports, Ms. Lizzie Grubman had had one too many of a variety of interesting things. She was approached by Mr. Scott Conlon, a schoolteacher, who like many other mortal Americans was working evenings as a security supervisor to supplement his miserly income. Mr. Conlon asked Ms. Grubman to move her vehicle out of the fire lane, and as is often the case when royalty is confronted by commoners, this younger, prettier version of Leona just lost it. With a "Fuck you, White Trash!", New York's No. 2 on the Queens-of-Mean list put the pedal to the metal on her papa's $70,000 Mercedes SUV in reverse. God only knows what ticked her off (an unwanted taste of calories in her lobster salad perhaps), but whatever it was, it really did the trick. Injuring a grand total of sixteen people in the process. And in her haste to get somewhere else (an urgent midnight manicure?), she didn't even say "Good-bye." Not even an "Oh, sorry." Of course she may have just assumed the flesh masses caught between the bumper and the wall belonged to Latino dry-wallers or other working class peons and thought she could and should get away with it. *Injured? Give me a break! What were they doing there anyway! Just when will they ever clear the roads of all the trash?*

The little downtime outing did cost her though. After pleading guilty to several charges, she actually served a little time (before Hampton Hilde of custard, curtains, and do-it-yourself picture frames fame got there). Of course if the rewards from O. J.'s civil suit sentence were any guide, the injured should have considered themselves lucky even to get a box of Twinkies out of the ordeal.

It is indeed saddening to witness the suffering the nation's upper-crust gents and divas are subjected to in confrontations with those of the lower echelons. The very idea of having to face shareholders and one's devoted public as a convicted felon! "White trash" thrives in ample quantity in Red State America of course, but in up scale suburbia, the genus likely includes anyone who's under eight figures. Class warfare at its best.

Back in a West Coast branch of one of the country's favorite eco-friendly ice cream joints, a young part-timing student from Mongolia reported that his experience with suburbia's "professionals" had negatively colored his view of the country he'd dreamed of since he was a child. The young man was somewhat of a phenomenon in his own right. With a near-photographic memory, he could recite not only all the presidents and the dates of their terms in office in sequence, he also knew their vice presidents, most members of their cabinets, and what important legislation had been enacted during their years in the White House. He had then decided to better acquaint himself with the decisions handed down by the Supreme Court. Sadly, because of a persistent lack of money, all this intelligence was wasted in keeping America's own models of hubris customer king:

> One day this businesswoman comes in and orders a medium-sized ice cream, so I got right to it and started scooping it out. For some reason she thought I'd taken a small cup, so she starts screaming, "I told you I wanted a medium-size, not small!" and she takes her hand and slaps me on the back of the head and I mean hard; it really hurt. She said "Are you really stupid or do you just look that way?" I felt like I wanted to kill her.

Asked how often he encountered people like that, he lamented that

> ... it's every day, sometimes three or four in one day. They don't usually get physical or anything but they yell and call you names. Sometimes they throw the money on the counter and I've had a couple of people threaten me because I guess they were in a bad mood and needed somebody to take it out on. What really makes me angry are people like this guy who walks in in a suit talking on his cell phone. Since it was his turn to order, I asked him what he wanted and he raised his hand and said, "Shh!" So I walked toward the back and he starts yelling "HelLO! HelLO! Does anybody work here?" Oh my God, I just really wanted to hit him. You can't believe how much I hate that word "Hello!" The same thing happened with another guy on his cell phone and we were just trying to tell him to take his $14 in change on the counter. He got angry because we were trying to help him but he felt he was being interrupted. We should have just kept the change I guess, but most of us are too honest to do something like that.

The pattern is persistent. In a *Newsweek* essay aptly titled "Can I Get You Some Manners With That?" journalist Christie Scotty criticized the despicable lack of civility displayed by the "professionals" she served while waiting tables one year, with customers barking orders in drill sergeant mode, all while refusing to make eye contact or otherwise acknowledge her existence.[29] With all the reserve and humility of invasive surgery, the nation's summa cum laudes of self-esteem and assertiveness training are incapable of ordering a drink or a meal without sounding like O'Reilly with prickly heat. For many no doubt an admirable title to bear.

Jane Jacobs[30] spoke of the blurred boundaries between public and private that accompany the disintegration of the densely populated metropolis and the resultant absence of feedback. This fact is demonstrated daily in the blatant disrespect for others thought to belong to a lower social status. Once, when families had the time and willingness to think and converse with their offspring, courtesy and the importance of empathy as an extension of the "Golden Rule" were taught in the sanctity of the home. Today, the walking vestiges of a public are rapidly losing the ability to distinguish between the appropriateness of context and measured actions and responses.

Most of us prefer not to have sex on stage or to rid our bowels and urinary tract in full view of others. Stubborn socio-biologists will surely try to find the "hard wiring"/"genetic component" responsible for this diffidence, or as the case may be, for the reverse inclination to "let it all hang out" in a complete dismissal of social taboos, but it is with careful parental guidance that we learn at an early age the societal "norms" (however questionable and rational they may be) that our peers require of us. Through combinations of positive and negative feedback, children learn to overcome their natural urge to pick their noses and to chew on the "boogers" (or peruse their fingers for the find). Most of us eventually become so well toilet-trained that we successfully repress the urge to pee in the corner of the dining room at a dinner party and "hold it" until we've found the nearest toilet bowl. Many males have even mastered the art of precision urination to avoid telltale yellow stains on a white porcelain backdrop. Failure to conform to the array of tacit rules and regulations we normally take for granted could lead to behind-the-scenes chatter that can be very detrimental to one's social life and career plans. Admittedly, these are social conventions and as such are founded in historically mediated developmental patterns that display wide variation from culture to culture. Within each culture, however, members learn to conform to a compendium of mores and customs to ensure acceptance and respect. It should be desirable that individuals question these traditions by articulating their objections and show willingness to throw customs and behavioral patterns overboard in instances when outdated norms hinder societal development or function as oppressive control mechanisms of illegitimate authority.

In the case of the suburban mind however, the fusion between public and private has proceeded haphazardly to the detriment of social consciousness and communicative action. If *I* am the center of the universe, it's quite natural to regard all others as nothing but instruments to be discarded after use or as useful background noise to lengthen the intervals between phases of unwanted boredom *I* might experience. Fully in keeping with this newly formed suburban character is the willingness to receive the ubiquitous very important call. The interlocutor is reduced to a casual tidbit among countless others in a deceptive openness to what is ostensibly the entire world, but one in which no one is permitted an exalted status—*Sorry, I think I should take this call.* Spheres of intimacy melt away as the most heart-felt confession takes a back seat to that casual glance at the front pants pocket, signaling an incoming message, which, *eo ipso*, is more important than anything offered up in a face-to-face encounter. The chime, hum, buzz, beep and *Für Elise* of cell phones occupy the totality of interpersonal space, inserting what should be private into the public sphere for all to hear, but all the while precluding active participation. By the very nature of cell phone interaction, the passer-by is forced into the role of social voyeur, an intolerable situation of being teased by a conversation he/she isn't allowed to participate in. *Look at me and listen to me as I do something you can't. It's my party and you're not invited!* Even in places one might least expect to hear truly embarrassing confessions (the UPS package pick-up station, in the waiting room at the dentist's office), no holds are barred: *Yeah, I'd really like to have the job and I think the interview went pretty well but if they like find out about all the drugs I've taken and stuff it like might not be so good.*

The problem is now so pervasive that various pay-per-call services are springing up to exploit the ever-ready gadgets, and the potential seems limited only by the imagination. How about the incoming call functioning as a handy *coitus interruptus* birth control device? Software programs could monitor respiration rate and muscle contractions, and at just the critical moment, place that important pullout call. For-fee agencies have already been created to allow an incoming call from an anonymous person to interrupt a specified activity at a given time as a form of "polite excuse" to get away from that unwanted date or to get out of the arduous task of helping a friend move into a new apartment. With the push of a button, in comes the anonymous call pretending to be the boss demanding that the answerer come in to finish up some work, or the father insisting that those errands be done without further delay. (One wonders whatever happened to honest talk.) Cell phones of the future will no doubt be equipped with different modes to

adapt ring patterns to the situation at hand and remind recipients of corresponding protocol: funeral mode at the grave site with the Dirge ring with instructions
not to giggle or scream.

Fully in keeping with other trends in social autism, America's suburban elite
also prides itself on its workout enthusiasm, a mania that has infected men,
women, and children of all ages and ethnic backgrounds. As seemingly innocu-
ous as a picnic outing (and judging from the expressions of the ab-flex gym glit-
terati, a lot less fun), fitness passion has established itself as the Platinum Visa
Card of America's Body Cult Dotcom. As common in Brentwood as cows in Cal-
cutta, pasty Lycra ladies replete with bounce-proof, self-basting pony tails, hy-
drating suck-on bottles, head- and cell phones, plough through traffic in the
palm-lined avenues of L.A.'s caviar corner, jogging their bods to perfection as part
of a cult-like daily ritual. With pre-puckered lips cast in hardened determination
and palpable contempt, they proudly convey the aura of distance that only success and money can buy. Pumped-up bench-pressing biceps boys, whose testos-
terone-laden confidence tops anything Ollie North or an Abu Ghraib interrogator
could ever live up to, babble tidbits of cool in series; their personal histories, life
goals, and destinies neatly summarized in dippy combinations of pecs-specs and
investment returns. What remnants of critical thinking might still exist beyond
the layers of WYSIWYG confidence are devoted solely to endless chatter about the
expanding ego's preferred topics of importance: the work-out routine and financial portfolios. Replace the "mind" and "soul" of these jiggling-jogging, hop-
ping-bobbing, push-up/pull-up human pop tarts with an "Intel inside" and no
one would know the difference. Except that the computer version would be less
preoccupied with its own Adonis image in the rearview mirror. Single-mindedly
committed to a GQ face and to butt muscles that could stop a Ford Excursion in
three yards, these workout buddies have reached pinnacles of self-esteem unknown to previous cultures. Equipped with a Saddam-esque sense of remorse,
this web-page age *Übermensch* has a veritable global arsenal of options at its dis-
posal with which to prove itself *numero uno, sans* head, *cum* Bimmer.

In countless numbers of dating profiles flooding the Internet, suburban values dominate, as if the muscles and credit scores themselves were on the meat
auction block. A smoking Toyota Corolla driver would stand about as much
chance of landing a date in this crowd as a necrophile's being appointed Supreme
Court justice. Probably less. *Apropos* smoking: dare to light up in the lean-mean
environs of California's royal Arcadia and instantaneously reality surpasses any-

thing *Saturday Night Live* could ever dream up. The self-appointed keepers of institutionalized bliss begin a fixed ritual of tics, twitches, and convulsions at the mere sound of a match being struck or a lighter wheel scraping the flint. All remnants of civility (not that there were ever that many to begin with) are quickly discarded amid violent throes of artificially induced asthma attack simulations. Calls for tobacco extermination programs surface as the non-fat Wi-Fi-fanatics arrogate for themselves a judicial monopoly status governing the do's and don'ts of environmental pollution. An ironic fact, considering the millions of tons of noxious car and SUV exhaust fumes they willingly ignore while sipping their decaf lattes.

Of course it isn't the toned and buffed corporal armamentarium per se, but rather the chronic mirror voyeurism that is so disconcerting among America's diamond-studded suburban elite, especially when one considers that at any single busy gym-hour across the country there are probably more "bodies" doing "their thing" than there are books and newspapers in the hands of the under-50 cohort. In terms of zeal, the workout regimen has become as much a ritualistic part of that vast reservoir of profound gasconade among nouveaux riches Americans as has the mandatory rundown of NBA scores and bust-size stats among dapper double-comma dudes.

The bold and immortally beautiful have also managed to turn dieting into an art form. In upscale suburbia, where no master of the stair machine would be caught dead chomping on working-class grub, the no-fat fad is more enduring to the anorexic gourmet than special effects in Hollywood cinema. The same holds true of course for Miami's own version of a catwalk world, South Beach, where the quest for eternal beauty has even served to gentrify the neighborhood and spruce up the landscape. No room for any plain Dicks and Janes here either;[31] this mindset's quest is universal. One perennial regular to L. A.'s famed Farmer's Market commented that if Nicole Brown Simpson (whose own Giacometti physique could hardly have been accused of midnight raids on the cookie jar) had been obese, no one but her immediate family would have cared one way or the other.[32] The same no doubt applies in inverse proportion to her former bank account figures. In the world of the perpetually cool and ravishing, there can be no room for imperfection. In The Hamptons and Brentwood 90049, even the common fart comes in designer scents. *Egoiste*, no doubt.

Among the elite, beauty and power instill unshakeable confidence in those who possess them (or feign to). By the same token, there is little tolerance for anything reminiscent of mortality, or God forbid, poverty! *Like yuck!*—a fact the author saw painfully confirmed one early fall morning while walking through Westwood Village. Parked in a wheelchair on the opposite corner was a man, about forty-five, with both legs amputated just above the knees, a doppelgänger for Tom Cruise in *Born on the Fourth of July*. A paramedic van in the accompaniment of a police car pulled up beside the curb in front of the man. Four men got out, approached, and asked what his purpose was in sitting on the corner so aimlessly. "I'm homeless," responded the man.

While inspecting the ID the man had displayed, one of the policemen explained that a number of complaint calls had gone in from people living in the area. "Just look around and see what a beautiful neighborhood this is," the concerned officer explained. "But you are not beautiful and people don't want to have to look at you. So if you're homeless, at least park your wheelchair in one of the alleys behind the building so people can't see you."

And indeed, what a beautiful neighborhood it is.

Like most other Americans, the upper-crust homeowners have far more important things to concern themselves with than with homeless tramps, amputees or otherwise. *We just love the feel of our new SL500.*

As for empathy for a fellow? Take it as taught in the Ozarks: America's Martha's and Lizzie's wouldn't "piss in your ass if your guts were on fire," unless it came with an appropriate tax write-off. In fact, in the summer of 1994, a Los Angeles-based KFI AM radio talk show host actually suggested that the government implement a final solution to the city's human eye-sores by putting homeless people to sleep like dogs. Particularly revealing was the number of listeners calling in to support the idea. Someone must have had plans for a new type of diet for the family German Shepherd.

In September of 2005, the whole world got to watch as America's contempt for the poor was put into practice. Two devastating hurricanes in series, "Katrina" and "Rita," swept through the parishes of Louisiana, destroying the infrastructure of New Orleans and rendering hundreds of thousands homeless. For decades, New Orleans city planners, politicians, and civil engineers, all too familiar with the real threats a large storm posed to the city, pleaded for federal funding to fortify the city's levee system. Many areas of the metropolis situated between the Mississippi River and Lake Pontchartrain lie below sea level and hence have been especially vulnerable to storm surges. In 2004, Louisiana legislators Landrieu, Jefferson, and Vitter put in a request for $60 million to strengthen the city's floodwalls. The George W. Bush administration not only did not heed the warnings that a major hurricane targeting New Orleans was a disaster waiting to happen, the Republican budgeters at the White House even slashed what little funding was earmarked for the city. That summer, the project director for the Army Corps of Engineers, Al Naomi, complained that only fifty percent of the Corp's requested funding was being approved. The total Bush had foreseen for the flood prevention measures was a paltry $3.9 million. According to a September 2, 2005, report in the *Washington Post*, Bush had "essentially frozen" funding for the Corps of Engineers.[33]

Faced with the possibility that the city's worst nightmare was about to become reality, on August 28, 2005, New Orleans mayor Nagin ordered the mandatory evacuation of the city's residents, setting in motion miles and miles of cars, trucks, jeeps, motorcycles, and buses trying to escape the oncoming storm. Several of the key levees, designed to withstand storms no stronger than a weak category 3, gave way as Katrina, weakened to a category 4, made landfall.

On August 29, just as hurricane Katrina was starting to unleash its force on New Orleans, Michael Brown, Federal Emergency Management Agency (FEMA) director and a friend of a friend of a … in the Bush *cronycracy*, received an important email from a co-worker commenting on the director's clothing: "You look fabulous." Brown responded: "I got it at Nordsstroms (sic) … are you proud of me? Can I quit now? Can I go home?"

In answering an email later from an employee directly in the path of the storm in New Orleans, Brown confessed that "I am a fashion god." Days later, as the extent of devastation and chaos in New Orleans became clear for the world to see, a FEMA employee fired off another email to inform Brown that the "situation is past critical … thousands gathering in the streets with no food or water … estimates are many will die within hours." Brown replied: "Thanks for update. Anything specific I need to do or tweak?"

In response to a brief query from a co-worker ("U OK?"), Brown wrote that "I'm not answering that question, but do have a question. Do you know of anyone who dog-sits? If you know of any responsible kids, let me know." George W. Bush was quite right in his assessment: "Brown, you're doing a heck of a job." On a par with the president himself ("It's hard work; it's hard work.")

As the tragedy unfolded, viewers around the world came to realize that somehow, for some strange reason, more than 100,000 people, almost all of them black, were still in the city. Why had they not evacuated? Brown, as capability-challenged as ever, expressed his dismay at these unwise choices during an interview with Ted Koppel on ABC's *Nightline*. Luckily, Koppel's rage was audible as he desperately tried to adjust the *Car-54-where-are-you*? version of reality Brown presented. The thousands who were at that very moment clinging to trees and rafters or stranded on sinking roofs with no water or food, had not *chosen* to stay; this was not a "lifestyle" decision so popular among proponents of the individual blame/responsibility ideology. Rather they had no means to leave. Contrary to popular belief among the country's mutual fund investors asleep in silk sheets, there sure as hell was no money there for even a bus ticket, much less for an Escalade in a paved double-car garage at the end of some tree-lined cul-de-sac. This was the reality of the millions of nickel-and-dimed Americans, the poorest of the poor, day laborers and hand-to-mouth make-do families, who somehow had all been conveniently forgotten. While a Chicago family was heading back home with the son they'd just enrolled in Tulane, courtesy of a $5,000 chauffeured limousine, the city's have-nothings were swimming through raw sewage in a cocktail of lead, benzene, poly chlorinated hydrocarbons, gasoline, diesel, and toilet bowl cleaner.

With hundreds of images of the desperate and dying flooding the media, the world suddenly became aware that at the heart of America's bedside glitter, a Third World lies abandoned, prey to the whims of corporate greed and the "compassion" of the country's market forces. As World Policy Institute research analyst Frida Berrigan so aptly put it, Hurricane Katrina had "swept away the curtain hiding the poor, confronting the richest country on the globe with its inner Third World."[34] *It's like, who are these people?*

The superficiality spawned by wealth is far more than a choice flavor among others; it is an acquired trait of the upwardly super-mobile, the *modus vivendi* of a society in which, as Christopher Lasch implied, the aspirations of success are devoid of any other significance outside the vision thereof and its manifestation in the successful public image.[35]

Among the avant-garde of the dubya-dubya-dubya Nasdaq moguls, money has become a life-fulfilling goal, the sole surviving *entelechia*. The acquisition of wealth has successfully replaced the concept of deity as the highest ontological category, with the hierarchical pecuniary totem pole grounded in the DOW and S&P 500 index, through which all "legitimate" references to Being are mediated. From the subordination of the entire realm of aesthetics under a potential market value at Sotheby's to the gradual disappearance of financially unrewarding intellectual interests, human endeavor is "colonized" (to paraphrase Habermas) by price and profit indices. This is a world of positive immediacy in which things of instantaneous *me-importance* take on an exaggerated, strictly utilitarian role defined by the underlying Hamlet question: *Is this what I want?* Perception is related solely to the Here and Now, defined by the center-stage ego. The distant (and even recent) past are seen at most as potential topics of academic research conducted for the sole purpose of *my* undergrad requirements, but highly unworthy of actually thinking about, much less discussing. Ideas and their history are somewhat hard to come by in a world dominated by *me*. The traditionally phobic response of the Anglo-Saxon mind to metaphysics (*nota bene*: the content of certain philosophical questions that originated in Greece, not a hypnotic past-life episode) has been entirely successful at expunging contemplation to the jurisdiction of society's "losers" who just don't know where it's at. *What good is conceptual thought if it doesn't relate to me? HelLO!*

In dozens of "Woods," "Glens," "Hills," "Oaks," and "Dales," society's cream goes to bed at night with dreams of the mega-merger waiting to happen, with a side order of soaring investment returns. The names themselves conjure up bucolic serenity and the tweed-inspired flair of English country gentility. Add an "Esq." suffix like "estate" to the upscale name, and you're moving on up the pecking order to one high fallutin' zip code. "Location, location, location" as the real estate stars were once so fond of saying in preface to their multi-million-dollar deals. What counts is a Babe-Watch figure, a cool car, major shares in the hottest stocks, and the Brentwood estate where the get-rich-quick fix is at home.

This land of blimp-sized designer breasts and hyper-terrestrial vehicles covering half the area of Liechtenstein has now made its way to the forefront of palatial dwellings. Green with envy at the sight of Saddam's former splendor, America's plutocracy set to work on recreating the abodes of the globally rich and famous on a friendly neighborhood scale. One chic suburban landscape after the next has been transformed, with nature giving way to the realized dreams of boundless egos in search of yet another scent of territorial marking. CBS's *60 Minutes* tracked the trend in a segment featuring downtrodden high-rollers, sadly thwarted in their missions of personal expression by communities such as Chevy Chase, Maryland, who finally said *Enough is enough already!* Thousands of attractive, perfectly solid houses were being snatched up all across the country at bargain-basement prices (i.e. in the upper six- and low seven-figures), only to be demolished. The four-bedroom, two-bath 2,000-square footer just doesn't cut it anymore. The "Levittowner" may have been the apple of many a suburban eye in the 1950s, but today's expansive personas demand breathing room in the likes of the "Hampton" (ring a bell?) with its familiar aristocratic floor plan spread out over 4,800 square feet.[36] The designers and constructors of the McMansions (as they're now fondly called) were averaging in excess of 8,000 new mega-house constructions per year. Owner Bob Toll explained to *60 Minutes'*s Morley Safer[37] that consumer demand had gone from approximately 3,200 square feet of living space in the mid-nineties to 4,600 feet in 2005.

That is of course a comfortable starting point. The Hummers of suburban living demand nothing short of ten, twenty bedrooms and so many baths; swimming pool; bath house; billiard room; cinema-size entertainment center; family room; study; library (*they do look so nice*); a formal dining room; several hundred square feet of kitchen space; a gilded foyer flanked by two marble staircases leading to private chambers. And that's not even counting the golf course and standard-size basketball court. All for one husband, one wife, and a single child, possibly two. One does so want to keep up with the Windsors.

Life's motto: *Strut your stuff! Show the world who you are!*

Back in the Dishwater

Most Americans never make it past Levittown or *Pleasantville*. For whatever reason, the dream usually gets stuck on page 11 of *Better Homes and Gardens*, still very much "in the dishwater." At home in mainstream suburbia with its endless rows of detached houses, each vying for first prize in any number of one-upmanship categories, the wannabes have mortgage payments to make and utility bills to pay; kids to clothe and feed, and college tuition to save for; groceries to buy and laundry to do (if there's no maid). There's the never-ending struggle to keep the kids out of crime and off drugs in an era when "just say 'no'" is utterly laughable. Most of all, there's a job to hold down, as long as it lasts.

Here in America's commoner wastelands, even nature's most beautiful corners have been tragically marred by thousands of strip malls—hideous clumps of monotonous functionality that are home to a combination of faceless doughnut shops, shoe stores, locksmith services, what-not/convenience stores, and a brand-name franchise specializing in gas, computer games, pizzas or fried chicken. Strip malls have taken up residence in every nameless thoroughfare in every nameless town between the Atlantic and Pacific oceans. As symbols of provincial lifelessness, void of personal history, a global presence, or human future, they are the twilight zones of existence, trapped in a mindless rut between life and death. Without exits.

Unlike those of Paris or Rome, suburbia's streets, corners, stores, and malls are never the objects of longing; they are never the destinations tourists dream of; they incorporate nothing that could even elicit memory. Unlike the silhouette of Venice's palaces on the Adriatic, the view of the Vatican and Tiber from the Pincio or the vista of Hong Kong Harbor from Victoria Peak, America's eerily identical suburbs offer no mnemonic aids to break the hypnotic spell of oblivion. Like the high school classmate whose only ambition in life was to become a full service attendant at the local gas station, suburbia casts its net in an infinite sea of mediocrity.

To be successful here means first of all putting on a happy face, real or feigned. Let your world be a smile! Meet travesty and bad luck with that good-ol' *Just-do-it!* spirit the world has seen demonstrated time and again in Olympic tradition. To be successful here is to put a religious trust in the power of positive thinking and the conviction that the course of human events is a Hollywood-scripted episode in a happy-end "surfin' safari" saga. Let other nations squeamishly retract in fear of a haplessly polluted environment; the U.S. has pioneered GM foods to meet the challenge. While pampered Europeans react to the prospects of permanent unemployment and drastic reductions in social services with threats of civil unrest, U.S. laborers emerge as paragon model employees—ever ready to sacrifice health, family, and sanity in a sixty-hour workweek. But oh my, can they ever smile!

Being at home in the suburbs often means battling a daily two-way commute, with "life" (as such) centered, as always, around work. For the lucky ones, that's fifteen to thirty minutes a stint; for the not so fortunate, it's an hour or two each way. The structural design of America's suburbs is centered around the car and its primary function to move individuals from one point to another.[38] In the Los Angeles metropolitan area alone a full twenty-five percent of all land area is devoted to the car: streets, freeways, parking lots, garages, gas stations, dealerships. Considering the distances that must be traversed just to complete the most mundane tasks and the time spent behind the wheel, Angelenos would doubtless be better off having a car but no apartment, rather than a place to live without a car. In the worst-case scenario, the back seat becomes a make shift bed, but driving the apartment to work is one Toyota will have to work on. On public buses (which may or may not come), or the world's most expensive subway system connecting Skid Row with nowhere, it's easy to see why "car hell" is the Angeleno's phrase of choice to describe the hours or days when the car is in repair. Just trying to navigate trips to the post office and back on the bus could easily eat up two precious hours. Combine that with grocery shopping and a quick trip to the dry cleaner's, and a good four hours has been wasted. And that's if there hasn't been a stabbing or rape in the seat in front.

But suburbia also has multiple built-in mechanisms to keep people off the streets on foot, effectively removing realistic chances of the casual encounter. To thoroughly "disrupt" (as marketing strategists like to phrase such things) any impending association with society's have-nots, walking is strategically integrated into the appearance of the workout routine, requiring special shorts, shoes, and an unmistakable look of hardened endurance, not to mention a trot in *molto allegro*. In suburbia itself, no one walks except desperate political campaign activists and religious sects warning of impending doom and Judgment Day. In many lovely suburban communities the police have even been known to stop pedestrians (Europeans usually) unaware of the tacit taboos, demanding to know what they were doing. Nor is it possible to just walk down the street, knock on a friendly door and greet the owner (who probably wouldn't open anyhow) with an innocent "Hi, I'm from the house over there. I'm bored and I'd like somebody to talk to." The response (thought, but not spoken among the polite) is already known: "This guy has issues,"[39] which summarily reduces all societal maladies lurking beneath the anomie of suburban contentment to a personal problem the individual will have to learn to deal with, most likely with the help of a therapist. What's more, a strong mistrust of the probable malicious "hidden agenda" (robbery? rape? murder?) of the poor soul would lead to the most likely course of action—getting rid of the guy ASAP.

For those lucky enough to own a car, the commute itself puts untold strain on body and mind, adding to the frustrations already mounting from an underpaid job with no paid vacation, no sick leave, and no medical insurance. And forget about spontaneously dropping by at that friend's house—there is traffic on the "surface streets" to consider; the time and condition of the freeways to think about; and the final question of whether there will even be a parking spot anywhere near the final destination. And that's only the trip there.[40] At the end of a long day of just making it, all that these tired impoverished souls want to do is to get home and "kick back." That often means fast-food pick-ups or a microwaveable entree from the frozen food section. At best there's a tossed salad to go with it. After fulfilling life's little necessities, each family member does his or her own thing by grabbing the cell phone, TV remote, videogame control, or internet-ready laptop. What more could one ask for in the way of a fulfilling social life?

With hundreds of hours per year spent behind the wheel, it comes as no surprise that the car has taken on an ideological significance all its own. Turning necessity into pleasure, the suburban mindset has transformed these lifeless humps of metal and plastic into the most petted, pampered symbols of arrival into various strata of the middle class. (Had Plato only known that in a later stage of human evolution the plain old common car would become synonymous with the highest criterion of earthly existence.) Put any random Tinker Bell behind the right set of luxury wheels and the instant extreme makeover is overwhelming, with nose and countenance reaching an elevated angle of attack that would thoroughly shame European royalty.

Confirming once again that erring is indeed quintessentially human, Americans in the mid-1990s bit into the marketing scheme cooked up by Detroit's "Big Three" to save money while fulfilling the average Jo and Flo Blo's insatiable hunger for omnipotence. The SUV (Sport Utility Vehicle) was born—a grotesquely monstrous überhunk of steel that promised to pulverize anything and everything that got in its way. Never mind the disastrous effects the beasts had on the environment as they filled the last remnants of breathable air with a cocktail of cancer-causing agents. The nation's consumer brats summarily dismissed out-of-hand their outstanding contributions to global warming and respiratory filth. Encased (all alone) in their ersatz-tanks, millions of Americans discovered the pleasure of playing God as they merrily roamed the freeways and highways, threatening everything in their paths with assured destruction.

Although the standards of measurement vary over time, "keeping up with the Sanchezes" is an intact, internalized value system that keeps the wheels of corporate capitalism spinning smoothly. Being is equated with having and flaunting. In the lower echelons of this simplified caste system, the objects required to prove oneself worthy of being seen as an authentic person are relatively restricted.[41] Usually the acquisition of a newer, truck-sized TV and the latest jeans are sufficient. But once you get to the suburbs and the totalitarianism of the home owners' associations, driving a shabby old car signals to the SUV-urbanites that either a) you can't afford a new car, in which case you've got a loser income and deserve nothing less than the American version of purgatory: a negative TRW Report (yes, there are new names in the credit reporting game ("Experian," "TransUnion," and "Equifax"), but the power of the ultimate authority on existence-worthiness to strike fear in the hearts of the helplessly hapless is so engrained in the American national psyche that it surely deserves its own Webster's entry as a verb like "to xerox" or "Will I be TRWed?"); or b) you can afford a car, but because it's an old beat-up Volvo, you are safety-conscious to the point of paranoia, which then implies that you're a graying Blood Type A introverted cat lover who spends weekends at art museums and/or foreign/independent films, votes Green, and has an Annie-Wilkes-style collection of glass dolphins from a Heal-the-Bay walk athon. Given either of these two alternatives, you have automatically reduced the number of potential friends and acquaintances to under 0.1 per cent, thereby greatly increasing the likelihood of finding someone to have a meaningful conversation with.

So much of the American personality and identity is based on the initial credit offer into exclusive membership into Mr. Bush's "ownership society"—the right car, the most desirable house in a presentable zip and area code; diplomas from just the right high schools and colleges. It's only logical that every effort is made to enrich and embellish that realm of things intrinsically linked to the social persona. But suburbanites can become real fussers when it comes to acquiring and maintaining the latest trends in furnishings, easily depleting that five-figure bank account. Style, placement, color pattern, material, price class, and popularity all figure prominently into the issue of self-esteem and one's image of respectability in the community.

Equipped with every conceivable electronic gadget, the chic and shiny stainless steel kitchen glistens with jet-setter modernity; the menageries of living room utensils, all carefully matched and color-coordinated with carpet, walls, lamps, and bookcases, secretly ponder their own raison d'être. (Because there's often no need for real books, fake (i.e. "blank") tomes are readily available for a fraction of the price of the real thing, with authentic titles in antiqued leather binding as a kind of Las Vegas version of erudition on the cheap.) The same applies to the "formal dining room" eagerly awaiting an elegant candlelight supper and its first guest butt. Even where financial restraints force the owners to omit the sauna and built-in Jacuzzi, the cleaning crew guarantees that the life span of a fallen pubic hair is measured in seconds. Basin, bowl, and tub glisten in aseptic pastels, with towels, bathmat, shower trimmings, toilet paper holder, and seat cover beaming in a chorus of chromatic harmony.

True to its deep-seated love of all things Arcadian, suburban America has also created something ostensibly quite unique in the world of home decor: *faux wood*. There are kitchen ranges, refrigerators, microwaves, intercom systems, dicta-phones, thermostats, and dishwashers pretending to be wooden. There are also air conditioning units and TV/VCR combo sets designed to fool you into thinking they're wooden, too. The company Oregon Scientific even offered a 48KB "revolutionary new data link organizer" that connected to the computer, encased, as the company described it, "in an attractive woodgrain" cover. Holding the winning Publisher's Clearing House number in this war of misfits was the uniquely mawkish "rosewood cordless phone/alarm clock" from Bell Phones. According to *TopiX*'s description, it was the most beautiful design they'd ever laid eyes on, one that was "destined to get attention." Indeed.

The one question that asserts itself immediately is *Why?* What earthly or other reason would any sane human being have in constructing something that is so utterly, indubitably not wooden now, nor ever has been, nor ever will be, to look as if it were?

How trust-inspiring would the space program be if the shuttle were also designed to look as if it had been made of maple or oak? (For that matter, how trustworthy is the space program period?)

There are certain things in life that simply don't "go together," as in "don't match"—the Queen defecating (although it's highly likely she does); the Pope "gettin' jiggy" with a Snoop Dog rap-along in a senior citizen outing, or posing as a Playboy Bunny. (In fact, nothing seems to go with the Pope except birth control/gay sex *Verbot* and rattling off "Be fruitful and multiply" in 197 different languages.) Or cars that look as if they had been manufactured out of wood. But alas, in the pre-silver-metallic days of visual manslaughter, suburban America's passion for the forest even produced several versions of station wagons and mini-vans whose sides were covered in a kind of grainy, middle-toned beech wood paneling all the way around the vehicles. The top and bottom of both sides, rear and front, were clearly and unpretentiously metal, probably steel, but there was that ostentatious, gaudy strip of awkward-looking wood placed there on both left and right sides. Did they use nails or Elmer's glue?

The trend even caught on with what one might call the "Neiman-Marcus" rendition of the wood-look, called *Burltech*—a grainy, glossed-up version of what might once have looked like the back of a Guarneri. It can be found even in imported luxury sedans (BMWs, Jaguars, Mercedes et al.). *Sharper Image* at one time offered a portable AM/FM radio "with Sound Soothers" which it sold in three different versions: graphite, metallic gray, and Burltech. The faux wood version was even $10 more expensive than the graphite version and $35 more than the metallic gray finish. What *Sharper Image* described as "the ultimate Sound Soother," in "handsome Burltech finish" of course, was even equipped with a SuperView screen. There was also a solid-state electronic "Memo Manager" in Burltech and an immaculate "Heart and Sound Soother relaxation system" which included sounds from the North Woods, California Coast, the Rain Forest, and a Tropical Cruise—all in Burltech, and all designed to evoke the placid images of the wagon wheels of yesteryear or a peaceful life *On Golden Pond*. Both charming and cozy in their own right, but not worthy of something whose inner soul is a silicon chip.

The suburban love of nature goes only so far though. At the other end of the spectrum is the suburban middle-class problem of dealing appropriately with all those nasty, odorous things humans have been known to emit. When it comes to the sometimes urgent need to hit the toilet, it's slim pickin's in suburbia. In fact, the traditional American phobia of unpleasant odors has even necessitated the widespread replacement of "toilet" with "restroom" to rid itself of any unwanted connotations, as if the true purpose of the quick trip there were to doze off (not surprising with the hours these people put in at work).

Toilets can be found in abundance in every European village, town, and metropolis, and asking a stranger for the quickest directions there will evoke nothing more than either the correct answer or a casual *I don't know*. In the United States, in contrast, toilets, *ehem*, "restrooms" are few and far between. Asking a stranger the whereabouts of one is often met with sheer shock and suspicious glares. "In public," there are none (consistent perhaps with the fact that there is no longer a public to speak of). For those poor souls who should ever feel the "gotta-go" urge for bladder relief while dilly-dallying about in the streets of suburbia, an unpleasant surprise awaits. For the urologically challenged, American suburbs are ripe with near-miss situations. It isn't necessary to have already entered the phase of life in which incontinence is the norm and fellow commuters stare with gleams of hope for "Yes" votes on the newest euthanasia measures; all that's needed is to have those extra cups of coffee. Since stopping at one of the anonymous houses on an equally anonymous street is out of the question, the next logical solution would seem to be one of the dozens of convenience stores or fast food joints. For those uninformed enough to be on foot, the situation is dire from the start; the nearest bush will have to do. Such desperate measures however carry potentially serious consequences as neighboring friends, families, watch group collectives, and members of the armed Home Owners Associations are acutely vigilant to the dangers of indecent (when is it ever not?) exposure of body parts "in public" and seem to be in direct link 24/7 with offices of Homeland Security.

The promising quick drive to the nearest bun and burger adds mounting pressure on the urinary tract in anticipation of relief—which is just not to be because of the sign that says either a) *Out of service* or b) *For customers only*. Given choice a), it's back in the car and off to the next burger, chicken, pizza, sandwich or bagel shop. For those lucky enough to have been dealt option "b," the next obstacle is either to stand in the never-ending lines behind the nation's famished three-hundred-pounders, or to attempt direct entry without further ado. Direct access to the restrooms is normally not possible, however, without a token, obtainable only from the cashier, who is not to be interrupted unless one has waited patiently in line and ordered something. It just wouldn't do to simply ask for the token or key. That would be even worse than asking for a "large cup of black coffee" at Starbucks. Here, the restroom has issues—something nasty, degrading, dirty, sexual, un-Christian. And oh boy, the kinds of glares that can be thrown one's way when asking to go to the toilet. That's where dirty old men try to lure in little boys and girls for unspeakable acts. It's where the nation's crack addicts retreat for a quick fix. A place where Al Qaeda sleeper cells might congregate. So to prevent such activities from occurring, "toilets" don't exist, only "restrooms" linked to bona fide paying customers who've left a whiff of their traceable credit history with the cashier.

Inside, a new experience awaits the first-time restroom visitor in American suburbia. Cleanliness is indeed right next to ever-present godliness. What's more, the places have all the privacy of an open-air Chinese market. Cubicle walls are equipped with virtually see-through doors ("the eyes of Texas are upon you"), allowing complete recognition of anyone unfortunate enough to be suffering a Maalox moment without the goods, leaving the poor victim to ponder who among the throngs of customers has recognized me?

As a nation, Americans are distinctly phobic when it comes to all things related to the excretory organs nature has equipped us with. And this is where blue comes into play. Nowhere else is it possible to find so many sundry things colored blue. If it's edible, potable, sniffable, washable or wearable, there's a blue version of it in a store near you. Non-blue dominant bathroom motifs are as rare as realism in the GOP, and cosmetic firms even seem convinced of blue's superior power to wash and condition human hair. There's blue added to many brands of chewables (gums, mints, M&Ms), suckables (Lollipops (the high-tech kind)), soft drinks (Pepsi, Gatorade), cookies, cakes, cereals, vitamin pills, prescription drugs, toilet bowl cleaners ("restroom bowl" would be stretching it a bit), laundry detergent, condoms, floor scrubs, sanitary napkins, toothpaste, mouthwash, and casket linings. Blue is a simple, effective means of ridding the mind of sordid sins involving body fluids and solids that normally fall in the opposite end of the color spectrum between yellow and brown. Blue is high-tech, clean, space-age.

Like that of all of suburbia, the essential purpose of the carefully orchestrated coterie of things is to project the persona of the owner. But somewhere along the way, the ceaseless longing for fulfillment and the endless search for meaning in life seem to have taken a wrong turn. The quest to shine as an individual and to be free of the dictates of traditions has become blind to the world, recognizing only its own image in the reflecting pool. For a sad many, after all the years of tears, toil, and worry, all they've got to show in that final breath of seventy-plus years is the larger-than-life house, a son who's the regional manager at Wal-Mart, and the bathroom in baby blue with co ordinated ceramic tiles. If at least one purpose in life is to create meaning, these people have pretty much missed the boat. And it ain't coming back.

Pathology of the Mundane

Suburbs chip away at the world, leaving in their wake minds nourished on gadgets, the texts of cereal boxes, more gadgets, and the local news. Place and time are connected in ways few of us ever become conscious of. In America's outback, where signs still flank the entries of old redbrick hotels advertising "Rooms with Color TV," modernity has passed the public by. Who we are depends so much on the public that exists (*or doesn't*) out "there," external to ourselves. For all their talk about individuality, too many Americans have bought into the same plugged product line, hook and sinker. To be sure, the goals have a foundation in the real economic benefits of home ownership, the need for acceptable schools, and a safer, more pleasant environment in which to raise a family. But it's what is missing from this semblance of life that should seem disconcerting: *the world* as an open-ended context of learning, experience, and engaged involvement, in which the personal realm is examined in terms of its historical evolvement within a larger societal sphere of inter-subjectivity. Without this expansive and critical political involvement with *the world* in its both most fascinating and most disturbing sides, independent of the individual ego and its enriching hangout at the local mall, reality becomes a bonsai version of a bad movie that relates the perpetual story of a baseball team's winning season. When the world is defined by the form and content of the local news, what the people see is pretty much what they are. When the public itself becomes detached from the larger realms of nations, their relations to each other, and the global community of knowledge, reality itself is stunted. Few of us spend sleepless nights fretting about the design of yogurt containers in northern Australia; we worry instead about problems and solutions that affect our own realm of concerns. But the smaller the horizon of vision and influence, the more particular, singular those levels of concern are likely to be. With the usurpation of reality by the marketing forces of politics and entertainment, the event horizons capable of arousing curiosity, concern, and action, are reduced to items of momentary personal interest that lack any ability to excite inter-subjective enthusiasm. The effects then become the cause for as yet a further spiraling turn away from global, human concerns toward the ignorance of the mundane and banal.

The loss of global horizons is a product of group-think on a massive scale—a closed system of reference and interpretation in which the only substantial new input arrives in the form of three hijacked airplanes used as lethal missiles. After an initial period of profound *Why us?* bewilderment, it was back to the mundane world of daily routines, paralyzed in the insularity and ignorance that develop from the loss of the world context in which the personal is understood in terms of its interrelatedness with the political. The wake-up call proved to be nothing more than a temporary blip in the contents of daily public talk and two more additions to the growing list of countries now taught in public geography class. The personal ersatz-world consists of endless acquisitions from the rational catalogue of the hottest consumer must-haves. *Plus c'est la meme chose...*

When populations turn their backs on the elbow-to-elbow hustle of the asphalt-grind for better vistas of green lawns and shade trees, they also leave behind the most essential feature of community: the city center as a place of encounter. That one single-most important locus of city identity—Trafalgar Square, the Champs Elysees, Times Square, Red Square, the Piazza San Marco, the Brandenburger Tor, where people meet, talk and experience a mutual encounter with a common focus.[42] Without a defining center as a central focus of interaction, there is little commonality, no defined agora around which all can congregate to share experience.[43] As the clocks around the world successively struck midnight to ring in the new millennium, millions thronged together to share the excitement simultaneously. But in the world's quintessential suburb, the "call of the mall" was suddenly silent. The sprawl of sixteen million church mice was treated to the rare climactic experience of seeing the Hollywood sign lit up at night. For millions who had missed the flight to

Paris or the Big Apple, the answer to the question *Where were you at the dawn of the new millennium?* turned out to be *Nowhere in suburbia*.

In the absence of daily encounters with a greater social-political context, the individual is thrown back to more archaic forms of personal interaction. Aside from the constant "new arrival" of video games such as *Underground 2, Grand Theft Auto, Call of Duty,* and *The Incredibles,* whose popularity wanes as more elaborate and challenging titles hit the market, suburban teenagers center their lives around activities designed to make them look cool. Gone for many are the ah-so-touching Kodak moments of father and son throwing the ball to each other until the cows come home, replaced by cooler things like text-messaging while driving through the 'hood in a suped-up car sporting screaming wheeling hubcaps that cost a couple of grand apiece,[44] and a look even Antarctic penguins unerringly recognize as *Made in USA*. More often than not, the eyes are glazed over either as an effect of the latest dope content, or as a byproduct of natural selection. With windows rolled down, the homie-cabs cruise aimlessly through highways and byways, the sole purpose being to attract attention through the latest hip-hop artist blaring through the suped-up speakers at such decibel levels that the neighborhood aquariums are disrupted by sonic tsunamis. The only message of this wonderfully creative pastime: *how cool and tough I am*. Like the piss from a non-neutered tomcat, the relentless bass from the *50 Cent Dr. Dre* drones *Straight Outta Compton,* marking the *Phat Farm* identity of the cruiser as one of the in-crowd that oozes cool. He may not know the difference between DNA and JFK, but hey, he's cool with that. He may even pull out an AK47 to prove the point.[45]

The female popularity contest is won by dating the raddest guys, sporting the hottest and most exclusive jeans, and having a to-die-for figure that's the envy of the Myplace dot world. This of course requires parents with the appropriate in-town positions of influence, corresponding income brackets, house, car, and attitude. In small-town USA, she's tops on the cheer-leader squad, gets invited to every party worth going to, and drives the latest model car in the $45,000 plus price range. She likely spends every waking minute texting or gabbing with someone on the cell phone, busying herself with linking up with those who can reinforce her status as potential queen bee among the coolest of the hive.

Lacking the common status-related tendency to hang out with those of the same age group after work or on weekends, the suburban American adult is more often than not at home alone with the shopping trophies and an unfulfilled quest for personal satisfaction. The death of the suburban spouse or separation through divorce often leaves the widow(er) grieving and incapacitated, sending those who can afford them into years of therapy sessions. If the separation comes at 50+, good luck! The life spent devoted to the kids, in a close emotional bond with that one significant other, has meant relegating past friends to the back seat. They become much harder to find as the years go by. Most of those old friends have devoted themselves to marital bliss as well.

By the time its Splitsville between the married couple who bought into the suburban dream, emptiness consumes much of what remains of hope, even amid the latest camcorders, giant plasma screens, and patio design schemes.

Loneliness breeds desperate measures, including "speed dating," in which the tradition of involved conversation is reduced to a quick-paced sales pitch of sound bites and pixels, and scads of online meet-a-date services. Nature is such a novice playwright: One would think that evolution's bromide plot of catch-me-if-you-can and I'm-yours for-the-taking, that ceaseless flirtatious interplay between the sexes would at last heed the call for novelty. But when in the mood for love, those in heat experience every song, poem, film, and stroll through the mall as a unique experience shared for the very first time between two soul mates.

And yet it's no more sublime than the humping of rats, dogs, lizards, and countless other living things that share the same natural version of this Microsoft beta release. The romantic search for that significant other sometimes lasts a lifetime; so, too, do the devices dreamed up to force the spotlight on oneself—to bask in fame and universal recognition; to be the one-and-only, the alpha and omega for that one special person. When online date number ninety-seven turns out to be another instance of false advertising, hope dreams on in spite of itself. Self-doubt argues that the digital photo, or maybe the wording was to blame. Or was the income too low? Hobbies and interests? *Something I said in an email?* And one day it hits home that the only other person who will ever share the pillow-for-two greets the morning with the warmest *Meow.*

Where the goals of being Julia, J Lo, Cameron or Oprah; Brett Favre, Ben Affleck, Tiger Woods or P. Diddy, are ceded as out-of-reach, the middle-class mind of the suburban burgher invents its own set of instruments and rules in its ceaseless struggle for admiration—from the most heavily invested stock portfolio at the Fairwood Country Club to the house with the most often photographed daughter at the Summer Wood High School prom. The lack of stimulating mental tasks to challenge both thought and passion in a world beyond the Self causes discourse to atrophy into the states of animated bubble-babble known to us all: "So I'm like 'no way' and he's like all 'yeah, right' and I'm like 'whatever!' "

Life in suburbia has led to a curious reversal of "public" and "private." What should rightly be public—the articulation of the complex array of social and political factors determining a citizen's ability to receive fair and livable wages for work expended, quality schooling, housing, and health care—is relegated to the outcome of the personal success (or failure) story, leaving those affected to seek out appropriate therapy groups or go on TV if needed. Conversely, what shouldn't be, and isn't, of any interest to the public asserts itself as unmitigated chatter into daily life. TV cameras are just a cell phone flick away from that catchy personal sob-story involving the heroic triumph over personal tragedy or the plea for the public's help in one poor soul's struggle against adversity. Halls and malls, freeways and fairways are all one continuous locus for chatter about "the new sweater I bought," the reasons "I'm breaking up with my boyfriend," or why "the pasta at Todd's last night was like so not *al dente*." In the hierarchy of knowledge, much of suburban emptiness is manifested in the permanent empirical observation report, while reflection and collective reasoning are replaced by the banality of the immediate here and now. Both form and content of this publicly private chatter reflect widespread streams of consciousness whose object-orientation fails to lead beyond particular, nominal meaning. The opportunity is rarely given for the conversation to evolve into discussion with relevance beyond the car, bar, classroom, bedroom or *eBay* bid.

In keeping with the central narcissistic focus, albeit in more studied, refined form, the present-day suburban employee gets together after work to gab about personal issues generally void of any wider significance. "Closeness" then develops when both participants have the feeling they can drop (with no fear of reprisals) the interview mask, i.e. the suitable employee persona that got them through the HR door in the first place. Water-cooler chat serves to break the ice and test the water for any commonality that might set up an evening at home together or a couple of hours in the sauna or fitness center.

Meaningful discourse is clearly dependent on the appropriateness or relatedness of a given set of utterances to the context in which they are made and to the underlying intent involved. Speakers of any given language community must therefore adapt both to the given situation and to other speakers involved by being able to employ changes in register, intonation, stress patterns or other similar linguistic devices. But suburban discourse is predefined and pre-contextualized to exclude wide variations in content and intent. The prevalence of and preference for the emphatically positive in personality patterns, which results in part from the broad success of the studied and internalized "knock-'em dead" interview pitch, has successfully corroded character-based deviation[46] that in pre-suburban periods of history may have offered up refreshing forms of defiance of the established order. The mutually reinforcing nature of speaker intent and listener expectation serve to perpetuate the colonization of discourse through media content which has attained a saturation level approaching one hundred per cent. The results of this uneventful symbiosis of banality are most apparent in the demise of *communicative action* evidenced by the disturbing dearth of in-depth political argumentation about issues that should be of common concern, and in the absence of justifiably negative critique of the status quo. The latter is immediately cast aside as the markings of the notorious "disgruntled employee" (who by implication is mentally imbalanced). With language at the workplace (the only area in which suburbanites might actually find regular human contact) restricted to obligatory small talk, it follows that uncomfortable political/public policies remain unarticulated and un-reflected.

As the *Play Station* generation nears grandparent age, some of the long-term effects of suburbanization are becoming increasingly evident. Isolated, insulated, privatized—entire generations of suburban babies, parents, and grandparents now constitute the bulk of the U.S. population. Structure and content of suburban life have led to an absence of concrete, negative feedback from what remains of the public at large. How and where could honest feedback arise when the pre-defined content and context of speech acts preclude most forms of deviation and when "the public" has no forum outside the sports arena, concert hall or internet chatroom? (Community-based political events and occasional grass-roots election rallies are welcome exceptions to the rule.) In this context, Habermas's notion of colonization describes a societal framework that, at its best, formally affirms the tenets of liberal democracy while giving citizens so much room for fun and games that they hang themselves in the void of communicative/political action. The individual ego is free to determine time and place, form and content of the "conversation," which has none other than mundane singularities of empirical observation. In fact, the prefix *con* implies a dialogue between two or more; the disturbing reality, however, is the absence of dialogue. What has quickly established itself as the norm is the omni-directed utterance typical of cell phone gab:

So I like just walked into the hallway in the basement and I like turned on the light but it's still really dark down here. Weird. The attentive listener accustomed to "a point" might be hard-pressed for a sensible response to this statement, but one possible answer might be: *You probably need to put in a brighter bulb.* The speaker complaining about the dim light is not really talking "with" anyone; rather, the utterance is simply an immediate expression of an item of mental content, however disconnected from previous statements it may be. The speaker might be just as capable of talking to any randomly selected person off the street. This is also confirmed by the fact that any type of "clueless" "Wayne's World" response given *ad libitum* would be tolerated without even a hiccup. *Dude, we saw this like awesome accident last night and like the top of this car was completely gone.* Coherence and cogency are not necessary because none is called for. There is no negative feedback; there are no meta-level commentaries. An eavesdropper could possibly pick up right in the middle of the exchange and be clueless as to what preceded or what might follow a given exchange. The speech patterns increasingly take on the quality of isolated reports of the immediate thought content of the speaker, given in monologue, irrespective of any connectedness or absence thereof. Rambling reports of this nature lack direction precisely because suburban isolation has robbed its inhabitants of higher-order contexts of communicative (inter-)action. There is no direction because there is no topic; there is no topic because life itself is utterly one-dimensional. Only the immediate, spontaneous, un-reflected report of what "I'm" thinking, hearing, seeing at any given moment, registers as acceptable discourse.

The resultant quick-pick society is defined by built-in attention deficit disorder, with no one left to talk to. With the world yakking away at those fingertips, present company is never enough. The focus of mundane content and discourse is de-coupled from the *life-world*[47] and the global scope of human development.[48] Suburbia is by nature utterly provincial; its inherent defining structure precludes sophistication as the articulate expression of cosmopolitan concerns to us all.

And so, there they are, the homeowners of America, safely secluded behind their own suburban walls in a place that's officially *all their own* (the phrase in itself suffices.) Where everything is truly hunky-dory. Until one day when it dawns on them that it's pretty quiet inside the house. A quick look outside reveals more of the same: nicely trimmed lawns and gardens, but not a living soul in sight. Not even screaming kids playing ball on the street (video games are the only fun in town these days.) As Kenneth T. Jackson chillingly remarked, "There are few places as desolate and lonely as a suburban street on a hot afternoon."[49] (William H. Whyte referred to the street as "the river of life of the city" but the key word there is *city*.) The silent wish to have another person there to "talk to," to confide in, becomes discomfortingly demanding. The mind sorts through old photos of better homes for new ideas: tile patterns for the kitchen floor, drapes for the living room, a high-tech tub for the guest bedrooms, thinking that all the tweaks and frills will somehow do the trick. Hope floods the silence with defining images of the Self amid an exuberantly appreciative crowd. The thumb hits the ON button on the TV remote. At least there's the sound of what looks like another person, with "contact" re-established with the outside world.

In an instant, the desperate housewife is treated to a salad of attention-grabbers with the science of image-perfection reaching depths far profounder than any mere pluck or tuck could attest to. From bird's-eye to fisheye views, *we're-there-live* quick-cams zoom in on areas that hold the promise of being hot spots of action, blood, gore, or celebrity semen seepage. Never far behind: the Highway Patrol as Will Smiths of the turnpike lanes with live details of rubber-to-asphalt street chases or bank heists. These mini-orgasms of suburban excitement are the ties that bind the otherwise desperately lonely, providing a meaningful photogenic context of imagined connectedness. The conviction that *image is everything* is indeed just that: abandoning truth and genuine comprehension for the typecast appearance of such.

Occasionally there's even the chance to perform that one act for which many Americans seem to need no rehearsal: the display of public grief. Whether at the loss of the world's most beloved princess or the country's own Camelot reps, Americans are true masters at public tearful one-upmanship. With anything in sight that looks re motely like a TV camera, it's *"Here's-Johnny!-Come-on-down!"* time in which the individual griever can show the world the loss *I feel*. With heads raised to the heavens, the Amazon streaming from one eye, the Nile from the other, grimaces of pain are carefully coupled with what appears to be gallantly futile attempts to gain control. Like Christians on the verge of martyrdom in the mouths of Roman lions, these woe-is me starlets of day-time drama conjure up inner images of all the grand dames of cinema and stage in one camera-ready moment: *Ah, look at the dignity, the poise I display, despite my tragic loss. The floods of tears I shed are visible proof of my closeness to the deceased. Now we can both live on forever in the hearts and minds of all who are watching.*

Particularly noticeable among the nation's TV journalist fledglings is the "I'm on the ball" quick-fire gung-hoism that characterizes the smile-infested lines read off the teleprompter. Here, American journalistic science has elevated the fake flake to a status symbol. All share a puzzling inability to realize that there is something quite uncanny about the hyperventilated stress patterns used democratically to lend equal attention and emphasis to all items of news, irrespective of relative importance, whether those reports concern growing numbers of dead in a natural catastrophe or the projected profit figures for the latest fad toys for the country's beloved playpen poopers. Were these super-emoters of the "breaking news" super-sale genre genuine people as opposed to empty image functions, one would undoubtedly be convinced of a schizoid tendency on the loose. But the explanation is far more pernicious. The savvy local viewer somehow knows that, absent the electronic prompts, those eyes and the gray cells behind them betray the one in a billion likelihood of their knowing the difference between soufflaki and Slovakia or between a carboxyl and a carbuncle. The hammed-up concern about events in country X and the flood victims in country Y; the passionate eagerness for knowledge feigned in that focused squint towards the camera in discussions of politics and science; the smiles in permanent readiness from the self-absorbed camera-cozy debutantes firing off an upbeat report about a new line of cell phones, all feed the big-time ratings vampires in charge of developing an action-packed combo of news and reality TV to keep the public informed and tuned in.

All reality is pre-constructed through the form and content of market(ing) forces. It becomes impossible to step back from the given, presented in endless cascades of windows via the screens of TV, the Web, the cell phone, or the iPod video's digital display. The icons and scenarios projected via ubiquitous gadgetry reveal an interpretation of reality centered on success defined as material wealth and coolness. Silence, critical reflection, and analysis become the domain of those unplugged from "reality." "Normal" citizens are integrated into the wealth-proliferation scheme with every fiber of their optic being. The reality of the *societas* is thus exceedingly one-dimensional, admitting only pre-recognized variants of clearly established themes. The *Price is Right* treats its viewers to an ensemble of excited participants eager to enhance their mediocrity with more furniture, appliances, vehicles, and electronics by guestimating the retail prices of common consumer articles. The cable news channels create unity in diversity by setting the scenes for fast-paced displays of what "everybody's" talking about at the water cooler. The frameworks, ranging from the latest *EXTRA! EXTRA!* or *Entertainment Tonight* love-gone-sour item to shark attacks on the Florida coast are updated to be "hot" items of interest, ensuring that this carefully constructed slice of all that's real encompasses a totality of viewers.

One has to wonder whether all these people in all these suburbs are just pretending to be contented, self-sufficient happy campers. There are indeed genuine recluses out there among the stoic poets, writers, mathematicians, and artists, who truly couldn't care less if they ever saw another human being. Most of us, however, are not Ted Kaczynskis, and as sad as it is to admit, this is not what we bargained for or knew we were getting into. *But gosh, with the mortgage already locked in, with the whole world of friends, family, and colleagues in full awareness of how much we were looking forward to having this place of our own, what kind of nut are they going to think I am if I start complaining about being unhappy?*

The interminable suburban preoccupation with the personal image and the corresponding acquisition of things that promise attention and esteem define an impoverished world often lacking in even the semblance of a genuinely fulfilling life. There is perhaps the secret longing for the days of exchanging intimate secrets and soul-searching, when that "closest" childhood friend would sleep over, or for the antics and foot-loose days in the college dorm. Alas, grown-ups, it's "until death do you part" time, with only nineteen more years to go on that mortgage and home equity as a stairway to heaven.

Industrial society's promised grant of independence has sent the individual out on a search whose fulfillment is always just over the horizon. Driven by that un-stilled, infinite longing to unite what is with what could and should be in the name of happiness, the quest often ends in loneliness, with age and thwarted social extension putting the brakes on the important and expected personal capacity to change one's situation through the power of sheer will. Being trapped in the suburban dream is ultimately at odds with the relentless American urge to leave it all behind, to ride off into the sunset and never look back.

The fading embers of life awaken dreams unfulfilled and fears previously contained. Jews who have deleted the Almighty from their BlackBerry might still have the joy and comfort of tradition based on the law and maintained by the family; Catholics, too, may relish the closer bonds of kinship in the absence of faith and genuine belief. But the outcome effected by Protestantism's radical independence and denial opens up the door to the horror of nothingness, for which there is no remedy. For them, spring does not follow the gray sorrow breathed upon life by the chilling silence of November. Is it any wonder then that so many of America's games and plans for busyness often come with a leap of faith?

Like the two tired faces of American politics, suburbia's happy families seek relief from universal boredom and despair in often opposing lifestyles, values, and mundane clichés. Those who sense an inner longing for a bigger world of changing ideas, the latest gossip, and engaged public interaction, have returned in their search for greater fulfillment to one of the cornerstones of the modern public sphere: the coffeehouse. Chapter 2 examines the information age's version of this great treasure of civil society and contrasts it with its noble ancestors of the great European tradition.

Turning their backs on the world's evil ways, America's red-state opponents of modernity and the cosmopolitan savoir vivre have joined the ranks of many around the world who bow to the dictates of a totalitarian understanding of all that earthly existence has on offer. As we shall see in Chapter 3, for those who have found it, belief appears to still all longings, answer all doubt, solve all problems, and numb all worries. Knowing that salvation is here at last, life becomes one unified, blissful day.

America is largely shaped and defined by those who cling to the suburban dream—one that has become a never-ending path to nowhere.

Notes

1 Simon Schama, *Landscape and Memory* (New York: Vintage Books, 1995) 529-530. See also James S. Ackerman, *The Villa: Form and Ideology of Country Houses* (Princeton: Princeton University Press, 1990).

2 Kenneth T. Jackson, *Crabgrass Frontier. The Suburbanization of the United States* (New York and Oxford: Oxford University Press, 1987) 13.

3 Simon Schama, *Landscape and Memory*, 572.

4 *Ibid.,* 558.

5 See Kenneth T. Jackson, *Crabgrass Frontier*, 36.

6 *Ibid.,* 101.

7 Cited in Kenneth T. Jackson, *Crabgrass Frontier*, 27.

8 *Ibid.,* 30.

9 *Ibid.,* 13 and *passim*.

10 See G. Montagu Harris, *The Garden City Movement* (London: Garden City Association, 1906) 17 and *passim* as well as Stanley Buder, *Visionaries & Planners. The Garden City Movement and the Modern Community* (New York and Oxford: Oxford University Press, 1990).

11 Lewis Mumford, "The Garden City Idea and Modern Planning," in Ebenezer Howard, *Garden Cities of Tomorrow* (London: Faber and Faber Limited, 1965) 34.

12 See Kenneth T. Jackson, *Crabgrass Frontier*, 79.

13 Cf. F. J. Osborn, "Foreword" to Ebenezer Howard, *Garden Cities of Tomorrow*, 7.

14 Lewis Mumford, "The Garden City Idea and Modern Planning," in Ebenezer Howard, *Garden Cities of Tomorrow*, 29.

15 F. J. Osborn, "Foreword" to Ebenezer Howard, *Garden Cities of Tomorrow*, 26–27.

16 See Stanley Buder, *Visionaries and Planners. The Garden City Movement and the Modern Community* (New York and Oxford: Oxford University Press, 1990) 161.

17 *Ibid.*, 166.

18 *Ibid.*, 165.

19 See Barbara M. Kelly, *Expanding the American Dream. Building and Rebuilding Levittown* (Albany, New York: State University of New York Press, 1993) 22.

20 See *Levittown PA. Building the Suburban Dream* at http://fandm.edu/levittown/one/b.html.

21 *Ibid.* See also the documented history of the community in photographs in Margaret Lundrigan and Tova Navarra, *Images of America: Levittown* (Volume II) (Charleston, South Carolina: Arcadia, 1999).

22 *Levittown PA. Building the Suburban Dream* at http://fandm.edu/levittown/one/b.html.

23 *Ibid.*

24 For an interesting childhood perspective of life in Levittown written from the memories of someone who actually grew up there, see Pam Conrad, *Our House. The Stories of Levittown* (New York: Scholastic Inc., 1995)

25 See *Levittown PA. Building the Suburban Dream.*

26 Cf. Lewis Mumford, *The City in History. Its Origins, Its Transformations, and Its Prospects* (San Diego, New York, and London: Harcourt, 1961) 485–486.

27 For actual figures pertaining to the demographic shift and its impact on society see Robert D. Putnam, *Bowling Alone. The Collapse and Revival of American Community* (New York: Touchstone, 2001) 209. See also Alex Marshall, *How Cities Work. Suburbs, Sprawl, and the Roads Not Taken* (Austin, Texas: University of Texas Press, 2000).

28 Gwendolyn Wright provides a detailed history of housing in the United States in *Building the Dream: A Social History of Housing in America* (New York: Alfred Knopf, 1981).

29 Christie Scotty, "Can I Get You Some Manners With That?" *Newsweek*, 18 October 2004.

30 See Jane Jacobs, *The Death and Life of Great American Cities* (New York: The Modern Library, 1993) 72–86.

31 For a first-hand account of this giant reflecting pool, see Rick Bragg, "Beauty Reigns Supreme in a Florida Enclave," *New York Times*, 28 May 2000, 1.1.

32 For all the phobia about obesity, many seem to have difficulty understanding the correlation between sitting in a car all day and getting fat. Those who have grasped the connection have solved the problem in what is thankfully a uniquely American way: the walking machine or stair master. These novel contraptions allow humans to exercise in the comfort of their own homes, which of course have to be big enough to accommodate the things. Since walking itself is the prerogative of the poor who can't afford a car, few want to walk because of the shameful association. Besides, it's so much more upscale to have to pay to walk. The only acceptable movement afoot in public is jogging, which needs to be scheduled in the weekly personal planner, and requires a short drive to a suitable jogging course. This is a bit similar to the American invention of seedless grapes (the only

type now available in average supermarkets). With the seeds removed, the public is now able to buy the seeds (because of their powerful anti-oxidant properties) in separate containers for roughly $10-$20 a bottle. The wonders of technology.

33 Jim VandeHei and Peter Baker, "Critics Say Bush Undercut New Orleans Flood Control," *Washington Post*, 2 September 2005, A16.

34 Frida Berrigan, "America's Third World" (full text available at: http://www.tompaine.com /print/americas_third_world.php).

35 Christopher Lasch, *The Culture of Narcissism. American Life in an Age of Diminishing Expectations* (New York and London: W. W. Norton, 1991) 59.

36 Toll Brothers, who actually build these fast-track versions of Windsor Castle and Versailles (made in USA), provide a virtual tour of the beasts at http://www.tollbrothers.com.

37 "Living Large," *60 Minutes* (November 27, 2005).

38 For a remarkably good analysis of the demise of community as a result of automobile-based suburbanization, see Andres Duany, Elizabeth Plater-Zyberk, and Jeff Speck, *Suburban Nation. The Rise of Sprawl and the Decline of the American Dream* (New York: North Point Press, 2000). See also Alex Marshall, *How Cities Work. Suburbs, Sprawl, and the Roads Not Taken* (Austin, Texas: University of Texas Press, 2002); Jane Holtz Kay, *Asphalt Nation: How the Automobile Took Over America, and How We Can Take It Back* (New York: Crown, 1997); James Howard Kunstler, *The Geography of Nowhere: The Rise and Decline of America's Manmade Landscape* (New York: Simon and Schuster, 1993).

39 Geoffrey Nunberg has identified the "psycho babble" of various "human potential" trends during the 1960s as the origin of this phrase. See Geoffrey Nunberg, *The Way We Talk Now. Commentaries on Language and Culture from NPR's "Fresh Air"* (Boston and New York: Houghton Mifflin Company, 2001).

40 Sprawl has made the trek with the family cars not much better than the hours spent hoping for a bus to arrive. According to the U.S. Census Bureau's figures based on data from 2000, the nation's commuters spent an annual average of 120 hours getting to work and another 120 getting home. Numbers released by the U.S. Department of Energy revealed that Los Angeles drivers spend an annual average of four full days idling in traffic. In monetary terms alone, the nation racked up a loss of $63 billion in lost time, productivity, and fuel due to traffic gridlock. One can only imagine what effects a lifetime of going nowhere must have on cognitive development and the relationships with family and friends.

41 See Thorstein Veblen's seminal study of the interplay between social status and "conspicuous consumption" in *The Theory of the Leisure Class* (1899) (New York: Random House, 2001). Duany, Plater-Zyberk, and Speck provide an interesting analysis of the role house prices play in determining the social status of suburban co-inhabitants, *Suburban Nation*, p. 43 and *passim*. Paul Fussell offers a light-hearted look at the role of the car as status symbol in American society, in *Class. A Guide Through the American Status System* (New York: Touchstone, 1983).

42 Marshall Berman has successfully captured the importance of Times Square as such a central locus of urban encounter in his recent *On the Town. One Hundred Years of Spectacle in Times Square* (New York: Random House, 2006).

43 Among the first to actually study the observable effects of place and social behavior and adaptation was William H. Whyte. Many of his very relevant conclusions can be found in *The Social Life of Small Urban Spaces* (New York: Project for Public Spaces Inc., 2001) and in *City: Rediscovering the Center* (New York: Doubleday & Company, Incorporated, 1990). See also the Web site: http://www.pps.org.

44 Since MTV first aired the show "Pimp My Ride" in March of 2004, the enthusiasm for pumped-up cars has skyrocketed as yet another fad among the country's teens.

45 Detailed studies of the effects of the suburban environment on the developmental patterns of teens can be found in Donna Gaines, *Teenage Wasteland: Suburbia's Dead-End Kids* (Chicago: University of Chicago Press, 1998). See also William Hamilton, "How Suburban Design is Failing American Teen-Agers," *New York Times*, 6 May 1999, B1, B11; Jonathan Rose, "Violence, Materialism, and Ritual: Shopping for a Center," *Modulus 23: Towards a Civil Architecture in America* (August 1994): 137-151.

46 For a detailed study of the corrosive effects of a labor market based on temporary, expendable "flexible" positions on the character development of wage earners see Richard Sennett, *The Corrosion of Character. The Personal Consequences of Work in the New Capitalism* (New York: W. W. Norton, 1998). Of earlier date are the changes William H. Whyte observed in *The Organization Man* (1956) (Philadelphia: University of Pennsylvania Press, 2002).

47 Thorough treatments of this important philosophical operative can be found in Alfred Schutz and Thomas Luckmann, *The Structures of the Life-World* (Evanston, Illinois: Northwestern University Press, 1973); Thomas Eberle, *Lebensweltanalyse und Handlungstheorie. Beiträge zur verstehenden Soziologie* (Konstanz: Universitätsverlag Konstanz, 2000); Jürgen Habermas, *The Theory of Communicative Action. Lifeworld and System: A Critique of Functionalist Reason*, translated by Thomas McCarthy (Boston: Beacon Press, 1989).

48 See Andres Duany, Elizabeth Plater-Zyberk, Jeff Speck, *Suburban Nation*, x.

49 Kenneth T. Jackson, *Crabgrass Frontier*, 280.

Chapter 2
Starbucks And The Public Sphere

JUST AFTER DAWN IN EVERY AMERICAN city and suburb of name, a carefully choreographed routine springs to life. Guided by the invisible hands of image grooming and identity maintenance, hordes of fussy taste-tester divas swoop in on stage sets universally recognized by their green and white logo. An integral part of mundane experience, the Starbucks ritual has now come to symbolize both manner and content of a class-specific form of (sub)urban encounter. This metropolitan scene of sociality is habitually populated with the images of personas familiar to us all, each attesting not only to the insidious power of the media to orchestrate "individuality" to its own advantage, but also to our own complicit willingness to believe that such customized displays of busyness are somehow an adequate substitute for meaningful conversation and a fulfilling social life. Whatever may be said about the coffee itself, as the authoritative Valhalla of mocha habitués, this icon of blue state life provides us with valuable evidence of the transformations occurring in the public sphere and with clues to the identities that constitute the (sub)urban scene. Transcending its own original function as an alternative watering hole for the espresso connoisseur, Starbucks has become a focal point of human interaction in a to-go society, hinting at what we have become, and where we are headed. The cold, hard numbers tell only part of the story.

From its humble birth in Seattle's open-air Pike Place Market in 1971, Starbucks had spread to encompass more than 2,200 branches worldwide by 1999. According to a CNN Financial News report that aired that year, Starbucks had wanted to achieve a global name for itself. Following Coca-Cola's model of success in the beverage industry, Starbucks' Howard Behar had planned to expand the firm's Asian presence to 500 stores. As Behar saw it, the company needed to face the challenge that more than eighty percent of all coffee was consumed outside North America, with the Asian market in particular looming as an enticing target for the taking. Market analysts expressed doubt at the time that Starbucks would succeed in changing many Asians' preference for tea into a full-fledged mocha addiction typical of the U.S. consumer base, where ten percent of all customers frequent the scene twice daily. That was then.

In 1982, Starbucks came under the leadership of Howard Schultz, *il duce* of the company's *Hauptquartier*, and the growth rate became exponential. According to a *Business Week* cover story in September 2002, in just fifteen years Starbucks had expanded from an already impressive seventeen shops in its home base of Seattle to more than 5,680 branch stores in no fewer than twenty-eight countries,[1] with an average annual sales increase of twenty percent and profits climbing at a rate of thirty percent per year. In the first three quarters of 2002, sales had risen to $2.4 billion, with profits totaling $159.5 million, excluding capital gains and one-time charges. The number of branches had easily exceeded 10,000, tendency climbing.

Even in staidly elegant Europe, the company's growth was unstoppable. The *New York Times* reported in June of 2002 on the unexpected success Starbucks was enjoying in Vienna of all places, the very epitome of the European coffee soul. The city's cafes once conjured up black and white images of relaxed conversations about world affairs between bites of sumptuous Kaiserschmarn and smoke rings pirouetting from behind discreetly positioned daily rags. Not much room, one would think, for the sanitary perkiness mastered by the Starbucks crowd, but there they were: not one, but four different versions of America's *latte paradiso*, complete with strictly enforced bans on puffing.[2] What's more, the numbers were impressive yet again, with the store registering more than 100,000 guests in the first two months alone. In much the same way that the indelible golden arches once imposed their fast-paced American-style nutrition plan on the culinary world, Starbucks has succeeded with its caffeine quick-fix in upstaging even the most venerable of old world establishments. Germany's *Der Spiegel* referred to Starbucks's conquest of the Old Continent as nothing but frothy milk[3] and declared that the Europeans were quite well provided for without American coffee. But the trend didn't stop.

As reported in the *Korea Times* in March of 2002, Starbucks not only succeeded in breaking even two years after its Seoul debut in 1999, achieving the fastest growth rate in the entire Starbucks magic kingdom, it had also established thirty-two other shops in Korea, two of which were located in Pusan and Taegu. Meister franchiser Chung Chin-Koo, CEO and Director of Starbucks Coffee Korea had even managed to step on a few traditional toes in the process by setting up shop in Insadong, one of Seoul's most cherished historical sites, in close proximity to centuries-old buildings. The franchise planned to open twenty-six more shops in 2002 in strategically located shopping areas with high concentrations of businesses.[4]

The same pattern emerged in China, with nine or more branches in Beijing and Shanghai, where the company had planned ten new stores annually over a five-year stretch. The largest of Beijing's Starbucks branches, located in the Eternal Chao Yang Boulevard, sported comfortably large seating areas, the usual bar, and service personnel trained in Seattle. Not surprisingly, literally everything from the beverage lingo to the striking decor is cloned after the U.S. original. As expected, even for the throngs of young Chinese who frequent the place, the Starbucks experience is not about the coffee but the inimitable "atmosphere."[5]

By the end of 2005, Starbucks had expanded to just over 15,000 stores worldwide, catering to some thirty-four million customers per week. The corporation added another 1,342 stores to its fleet in 2006, and in 2007 yet another 2,571, bringing the total to just over 18,900. Its revenue growth rate for fiscal year 2007 alone was twenty-one percent or some $8.0 billion from $6.6 billion in 2006 (source: The Starbucks Coffee Company). Starbucks has since become as mundane and accepted as Spanish for gringos on American primetime TV.

More critical spirits can't help but wonder what the source of the miraculous Starbucks appeal really is.

Rites of Passage

In many ways, the Bohemian coffee pundits in regular attendance at this distinguished institution are a remarkable bunch, neatly positioned in a social class or two above and beyond fast-food broadsides, homophobic holy-rollers, and the high-fivin' skateboard crowds. Starbucks patrons (at least the American variety) tend to be neatly groomed, well-informed citizens who study the scads of self-help guides rolling hourly off America's publishing presses. They display impressive knowledge of historical events, literary masterpieces, and community politics (*Utne Reader* subscribers are often among the first to compete in America's morning siege on double decaf lattes.) And unlike their generic workout compatriots over on aisle five looking for Kafka between the tabbouleh and rice pilaf, most Starbucks devotees have also outgrown the phase of mistaking Auschwitz for a Nike competitor. In fact, the intellectual prowess of this certified caffeine nobility is so impressive that one could almost be inspired to a glimmer of that most fleeting and unaudacious of human emotions: *hope.*

Starbucks sophisticates are among the first to chide themselves for failure to recycle, and although the self-knitted tampon is not yet listed among the assortments of Starbucks offerings, environmental consciousness is rightly a persistent theme to be reckoned with as a brief browse through the "Mission Statement" at the Starbucks Web site reveals. In addition to preempting possible lawsuits filed by unwitting victims assaulted by the temperature of fresh coffee, the convenient insulating sleeve surrounding the Starbucks paper cup even reminds customers that it is "made from 60% post-consumer recycled fiber and uses approximately 45% less material than a second paper cup."

Toadying to the professional (sub)urban aspirant who has not quite lost the flair s/he so admires in Europe's cultural elite—the ones that really *parlano italiano* —Starbucks caters to throngs of regulars who often follow clearly recognizable patterns. Ahead on your left: a mid-thirtyish, adroitly dressed female career climber of the BMW 5-series with a corporate law firm scowl, just brimming with latte expertise; behind you, the gesticulating T-mobile vanity bonfire: art buff, film script writer and critic, would-be actor/editor/director, Kevin Costner-type multi-talent rolled into one, who has instantly sized you up as a nobody; at the front of the line, America's favorite icon of polit-punditry: the pony-tailed suburban soccer mom with frequent-flyer miles, in for her third post-workout decaf no-foam latte. Surrounded by such clinched-lipped exemplars of society's upper cream, the innocent novice can easily be made to feel like an ask-and-tell drag queen at a Mississippi Bible reunion.

But apart from its regulars, what truly distinguishes the Starbucks institution from other caterers to the tongue is the Gestapo-like efficiency and Masonic seriousness with which its scientifically calibrated, typologically categorized, and no doubt patented concoctions are brewed and distributed. The first-time customer is also overwhelmed by the magical unanimity that reigns between latte lappers and the deacons and elders of the espresso machines. Scientology has all the openness of a local Wal-Mart by comparison. But this is precisely where part of the irresistible appeal lies for the endless queues of pilgrims to the sanctum sanctorum of mocha bean rapture.

After careful scrutiny of the menus and possibly a couple of choking dry runs, one is finally initiated into the arcane fraternal order. The social mechanisms that generate tacit complicity among the bona fide espresso illuminati offer interesting insight into both our national character and the American need to be

recognized as belonging to an identifiable group. As assuredly as German and Soviet spies were once exposed in Hollywood post-war cinema through trick questions—*What was the score at the bottom of the 3rd inning in the first game of the 1928
World Series when New York beat St. Louis?*—Starbucks cult misfits become instantly
apparent either through their pitiful lack of insider competence, or by committing
the ultimate faux pas among the Knowing: asking for help from friends or fellow
attendees. The anomie that can ensue from such breaches in protocol arouses
memories of Hollywood at its best: A zen-like silence engulfs the room as collective heads, rubbernecking in unison to announce the alien presence, emit
high-pitched poked-piggy squeals in chorus. So a word to the wise: Starbucks is a
haven for lovers of order, procedures, and tradition.

Among the most effective of the institute's corrective measures is surely the
glance of omniscience mastered by all Starbucks employees worldwide (the politically correct Starbucks term is "Barista") and admirably emulated by the armada
of twice-a-day show-offs. The corrective Barista-stare will alert you to the error of
your ways, which is particularly often the case with mistakes in the syntax that
governs beverage orders. Much like English as we once knew it, Starbucksese is
also characterized by a strict order of adjectives pre-positional to the noun they
modify. But this is where it gets dangerously tricky for the uninitiated: Does
"half-fat" precede or follow "no foam," "decaf," or "half caf"? And how about
"non-fat"? (*Would you like to call a friend?*) Given the estimated 90,000 possibilities
of combinations, ordering a simple cup of coffee could theoretically become a task
as daunting as accurately reporting a vote count in the state of Florida.

"What does it take to be a Starbucks Barista?" is the question found in
reader-friendly print on the side of the paper cup, along with the answer:
"Baristas are trained thoroughly at Starbucks. To earn this important title, every
barista-in-training must first attend Starbucks Coffee School where the art of coffee preparation is mastered." That is where the seriously career-minded learn to
survey-sniff their noses into trained appreciation for all the subtle differences that
ostensibly characterize the drinks.

In the late 1990s, the creative strategists at DDB Worldwide Marketing cleverly used the Starbucks syndrome to their advantage in a TV ad for Café de Columbia (the brand with the picture of that nice Mr. Juan Valdez on the front). The ad,
appropriately titled "Café Bar," featured three thirty-somethings (two men, one
woman) entering a Starbucks look-alike. In yuppie-style survival-of-the-fittest
brusquerie, the two men (stylishly dressed, and judging form their scamper, *tres,
tres* busy), edge out the young woman and proceed to order. The first rattles off "a

double espresso latte, half decaf, medium foam, and a dusting of Dutch chocolate." Not to be outdone, the second man places an order for "an Austrian goat milk cappuccino with a touch of Madagascar cinnamon." The pleasantly Londonish-sounding narrator comments on how difficult it is just to order coffee these days.[6]

Starbucks is the next-best thing to an introductory course in the semantics of commercially imposed Newspeak. Where possible, Italian names have been introduced for sizes—*grande* and *venti* to create the appropriate ambiance (clearly always a strong point at Starbucks) and a potential class-defining debut standard. Translation: "large" and "twenty". (NB: The smallest coffee most commonly found on the menu offer is designated in plain, unadulterated English: the "tall". Being the least expensive cup size, the "tall" order punishes the cheapskate by not permitting her to preface her fluent make-believe Italian with two additional syllables of Mediterranean savvy. But under no circumstances is it advisable to engage in unsolicited creativity by substituting "large" or "the largest" for the previously mentioned Latin root equivalents.)

Prior to the Empire's (not the British) expansion to all corners of the globe, a teacher trainer for the University of Cambridge Local Examinations Syndicate was sent to Portland, Oregon, on a temporary assignment and suddenly found herself trying to cope with two unfamiliar jargons at once. After she had placed her highly RP-accented Starbucks order for a plain coffee—in itself tantamount to letting nasty nasal things drip onto a portrait of Di—the Beanmeister fixated her with a *just-say-no* gaze and queried, "With room?" Thinking she had possibly come face-to-face with a tabloid-worthy American psycho, the woman swallowed, then answered courageously, "I have accommodation, thank you!"

A quick immersion course via the Web (double click on "Latte Lingo") would have revealed the nature of the error: "with room" is convenient insider code to alert the barista not to fill the cup all the way to the brim but rather to leave "room" for extra goodies such as cream and things. *Alles klar, Herr Kommisar?*

To really appreciate the subtle nuances at least nominally in place among the thousands of combinations and meta-combinations of espresso-based drinks at the NASDAQ of coffee lovers, one must surely be of an exceedingly cultivated palette; nothing ordinary will do. And as far as the lingo among the die-hard fans goes, even former CNN reporter Farlan Chang goofed when he surmised that "with long lines of Asians ordering tall grandes (sic), Starbucks says its ready to turn Asia's recovery into a pot of gold."

The company is the quintessential American success story and one more name in a long list of exporters of distinctly American culture. But what prompts this daily hajj among the otherwise ostensibly sane? Writer Maryann Hammers insisted there was something positively "classy" about the place, the smells, the ambiance, and the very personable TLC approach the baristas have with their customers.[7] There is also perhaps a hint of the past, a subconscious atavistic need for more intimate, manageable surroundings. But whatever guides the thirsty throngs, Starbucks contrasts considerably, as we shall presently see, with the form and function of the historical coffeehouses that came to exert such an immeasurable influence on the development of the political, commercial, judicial, and cultural institutions of Europe.

Like the structural fabric of cities themselves, the evolution of coffeehouse culture mirrors the transformations that defined the growing pains and pleasures of society, from the last vestiges of feudalism through to the essence of modernity. And it was nothing less than the collective *zeitgeist* of an entire epoch, defined by the provocative discourse of an evolving public sphere, which gave rise to the first coffeehouses in Europe and to the forms of interaction that developed within. Many of civil society's most treasured institutions and traditions emerged in and around the humble coffeehouse. The impact it had in shaping the public sphere can be understood only within the context of the upheavals transforming Europe at the time the first establishments began to appear. What motivated the seventeenth-and eighteenth-century patrons who called Europe's coffeehouses home? What engaged their minds? What did they talk about during their dusk to dawn sojourns?[8] Let us briefly examine the mindset that characterized this era and explore the origins of the coffeehouse as a seat of enlightenment and engaged public encounter.

Places of Interaction and the Genesis of the Public

Ushered in by one of the most profound paradigm shifts in human history, the Enlightenment was predicated on the Age of Reason's dynamic dissolution of totalitarian religious canons, entrenched social structures considered ordained by God, and dogmatic epistemological premises that had dominated European thought since the fall of the Roman Empire. In just a little over a century, the continent had experienced a fundamental change in perspective—*away from* the centralized paternal authority of the Catholic Church and the institutions it supported, *toward* the individual as an agent of independent thought and action. This paradigm shift was supported by changes in commerce that had already gained a foothold through much of Europe in the sixteenth century. The discoveries of new lands and continents had brought new wealth and splendor to the populations, which were gradually beginning to increase again after the widespread decimation caused by the Black Plague in the 1300s. Widespread labor shortages resulting from this population decline were particularly noticeable in cities and ports, where the rapid growth in commerce and merchandising was in full swing. Increasing numbers of people were drawn into the urban centers, where, as new classes of merchants and wily entrepreneurs amassed vast amounts of capital, work became plentiful.

One of the direct effects of mercantilism's policy of population growth, particularly in England and France, was the massive influx of rural segments of the population into the hubs of trade in the capital cities. London and Paris were literally exploding at the seams. Within just over a century, the population of London had gone from 150,000 to about 700,000 in 1700. While the population of France as a whole was in decline (as was the case in many other parts of Europe), Paris itself saw an increase in population to about 500,000 by the mid-eighteenth century. Toward the end of the eighteenth century, according to Lewis Mumford, the populations of Naples, Paris, and London had grown to more than 433,000, 670,000, and 800,000 respectively.[9] Richard Sennett points out that in this phase of expansive growth a novel type of human individual emerged, dissolved of traditional bonds to family and place of birth.[10] Sennett cites three distinct features of the urban environment which played critical roles in the urbanization process and which were key in socializing the wide assortment of the city's individual inhabitants during the *ancien regime*: the theater, urban street life, and the coffeehouse.

The *theater audiences* of the mid-eighteenth century played an important role in defining the boundaries between what was gradually being defined as public, and the more natural forms of behavior handed down from generation to generation in accordance with static, pre-defined social roles.[11] No longer the exclusive domain of a particular group of elites, the theater gradually became a general forum for civic engagement and an open arena for public encounter.[12] Because stage actors were deemed to be underlings of questionable character, the spectators were able to let themselves go with an extreme display of emotion in response to particularly moving segments of a play. An intimate, interdependent relationship developed between the stage actors and the audience, and if the performance was felt to be good, a palette of passions filled the halls with approval and calls for an encore.[13] Less than stellar portrayals were accordingly hissed down with catcalls.

This mid-eighteenth-century symbiosis between actor and audience contrasted sharply, as Sennett observes, with the more transient lifestyle of seventeenth-century thespian troupes whose performances were constantly on the road looking for new gigs.[14] Roaming town and countryside during most of the 1600s in search of engagements, both actors and directors were essentially nothing more than miserably paid stand-up performers for select groups with particular and often highly specialized tastes.[15] Acting on the advice of Madeleine Bejart, a notable French actress at the time, Moliere had tried but failed to establish his own theater company, and actually served time in prison twice in 1645 for debts incurred in trying to get the project off the ground. The theater company he had helped form with nine others, the *Illustre Theatre*, then toured the French provinces for thirteen years (1645 to 1658) before ever being able to settle into premises of its own back in Paris.

In spite of the fact that in both Britain and France common people had been admitted "even as far back as the seventeenth century to the Globe Theater and the *Comedie*," this audience of "domestic servants, soldiers, apprentices, young clerks, and a lumpenproletariat who were always ready for a 'spectacle'" was still, as Habermas has observed, "part of a different type of publicity in which the 'ranks' paraded themselves, and the people applauded."[16] By 1750 the theater had emerged as an established institution and even received the financial backing of public funds. No longer forced to hit the road for short-term engagements, the performers began to settle into permanent positions[17] that in time evolved into genuine centers of entertainment and hubs of interpersonal interaction for city dwellers.[18] According to Habermas, the extension of the royal edict of 1641, issued "to combat the noise and fighting and, indeed killing," to the main floor theater audience, "the bourgeois part, whose first typical representatives were the *marchands de la rue St. Denis* (the owners of the new fashion and luxury shops: jewelers, opticians, music dealers, and glove makers"[19] was a decisive moment in the way the merchant classes perceived their role within an increasingly class-differentiated society. This shift produced, as Habermas maintains, "not merely a change in the composition of the public but amounted to the very generation of the 'public' as such ... ."[20]

In much the same way that movie audiences today can become so enraptured in the plot and characters that they begin to feel the entire gamut of human emotions depicted on the screen, so, too, did eighteenth-century theater audiences enter into complex patterns of emotional empathy with the characters and their roles. The passions were so deeply felt that particularly dramatic scenes often ended with the entire audience in tears.[21] These spectators were quite willing to see the same play performed repeatedly and hence grew to know the lines almost as well as the actors did. We find here again parallels to modern movie audiences who freely admit to having seen a particular film they like ten or twenty times. The plays themselves contributed immensely to civil society's increasing awareness of itself as a public. As Hegel described in the *Aesthetics*, the internal conflicts of the literary subject ("collisions," in Hegel's words), functioned as vehicles of an ongoing struggle among contradictory moments for individual freedom and independence, with each collision demanding resolution. Reaching new heights in the romantic period, the seedlings of this emancipating development of the human subject were nowhere more evident than in Greek tragedies.

The French theater audience hence became reacquainted with the inner and outer struggles of Greek drama in the plays of Pierre Corneille and Jean Racine, such as *La Thebaide* (first performed by Moliere's troupe at the Palais-Royal Theater on June 20, 1664), which portrays the dark struggle between the identical twin sons of Oedipus, one of whom chooses to attack, the other to defend his home town of Thebes, and in *Andromaque* (1667, with the renowned Henri-Louis Lekain cast as Oreste), in which a complex web of power, love, and emotional extortion ensues among the four characters, revealing a sobering political reality at the roots of human relationships. The drama of the dichotomous human also became powerfully evident in Racine's crowning masterpiece, *Phedre*. Being erroneously informed of the death of her husband (King Theseus), Phaedra declares her passionate obsession for her stepson, Hippolytus, who is tortured by the very idea. Returning home, Theseus is told that it was Hippolytus who tried to secure the love of Phaedra. Enraged, Theseus pleads with Neptune to kill his son. Heart broken at the turn of events on all sides, Phaedra then takes destiny into her own hands and kills herself.

The theater was beginning to reflect the enormous changes brewing at the core of French, German, and English societies. Denis Diderot believed it was time for dramatists to get off their crusty high horses and get with the programs that concerned what this new breed of citizen was really thinking and feeling. The *querelle des anciens et des modernes* pitted conservative thinkers, who clung to the notion that the stage should reflect classical themes of antiquity, against representatives of a modernist vein such as Fontenelle, who felt that audiences had in fact matured beyond the problems reflected in traditional plays. Racine's neoclassical staging of Greek tragedies was gradually replaced by what Diderot called the *drame bourgeois*. As a leading author of the *Encyclopedie*—in both intent and content an epochal achievement of the Enlightenment—Diderot was relentless both in his efforts to further knowledge and critical thinking and in his endeavors to unseat moral hypocrisy and religious superstition from the sway it held over his fellow citizens. This purpose is also reflected in his *Discourse on Dramatic Poetry*, which was influential among dramatists in France as well as in Germany and in England. It was the common people in their ordinary lives, not the figures of society's higher ranks that should be the focus of dramatists' efforts, Diderot insisted. This transformation is reflected in the fact that the traditional forms of theater were becoming less and less attractive. The audiences were eager to see plays they could relate to, whose content reflected the changes in psychology emerging within a distinctly public body of citizens.[22] This trend toward realism had already manifested itself in the *comedie larmoyante* ("tearful comedy") in France and in the tragicomedy form in England, with middle-class individuals prominently featured in the novel *Pamela and Clarissa* by the English author Samuel Richardson and in the groundbreaking play *The London Merchant: or, the History of George Barnwell* (1731) by George Lillo. In Germany, *The London Merchant* became the model for Lessing's *Miss Sara Sampson*, which premiered in Frankfurt an der Oder in 1755. This highly popular *bürgerliches Trauerspiel*[23] followed Diderot's plea that dramatists should break with the neoclassical tradition that had also dominated the German stage by quite successfully developing characters from the common bourgeois social milieu. Lessing's *Miss Sara Sampson* depicts in exquisite detail the inner conflict of a woman of a traditional bourgeois household who is torn between her own conscience, steeped in established social norms that extolled feminine virtuosity, and the passionate love she feels for a wuss. Both plot and character development are reminiscent of Mme. Lafayette's *La Princesse de Clèves*, set a century earlier, whose heroine is inescapably trapped in her love for the Duc de Nemours. The courtly mademoiselle succumbs to her inner piety by sublimating all feelings of worldliness and flees to a remote monastery to begin a new life.[24]

In two important ways, the theater had thus become in little more than a century an essential public forum for both established and emerging classes. First, behavioral expectations and patterns developed from the public's encounter with the theater as a mediator of form and substance of interaction. These acquired behavioral patterns, which often included emancipative conflict resolution, eventually became part of a standardized code of conduct within that forum of interaction. Audiences were permitted and even encouraged to become involved in what they witnessed. Secondly, the sheer numbers of regular playgoers (more than 150,000 per year by the mid-eighteenth century) served to consolidate this ritual into an essential feature of public life, thereby allowing the participating public to internalize the limits and expectations associated with a variety of social roles (William Blake's "mind forged manacles") developing at that time. The theater experience enabled the newly formed public to sense and to know what was possible.

At the other end of the spectrum of urban life, public places provided a concrete chance for meaningful encounter. The massive Bernini-inspired restructuring of Paris in the late seventeenth and early eighteenth centuries had transformed many of the city's established focus points of public life into architectural squares such as the Place Vendome, the Place des Invalides, and the Place de la Concorde, in order to create the feeling of vast openness within the confines of the densely populated, cramped urban environment. One unintended result of this approach to urban planning was that these public places did not beckon the public to stay and mingle.[25] At the same time, the explosive growth of the urban population had profound and lasting effects on the cities' newly acquired inhabitants and on the continuing development of the nation states. The depth of change effected by this mass movement from the countryside to the crowded streets of Europe's major city centers is best understood by contrasting it with traditional rural forms of existence.

Nothing ever really changes in rural or village life, except the seasons and the weather. Individuals are fettered to family traditions generation after generation. Moreover, every member of the community is thoroughly transparent. Folks are neighborly, ready to help out with a loaf of bread and household chores; families are close-knit, and no one gets left behind. The "private" lives of villagers are worn inside-out for the community to scrutinize and assess, as private concerns cede to the general will of the harmonious communion.[26] Barely perceptible, amendments to life's given ways are rarely wanted, and tolerated only in very small doses. Bonds of trust last a languid lifetime, and failure to comply with tacit order and norms spells disaster for the nonconformist. Predictability and sameness guarantee safety and coziness, assuring village inhabitants that no dark surprises lurk beyond life's foreseeable horizons. Things are what they seem, as they always were, as they always will be. Time itself seems to stand still in country villages, and the biggest news is likely to be the annual arrival of a nearby county fair, the unexpected pregnancy of a logy teenage girl, or the timely death of the local grouser.

By the mid-eighteenth century, London comprised the largest concentration of people Europe had ever known. In the memorable words of Samuel Johnson, "the full tide of human existence is at Charing Cross."[27] London offered, he contended, "all that life can afford."[28] For countless numbers of migrants from England's countryside, resettlement in the city par excellence must have been truly overwhelming. The city was vast, incalculable, unforgiving in its irascible inconsistency, and demoralizing in its refusal to acknowledge even the existence of the individual fish caught up in its immense net of anonymity. In its bowels, the city harbored con artists and urban gangs specialized in every known form of chicanery. At the same time, London had become the unchallenged financial center of the world, the hub of a vast network of overseas trade, and home to investors and insurers from around the globe. The city encompassed squalor and splendor, dens of iniquity and salons of grandeur, all in close proximity to each other. This wasn't Kansas anymore.

Because of the sheer size of the city, anonymity became the rule rather than the exception. At the same time, the anonymity of the urban jungle represented an enormous opportunity to escape the confines of immutable, dogmatic traditions of family, friends, and church. In the city, individuals can shed their old skin by casting off a predefined destiny and in fact becoming a new person, reinvented according to the individual's own inner longings. The same obviously held true in Paris because as Simon Schama has documented, even within the distinctly defined public spaces of the street theater it became virtually impossible to rely on traditional class-distinguishing criteria. More sophisticated modes of behavior were copied by commoners just as often as was the expensive jewelry worn by the aristocracy. It became exceedingly difficult to tell whether a couple parading through the Palais-Royal really was a genuine exemplar of society's upper crust, or mere wannabes.[29]

Whereas village life has always been predicated on the mutual trust that develops from accepting one's neighbors as part of a familiar, quasi-familial circle of predictable confidants, life in the city is there only for the taking, giving nothing in return to those who can't fight for it. As society as a whole was liberating itself from the dogma of religious superstition and the unjust tenets of absolutism, individuals were awakening to new inner yearnings to become more than the lack of birth privileges and an inherited social station allowed them to be. This paradigm became particularly visible in the literature of the period.

This intra-national clash of cultures was perhaps nowhere better depicted than in the writings of Daniel Defoe. Often hailed as the "father of the English novel," Defoe was an enigmatic man with an enormous range of interests and talents. His extraordinary insight into the eighteenth-century urban *zeitgeist* is nowhere more poignantly developed than in his character portrayal of *Moll Flanders*, the female picaro in the novel of the same name. Born as an orphan in Newgate prison, Moll Flanders is just one of the masses of nameless, pitiful country bumpkins who is swept into London at the turn of the century. Destiny has provided Moll with about as much escape velocity as that of a modern inner-city crack baby found in a back-alley Dumpster. With an uncanny sense of survival, ruthless guile, and relentless willpower, this femme fatale lies, cheats, steals, and weds her way into the heights of wealth and personal security—an eighteenth-century version of today's corporate executive. As a literary preview lesson in GOP-style Social Darwinism, Moll Flanders utilizes cold reptilian manipulation to escape the "frightful spectre" of poverty she experienced in her youth. Like a stealthy arachnid, she unscrupulously slips in and out of carefully studied social roles, shunning no means to justify her goal of becoming a "gentlewoman," independent of the ignominious dictates of any employer and subject to no one's will but her own.

Moll Flanders prototypically embodies all the traits of the nouveaux riches, the poor souls who for most of their wretched lives never have a "pot to piss in," but who become so successful at wheeling and dealing, at beating the odds against them by exploiting the good will of others, that they come to regard the bright, new, alluring world of consumer goods as theirs for the taking, literally.[30]

Pierre Marivaux's novel *Le Paysan parvenu* (1735) presents a similar motif. The story's gigolo protagonist, a "fortunate peasant," consciously uses his beguiling charm and erotic appeal to older women to climb his way up the social ladder. Even as early as 1665 the image of the thoroughly duplicitous, self-loving (*l'amour-propre*) master of the social survival persona dominated the Maximes of La Rochefoucauld: *Les vertus se perdent dans l'interêt comme les fleuves se perdent dans la mer* ("Virtues are lost in self-interest as rivers are lost in the ocean"); *L'hypocrisie est un hommage que le vice rend à la vertu* ("Hypocrisy is the hommage that vice pays to virtue.")

The rules of life that had held sway over Europe's populations were eroding; birth rights and privileges, sacrosanct and unalterable under feudalism, were giving way to the power of money and property, both of which could be acquired through scheming and conniving. Moll Flanders demonstrates the power and plasticity of the social persona, that malleable facade that works wonders for those who masterfully manipulate it. Most importantly, Moll Flanders was born as one of the countless numbers of other "nobodies" who somehow learned to do their best with the circumstances fate had dealt them.[31] *As no one in particular, Moll Flanders was, in effect, everyone in potential.*

Eighteenth-century urban life was predicated on the social encounter—in the theater, in the streets, in the parks, in shops and offices—and so the ability to maneuver through the diverse subtexts and strata of society's expectations became vital to getting ahead. Whereas the populations of previous centuries had been officially obliged to abide by sumptuary laws that defined dress codes as well as food and drink in accordance with one's social status or trade, the eighteenth-century urban burgher was de facto at liberty to choose attire appropriate to a given occasion, but not necessarily with regard to his or her background or occupation. Whether or not one was meeting a person of substance or a great pretender became increasingly difficult to answer. With the demise of the guilds and the necessity of generating an enormous, diversified workforce to keep pace with the rapid growth in international trade, in financial markets, and in the administrative sector of society, the classical means of defining a person's identity became increasingly blurred. This lack of a clear-cut class identity intensified the growing perception that the people one encountered on a day-to-day basis were no longer transparent.[32] For the landed gentry and those of means, identity was given by the stations they held, the recognition they received, and the influence they exerted; for the multitude of commoners, ubiquitous anonymity had created such an extreme sink-or-swim environment that the underlying question of authenticity became less important than the overwhelming desire to define oneself.[33]

The Penny Universities

There is a prodigious number of Coffee-Houses in London, after the manner I have seen some in Constantinople. These Coffee-Houses are the constant Rendezvous for Men of business as well as the idle People…They smoak Tobacco, game and read Papers of Intelligence; here they treat of Matters of State, make Leagues with Foreign Princes, break them again, and transact Affairs of the last Consequence to the whole world. They represent these Coffee-Houses as the most agreeable things in London, and they are, in my Opinion, very proper Places to find People that a Man has Business with, or to pass away the Time a little more agreeably than he can do at home… .

—From *A Brief and Merry History of Great Britain*, 1697[34]

Nowhere within the smoldering metropolis was there more to be discovered than in the coffeehouses, the true urban centers of public life, which played the most pivotal role in strengthening the currents of social emancipation that revolutionized the Western world. The coffeehouses fulfilled many important needs in the people who frequented them. As the cement that held together a social fabric in disarray, the coffeehouse of metropolitan Europe became the central point of orientation in a sea of change, personifying both parts and labor in the arduous process by which an educated citizenry arose from the quagmire of impotent ignorance, superstition, and feudal servitude. The multi-layered process by which individuals emerged within distinct social classes as dichotomously public-private, quasi-autonomous free agents, was rooted in the structural changes that accompanied the increased dominance of the bourgeois class.

After the Glorious Revolution, the role of the stately court was eclipsed in importance by an extraordinary expansion of towns and cities. In France, the *salon*, which already enjoyed a solid tradition of providing a grandiose space devoted to exhibitions and discussions of taste, brought together men and women of various social stations in an atmosphere of free and open interaction.[35] By 1750, this public cultural institution had been enhanced by more than 600 coffeehouses. Common to all were themes representative of the political and personal concerns of the emergent middle class.[36]

According to Ellis, of the 3,000 penny universities (as coffeehouses had come to be known) that existed in London by the end of the seventeenth century, none was of greater influence than *Will's*, established by William Urwin in Covent Garden, one of the tonier areas of the city in those days. Home to a number of writers of the time (foremost among them John Dryden), *Will's* functioned for more than thirty years as an institution of impromptu learning on all matters of public discussion, whether political, financial, or aesthetic in nature.[37] Ellis also notes that Alexander Pope's famous *Rape of the Lock* was based on gossip traded at *Will's*.[38]

When Dryden died, *Will's* was no longer able to attract the same intellectual caliber of clients it once had and reportedly became a gaming hall. In a location situated (according to Pope) directly opposite *Will's*, Addison appointed a Mr. Daniel Button to run a coffeehouse that became fittingly known as *Button's*. Like *St. James's* (already known for its focus on all the news sources of the day[39]) and the *Smyrna*, *Button's* soon became one of the favorite hangouts of both prominent Whigs and talk-of-the-town regulars such as Alexander Pope, William Hogarth, and Jonathan Swift. The Tories flocked to *White's Chocolate-house* and the *Ozinda*.

The highly influential Royal Society was founded in 1662 by England's brightest devoted clients of the *Grecian* and included none other than Christopher Wren, Robert Hooke, Joseph Glanvill, and Bishop John Wilkins. Isaac Newton, who became an elected member in 1671, might never have pieced together all the paper work stuffed away in the backs of his desk drawers if the ongoing discussions at the *Grecian* concerning centripetal force and linear motion had not prompted Edmond Halley (also a member of the prestigious club) to seek out Newton's advice on the matter. Realizing that he had in fact a number of years earlier solved the problem Halley was referring to, Newton promptly began work on the reconstruction of his solutions, the result of which was the epochal *Principia Mathematica*.

From the outset, the coffeehouses shared one significant trait: they were all remarkably egalitarian. Irrespective of the social standing of the clientele, these establishments rapidly became the locus of intense social interaction (albeit exclusively among men) and thereby set the stage for discourse patterns that became crucial in the transformation of the public sphere. Along with *Tischgesellschaften* and *salons*, coffeehouses generated, as Habermas has observed,

> ...a kind of social intercourse that, far from presupposing the equality of status, disregarded status altogether. The tendency replaced the celebration of rank with a tact befitting equals. The parity on whose basis alone the authority of the better argument could assert itself against that of social hierarchy and in the end can carry the day meant, in the thought of the day, the parity of "common humanity" ("*bloss Menschliche*"). *Les hommes*, private gentlemen, or *die Privatleute* made up the public not just in the sense that power and prestige of public office were held in suspense; economic dependencies also in principle had no influence. Laws of the market were suspended as were laws of the state. Not that this idea of the public was actually realized in earnest in the coffee houses, the *salons*, and the societies; but as an idea it had become institutionalized and thereby stated as an objective claim. If not realized, it was at least consequential.[40]

The realm of learning had largely been the privilege of the well-to-do. With little interaction between society's upper-crust intelligentsia and the working class, the latter was defenseless against those who (to paraphrase Plato) fought with words and ideas. For each world, the coffeehouse provided exposure to at least glimpses of the mindset of the other. Ellis likened the early coffeehouses to Noah's Ark as representative of all species in the human circus.[41] Sharing this assessment, Heise reports that the coffeehouses were unique in providing a relaxed atmosphere completely void of any concern for manners, personal profile or family status. Men (this was long before Gloria Steinem's days) who normally led lives segregated by profession and family background, found themselves in the delightful company of every mutt, mongrel, and aristocrat society had to offer, for nothing more than a mere penny entrance charge.[42] This function as a universal gathering place was not unlike that fulfilled by the Hellenistic *agora* and the Roman *forum*. The coffeehouse was an icon of urban civility, public interaction, intense learning, and endless discussion.

Twenty years after the opening of the first coffeehouses in England (1650 in Oxford, 1652 in London), the magnetic influence of the participatory social forum they provided had become so powerful that a petition sponsored by women sought to have coffee and the establishments serving it banned entirely. There were, as Heise notes, presumably other economic interests behind the petition, such as the concerns of the gin and ale house owners that their businesses might continue to suffer from the popularity of cheap coffee. It is noteworthy that in prudish England of 1674 *The Women's Petition Against Coffee Representing to Publick Consideration the Grand Inconveniencies accruing to their Sex from the Excessive Use of that Drying, Enfeebling Liquour* outlining the complaints of "thousands of buxome good women, languishing in extremity of want" cited the "brisk activity of men who in former ages were justly esteemed the ablest performers in Christendom," apparently in reference to an un wanted Viagra-like speed-effect that coffee had on English men. Instead of taking their good old romantic time, these once master performers had become "to our unspeakable Grief ...*Frenchified*... meer Cock-sparrows, fluttering things that come on *Sa sa*... ."[43] In response, King Charles II issued a proclamation in 1675 on the closing of the coffeehouses, in essence arguing that the establishments represented hotbeds of inflammatory, anti-government gossip, and that they kept men from an honest day's work.[44] The ensuing furor was so vehement that the edict was rescinded in January of 1676 when the coffeehouse proprietors gave their written promise ensuring they would guard against the dangers posed by negative chatter.

By the mid-eighteenth century, coffeehouses had begun to diversify in unison with the increasingly specialized interests and occupations represented among the social classes. Even within given establishments, certain tables or areas of the house often arranged themselves automatically into cozy corners of like-minded feathers, prompting this remark from Malone in one of his plays:

> In a coffee-house just now among the rabble
> I bluntly asked, which is the treason table?

Ellis provides a lucid portrait of the comings and goings that characterized the typical coffeehouse of the day in his citations of an eight-page account, entitled

Coffee Houses Vindicated, which clarifies the advantages the coffeehouse had over the "publick house," where primarily ale was served:

> Lastly, for Diversion…Where can young gentlemen, or shop-keepers, more innocently or advantageously spend an hour or two in the evening than at a coffee-house? Where they shall be sure to meet company, and, by the custom of the house, not such as at other places stingy and reserved to themselves, but free and communicative, where every man may modestly begin his story, and propose to or answer another, as he thinks fit…So that, upon the whole matter, spight of the idle sarcasms and paltry reproaches thrown upon it, we may, with no less truth than plainness, give this brief character of a well-regulated coffee-house, (for our pen disdains to be the advocate of any sordid holes, that assume that name to cloak the practice of debauchery), that the coffee-house is the sanctuary of health, the nursery of temperance, the delight of frugality, academy of civility, and free-school of ingenuity.[45]

The free-spirited discourse among "equals" contributed immeasurably to the education of the citizenry as a whole, despite the puritanical nature of the "rules of order" that held sway in the coffee establishments at the time. At least in the earliest stages of their development, prior to widespread separation according to the political leaning of their "regular" clientele, these penny universities were the one place where "a man might pick up more useful knowledge," as Cambridge Professor John Houghton was quoted as saying, "than he could if applying himself to his books for a whole month!"[46] Ellis also emphasizes that the literate educated people among the crowd would normally read aloud items of interest found in the government's Gazette so that the illiterate among the patrons could be informed of the latest events. The early coffeehouse was a grassroots forum for the unsuppressed exchange of ideas. The associations and friendships formed within its walls had an immense impact on society at large.

As hotbeds of both gossip and knowledge, many of the established coffeehouses soon became the primary sources and distributors of various types of printed matter and newspapers themselves. By 1661, the Public Records Office was able to list the London-based coffeehouses that received the *Newsbook*, a compilation of notes taken in Parliament by a certain Mr. Muddiman, an ex-school principal. The Licensing Act of 1695 brought an end to censorship in England, precipitating an immediate and massive expansion in printed media on offer to the public, with the first daily (appropriately titled *Daily Courant*) appearing in 1702. In each case it was the coffeehouse discourse that shaped both form and content of the publications. At the same time, newspapers became increasingly influential and the public began to regard journalistic writing as an important form of discourse,[47] with such renowned men as Sir Richard Steele and Joseph Addison (*The Tatler* and *The Spectator*), John Dunton (*Athenian Mercury*), Jonathan Swift (*Examiner*), and the "first professional journalist," Daniel Defoe (*Review*) joining the ranks of literary greats whose exemplary essays, dialogues, and commentaries contributed immensely to the formation of rational-critical argument as an instrumental pillar of burgeoning civil society.

Like many other periodicals of the day, *The Tatler* was conceived as a regular account of newsworthy items ranging from reports on political events at home and abroad to discussions of plays and poems. Over time the publication devoted itself increasingly to a type of run-on commentary and critique of public behavior and taste in middle-class English society, setting as its goal the education of the less-learned in questions of manners and taste—a forerunner of *Martha Stewart Living, sans* aftertaste.

When *The Tatler* closed shop in 1711, Steele and Addison devoted their eminent talents to *The Spectator*, which first went to press in March of 1711 and appeared six days per week. Like *The Tatler* in its later stages of development, *The Spectator* sought to educate the public through discursive tracts, particularly the critical essay, for which Addison became famous, and to transfer knowledge from the ivory tower of academe into the quotidian world of middle-class English society. By directly addressing the majority of topics being discussed in the coffeehouses at the time, *The Spectator* became a cornerstone in the formation of public opinion. Many of the essays, commentaries, reports, and letters published in *The Spectator* seem quite modern. In issue No. 337 from Thursday, March 27, 1712, we find a devoted reader's commentary on the benefits of public versus private schools and on pedagogical principles that stimulate independent, philosophical thinking among young pupils:

> You may please to remember, that in my last Letter I endeavoured to give the best Reasons that could be urged in favour of a private or publick Education. Upon the whole it may perhaps be thought that I seemed rather enclin'd to the latter, tho' at the same time I confess'd that Virtue, which ought to be our first and principal Care, was more usually acquired in the former.
>
> I intend therefore, in this Letter, to offer at Methods, by which I conceive Boys might be made to improve in Virtue, as they advance in Letters.

I know that in most of our public Schools Vice is punished and discouraged whenever it is found out; but this is far from being sufficient, unless our Youth are at the same time taught to form a right Judgment of Things, and to know what is properly Virtue.

To this end, whenever they read the Lives and Actions of such Men as have been famous in their Generation, it should not be thought enough to make them barely understand so many Greek or Latin Sentences, but they should be asked their Opinion of such an Action or Saying, and obliged to give their Reasons why they take it to be good or bad... .[48]

A number of discussions involved the status of women in society and the best approach to educating them into ladies. One reader, "Anabella" (perhaps Phyllis Shlafly in a previous life), suggested that one of the best ways to better educate women was to make sure they stayed at home and left higher education to men.[49] It is important to remember that these rags reflected the *zeitgeist* and its interests, which ranged from Locke's lofty thoughts on happiness to Hobbes's theory of the state and human society, from questions regarding the best forms of government to the newest trends in music, and nowhere was the spirit of the era more manifest than in the coffeehouses that brimmed with curiosity and flourished with the pursuit of knowledge.

Freed from previous heavy-handed constraints of censorship, the wider press emerged as an instrument of politicization. Habermas observes that with the appearance of Bolingbroke's *Craftsman* in November of 1726 and the subsequent *Gentleman's Magazine*, "the press was for the first time established as a genuinely critical organ of a public engaged in critical political debate: as the fourth estate."[50]

Coffeehouses gradually began to diversify in unison with the increased specialized interests and occupations represented among the social classes. Lawyers and legal scholars tended to frequent either *Nando's* or the *Grecian*; bankers involved in the City congregated at *Garraway's* or *Jonathan's*; the world of academe flocked to *Truby's* or *Child's*.[51] Because society's learned met at the coffeehouse to grab the latest news and gossip related to every conceivable vein of interest a person might have, it was a natural development that bookstores snuggled up in close proximity to these seats of erudition. In some areas, the combinations of coffeehouses and bookstores made up more than half of an entire city block.[52] Many proprietors of coffeehouses also became actively involved in the book trade, with each establishment symbiotically complementing the other, much like many Barnes and Noble or Borders outlets today—(with a different public). The latest books to hit the shelves quickly became the hottest topics of coffeehouse talk, prompting in turn an expanded public interest and sales, which then led to a need for further discussion and so on.

Coffeehouses were the seats of political journalism during most of the seventeenth and eighteenth centuries. Samuel Pepys, whose extensive *Diary* from January 1, 1660, through May 31, 1669, encompassingly reflects the spirit of the era, knew all the ins and outs of the London coffeehouse scene. Pepys' notes, many of which have now been reproduced digitally, detail the use of the ballot box which was called into play at the *Coffee Club of the Rota* when discussions had become so intense and entrenched that one or both sides of the debate decided to put the issue to a vote. John Aubrey (like Pepys a universal man-about-town who always heard the grass growing) described the political discourse in the "Amateur Parliament" as "the most ingeniose...that I ever heard, or expect to heare, and bandied with great eagernesse: the Arguments in the Parliament howse were but flatte to it."[53] Political debates of this type had become commonplace forms of civic involvement. The questions posed and answers pondered eventually led to grassroots organizations and associations as precursors to more clearly defined political action units that developed at the turn of the century.[54]

In late eighteenth-century England, the coffeehouse gradually ebbed in importance as increasing numbers of patrons found themselves hanging out with like-minded individuals from similar social or professional backgrounds, adding to a trend already visible in the 1720s. This process of segregation by interest and status gave rise to the much more private club, whose members more often than not had to be nominated by a standing member and subsequently approved by the others before admission could be granted. By this time, general identifying markers of social class such as verbal skill, accent, posture, profession, and "taste" had become internalized to such perfection that it became quite difficult to switch masks in order to pose as a member of a higher ranked class. The clubs became domains of exclusivity that precluded the egalitarian openness and freedom to mix-and-mingle that had characterized the coffeehouses in their formative years, thus strengthening the very mechanisms that served to perpetuate the sharp divisions among classes, whose lives were worlds apart.

Like England, France was an extremely class-oriented society with the nobility of lengthy pedigree forming the upper crust of society. The educated public sought out every conceivable opportunity to acquire and perfect the savoir-vivre typical of members of the ruling aristocracy. The wealthy bourgeoisie had developed a love-hate relationship with nobility in part because the aristocracy refused to acknowledge the newly-acquired wealth as an indicator of social stature; the noble classes, even those of little or no means, looked down on the merchant classes. The latter were envious of the special privileges nobility enjoyed such as its being exempt from *taille* or common taxes. Of all the strata found within the class of merchants and professionals, the most highly respected were independently wealthy. Whether through capital gains or the interest earned on property or investments, those of means were free to enjoy life at its fullest without ever having to lift a finger.[55] Quite often, however, the wealthy merchant simply chose to buy a title of nobility from any of the more than 3,700 offices that were up for grabs as part of a buy-to-be-the-best scheme. William Doyle has reported figures of anywhere between 5,500 and 7,500 individuals who achieved nobility status by buying an appropriate office. But the practice infuriated members of the higher strata of the bourgeoisie employed in more delicate intellectual jobs because they considered their professions to be superior to those found among mere merchants having nothing else to show for their work except money.[56] In their limitless efforts to keep up appearances, the market-price nobles exploited every avenue to perfect their diction and mannerisms, and to exude a courtly aura of erudition and eloquence. The coffeehouse was but one among several public sites that appealed to the would-be aristocrat as well as to the comparatively large literate population of France. Others included the salons, reading rooms, libraries, and literary societies. At the top tier were the *academies*, in which membership was restricted to an elite few.

The level of public involvement in eighteenth-century France was no doubt comparable to that of England. Procopio dei Cultelli's coffeehouse *Procope*, founded in 1689, functioned as a forum of philosophical debate for Fontenelle, Voltaire, Diderot, and Rousseau, to name only a few. As Georges Lefebvre stressed in his study of the Revolution of 1789, the ideas of these writers and the work of the encyclopedists became central topics of discussion at all the salons and cafes of the day, reinforcing in turn the political impetus that was brewing among the critics, ideologues, and their attentive listeners.[57] As early as 1721 Montesquieu had praised the opportunity the coffeehouse provided for literally round-the-clock discussions with people from every walk of life. Like their English counterparts, the coffeehouses of Paris and above all Amsterdam (long the center of a liberalized press that informed readers of happenings around the globe) were located in close proximity to bookshops.

Although the German press evolved quite independently of the coffeehouses, these institutions soon became the focus points for writers and editors of various publications such as *Der Patriot* (Hamburg, 1724), *Die Vernünftigen Tadlerinnen* ("The Rational Tatlers") and *Der Biedermann* (both Leipzig, 1728).

Later in the century, Milanese economist Pietro Verri and his brother Alessandro founded the Società dei Pugni, a literary circle of intellectuals. Highly influenced by both Montesquieu and the Encyclopedists, the Società, which now included the economist Cesare Beccaria, began publication of *Il Caffè* ("The Coffeehouse"), whose literary style and general appearance mimicked *The Spectator*. Like its English predecessor, the relatively short-lived periodical (1764 - 1766) included articles and essays on a wide range of topics, but was devoted to propagating the spirit and content of the Enlightenment. Beccaria acquired international renown in his own right for his extensive and highly acclaimed writing on crime and punishment (*Dei delitti e delle pene* (1764)), in which he persuasively argued for humane forms of punishment and against the use of the death penalty.

In one form or other, coffeehouses have been a permanent feature of Western urban culture for well over 350 years. The inns, alehouses, and coffeehouses were true windows on the world, registering the pulse of urban life at leisure and inviting clients to come in and stay. Here is where people came to meet each other, welcome newcomers, and discover and discuss the latest news.

The educated public emerged within the walls of the coffeehouse in a tightly woven web of mutually reinforcing factors, all of which synergistically combined to crack open established authority and dogma in order to subject reality to the critique of reason. The coffeehouse became the home-away-from-home for vast numbers of lesser and greater writers, poets, artists, politicians, refugees, and public intellectuals all over Europe. The establishments themselves ranged from the sublime *Café Bauer* in Berlin, the political arenas of the *Rote Stube* and *Stehely* (home to Marx and the Young Hegelians), the intellectual (as depicted for example in Gustav Taubert's 1832 painting) *Berlin Reading Café*, to the cozy *Café Hoppe* in Amsterdam or the *Café de la Paix* in Audierne.

The era that gave birth to and nurtured the culture of the coffeehouse was one of dramatic change as religious doctrines violently competed for legitimacy, as scientific method sought to overcome ignorance and dogma in its quest to make sense of the world, as the power of money and commerce replaced the traditional scheme of political power based on birthrights. This was the origin of bohemia and its quest for unencumbered poetic expression and unbridled reflection on the world. Throughout the eighteenth and much of the nineteenth century, the pattern was repeated all across Europe as citizens gathered with their cups around wooden tables laden with pots of coffee to ponder the changing world and to challenge the status quo with the enlightened hope of creating something better. Seen from the vantage point of today's freeways, drive-thru's, super-malls, chat rooms, and text messages, the coffeehouse ponderings and "reflections," as Russell Jacoby put it, represent an irreplaceable break with an era in which language actually meant something.[58]

Starbucks and the Water Cooler

The quest for individual fulfillment anchored deep in the Western mind has its roots in the enormous challenges and transformations that defined sixteenth-and seventeenth-century Europe. In turn, these changes opened up new vistas of knowledge, ushering in a new stage in the enactment of human events. A new type of human being emerged on the scene, endowed with self-assuredness and a growing trust in the rule of law and capacity of the individual to change the course of destiny.

The "dialectic of Enlightenment" (to use the phrase coined by Adorno and Horkheimer), effected changes of another, unforeseeable kind. Symptomatic of the form and power of interpersonal communication that dominates public America 350 years after the first coffeehouses opened in Europe is a metaphor that has arisen among the chatting classes as a ubiquitous symbol of conversation: *the water cooler*.

What does it say about a culture when the essence of meaningful discussion and human interaction is symbolized by the scant two or three minutes needed to grab a cup of water from the office Sparkletts bottle? How cognitively emaciated has society become when the highpoint of public discourse is limited to a brief belch of banality in a chance encounter?

The ability and eagerness to talk, discuss, and argue about anything was in both antiquity and the formative years of the coffeehouse culture a completely natural expectation participants in social encounter had of both themselves and each other. The very concept of the human being as "that living being in which speech is inherent" was inexorably linked to this most cherished faculty and a *conditio sine qua non* of a functioning society. The formation of a citizenry, a public, was predicated on the creation of mechanisms that enabled the achievement of common interests through active civic participation, mediated every step of the way through discussion, dialogue, and active engagement.

Limited by busy schedules and never-ending hours at work, with little if any paid vacation or sick leave; isolated in the deceptive quietude and serenity of

American suburbia; stuck in the daily traffic jam to and from work; sober to the realization that being married with children just ain't all it's cracked up to be, we have nothing left at the end of the day but the habitually ominous one-liner. "Have you found another place for your backpack?" yells a suburban mom to her kids in one of those Bank America TV spots depicting the icons of American norms. As she puts a bag of popcorn into the microwave and boots up the kitchen computer to pay her bills online, her son yells from the family den that the movie is starting. That's most likely the only conversation the two will have—complemented perhaps by important additions—"It could use a little more salt."

In a society that goes "bowling alone,"[59] public intellectuals engaged in open-ended dialogues that address issues of importance and reveal the extent of discontent dominant in daily life are a dying species. Realizing the need for an open exchange of ideas, Seattle resident Vicki Robin, co-author of "Your Money or Your Life," committed herself to reawakening the lost art of good conversation by opening up "Conversation Cafes."[60] As the Associated Press reported in "Coffeehouse Chatter Grows Across Nation,"[61] city residents actually started conversing in what became a revival of the salon concept, a modern attempt at resurrecting the original coffeehouse. According to the article, after the first Conversation Cafe opened in 2001, the movement quickly gained momentum, with cafes spreading from coast to coast in major urban areas. After the September 11 attacks the movement quickly gained a fair share of regulars, many of whom felt the need to verbalize the anxiety they felt. The trained host of one of the joints commented that there was clearly a need for meaningful conversation.[62]

The motley groups that initiated and inhabited Europe's historical coffeehouses were often driven by an insatiable curiosity to understand everything that was happening around them. In our "culture of narcissism" by contrast, the primary motive in meeting others is often to have an outlet for venting frustration, to unload weeks of pent-up hostility and anxiety on an ersatz-therapist who becomes trapped in a never-ending "dinner with Andre." When narcissism becomes perpetually impeded by suburban loneliness, the Starbucks routine sets in with a cast that responds to an imaginary audience, as if the participants were being recorded on film for public broadcast.[63]

More than anything else, it is Starbuck's cult quality, its suitability as a forum in which to be seen, and its status as a Boy Scouts-style standard-bearer to which far too many must (and gladly do) adhere that is indicative both of America's dreadfully impoverished forms of social interaction and of public discourse that lopsidedly refuses to acknowledge anything outside the realm of the speaker's own loquacious ego. The Starbucks scene embodies a set of accepted ritualistic behavior patterns[64] that have now become second nature to many of the hubristic middle-class success stories who pride themselves on their ability to sound suave and debonair. When the S-Class Mercedes no longer suffices for public attention and brow-beating the there-to-serve-me waiter or nanny fails to fulfill that insatiable appetite for power, what better way to start the day than standing in line and spouting off in staccato cadence the script of allegiance the urban narcissist has learned to love? For many a sad soul, this is surely the height of a day otherwise void of human contact. Much like the mastery of complex verbal and behavioral rituals of religious sects or the spontaneous togetherness of the gone-tomorrow flash mob fad, the Starbucks experience is the initiated member's chance to bask in the light of peer acceptance and admiration, merely by belonging. The narcissistic thirst for recognition in a society deprived of human contact has created an outlet that is eerily normal.

As unique and distinctive as a Best Western, the Starbucks "atmosphere" is wonderfully predictable and well suited to entire leagues of cell phone clones in a rush. For the patient patrons-in-waiting, whose daily routines would otherwise be askew without that thingamajig brew, there's an inner yearning to be admired for that cosmopolitan savoir-faire and accompanying jet-setter multilingualism. The fleeting moments spent as devoted connoisseurs are nothing more than courageous attempts to counteract the consuming anonymity and isolation suffered by countless numbers of Americans who are no longer part of an encompassing social network. Nowhere is this need more pronounced and unfulfilled than in America's wealthier suburban communities.

One question nags in particular: Why is it that Starbucks branches are always located in neighborhoods whose residents belong to higher income brackets? Why is it that the to-go cups pop up predominantly in the hands of incandescently white, fussy, skinny-fast yuppies? One could of course apply the same line of questioning to countless other name-brand retailers and consumer outlets. After all, Macy's, Saks Fifth Avenue, Bloomingdales, Neiman-Marcus et al. are hardly competing for parking space on Chicago's South Side, in Bell Gardens, Bell Glades or Compton. But there the reasoning seems far more transparent. In impoverished neighborhoods where family income brackets scarcely peek above the poverty line, paying hundreds of dollars for a sweater, jacket or pair of pants is out of the question; K-Mart, Wal-Mart, Target, and Goodwill are there to fulfill such needs. But contrary to wishful thinking, a grande nonfat half-caf latte does not enjoy the same degree of monetarily defined social exclusivity that a bespoke three-piece Kiton might. Marketing logic would have it that paying a tad more for the pleasure of conversing in pseudo-Italian while sipping away at a paper cup just might not go over well among more down-to-earth Americans who have three jobs, no health care, and still can't make ends meet. Throw in the higher literacy scores needed to even order at the joint, and the scenario reeks of class warfare, a term now as taboo as a political operative as pedophilia is as a practice. As an innocuous-looking oasis of upscale serenity, Starbucks is virtually guaranteed to be perfumed and beggar-free. Unlike Coca-Cola, Starbucks has succeeded in surrounding itself in an aura of class-defining ritual that no longer recognizes itself as such.

What is remarkable about Starbucks has nothing to do with coffee. As apparent from the historical exegesis, the coffeehouse as an institution of civil society had its roots in the vast uncertainty that gripped the continent during an era of unprecedented change. People were questioning everything, and they felt a deep anxiety and sense of alienation. For them, discussions and companionship became essential for survival; they were there to find answers to their questions. What is especially disconcerting about the mentality hidden behind the Starbucks phenomenon is that *there are no questions* (and hence, to paraphrase Heidegger, no piety of thought). The Starbucks experience mirrors a society in which curiosity has died and critical inquiry has succumbed to *media*ted versions of truth. Temporary solutions to petty problems, dictated by the command centers of market-mediation, have taken on global importance. It is no longer the process of learning and discovery that is important, but the goal of arriving, one way or the other. For countless numbers of individuals defined by the relentless pursuit to "make it," all roads lead to money and the dream destination of being able to tell the whole world to shove it.

The coffee concoctions themselves might prove to be nothing special, on a par perhaps with those offered by your local greasy spoon down the street. But, oh, the Starbucks ambiance! Where else in America could you go on a daily basis and feel as if you were a real part of the scene? For want of a speaker's corner or other public forum in which to taunt and flaunt, to prove oneself a cut above the working classes, all the thwarted taker-types, each a potential "line out for a walk" (to borrow a title from Joseph Epstein) gather every morning at postmodernism's Ikea-style answer to the classical agora in a well-meant effort to remind us that we are indeed social animals. It need not surprise us that the tingle to mingle has been greatly restricted in a culture of saturated appointment books and soccer moms with just enough time for a sip before their screaming kids start ripping the seats out of the family SUV. The chance to see and hear authentic (to say nothing of interesting) people outside of Dilbert space or away from the ritual of Thanksgiving turkey and football games has become a rarity among Americans.

In consequence, the thousands of fast-food chains and convenience stores that pockmark the American landscape are hauntingly deceptive. Silhouetted against the backdrop of plastic pastel pleasantries, cloaked in the chipper stir of meaningless, torturous Muzak, are the figures of death-at-the-doorstep. Abandoned by the security of spousal companionship and the openness of youth, those who have already served their utilitarian purpose pitifully seek out human contact among the hurried scamper for burgers, fries, or original recipe chicken thighs. With all aims in the past, these last embers of hope linger for hours over a cup of coffee, the intended keeper of face. With the doors to new friendships and promising glances firmly shut, this, too, is the price we pay for the independence and freedom we treasure.

The loss of bohemia in that unbridgeable distance to the past has left us with a one-dimensional world of coldly uninviting monuments to consumerism.[65] In a system in which the wants and needs of the individual consumer ego have become the absolute standard by which all else is measured, one might rightly ask *What is left to discover? What is left to talk about?* Perhaps the never-ending conundrum of a failing education system? an all-work, no-play lifestyle that leaves little room for speculation? the lack of a sane and effective national health insurance system? But solutions of such magnitude assume a political consciousness and a willingness to become involved. They require, as Carl Boggs put it in *The End of Politics*, a vision to transform given conditions as well as the political will to look beyond one's own financial interests.[66] One might have to look far and wide to find a hint of that among the Starbucks crowd.

The ideal citizen as *homo cosmopoliticus*[67] has long ceased to play a leading role in quotidian America, as curiosity and learning have given way to fun and the individual's focal points of mediated consumer interests. When the entire world of knowledge and the perspective of the human role in history have been replaced by vapid gimmicks, fads, and an endless pursuit of entertainment, meaningful content in discussion and even in life cease to exist as anything other than the one-liner: *Make that a grande half-caf no-foam latte.*

Notes

1 Stanley Holmes, Drake Bennett, Kate Carlisle, Chester Dawson, "Planet Starbucks," *Business Week*, 9 September 2002, 100 and *passim*.

2 Steven Erlanger, "An American Coffeehouse (or 4) in Vienna," *New York Times*, 1 June 2002, A1.

3 Thomas Hillenbrand, "Starbucks-Offensive: Nichts als aufgeschäumte Milch?" *Spiegel Online*, 22 May 2002. Full text available at http://www.spiegel.de/wirtschaft/0,1518,197286,00.html.

4 Seo Jee-yeon, "Starbucks Changes Culture in Korea Coffee Market," *The Korea Times* (4 March 2002). Source: http://www.siamfuture.com/asiannews/asiannewstxt.asp?aid=2241.

5 Haili Cao, "Starbucks in Beijing," Asia Pacific Project (UC Berkeley Graduate School of Journalism). The text of this contribution can be found at http://journalism.berkeley.edu/projects/asiaproject/cao.html.

6 The entire ad can be seen online by selecting "Café Bar" at http://www.juanvaldez.com/menu/advertising/tv_90s_frame.html.

7 Maryann Hammers, "Starbucks is Pleasing Employees and Pouring Profits," in *Workforce Management* (October 2003) 58–59.

8 See in particular Liza Picard, *Dr. Johnson's London. Coffee-Houses and Climbing Boys, Medicine, Toothpaste and Gin, Poverty and Press-Gangs, Freakshows and Female Education* (London: Weidenfeld & Nicolson, 2000) as well as Edward Forbes Robinson, *The Early History of Coffee Houses in England* (London: Kegan Paul, Trench, Trubner & Co., 1893). Probably the best commentary and research on the early coffeehouses in England is to be found in Aytoun Ellis, *The Penny Universities. A History of the Coffee-Houses* (London: Martin Secker & Warburg, 1956).

9 Lewis Mumford, *The City in History* (1961) (New York: Harcourt, 1989) 355.

10 See Richard Sennett, *The Fall of Public Man* (New York: Norton, 1992) 51.

11 *Ibid.*, 73.

12 *Ibid.*, 78.

13 *Ibid.*, 75-76.

14 *Ibid.*, 77.

15 *Ibid.*

16 Jürgen Habermas, *The Structural Transformation of the Public Sphere. An Inquiry into a Category of Bourgeois Society* (1962) (Cambridge: MIT Press, 2000) 38.

17 See Sennett, *The Fall of Public Man*, 77.

18 *Ibid.*, 78.

19 Habermas, *The Structural Transformation of the Public Sphere*, 38.

20 *Ibid.*, 39.

21 Sennett, *The Fall of Public Man*, 75.

22 Cf. Simon Schama, *Citizens. A Chronicle of the French Revolution* (New York: Vintage Books, 1990) 133.

23 See Peter Szondi, Wolfgang Fietkau, Gert Mattenklott, *Die Theorie des bürgerlichen Trauerspiels im 18. Jahrhundert* (Frankfurt a.M.: Suhrkamp, 2001); see also Walter Benjamin, *The Origin of German Tragic Drama* (New York / London: Verso, 2003).

24 See Peter Brooks, *The Novel of Worldliness: Crébillon, Marivaux, Laclos, Stendhal* (Princeton: Princeton University Press, 1969).

25 Sennett, *The Fall of Public Man*, 54.

26 Habermas, *The Structural Transformation of the Public Sphere*, 43-44.

27 James Boswell, *Life of Johnson*, ed. G. B. Hill and revised by L. F. Powell, vol. 2 (Oxford: Oxford University Press, 1934) 337.

28 *Ibid.*, vol. 3, 178.

29 Schama, *Citizens*, 136.

30 The enticing glitz of the material world was a hallmark of eighteenth-century London. Gone were many of the homely open-air shops that had catered to medieval customs, replaced by a new type of store that beckoned through the window glass. As both Mumford and Sennett observed, Defoe gives us perhaps the first written account of window shopping, in which he expresses (through the grapevine) surprise at the reports of some ladies actually spending an entire afternoon in Ludgate or Covent Garden browsing through the glass without ever buying a thing. Cf. Mumford, *The City in History*, 435.

31 Dastardly as Moll's behavior may seem, Bernard de Mandeville actually attempted to defend the viciously selfish motives that were insidiously infiltrating society as expedient means to an end. His highly acclaimed *The Fable of the Bees* (1714) carried the revealing subtitle: *Private Vices, Publick Benefits,* and argued that the expedient coordination of what were essentially selfish interests actually benefited society as a whole. Both David Hume in *A Treatise of Human Nature* (1740) and Adam Smith in *An Inquiry into the Nature and Causes of the Wealth of Nations* (1776) later constructed similar arguments. A modern parallel is seen in Richard Herzinger's *Die Tyrannei des Gemeinsinns. Ein Bekenntnis zur egoistischen Gesellschaft* (Berlin: Rowohlt, 1997), and of course in the influential work of Ayn Rand.

32 Sennett, *The Fall of Public Man*, 57.

33 *Ibid.*, 67.

34 Cited in Ayton Ellis, *The Penny Universities. A History of the Coffee-Houses*, 270.

35 Schama, *Citizens*, 131.

36 Cf. Ulla Heise, *Coffee and Coffee Houses* (West Chester, Pennsylvania: Schiffer Publishing Ltd., 1987) 128.

37 Aytoun Ellis, *The Penny Universities*, 58.

38 *Ibid.*, 59.

39 *Ibid.*, 159.

40 Habermas, *The Structural Transformation of the Public Sphere*, 36.

41 Ellis, *The Penny Universities*, 46.

42 Heise, *Coffee and Coffee Houses*, 127.

43 Pamphlet published in London, 1674, kept in the archives of the British Library, London, accessible at http://staff-www.uni-marburg.de/~gloning/wom-pet.htm.

44 Heise, *Coffee and Coffee Houses*, 108.

45 Cited in Ellis, *The Penny Universities*, 57.

46 *Ibid.*, 28.

47 *Ibid.*, 165.

48 *The Spectator*, No. 337, Thursday, 27 March 1712. The complete editions of both *The Tatler* and *The Spectator* are available from the Rutgers University website http://tabula.rutgers.edu/tatler.

49 *The Spectator*, No. 351, 19 June 1711.

50 Habermas, *The Structural Transformation of the Public Sphere*, 60. See also Jean L. Cohen and Andrew Arato, *Civil Society and Political Theory* (Cambridge: MIT Press, 1999) 658 note number 40.

51 See Heise, *Coffee and Coffeehouses*, 127.

52 *Ibid.*, 137.

53 Cited in Ellis, *The Penny Universities*, 38.

54 See Jean L. Cohen and Andrew Arato, *Civil Society and Political Theory*, 218-219.

55 William Doyle, *The Oxford History of the French Revolution* (Oxford: Oxford University Press, 1988) 26.

56 *Ibid.*

57 George Lefebvre, *The Coming of the French Revolution* (Princeton: Princeton University Press, 1988) 49.

58 See Russell Jacoby, *The Last Intellectuals. American Culture in the Age of Academe* (New York: Basic Books, 1987) 30.

59 Cf. Robert Putnam's remarkable study of the decline in civic activity across a wide spectrum of indicators: *Bowling Alone. The Collapse and Revival of American Community* (New York: Simon & Schuster, 2000).

60 See <http://www.conversationcafe.org/>.

61 "Coffeehouse Chatter Grows Across Nation," Associated Press, 21 December 2002.

62 *Ibid.*

63 See Christopher Lasch's seminal analysis of this phenomenon in *The Culture of Narcissism. American Life in An Age of Diminishing Expectations* (New York: Norton, 1991) 239.

64 In his study of *Language and Symbolic Power* (Cambridge, Massachusetts: Harvard University Press, 1993), Pierre Bourdieu explored the complex process by which identifiable discourse sets derive their efficacy. In his treatment of rites and ritual discourse, Bourdieu emphasized the fact that the authoritative language of ritualistic behavior derives its power from the willingness of the governed to go along with the rules and content of the game. This willingness, in turn, is predicated on mechanisms rooted in the social history complex of the governed. See Pierre Bourdieu, *Language and Symbolic Power*, 113.

65 Russell Jacoby, *The Last Intellectuals*, 31.

66 Carl Boggs, *The End of Politics* (New York: The Guilford Press, 2000) 277.

67 See Reinhart Koselleck, *Kritik und Krise* (1959) (Frankfurt a.M.: Suhrkamp, 1973) published in English under the title *Critique and Crisis: Enlightenment and the Pathogenesis of Modern Society* (Cambridge, Massachusetts: MIT Press, 1988).

Chapter 3

Onward Christian Taliban

Mr. President, the times call for candor. The Philippines are ours for-ever, "territory belonging to the United States," as the Constitution calls them. And just beyond the Philippines are China's illimitable markets. We will not retreat from either. We will not repudiate our duty in the ar-chipelago. We will not abandon our opportunity in the Orient. We will not renounce our part in the mission of our race, trustee, under God, of the civilization of the world. And we will move forward to our work, not howling out regrets like slaves whipped to their burdens, but with grat-itude for a task worthy of our strength, and thanksgiving to Almighty God that He has marked us as His chosen people, henceforth to lead in the regeneration of the world.

> —Senator Albert J. Beveridge, *Congressional Record*,
> 56th Congress, 1st Session Vol. XXXIII, p. 705

HOME TO THE LARGEST NUMBER OF religious zealots outside Iran, Saudi Ara-bia, and the hinterlands of the Hindu-Kush, the United States of America shines as a self-proclaimed beacon of light and messenger-megaphone of the gospel of Judeo-Christian scripture. Even though the Bible nowhere mentions the country by name (*why not?*), it is clear to most of the citizens of this God-fearing nation that the Good Lord "shed his grace" on the land and its people, from "sea to shining sea."

God is praised at the drive-through for the Big Mac and large fries; in the opening minutes of the new season for the Little League coach who brought the local team to state-wide victory for the third year running; at the gym for the best-looking biceps on the block; at the scene of a plane crash for allowing prayers to be answered for some, while justly punishing sinners or sending others right on up to heaven; at breakfast, lunch, and dinner for leading this blessed country back into the Lord's fold of the Republican Party. The plea to God for that coveted promotion is met with extra tithes and smiles; setbacks confirm that the Almighty works in ways not always to our liking—*quod licet Jovi, non licet bovi.*

Heeding the message of the nation's outspoken evangelicals, God has apparently even become actively involved in setting foreign and domestic policy by appointing presidents (through the "mysterious ways" of malfunctioning voting machines and friends and family in just the right places), congressional representatives, and Supreme Court justices. Influenced perhaps by a sighting of the Virgin Mary holding Dick Cheney inside a McDonald's breakfast biscuit, even Catholics turned out in droves in 2004 to support George W. Bush of the Christian vanguard. By standing watch over the media, school curricula, Super Bowl halftime, and the Oval Office, God is alive and well in shaping the bodies and souls, hearts and minds, habits and lifestyles of tens of millions of American believers, and *nolens volens*, the lives of all others as well.

Religion in America is much more than a trust in God or Monday-Wednesday-Sunday get-together. Religion brings consolation in troubled times; it provides one of the few legitimate motives to meet with strangers and acquaintances, connecting with other members of the community in ways that allow the individual to experience a sense of belonging. The church serves as a network hub in the creation of social capital. For the super-faithful, life itself is devoted to worship of the Lord and to fellowship with peers of the pew. Particularly in "red-state America" and in rural/ex urban communities all across the country, the church community is a bedrock value in a tumultuous, tormented world. The services offered in communion with kindred spirits are an invaluable source of interpersonal fellowship and bonding (something not yet on the menu at Starbucks, but give them time).

The more radical fringe of the Christian right would like to transform the United States into a righteous theocracy. From its base of millions of wholeheartedly devout, the right-wing Christian agenda schemes to reshape government in strict adherence with the Good Book (not the *Qu'ran*). The Christian communications networks are also a formidable force in reaching millions of receptive listeners. Politicized to the core, the devoted turn out in respectable numbers to cast their ballot for the pulpit picks[1] nearest and dearest to the televangelists' moral agenda. The tacit prescription for all that ails America includes a judiciary whose verdicts uphold Biblical truths and expunge all forms of liberalism.

The United States boasts in addition to an estimated 63,000,000 Roman Catholics, dozens of Protestant denominations ranging from traditional Baptists, Methodists, and Presbyterians, to the now defunct Jonestown Kool-Aid kids and the debunked Waco wacko Branch Davidians. According to the U.S. government's 2000 Census, there were no fewer than fourteen denominations of Baptists alone, comprising more than 96,200 churches and memberships exceeding 30,700,000. The census listed more than 13,000 Presbyterian churches with some four million members; 15,000 Churches of Christ; 15,300 Churches of God in Christ; 1,908 Churches of God of Prophecy; 36,170 United Methodist Churches with 8,400,000 members; thousands of Episcopal, Pentecostal, Full Gospel, Lutheran, Copts, and Jehovah's Witnesses. The list goes on to include denominations exclusive to the United States as well as Buddhists and Hindus, Jews and Muslims.

By far the most vocal of America's millions of worshippers are those that enjoy a "personal relationship" with Jesus Christ. "Born again" evangelical Christians have included not only a number of politically and socially influential denominations, but also star personalities such as Bush 43 and his mentor and pastor-to-the-nation, the Reverend Billy Graham. Sects are separated by what outsiders might deem trivial differences concerning the interpretation of this or that scripture, debates concerning the role of the preacher to the congregation, or the role of women and music in the church. Nevertheless, it is the belief in God and in Jesus Christ as God's "only begotten son" and sacrificial personal savior that unites the members of these denominations and determines the societal roles performed by the church covenants.

Straight from the Heart

America's evangelical Christian movement was shaped in no small measure by the patterns of ministry that emerged during the Great Awakening (1735 – 1745) as the population of pre-revolutionary America expanded westward from the eastern seaboard of the thirteen original colonies into Appalachia and the Delaware River regions. Both pre- and post-revolutionary America was home to a variety of denominations living in close proximity to one another. Except for skirmishes directed at Quakers for their doctrine-based refusal to take up arms against the forces of the British crown, religious differences were rarely met with violence.

Specific denominations were dominant in each region of the colonies. New England was profoundly influenced by two groups of Puritans, distinguished by the stance they had originally adopted toward the Church of England and its

Thirty-Nine Articles. The more radically Calvinistic adherents of the Reformation openly opposed the Church of England's doctrines and rituals as tainted by remnants of Catholicism and chose to sever relations with the church by immigrating to America, where in 1620 they established a settlement for the like-minded in Plymouth, Massachusetts. The majority of the reform-minded chose to purify the church from within, but many still opted to do so from the American side of the Atlantic where they established the Massachusetts Bay Colony. Common to both branches of Puritanism were the Calvinist doctrine of predestination and strict adherence to a rigid lifestyle governed by an intolerant religious codex. The mid-Atlantic colonies gained renown as centers of religious tolerance for a number of Protestant denominations. Chief among the Pennsylvanian religious groups were the Quakers, who were so opposed to established church structure that they were not even permitted within the boundaries of Massachusetts. Under the leadership of Cecil Calvert, English Catholics established the colony of Maryland in 1634. Greatly outnumbered by surrounding Protestant settlements, the colony adopted a tactically wise platform of religious tolerance. Protestants eventually gained the upper hand and officially ended the peaceful symbiosis in 1689. Virginia and the Carolinas remained predominately Anglican, interspersed with settlements of Scots-Irish Presbyterians.

Whereas Christian Americans today lament the absence of religion as a societal force in Europe, and Europeans bemoan the infiltration of religious fundamentalism into all spheres of American society, the situation was the opposite for a brief period in pre-revolutionary America. European men of the cloth (particularly Anglican clergy) who visited the colonies frequently complained that the role of religion in America was waning and that the population was losing its way. That situation soon changed, though, with the arrival of George Whitefield, a British Anglican minister who toured the colonies on a number of occasions in the 1740s.

In stark contrast to the contained cerebral study of scripture advocated by traditional Anglicans, Puritans, and Presbyterians, Whitefield was a rabble-rouser for Jesus, traversing the colonies from one end to the other and drawing crowds in the thousands wherever he went. He spoke extemporaneously from the pulpit, memorizing in advance the riveting sermons which he spiked with vocal quakes and quivers and theatrical gestures designed to quicken the hearts and shake the minds of his spell bound audiences. Shakespearean great David Garrick was quoted as saying that Whitefield "could send an audience into paroxysms by pronouncing 'Mesopotamia'."[2] In Chapter X of his autobiography, Benjamin Franklin expressed astonishment at the "multitudes of all sects and denominations that attended [Whitefield's] sermons." Franklin was equally amazed by the "extraordinary influence of his oratory on his hearers, and how much they admir'd and respected him, notwithstanding his common abuse of them, by assuring them that they were naturally half beasts and half devils." Whitefield was also the first evangelical PR whiz who knew how to exploit all the commercially available options of his day to the best of his advantage.[3]

Echoing the refrains of Whitefield's ministry was Gilbert Tennent, one of the minor hell-raisers of the Bible-belting crowd[4] who routinely scared the congregations into conversion. Timothy Cutler, an Anglican who felt particularly bemused by the spectacle of Tennent's (the "monster") hell-fire and brimstone saber rattling from the pulpit noted that the audiences were in fact charmed by the awe and fear preached into them "and in the most dreadful winter I ever saw, people wallowed in snow, night and day for the benefit of [Tennent's] beastly brayings; and many ended their days under these fatigues."[5]

The Great Awakening effected both heated theological discussion and structural changes in the church at the regional level. New England's Puritans split into distinctive camps represented by men who had attained a certain degree of star status in their own right. Traditional "Old Lights" such as Charles Chauncy (a.k.a. "Old Brick") saw the exceedingly dramatic revivals as hot air appeals to vulgar emotion at the expense of reason and serious study.[6] The traditional clergy saw a debasement of theological learning taking place as thousands became entranced by the rabid exhortations of fear and trembling, salvation and damnation spewing from the foaming mouths of the traveling circus ministers. The whipped-up enthusiasm for the new revivalist approach to conversion had occasionally even reached the tipping point as Whitefield and followers called for book burnings.

"New Light" theologians such as Jonathan Edwards were greatly encouraged by the sheer numbers of conversions that could be traced back to the revivals and by the newly-found forms of religious activity among the congregations throughout the region. As hams with this much theatrical talent, the ministers were no doubt wallowing in the sense of power their sermons endowed them with as they stood before thousands personifying God's immutable omnipotence. Advocates of the revival movement viewed the Old Light prescriptions for salvation and its platforms of piety as cold, sterile, and cerebrally aloof. If Chauncy's list of epithets attributed to Gilbert Tennent is to be believed, there's hardly anything the traditional learned men of the cloth were not accused of being, including "children of Satan" and "Rebels and Enemies of God."[7]

The theological points of departure were virtually the same for both groups: original sin would automatically lead to eternal damnation in the fires of hell for all who did not find salvation in Jesus Christ through conversion. Whereas the Old Lights emphasized thorough study of scripture through the guidance of the educated clergy, repentance from sin, and faith in Jesus Christ as savior, the New Lights sought the same end results by way of conversion through the fear of hell and the heart-felt longing to perform God's will. Self-contained traditional thinkers were more inclined to side with the Anglicans; those enthralled by the emotional epiphanies on offer at the revivals often became Baptists and Methodists (beginning in the 1770s). Congregations that had rallied around the scornful reproach expressed by Chauncy often held liberal theological views, but were quite traditional in their contempt of the ostentatious display of extreme emotionality whipped up among those mesmerized by Whitefield et al. These skeptical groups eventually formed the cornerstones of Unitarianism.[8]

Most importantly, the revivals of the Great Awakening were the first major events that the country experienced as a unified nation.[9] The revivals were thus phenomenally successful in bringing together large numbers of people from the Native Americans and black slaves, to the learned ladies and gentlemen from society's upper crust, all with one common interest: experiencing first-hand the power of God's words of warning and the only acceptable prescription for salvation. The Great Awakening was in effect a populist revolt against the elitist approach to salvation and the Christian life, which the revivalists regarded as overly intellectual and exclusive. A number of the clergymen affiliated with Jonathan Edwards openly expressed their doubts as to the moral rectitude and legitimacy of slavery. Samuel Hopkins deplored the blatant hypocrisy of the colonists' cries for liberation from the tyranny and oppression they experienced as subjects of the British crown, while callously "oppressing and tyrannizing … many thousands of poor blacks, who have as good a claim to liberty as themselves."[10]

As a perhaps logical continuation of the emancipation process that began with the Reformation's insistence that individual salvation could be attained *sola scriptura, sola fide,* without the intermediary priest, the evangelist movement went one step further in putting all sinners on an equal footing, with God's message available to all, irrespective of any ability to read the Bible or intellectually to grasp the theological intricacies involved. If the heart was right and ready for conversion, salvation was potentially just a baptism away. The liberating enthusiasm for a more natural path to salvation through "down-home" religion was thus also a revolt against book-learning and the primacy of intellect over the gut-wrenching pathos of the common people. The central message of the Great Awakening united tens of thousands around a common cause, from the bottom up, and is thus often seen by scholars as an important precursor to the republican ideals of the American Revolution itself.[11]

During the revolutionary period the Puritan foundations of American religiosity gradually metamorphosed into a type of Protestantism that Mark A. Noll has characterized as distinctly American, with theological underpinnings that served as an ideological basis for the violent separation from Britain.[12] On both sides of the political divide, the Bible was exploited to the fullest in order to shore up support for the respective position. Among those favoring independence, principles of Christian virtue and republican ideals became mutually supportive, with scripture after scripture evoked to bolster the struggle for freedom from tyranny. John Witherspoon, then-president of Princeton University, was a Scottish Presbyterian who supported the revolutionary army in his sermons by arguing that the quest for freedom from tyranny was simultaneously a battle for religious liberty and vice versa. Tom Paine's *Common Sense* made extensive use of the Bible, particularly the Book of Judges, to demonstrate God's distaste for monarchies per se. Of particular note was the emergence of millennial thought, which saw parallels in the showdown between the new Republic and the oppressive British king on the one hand, and the battle against the evil forces of the Beast as depicted in the biblical saga of Daniel on the other.[13] The Apocalypse of John was used to convince any doubting Thomas that the political upheavals of the Revolution presaged the imminent end of time. (Convenient convictions of this type have surfaced again and again throughout the country's short period of development, most recently in Reagan's invocation of America's messianic role in human history, and, one might reasonably conclude, in the eight years of foreign policy during the administration of Bush 43 under the auspices of radical Dispensationalists.) Jonathan Boucher, an un-repenting royalist, argued equally persuasively on the basis of scripture that the "disobedience" of human ordinances was tantamount to disobedience of God. In a similar vein, Miles Cooper believed that the violent overthrow of the established government would eventually lead to a type of perpetual domino effect and a permanent state of upheaval. Such chaos, he reasoned, flew in the face of divine plans for human societies.

Understandably, religious activity reached an all-time low during the Revolution as people throughout the colonies were distracted by political upheaval and the violent attacks that ensued. This was also the era in which the ideas of the French *philosophes*, English rationalists, and Scottish "common sense" philosophers made their debut on American soil. The concept of an impersonal God, embodied in the notion of a highly rational, Newtonian universe, left little room for the message of eternal damnation that had guided the Great Awakening. Chief among the stateside proponents of a deistic universe was none other than Thomas Jefferson, primary author of the *Declaration of Independence*. Jefferson's break with the versions of Christianity put forth by traditional Catholic and Protestant interpretations of the Bible was so radical that he planned a more rational version of the Bible, cleaned of much of the "absurdity," "charlatanism," and "superstition" he attributed to many of its passages. While Jefferson considered himself a true Christian in a moralistic sense, he rejected outright all claims of miracles and biblical references to supernatural occurrences. In a letter to General Alexander Smyth on January 17, 1825, Jefferson referred to the Apocalypse of John as the "ravings of a maniac, no more worthy nor capable of explanation than the incoherences of our own nightly dreams." "Nature's God," anchored in the *Declaration of Independence*, was thus a somewhat "un-Christian" deity: infinitely benevolent, rational, impersonal, neither acknowledging, nor favoring, any creed.

Like Jefferson, Thomas Paine ("the English Voltaire") openly embraced deism and the Enlightenment's interpretation of perceived reality as the clockwork of rationally accessible mathematical laws. The advocate of common sense went beyond given critique in his assessment of the faiths of organized religions, regardless of creed or denomination, as "human inventions set up to terrify and enslave mankind, and monopolize power and profit" (*Age of Reason*, Chapter One). Deists, but also agnostics and atheists found solace in the writings of revolutionary hero Ethan Allen, whose 1784 *Reason, the Only Oracle of Man*, lambasted established religions and the "tyranny of Priests" who made every attempt "to invalidate the law of nature and reason, in order to establish systems incompatible therewith." The common plea among these learned men was that society as a whole free itself from the shackles of religious superstition and embrace human reason as a guiding beacon of liberty and justice. The *zeitgeist* succeeded in establishing the freedom of worship under the auspices of a neutral, secular government. The American love affair with the Enlightenment was brief, however, as new voices of religiosity began to stir in various areas of the country.

Whereas the Great Awakening had unlocked the primordial terror of the prospective eternal flames of damnation and the passion for salvation in "common" people, the so-called Second Great Awakening firmly established entire networks of religious organizations and associations with the explicit goal of spreading the word of God as interpreted by leading clergy and theologians, and of cleansing minds of lingering deistic influence. At the close of the eighteenth century, traveling ministers began to hit the trails again, preaching the gospel to farmers and mountain folk cut off from established churches in larger towns and cities. In 1801, Cane Ridge, Kentucky, became the venue of choice for the largest Christian revival the continent had ever seen. Estimates of as many as 30,000 Baptists, Methodists, and Presbyterians, black and white, streamed into the area to hear the gospel delivered by traveling preachers. Participants witnessed an entire array of curious physical manifestations of religious enthusiasm as many of the faithful fell as flat as a fritter to the ground, only to begin a series of shakes and convulsions, hoots and hollers, moaning and barking, as clear "indications" that they had been touched by the powerful word of God. The seminal event laid the groundwork for hundreds of community churches and religious associations that mushroomed in the years that followed in all regions of the States. The Baptist and Methodist denominations grew by leaps and bounds and overtook in numbers all other religious affiliations. Services themselves were transformed as more theologians gradually abandoned the hard-core Calvinist doctrine of predestination in favor of the Arminian interpretation of scripture allowing for sinners to find salvation through conversion. The period also saw the introduction of the "anxious bench." The designated seat in full view of the audience allowed members of the congregation who felt particularly touched by the sermon to take their seat at the front in readiness for conversion and baptism.

In the first thirty years alone, the nineteenth century celebrated the birth of the American Bible Society with its large publication endeavors, the American Home Missionary Society, and the American Sunday School Union. Since a system of public education had not yet been created, the Sunday School Union was instrumental in providing literacy programs to young and old alike. Religious literature of various kinds began to circulate in increasing numbers as established churches and organized revival meetings became permanent fixtures of civic action and social networking. In modern parlance, these associations were largely interdenominational "faith-based initiatives" devoted to correcting social ills and to supporting missionary work both at home and abroad.

Targets of the Puritan urge to purge included lotteries, a previous source of funding for various buildings at Harvard and Yale as well as for many parishes,[14] parties and festivities that included dance, the theater, anything seen as indecent, and of course alcohol. One of the stated goals of the Connecticut Missionary Society, established in 1798, was to "Christianize the heathen" throughout North America. To that end the *Connecticut Evangelical Magazine* was set up in 1800 to take on the public relations task of obtaining needed donations and popularizing missionary goals. Baptists turned out to be particularly active in preaching the gospel abroad, with the "General Convention of the Baptist Denomination in the United States of America for Foreign Missions" leading the way.[15]

These charitable associations were also creatively involved in aiding the sick and needy, but especially noteworthy were the humanitarian strides they took against the most heinous institution in American history: slavery. The lines of conflict were clearly drawn between northern abolitionists who viewed the loathsome practice as deeply un-Christian, and slaveholders who profited immensely from free labor that encompassed everything from cleaning the bedroom piss pots, to exhausting, back breaking tasks like hauling timber and bricks. The hornier masters repeatedly raped women and their daughters with impunity. To add insult to injury, they often sold off the offspring at local slave auctions, separating the children from the mothers who had conceived and cared for them. In accordance with their economic interests and biological "needs," they selected from the Good Book passages that affirmed the legitimacy of the master-slave relationship: Exodus 21: 20-21: "And if a man smite his servant, or his maid, with a rod, and he die under his hand, he shall be surely punished. Notwithstanding, if he continue a day or two, he shall not be punished: for he is his money."

In other words, it was fully acceptable to beat the crap out of this human "property," just as long as "it" didn't die. Killing it would have been a sign of squandering God-given resources.

The version in Ephesians 6:5 wasn't all that much better: "Servants, be obedient to them that are your masters according to the flesh, with fear and trembling, in singleness of your heart, as unto Christ … "

This was the scripture Uncle Tom obviously took too much to heart.

For the thousands of southern slaves who often had to meet in secret hiding places for midnight whisper worship, the Gospel represented a subtle ray of hope that one day—despite all odds—their horrendous physical suffering and unspeakable emotional grief would end. If not on Earth, so in Heaven.[16]

Much of the abolitionist fervor to end slavery came from their spiritual convictions based in the teachings of Christ ("Love thy neighbor as thyself") and from a common sense of what was good and proper. Many of the movement's most vocal advocates were tireless in their efforts to put an end to the abominable practice. Congregationalist Theodore Dwight Weld employed his revival sermons and direct "appeal on behalf of the Oberlin Institute" to awaken the public's support "for the immediate, universal, and total abolition of slavery" (1830). Harriet Beecher Stowe used her powerful skills as a writer to enlighten readers in personable prose to the interminable suffering of the countless children, women, and men of all ages entrapped in the state-sanctioned system. Quaker William Lloyd Garrison's newspaper *The Liberator* was devoted in part to the abolitionist cause and to the "diffusion of universal knowledge." Though many of the efforts could have been characterized as "preaching to the choir," they did much to garner support for the just cause and to sway and solder public opinion against a practice increasingly viewed as barbaric and evil.

It was inevitable that the growing divisions within the country over the issue of slavery would eventually spill over into the structure of the churches as such, and nowhere was the bitter conflict more apparent than among the Baptists.[17] The Triennial Convention's Board of Foreign Missions came down unequivocally on the side of abolition by announcing in 1840 that slave owners would not be allowed into the fold as church missionaries.[18] The refusal by the Home Mission Society to accept James E. Reeve, a candidate selected by congregations in the state of Georgia, led to a complete schism within the organization. Incensed Southerners responded by pulling out of the Triennial Convention and establishing the Southern Baptist Convention in 1845. The new affiliation, which openly supported slave holders' rights to shackle human beings, remains the nation's largest single organization of Protestants.

The post-Civil-War era heralded the legal emancipation of the slaves, but among the incorrigible losers of the conflict, the ideologies brought forth to dehumanize the African-American population have been slow to die out.

Challenges from Science—Interpreting History

Christian America awoke to a new kind of threat in the second half of the nineteenth century from two directions in scientific research. The century distinguished itself as an era in which great philosophical systems examined the problem of progress and direction in history. Hegel's *Phenomenology of Mind* tracked the steady progression of both the individual's and the collective intellect's multi-faceted dynamic encounter with Otherness towards the final goal of unity in the Absolute. In the progress of human societies, each epoch or concretized stage in the advance towards a higher level of consciousness and freedom contains inherent contradictions. In Hegel's model, the motor of history drives inexorably toward resolution through the negation of these contradictions and the emergence of a new phase of development with its own inner conflict. The final destination is the rational state as the unity of what could be and should be with what is.

Like his friend Condorcet, Auguste Comte was convinced of an identifiable "progress of the human mind." Following his mentor Saint-Simon's three-stage model of historical development, Comte set out to show that human knowledge had evolved through three distinct stages in a vertical movement from lower to higher. Religious thinking or theological investigation, occupying the bottom rung, consisted of a three-tiered movement from animism to polytheism to monotheism. Philosophy and metaphysics eventually replaced the religious, mythical realm of thinking with conceptualized abstractions in a tightly woven system of logic. This, in turn, led to the highest phase in the progress of knowledge: science and the scientific method, with sociology (a term coined by Comte) the crowning jewel on the pyramid. In Comte's view, the new academic study of human societies and their places in the history of civilization was to be an exact science capable of resolving once and for all issues of conflicting belief systems or economic and political interests.

In turning Hegel "upside-down" (or putting him back on his feet), Marx, too, was in the process of delineating his expansive theory of historical materialism as the natural evolution of class conflict predicated on the ownership of and access to the means of production. Marx's ideology critique posited that religion and philosophy were the expressions of underlying class interests. Once those interests and the mechanisms by which they operate on the ideological level were exposed, Marx reasoned, those most alienated from their own labor would rise up in revolt. The vision of a society based not on exploitation, but on rational principles of collective ownership and the just distribution of all material goods became the clarion call of the *Communist Manifesto* as a blueprint for historical change.

Common to all these theoretical constructs was the idea that a new continent of knowledge had opened up based on the real need to steer the direction of human endeavors from a dangerously haphazard playing out of events and conflicts, in which the strongest rival always gets the upper hand, to a rationally organized, purposeful effort toward the common good: the best life for the most people.

At the same time, the history of the earth itself became the intensely debated focus of inquiry. First proposed as a theory by James Hutton in 1784, the principle of uniformitarianism posited that the same natural forces shaping the earth today sufficed completely to explain how things got to be the way they are geologically. Close examination of rock and sediment layers found in Scotland led Hutton to publish his hypothesis of uniformitarianism as a plausible explanatory geophysical model in his two-volume *Theory of the Earth*. Hutton's theory flew in the face of catastrophism, the view that the earth in all its geologic detail had come into being through acts of God as described in Genesis. In stating that all currently observable forces could completely explain the natural features of the earth's surface, the theory implied a much longer geological history than the estimated 6,000 years proposed by biblical scholars. The theory received sound support in the form of detailed observations documented by Charles Lyell in the *Principles of Geology* (1830–1833). Lyell noted that fossils found in various rock strata could be explained only if a much longer time span for the stratification process was assumed.

With the publication of Charles Darwin's *Origin of Species* in 1859, a paradigm shift occurred in the understanding of the genesis and historical transformation of diverse species and their inter-relatedness to their natural habitat. The Judeo-Christian scripture, specifically the book of Genesis, taught that God created the entire universe—all forms of flora and fauna, including the human being, in less than a week. Calculating back from distinct individuals identified in the Bible, biblical authorities had arrived at an age for the earth that was clearly grossly at odds with the numbers proposed both by Darwin and by the geological study of rock strata and fossil remains. Furthermore, Darwin's keen observations of the astonishing forms of adaptation visible in various species implied like origins but many divergent paths of development. Darwin's conclusion was that earth's abundant species of plants and animals had changed (adapted) considerably throughout a prehistory spanning eons. A "creator" was rendered superfluous because the motor of bio-history transformation was haphazard mutations that either furthered or hindered survival into reproductive age. Darwin's theory provoked enormous dissent among the Christian community who interpreted the scriptures as the literal word of God. It continues to do so, and not just in Kansas.

A second major challenge came from a series of philological analyses of the Bible itself by scholars employing the best scientific tools available at the time. Deeply embedded in the philosophy of the Enlightenment, these predominately

German thinkers precipitated an entire wave of biblical exegesis and critique, opening up a chasm particularly in the Protestant religious community. Hermann Samuel Reimarus, a professor of philosophy and Hebrew studies in Wittenberg, published a provocative analysis of the truth status of received Christianity entitled *(Apologie oder) Schutzschrift für die vernünftigen Verehrer Gottes*, in which he argued that much of the content of both the Old and New Testaments, particularly the miracles such as the parting of the Red Sea or the resurrection of Christ, were a product of human imagination and could not have occurred as depicted in the scriptures. The bulk of Reimarus's important writings was published through the efforts of Lessing in various stages and became known as the *Wolfenbüttel Fragments*. The first complete edition wasn't published until 1972. Even in its incomplete form, Reimarus's *Apology* was a source of intense debate among theologians for years to come.

In what appears to be an expanded adaptation of ideas first put forward by French physician Jean Astruc, Johann Gottfried Eichhorn (often referred to as the "father of Old Testament criticism") hypothesized that the entire Pentateuch or first five books of the Old Testament were collections of literary texts based on historical fables put together during the era of King Soloman. The bulk of Astruc's speculation derived from the two distinct and contrasting references to God in Genesis, namely to *Elohim* and *Jehovah*. Astruc (and later Eichhorn) conjectured that Moses had used two separate sources, each of which had employed one or the other name. In an attempt to explain the discrepancies in content and emphasis among the synoptic gospels, Eichhorn also proposed an original, primordial *Urtext* of the gospels as a basis from which each of the received versions was thought to have been paraphrased.

Eichhorn then cast a critical eye on other books of both the Old Testament and the gospels of the New Testament. This line of argument was then sharply enhanced by the work of other scholars in the field, including De Witte and Geddes. Historical considerations were then added to the literary critique, enabling them to conclude that the Pentateuch was solely of literary-historical character, essentially void of divine influence.

Attempts to undermine both the received view of the Bible and the factual nature of the Christian gospel were ratcheted up another notch in 1835 with the publication of David Friedrich Strauss's *The Life of Jesus Critically Examined*. Strauss contended that it was by no means his intention to discredit Christianity, its moral teachings, or promise of salvation, but rather to expose the mythological nature of Jesus and the body of scripture in which his life and teachings were re-vealed. Strauss maintained that the entire New Testament was replete with evi-dence that Jewish myths surrounding the promised Messiah had been the basis on which the gospels were written.

As might have been expected, Strauss's work was defamed by large sections of the clergy as "satanic verse" straight out of hell. He had anticipated perhaps a more open-armed reception among theologians, but had warned laic readers not to read the textbook so as not to lose faith. *The Life of Jesus Critically Examined* (the English translation was the commendable work of Marryan Evans (a.k.a. George Eliot) and her first published book) was reprinted three times with several revi-sions in the third, to dilute perhaps as some scholars have argued the full brutal brunt of his arguments, which were widely regarded as sacrilegious.

Here again, the net result of much of the wave of higher criticism was to call into question the accuracy of the single most important book in the history of West-ern civilization and to cast unsettling doubt on its status as the inspired word of God. The American religious community's reactions to these challenges reflected even at the time the enormous divide visible in red state—blue state politics and policies today. On one side of the chasm were northeast urban intellectuals, who proved ready and willing to adapt and amend their theological assumptions in ac-cordance with the newest scientific or philosophical findings. A number of leading universities had already begun extensive secularization in curriculum and faculty appointments, highlighting the need for specialized professionalization in the sci-ences, with industrial philanthropists such as Rockefeller, Duke, Vanderbilt, and Stanford paving the way financially. The role of religious studies and theology was waning. The clash of scientific evidence and theory with religious conviction was typified in the somewhat schizophrenic attitude taken by such prominent academ-ics as Harvard botanist Asa Gray, who described the scientific side of his character as Darwinian, while philosophically remaining an adherent of the Nicene Creed.[19] Liberal theologian Shailer Matthews, dean of the theological seminary at the Uni-versity of Chicago even went so far as to call for a re-thinking of the role of Chris-tianity and the emphasis of its teachings in a changed society "to meet human needs."

For the millions of Americans whose spirits had been quickened to the core by the power of the word of God during the great revivals, these changes were part and parcel of deeply unsettling transformations visible everywhere as the seeds of mod-ernism took root in the social fabric of Western industrialized countries. The opposition to Darwinian theory and the repugnance attributed to higher criticism's interpretive models of the Bible began to weave themselves through a broad spectrum of the population. For many, the church community was a safe haven in a complex world of unseen economic forces, shifting political/financial power structures, and increasingly de-personalized forms of social interaction. As communities interlinked along improved lines of transportation, the populations became more mobile and transient. Those of mental, social, and financial means managed to stay on top of things by "going with the flow" of change and adapting to the new requirements of the more urbanized industrialized society. The rapid shift in population away from rural communities into larger urban concentrations didn't spell the end of revivalism or the church-centered life, but for those who did make the move into the cities, mundane existence often took center stage over worries about the afterlife. For those open to change, the transformations were hailed as a chance to break into new frontiers while enjoying the fruits of mechanization.

But modernity also had its victims. Those "left behind" in the ways and means of by-gone eras would not or could not accept many of the challenges created by this fundamental restructuring of society. The power of God, his word, and the communion with others in worship of him had been the bedrock of personal and communal stability for several generations. And suddenly, here, too, modernity was raising its ugly head by casting doubt on the legitimacy of the faith itself, that one secure threshold separating salvation from eternal damnation. From a psychoanalytical perspective, the vehemence with which the deeply religious segments of the population attempted to counter the threats was commensurate with the anxiety and fear that grew in response to the perceived dangers. Cries of "atheism!" echoed among the inner chambers of theologians, pastors, and congregations who condemned evolution as blasphemous and biblical critique as the work of Satanists intent on sowing seeds of hellish doubt in the minds of the faithful.

Not surprisingly, modern science and biblical hermeneutics were most well received in the halls of academe. Established churches in the Northeast and poor rural areas of the country were far less welcoming or tolerant of the new ideas coming out of the cities. As with the issue of slavery, church communities were divided in their responses to the perceived threats. At the same time, new organizations with altered doctrines began to emerge. The National Camp Meeting Association for the Promotion of Christian Holiness resulted from the efforts of a large group of Methodists who believed that it was not only possible, but advisable for the individual Christian to seek complete sanctification in addition to prior conversion. The experience common to many of the new movements was an emphasis on "baptism of the Holy Spirit," demonstrated by such gifts as "speaking in tongues," a spontaneous series of utterances that to outsiders sounded like gibberish, but which could be "interpreted" by others who had received "the gift." The practice became central to the various branches of the Pentecostal denominations. Other signs still in practice in many rural communities include the challenge of picking up poisonous snakes in the faith-based conviction that they could have no effect on the truly saved. As shit does sometimes happen, many ostensibly devout souls continue to meet their untimely end through a potent hemotoxin.

The widespread opposition to higher criticism took on the form of a political tractate in 1910 with the publication of the first in a series of twelve books that took direct aim at the premises and interpretive conclusions of biblical scholarship. Entitled *The Fundamentals: A Testimony to the Truth*, the booklets consisted of dozens of articles written by leading clergy and theologians of the day, including Thomas Whitelaw, Charles Erdman, E. Y. Mullins, James Orr, Sir Robert Anderson, David Heagle, evangelist L.W. Munhall, Benjamin B. Warfield, George W. Lasher (author of "Theology for Plain People") and Cyrus I. Scofield of *The Scofield Reference Bible* fame. The Fundamentals constituted a well-executed attack on the higher critics. Moreover, the essays appealed in part to an ever-catchy tone of anti-intellectualism juxtaposed against the piety of "theology for plain people." The tracts set in motion an activist movement particularly among Baptists, Presbyterians, and conservative Methodists. Its tenets were the needed call to arms against the "blasphemous" contentions spewing forth from professional biblical scholars tainted by the "evils" of the Enlightenment. The fundamentalists first tried to expunge liberal elements from within the ranks of their own church communities, but often were ready to cut established ties altogether. During the 1920s especially, a growing number of churches completely broke ranks with their mother organizations, while other groups of like-minded faithful chose to set up their own places of worship.[20] Curtis Lee Laws is credited with using the title of the religious volumes in 1920 to describe loyal Christians who readied themselves to take on the forces of evil. Joining the ranks of the vocal militants was none other than Populist orator par excellence, William Jennings Bryan.

Of all the historically documented encounters between adherents of modern science and the Enlightenment on the one hand, and fundamentalist Christians on the other, none achieved the fame of the Scopes "monkey trial" of 1925 in Dayton, Tennessee, immortalized in Jerome Lawrence and Robert Lee's play, *Inherit the Wind*, thirty years later.

At the center of the trial was Dayton, Tennessee, school teacher, John T. Scopes, accused of having violated the state's "Butler Law" which had been passed early in 1925, forbidding the teaching of evolution in public schools. The trial itself was prompted by action from the American Civil Liberties Union, which had pledged in newspaper columns to pay for the legal defense of any teacher willing to serve as a test-case scapegoat in a legal challenge to the legitimacy of the law. The trial brought out the best not only in the opponents of the fundamentalism—modernism divide, but also in the sharp-witted reporter covering the case for the *Baltimore Sun*, H.L. Mencken. Arguing for the prosecution was William Jennings Bryon, the self-appointed voice of the common man and ardent defender of the fundamentals of old-time religion. A three-time loser in his bids for the White House, the "old buzzard," Mencken commented, who had "failed to raise the mob against its rulers, now prepares to raise it against its teachers." The defense team, led by Clarence Darrows, went all out in its efforts to soften public sentiment for the sensible new theory at the heart of the debate, at one point even putting Bryan himself on the stand. The verdict in the case had been a foregone conclusion, as Mencken noted, the result not of open deliberation, but of the unshakeable conviction of the entire community that the faith of the nation was true and anything that opposed it was inherently evil.

The courtroom ordeal displayed the usual bigoted insight characteristic of so many of the show trials in which all-white juries found an accused black man guilty, eo ipso, of any crime "justice" could cook up. The front of the "so-called minds of these fundamentalists" had, as Mencken commented, "leaped to the assault as one man," united in their unerring convictions that they were fighting "a battle-royal between unbelief that attempts to speak through so-called science and the defenders of the Christian faith, speaking through the legislators of Tennessee" (so Bryan). (It is astounding how very much in vogue this argument is today.) As Mencken astutely observed, this was justice delivered by people who were "simply unable to imagine a man who rejects the literal authority of the Bible" against a doctrine they perceived as nothing more than an expression of the "atheism of the great urban Sodoms and Gomorrah." As much as the fight against Darwin's theory aimed to uphold the sanctity and validity of a belief system lying at the heart of the rural American soul, it was also a battle against the threats of modernism oozing out of the citadels of urban society. The Tennessee courtroom was Billy Sunday territory, home to simple folk who didn't, and don't take kindly to city slickers with their fancy learning and high-fallutin' ways. Sounds like Bush territory.

America's Own Taliban

Little has changed over the decades in many of these God-fearing communities. The willingness to take up the fight for the same cause is evinced by decisions taken by local schools in the same back-woodsy communities all across rural America, where the public will is determined by unwavering faith in the unerring word of God. The big-name evangelists of the revival era have come and gone, replaced in large part by the comfort of the TV screen and the nationally syndicated messages of heaven's most famous reps such as James Dobson, Tony Perkins, and Pat Robertson.

What has changed is the expanded scope of religious opposition to include issues that have become acute with the enhancement of knowledge and more liberalized social policies: abortion rights, embryonic stem cell research, genetic engineering with the prospect of human cloning, and gay rights. Irrespective of the social and theological issues that do indeed distinguish fundamentalists from evangelicals,[21] both groups presented pretty much a united front in helping elect two of America's most important conservative leaders into the White House. Reagan was able to rely heavily on the voters stemming from the so-called "Moral Majority," a group that coalesced around the sermons of Jerry Falwell, the late popular televangelist. Dominant themes at the time included the ever-popular rants against the "evils of communism" as well as perennial favorites like abortion, pornography, the "gay agenda," and the "corruption" of school text books through the "brainwashing" strategies of the "radical left," by which was meant anyone to the left of Billy Graham.

The activities of abortion opponents reached a high point during the 1990s with a series of bombings targeting abortion clinics and the direct endorsement of the assassinations of gynecologists who performed abortions in their practices. The National Abortion Federation reported a total of forty-one bombings, 171 cases of arson, and more than 1100 cases of vandalism perpetrated against abortion clinics, in addition to seven murders and seventeen cases of attempted murder of abortion doctors and their associates. Particularly worrying were the Web sites established by radical pro-life organizations advocating the liquidation of abortion doctors by individual chapter-and-verse vigilantes. Several of these Internet domains contained the names and home addresses of entire lists of doctors known to have been carrying out the procedures, and activists were tacitly encouraged to follow through with any action necessary in defense of the fetus. Viewers were then able to check on the progress made in the struggle by means of lines drawn through the names of the physicians who had been successfully "re-moved" from service.[22]

Among the most prominent cases was that of former Presbyterian minister Paul Hill, who shot and killed Dr. John Britton and his unarmed escort, James Barrett, in Florida in 1994. Subsequently executed in 2003 for the crime, Hill stated before his death that he didn't "feel any remorse because I think it was a good thing, and instead of being shocked, more people should do what I did." Convinced he was acting in the will of God, Hill added that God had used and would continue to use the killing of the doctor "in a marvelous way."

Nonviolent evangelicals such as Richard Land of the Southern Baptist Ethics and Religious Liberty Commission and R. Albert Mohler, Jr., of the Southern Baptist Theological Seminary in Louisville were quick to distance themselves outwardly from Hill's pro-violent stance in defense of the unborn, but the anti-abortion drive remains a permanent emblem of the pro-life, pro-family agenda of virtually all evangelical and fundamentalist Christians.

It is noteworthy that the two issues most dominant in the conservative Christian agenda and most likely to sound the militants' battle cry, both center around sex and its effects. In the case of abortion, there is the (sub-)conscious desire to punish the woman for engaging in intercourse without suffering the consequences spelled out in the Bible's story of the Fall: "In pain you shall bring forth children..." (Genesis 3:16). With the advent of the pill, females were free to engage in sexual pleasures without the fear of unwanted pregnancies, adding to the "moral decay" widely perceived by moral high-roaders to be clutching the nation during the 1960s.

Those who were sidelined in the pews missed out on all the fun of free love and experimentation with drugs. It must be a truly unbearable burden to realize that all the other guys and gals in the most hormonally-driven age groups are out there getting some in the city, while one's own guilt-plagued conscience secretly wants to, but instead opts for a round of "Rock of Ages" as a widely accepted means of suppression. What better way to ensure at least some discomfort in the lives of all the licentious "whoring sluts" than to force them into retribution with an unwanted child. *That'll teach 'em!*

The concern for the life of a freshly formed egg/sperm combo or for semen stains left behind on a blue dress is noticeably absent in the thousands of homeless shelters across the country. Once the finished product is there, legislation patterns prove the oh-so-concerned pro-family fanatics couldn't give a hoot. In fact, it's largely back to the Social Darwinist drawing board of dreaming up ways to punish the poor. According to a detailed study conducted by Jean Reith Schroedel, those areas of the country that are most averse to abortion are also among the stingiest when it comes to providing for the basics of the neediest families and children.[23] In West Palm Beach, Florida, a thirteen-year-old foster child (identified by the initials "L. G.") had gone missing for over thirty days without anyone on the part of state family services becoming very worried at all, until, that is, the girl reappeared—pregnant and wanting an abortion. On the very same day that the procedure was scheduled to be performed in a local clinic, the Department of Children and Families filed for an emergency injunction in Tallahassee for the state to prevent the girl from having the abortion. During the court hearing the girl explained that she wouldn't even be able to get a job to support the child, and being all of thirteen, she was much too young herself to become a mother. Juvenile Court Judge Ron Alvarez of the First Judicial Circuit in Palm Beach County, who presided over the hearings and complied with the girl's request for termination of the pregnancy, explained in an interview for PBS's *NOW* that he had in fact been pressured from various elements of the religious right, not to grant the abortion. When asked if he felt that he had acted as an "activist" judge, Alvarez rightly commented that public opinion is not always correct and that if judges in the past had not been willing to take a stand for principles of equality and liberty, children in America today would still be attending racially segregated public schools.

When AIDS first made its stirring debut among the "sodomists," Jerry Falwell, founder of the sinless "Moral Majority," declared that AIDS was not just God's answer to homosexuals, it was also God's punishment for societies that tolerated homosexuals. And what pleasure there was among the Christian right at the sight of Kaposi's! What *schadenfreude* they felt as they piously spewed out the thunderous message to repent! For judgment is at hand! Caught in the act of spitting vitriol at gays and lesbians (some of whom have even regrettably turned out to be nice people), the proper moral line en vogue today is to "love the sinner but hate the sin."

Christian conservatives use every argument in the book, and then some, to condemn homosexuality as sinful, abnormal, and unnatural. The most interesting ploy however is the spin on sexual identity as a matter of choice, much like the "choice" of whether to wear a blue or red tie to the office. This choice of words is indeed most peculiar. A survey should be conducted among heterosexuals to find out just how many believe that they could perform the conjuring trick of changing their sexual identity at the drop of a hat. How many straight women could suddenly abracadabra themselves into true-blue lesbians at the swish of a passing skirt? How many tow-truck rednecks could suddenly belch and realize that the expelled gas from the gut had left them with an overwhelming hankering for a penis? There can be little doubt that any man or woman, sound and secure in his or her sexual identity, knows fairly well that it just isn't going to happen. That of course by no means precludes the possibility that people of both sexes develop feelings of affection and even longings for members of the same sex at times and that for them living out the fantasy really is a choice. Which is just the point. No normal thinking, feeling, sentient human being would ever dream of calling sexual identity a choice—unless it secretly really was one.

The Christian militia's singular obsession with sexuality leads inevitably to the suspicion that there are indeed ulterior motives at work here. Many aspects of modern life would appear to be questionable when judged from the basis of scripture, including the consumption of pork, lusting after the neighbor's spouse, "bearing false witness," even murder. There is also such clear evidence in the scriptures that Jesus himself was deeply moved by the conditions of poverty he witnessed, warning at the same time of the near impossibility for the rich to enter the kingdom of God. And yet none of these other "transgressions" against biblical law, not even murder, elicits anywhere near the phobic response from the nation's good Christians as does sex in general, gay sex in particular.

Especially disturbing was the vote by virtually all of the 13,000 representatives to a conference of the Southern Baptist Convention in June of 1996 to boycott the Disney Company and all movies, videos, and amusement parks under Disney ownership. The reason? Disney had decided to provide health insurance coverage for the partners of its gay and lesbian employees. Disneyland had also extended a warm welcome to homosexuals who frequented the parks in groups at certain times of the year—not for sex, as evangelicals surely believed. Things then got ugly in 1997 when Ellen Degeneres "came out" on her ABC show with a revealing kiss smooched onto the lips of Laura Dern. Christian conservatives went ballistic, as if the most heinous acts imaginable had been committed in full public view. (They are, of course, but those are just instances of harmless massacres or moves toward totalitarianism in Washington. *Let boys be boys*.) The moral apostles would doubtless have been infinitely more comfortable with public beheadings or quarterings, but a kiss on the lips between members of the same sex? (*God forbid!*) And he did. At least according to the smear campaign that ensued, with companies such as J.C. Penny leading the way by dropping its advertising efforts with

ABC. Inasmuch as the network didn't renew the *Ellen* series, the campaign was effective. The director of the Christian Life Commission at the time prided himself on the sudden surge of power running through his holy veins: "Disney is going to find out just how many regiments and just how many divisions of godly people Southern Baptists have." And how godly they are: What better way to silence the "homosexual agenda" than to cut off their funding and deny them that crucial mammogram for the early detection of breast cancer (unbeknownst to many evangelicals, AIDS isn't the sole cause of death among homosexuals.)

Further attesting to the perniciousness of evangelical morals was an almost identical line of political activism taken in 2005 by Ted Baehr, head of the Christian Film and Television Commission. As outlined in its "mission statement" (the United States is perpetually on a mission of some sort), the organization is "dedicated to redeeming the values of the mass media according to biblical principles..."[24] When research scientists announced in the summer of 2005 that a vaccine against human papilloma virus had proved effective in protecting women against cervical cancer (according to the World Health Organization, the second leading cause of cancer mortality in women worldwide[25]) and was ready for use, Mr. Baehr told news reporters that "the vaccine seems to endorse a profligate lifestyle," and that the real way to prevent the disease was to subscribe "to a healthy lifestyle." In other words, aside from being a necessary deterrent, cervical cancer is God's answer to having sex outside marriage. Sadly, the vast majority of those who succumb to the disease are faithfully married women in the developing world. Hardly a just reward.

The sullen pride and invidious glee radiated by Christian moralists at the sight of sinners (i.e. those engaged in sex) bear the hallmarks of socio-pathology: It is better to condemn the "sinners" to suffering and death through acute or chronic illness than to have them living without appropriate punishment. This also explains in part the Bush administration's policy of tying various types of aid to sub-Saharan Africa in its struggle against AIDS to official endorsements of chaste, while condemning efforts to educate the populations in the proper use of condoms.

There are also very concerned, kind-hearted Christians among American conservatives who offer their services "to cure" homosexual sinners of their "affliction" through the power of Jesus and prayer. Just out of curiosity, of course, heterosexuals should once again ask themselves what they would think of the prospects if the situation were reversed. But that thought would likely be construed as the first step in a gay brainwashing regimen.

There are indeed several legitimate reasons why gays and lesbians might want to straighten out their lives, but being gay isn't one of them. Try instead the never-ending onslaught of homophobic propaganda, conservative family-values based decisions to fire and harass gay employees, or the threat of physical abuse, murder, and torture. But there they are: such organizations as the Family Research Council and Exodus International, who advocate prayer and the grace of God as sure cures for same-sex attraction. The underlying assumption is that homosexuality is sin, pure and simple, for "the Bible tells me so."

In July 1998 Exodus International began flooding many of America's largest daily newspapers with bigger-than-life spreads of dozens of smiling faces on a permanent Prozac-kick. The reason for the elation: They'd all been "cured" of their errant sexual orientation through the power of prayer and faith in Christ. The message was clear: repent, seek forgiveness from God for your sinful thoughts and you, too, can be healed!

Gay men and women around the world have tended to support the hypothesis that sexual orientation is genetically determined. Taken to its logical conclusion in the hearts, minds, and hands of religious conservatives, this initially comforting explanation could become the basis for a God-inspired genetic cleansing campaign, a final solution to rid the world of the gay agenda once and for all. Genetic tests of embryonic fluid would over night achieve the breakthrough abortion rights activists could only dream of as conservatives tripped over themselves demanding that doctors prevent the little "queers" from ever seeing the light of day. Those of Fred Phelps's Westboro Baptist Church persuasion (http://www.godhatesfags.com) would no doubt up the ante by demanding round-ups and.....*perhaps one last shower together?* for those with the sin gene.

Like the witches of Salem, gays and lesbians are also often blamed for a host of evils. Just after the 9/11 attacks on New York and Washington, D. C., Reverends Falwell and Robertson sat down for a little fireside reflection on it all, and in safe distance from one another (wouldn't want anyone getting wrong ideas). Falwell reached a remarkable conclusion, with which Robertson agreed:

> I really believe that the pagans and the abortionists and the feminists and the gays and the lesbians who are actively trying to make that an alternative lifestyle, the ACLU, People for the American Way, all of them who try to secularize America ... I point the thing in their face and say "You helped this happen."

So much for the money spent on homeland security. With God behind it all, our puny little border patrol doesn't stand a chance. And just when we thought we'd seen it all, a massive tsunami struck Southeast Asia, drowning more than 250,000. And who was to blame? The "faggots," "Thai prostitutes," and lascivious libertine Swedes who flock to the region every year in search of sun and sin.[26]

Just when gays and lesbians started to think it was safe to hold hands in public, along comes the wrath of God in the form of a tsunami to remind folks back home that they'd better keep their pants on. The backlash was felt in the political arena as well. By 2004, even moderately liberal pseudo-Republicans like Dianne Feinstein had to admit that the acceptance thing had gotten a little out of hand with San Francisco Mayor Gavin Newsome allowing the city to grant marriage licenses to same-sex couples. The Massachusetts Supreme Court followed suit by lifting the restrictions on tied homo knots in that state. And to top it all off, the United States Supreme Court actually overturned a Texas sodomy law, in effect clearing Big Brother Sam out of the American bedroom and causing justices Rehnquist, Scalia, and Thomas to lose years off what little life they had left.

The hearts of conservative Christian America thumped in rage. Prayers went out from the pulpits and across the Internet, as grassroots "save marriage" and "save the family" campaigns popped up like cheapskates at a Wal-Mart fifty-percent-off sale. Smirkingly smitten with fatherly concern, George W. Bush strutted before the American people, courageously promising his full support for the Marriage Act that would define the union exclusively as a bond between a man and a woman. The voting populace in eleven red states promptly acted to ensure that the measure would find its way onto the November 2004 ballots. The states' amendments passed hands-down as voters flocked to the polls to save Ozzies and Harriets from becoming future Jeffs and Antonios.

Other groups such as the Article 8 Alliance in Massachusetts set out to remove (one wonders how?) the four state supreme court justices who had supported liberalizing the statutes for homosexual couples. In Washington, the Christian Right rallied around its entrusted do-no-wrong Congressman DeLay ("God is using me all the time, everywhere, to stand up for a biblical worldview…" (this was the pre-indictment era)) and Senators Coburn and Frist to rid the nation of "activist judges," i.e. those who saw/see no legitimate rhyme or reason to banish gays and lesbians to the realm of judicial otherworldliness.[27] Pat Robertson warned that the judiciary was in part responsible for the "assault on marriage" and the "assault on human sexuality." In keeping with Christ's teachings to love one's enemy as one's self, this same defender of marriage and family values went before the nation's TV audience on August 22, 2005, to express his views about Venezuela's democratically elected president, Hugo Chavez: "You know, I don't know about this doctrine of assassination, but if he [Chavez] thinks we're trying to assassinate him, I think that we really ought to go ahead and do it. It's a whole lot cheaper than starting a war."

The idea that killing was somehow OK, but gay sex was as pernicious as the demons of hell fitted in nicely with the general mood of Bush's Christian jihad backers, and to be sure, the mood in much of the red-state country in 2005 was that judges who opposed demonizing gays and lesbians were guilty of actively supporting an un-Christian, immoral lifestyle. Mr. Robertson just added an international touch in the crusade of goodness against "evil" (a somewhat recurrent theme among Republicans: Reagan's "realm of evil" and Bush's "axis of evil") by including the Venezuelan socialist in the queue. Those who had voted for Mr. Bush's "moral" agenda sought to have the black-robed pagans of the Supreme Court removed, one way or the other.[28] Republican Senator John Cornyn of Texas even expressed what many onlookers interpreted as a veiled threat when he chided Supreme Court justices (excluding of course the renowned Troika) for taking on this

> ...role as a policymaker rather than an enforcer of political decisions made by elected representatives of the people...I don't know if there is a cause-and-effect connection, but we have seen some recent episodes of courthouse violence in this country—certainly nothing new; we seem to have run through a spate of courthouse violence recently that has been on the news. I wonder whether there may be some connection between the perception in some quarters on some occasions where judges are making political decisions yet are unaccountable to the public, that it builds and builds to the point where some people engage in violence, certainly without any justification, but that is a concern I have that I wanted to share.[29]

As if transformed by ESP, many alert listeners immediately heard various synonyms for that key word "concern," and they probably weren't far off the mark. Across the airwaves, appeals for prayers and tough talk-and-action rang out from people like televangelist Reverend Rod Parsley of Ohio. In a devout rant broadcast on June 2, 2005, by the Trinity Broadcasting Network, the good man appealed for the like-minded to "stand up with me and say we need a center for moral clarity" by doing something about this "judicial tyranny." Thousands applauded the gathering voices of a second revolution whose aim it is to overthrow the "dictatorship run by federal judges." (*Sieg heil*, he should have said.) Echoing the sentiment, Dr. Rick Scarborough, president of Vision America, demanded in his Reclaiming America for Christ pulpit plea that "radical judicial activism must be confronted by the church of the living God now!"

Apropos the "assault on marriage": it has to be seen as the pinnacle of irony that the state with the highest percentage of divorces, Oklahoma, is also home to one of the largest concentrations of Christian fundamentalists anywhere. In a state where coyotes and hoot owls quote scripture, gays and lesbians have less public or political influence than a welfare mom at an Exxon board meeting. It thus seems odd that heterosexuals concerned with the sanctity of marriage should associate their troubles with any aspect of homosexuality. And trying to solve the problem of climbing divorce rates by banning same-sex marriages is somewhat like General Motors' trying to increase global sales by banning peanut butter. Unless of course all the deeply moved moralists looked at the gleefully gay couples leaving the ceremonies and whispered to their inner selves, *Gosh, if only I could have gone down that road.*

Perhaps this also explains the forced "outing" of none other than the Reverend Ted Haggard, former president of the National Association of Evangelicals and charismatic founder of the New Life Church in Colorado Springs, Colorado. After convincingly and repeatedly warning the flock of his *mega church* of the dangers of sinful same-sex relationships, the pastor had to fess up to the revelations of Mike Jones of Denver, Colorado, that the two men had engaged in sexual activity. Jones's motives for disclosing the affair were nothing if not noble. As he explained to the Associated Press in November of 2006, "My intent was never to destroy his [Haggard's] family. My intent was to expose a hypocrite." For his part, Reverend Haggard described his "sexual immorality" as a "part of my life that is so repulsive and dark that I have been warring against it for all of my adult life."

Who knows what dark secrets linger in the closets of God's earthly Chosen Ones such as James Dobson of Focus on the Family (http://www.family.org)? As the Christian auteur of an entire series of articles, essays, books, sermons, and bumper warnings about the "gay agenda" and the call-to-arms to save the traditional heterosexual family, Doctor James Dobson has accepted the challenge God has ostensibly laid out for him to rescue America's men, women, and children from the temptations and iniquities of same-sex temptations. In one of his more recent addresses, *Marriage Under Fire*,[30] Dobson warned that the movement to legalize same-sex marriages was casting America into the moral chaos on a road to Gomorrah and damnation. The scenes of looming gloom and doom conjured up by the hordes of lustful same-sex couples with "radical demands" such as adoption rights and partner-based health care, portended, he argued, the country's final destruction. The homosexual "master plan," he insisted, represented a "perfect storm in the history of western civilization and must be stopped—or else."[31]

Methinks the Lady doth protest too much.

Ironically, Dobson, Robertson, Haggard, and their fellow do-gooder moralists have seen no need to speak up about the legions of outcast men, women, children, and grannies who have been relinquished to the horrors of rats and repulsive, disease-infested streets with no exits. From the icy banks of the Charles River to the beaches of Santa Monica, the faces of human failure, wrapped in cardboard boxes and wool blankets, haunt the corners of American cities as nameless statistics whose births and deaths are as pointless and peripheral to the pulpit preachers as a colony of ants in an inner-city dump. Their human wants reduced to unrealistic fantasies about a can of tuna or a loaf of bread. Their bodies infested with a gamut of maladies. Their prospects of fulltime employment at a living wage about as feasible as a sudden cure for cancer. All living proof of the efficacy of capitalism shouldered on the decision-making power of the tax-abhorrent conservative Christian army who never tire of raging the same relentless wars against the "gay agenda"—all in the name of "family values."

If it is indeed their "deeds" by which these pious executors of Christian principles wish to be judged, one would have to conclude that for those at home on the city pavement and their brethren in the low-wage service industry who have never experienced the comfort of paid sick leave or vacation, whose existence can be forced into a never-ending downward spiral of squalor and homelessness by any prolonged illness, a mass conversion to militant socialism might be a sensible solution. What perverse logic perpetuates this paranoid *totalen Krieg* against the sins of sex while allowing countless instances of economic hardship to go unnoticed?

To more cosmopolitan citizens of countries that still pride themselves on a continued connection to the Enlightenment, conservative America's puritanical attitudes governing sexual identity, human relationships, and the human body, are quite simply repugnantly exemplary of grotesquely misplaced values and religiosity gone amok. Indicative of this pattern of skewed values is the public's reaction to one of the most beloved video games of American teenage boys: *Grand Theft Auto:*

San Andreas. Various versions of the *Grand Theft Auto* series had been on the market for over five years. The National Organization of Women (NOW) protested more than once in "action alerts" about the despicable training in violence teenage boys were receiving while playing the game. In one scene of *Grand Theft Auto III*, a player picks up a prostitute, takes her into the car, which then bounces to indicate sex going on inside. After the fun, the prostitute then gets out of the car, followed by her trick with a baseball bat, who then proceeds to bludgeon her to death in gory, bloody detail. The console of the video game is even equipped with sensors and feedback to allow America's good little boys to get the real feel of the bat smashing through flesh and bones, for an extra kick, understandably. Alas, NOW's warnings fell on deaf ears. *Boys will be boys!* That was until June of 2005 when it was discovered that the makers of the orgies of violence had included software tricks that allowed players to create animated sex scenes within the game. With the simple download of an additional program called "hot coffee," kids could create a little virtual quickie here and there to detract from the possible boredom of nonstop killing. Although game experts stated that they had been unable to find any actual genitals depicted, the very idea of America's pure-minded youth being exposed to material of a sexually graphic nature had the country up in arms. *That was the last straw!* With creamed-on, smeared-in piety, the country's holy of holies hit the ceiling in disgust—not at people being annihilated in creatively explicit scenes of smashed skulls, quartered bodies or bloody, bludgeoned heads worthy of Al Qaeda's Al Zarqawi. No, the uproar was about sex; no one gave a hoot about the vile scenes of youth's rapacious thirst for blood. In their ready-made pose as better Republicans, the Democrats sent Hillary to the front with a declaration of war on the game makers, "Take-Two." The Federal Trade Commission immediately went heavy-handed and slapped a full-scale inquiry into "unfair or deceptive" advertising by the makers. The *Dallas Morning News* interviewed a mother who had bought the game in good faith for her eleven-year-old son, knowing that he was "pretty mature" for his age, i.e. he would have no problems dealing with the slaughter-house fun of mutilating humans as an after-dinner treat. But when she learned that there was sex involved, she felt "shocked and angry" about the way the game makers had "deceived the public."

There is something deeply disturbing about the collective thought processes of a society that condones and partakes in the most hideous forms of violence and torture, but shrieks at the sight of a penis. When Janet Jackson's left nipple peeked out in 8.5 nanoseconds of national air time during the half-time of America's

Superbowl—the only event that could upstage the Second Coming—conservatives and liberals alike were falling over themselves with expressions of "outrage," "disgust," and "utter contempt" at network television, Justin Timberlake, and Janet Jackson. Saint Peter's personal reps in the GOP (a.k.a. as the "American Taliban" as Frank Rich so aptly phrased it[32]) called for punishment, retribution, greater censorship, and a return to the safety of Lassie-come-home media integrity with the ever-beloved American family foremost in mind. For far too many evangelicals this singular obsession with one aspect of life— sex—has become the alpha and omega of received Christian teachings, THE all-encompassing focus of ethics to the exclusion of serious social ills.

The conservative Christian social-political agenda is predicated on a concept of state and individual rooted in a plan perceived as pre-ordained and revealed in and through scripture. Its ideal-typical form of government is a theocracy founded in Judeo-Christian ethics, central to which are certain fundamental tenets defining the role of God, Christ, original sin, and the divine plan for salvation as interpreted from the scriptures of the New Testament. These tenets and the texts on which they are based are the subject of the following sections.

The Good Book: Defining Truth and Reality

Syndicated radio talk show host Dennis Prager pretty much hit the nail when he explained the roots of the culture war bitterly dividing Americans at the dawn of the new millennium. As the talk-meister put it, the fundamental issue at the heart of the red-blue divide was not whether one actually believed in God, but whether one took the Holy Bible (in his case the Torah) to be the definitive, authoritative word of God.[33] Like conservative representatives from the other monotheistic religions, evangelical Christians have very firm views about the truth status of the most significant body of writing in the Western world. One of the country's most conservative Christian institutes of higher learning, Bob Jones University, details the most important elements of its creed on the university's Web site http://www.bju.edu. There, visitors learn that among other academic tenets the university regards every statement contained in the holy scriptures as the literal word of God, "inspired" in the most literal Latin sense of the root or "breathed into" the material form of handwritten text. In like manner, Liberty University and Moral Majority founder Jerry Falwell described the Bible as "absolutely without error." Far from being unique, this conviction of the inerrant and absolute nature of every statement in the Bible enjoys broad adherence all across the country.

The effects of this belief will likely shape the social, economic, political, and judicial spheres of national public life for generations to come. It already exerts a stranglehold on communication channels and the content of public entertainment and political commentary.

Even die-hard believers have no doubt wondered just how God's word found its way into the manuscripts that later came to be collectively known as the New Testament. Did Christianity's one true God whisper into the apostles' ears the thousands of words of scripture? Did he appear in the form of a new burning bush with the texts already prepared for automatic dictation? And just how well do the claims of biblical inerrancy hold up under closer scrutiny?

Today, the New Testament consists of twenty-seven books commonly grouped into four distinct divisions: the four Gospels (Matthew, Mark, Luke, John); Acts; twenty-one letters ("Epistles"); the Book of Revelation. The New Testament was written in the lingua franca of its day—Greek. Church history has relied on more than 5,000 Greek texts, none of which have survived in original form. Instead, posterity has been treated to an assortment of copies and meta-copies.

Many of the faithful believe that these twenty-seven books somehow magically appeared in one fell swoop of the divine hand, representing the sum total of what God had to relate to the human species about his son and the path to redemption and salvation. That was not the case.

These twenty-seven books were selected by ordinary learned men of flesh, blood, and very specific theological (and likely political) interests to the exclusion of many more texts that laid equal claim to legitimacy. Although biblical scholars question the authorship of a number of New Testament texts (e.g. whether I Peter was really composed by Simon Peter the disciple, or whether Paul the apostle was the author of Colossians, Ephesians, and II Thessalonians), God himself does not appear as the signatory anywhere in the New Testament. One wonders why.

Far from being a monolithic bloc of beliefs, Christianity embodied from the start highly diversified schools of thought and teachings.[34] The process by which these twenty-seven texts were chosen and ultimately integrated into the Canon of scripture known to us today as the New Testament mirrored the struggle for legitimacy among these rivaling factions of Christianity with very differing views about the nature (and even number) of God(s), humankind, and the role and mission of Jesus Christ himself.

A number of issues that proved to be divisive among early Christians centered on the role of Judaism and Mosaic Law in light of the new teachings of Jesus, the Messiah, a Jewish rabbi. At one end of the tug-of-war were those who saw in Jesus a natural continuation and indeed fulfillment of Judaic laws and prophecies. These Christian Jews (or "Ebionites" as they came to be known) were indeed thoroughly Jewish in their beliefs and conduct in everyday life, but unlike the majority of Jews at the time who saw in Jesus nothing more than a blasphemous heretic, the Ebionites believed him to be the promised Messiah of God's chosen people. What little is known about the Ebionites (no samples of their writings have survived the centuries) derives from the written attacks for-mulated against the sect by early functionaries[35] representing the line of thought theologian and religious historian Bart Ehrman has termed "proto-orthodox".[36] The Ebionites reportedly restricted their use of Christian documents to amended versions of the Gospel of Matthew, arguably the most "Jewish" of the four Gos-pels in content. They regarded Paul's interpretation of Christ and the Christian mission as heretical since Paul had repeatedly insisted that Jesus' death on the cross obviated the need to live in accordance with distinctly Jewish practices. Since in the Ebionite school of thought Jesus was the Messiah promised in Old Testament prophecy, salvation could come to non-Jews only if they became Jew-ish first, which meant among other things maintaining exclusively kosher eating habits, keeping the Sabbath, Passover, and other holy days, and *berith* or *briss* (male circumcision). The majority of Ebionites did not view Jesus as divine; nor did they believe in the virgin birth.[37] With his death on the cross, Jesus became in the Ebionite view the ultimate sacrifice in the eyes of God, thereby ending the Jewish practice of sacrifice.

As might logically be expected in a battle of religious ideologies, there was also a very influential group of early Christians who held that Jesus and his teach-ings represented a complete and radical break from Judaism. The Marcionites drew their name from the second-century theological scholar and philosopher, Marcion, whose own father was a church priest in what is now Turkey. As a num-ber of biblical scholars have pointed out, Marcion must have grappled with issues that have subsequently been categorized as theodicy. Critical commentaries about his work (primarily the extensive attacks written by Tertullian) reveal an inner struggle to come to terms with the unacceptably acerbic character of the cre-ator God of the Old Testament. Marcion's solutions to these deeply disturbing questions represented a completely new direction in Christianity.

Although nothing survives of Marcion's own texts, a good deal is known about this group of thinkers, again from the extant texts of those "proto-orthodox" (to use Ehrman's designation) writers who saw the different approach to Christianity as threatening heresy. Claiming that Marcion's ideas were satanically influenced, Justin Martyr warned in the second century that the renegade teachings had already begun to influence the entire human race (*Apol.* I, 26). Marcion and his followers had become far more than a mere sect. What is known through the writings of important heresiologists such as Tertullian, Irenaeus, and Epiphanius, is that Marcion's primary work, *Antitheses*, set out to draw a clear distinction between the God of Creation who established a covenant with the Jews, and the God of the New Testament. Relying in great measure on the Pauline Epistles and an adapted version of the Gospel of Luke, the Marcionites were so extreme in their separation of Jesus and Christian teachings from anything Jewish that they actually ended up with two Gods. In radicalized language probably not seen until that time, Marcion juxtaposed the God of Jewish worship—wrathful, severe, and unforgiving in his treatment of the slightest transgressions—against the loving God that Jesus Christ called "Father".[38] The result in effect was two distinct religions. The whole line of thought was just too much for many believers at the time, particularly one might suspect for those converts to Christianity who had originally been Jewish or who had non-converted Jewish family. Marcion's own father expelled him from the church over which the elder presided.

The nice young rebel also spent five years in Rome, where he had hoped to convince others of the truth of his religious discovery. There, too, his ideas proved far too radical for the established Roman community, which promptly showed him the door. Upon his return to Asia Minor, Marcion began work on spreading his convictions among smaller communities of listeners. He proved so successful in spreading his message that "proto-orthodox" church leaders began to regard him as a true thorn in the sides of the Roman version of truth.[39] The Marcionite break with Old Testament soteriology simultaneously negated the historical continuum of Judeo-Christian experience up to that time. The communities Marcion established were centered on the Gospel of love and faith in Jesus Christ in adherence with Pauline interpretations of ethical conduct and salvation. The Sabbath became another day; pork and shellfish were free for consumption; and men were happily allowed to keep their foreskins.

Marcion's teachings were (and still are) often linked with another very important group of early Christians whose interpretations were perhaps even more radical in their departure from what we now know later developed into the orthodox party line than those of the idealistic preacher's son had been. What strongly differentiates the Gnostics, however, from either Ebionites or Marcionites is the fact that a major compendium of Gnostic scriptures miraculously survived the ravages of both time and orthodox efforts to banish the texts. Prior to 1945, what was mainly known about the Gnostic branch of Christianity was related through the writings of "proto-orthodox" heresiologists[40] as described above in the context of divergent beliefs. That all changed in late 1945 when an Egyptian farmer from Nag Hammadi was out digging for fertilizer on the slopes of a cliff and stumbled upon a large, mysterious-looking jar. Hesitant at first to open it up for fear of finding an evil *jinn* billowing out in a puff of smoke, Mohammed Ali finally allowed his curiosity (and the thought of finding gold) to get the better of him, but instead of finding a pot of precious metal he discovered thirteen leather-bound books containing a total of fifty-two papyrus manuscripts written in Coptic. After several way stations, the texts finally wound up in the hands of the Egyptian government's Department of Antiquities. An impressive number of scholarly treatments[41] provide details of both the actual journey the manuscripts took and the history of their translation and interpretation. Suffice it to say that the discovery of the Nag Hammadi Library[42] (as the texts have now been collectively labeled) has been one of the most significant moments in Western theology since the Council of Nicaea.

With a radically idealist ontology, Gnostics developed an entire mythological system to clarify their understanding of universal fundamentals. Elements of Greek philosophy, particularly of Plato's theory of perfect ideas as the primary substance, point to a pre-Christian origin of many Gnostic tenets. There were of course different branches of Gnosticism as the Nag Hammadi Library reveals; the uniting theme among these diverse schools of thought, however, was that the material world itself was an illegitimate offshoot of the perfect world of divine ideas.

The Gnostic scriptures encompass several different types of texts from sections of Plato's *Republic* and essays on the highest cosmic power and the origins of the world, to three different authored Gospels (of Mary, Thomas, and Philip), as well as the Gospels of Truth, the Gospel of the Egyptians, the Apocalypse of Paul, the Apocalypse of Adam, two Apocalypses of James, and the fascinating Apocrypha ("Secret Books") of John and James, among others. Among the most remarkable of these texts from the vantage point of the orthodox Christianity with which the modern world is so well acquainted is the Gospel of Thomas, consisting of 114 sayings of Jesus Christ ostensibly dictated to his twin brother Thomas (cf. John 11:16: *"Thomas ho legomeno Didymos"* as well as John 20:24 and 21:2) after the resurrection. (This is the same "Doubting Apostle" whom (according to

the apocryphal *Acta Thomae*) Jesus sold into slavery (a merchant sent to Jerusalem to find a carpenter on behalf of King Gundnaphor of India made the purchase) so that Thomas might spread the teachings of Christ to that region. The
other eleven apostles were given similar assignments in different areas.) The Gospel of Thomas begins with the enigmatic promise that anyone who finds the correct interpretation of the sayings will not die. Some of the verses such as the
parable of the mustard seed are familiar from the canonized Gospels; other at
times highly puzzling verses hint of an almost paradoxical, indeed Eastern, or
Buddhist way of thinking. Viewed as a whole, it is easy to understand why the
proto-orthodox exegetists would not want the minds of their congregations "corrupted" with the readings.

Another highly unusual text from the modern point of view is the
Apocryphon of John. To anyone breast-fed on the traditional televangelists' story
of Creation with its cast of characters all the way through to the birth of Christ, the
Secret Book of John is potentially quite disturbing. The book declares through the
testimony of Jesus Christ himself to John, the son of Zebedee and the brother of
James, that the God Almighty of Genesis was in fact a type of renegade god, the
demiurge Yaldabaoth, an illegitimate product as it were of a higher spiritual aeon
(Sophia), who wanted to create another entity without first getting permission
from the one true God, the Absolute, Infinite One. The narcissistic Yaldabaoth
then takes on a life of his own, creating legions of angels, the earth, all material
forms, as well as Adam and Eve. The rest is "history."

According to this version of things, all is not completely lost. Some humans
have elements of the divine "spark" trapped inside their material bodies. Salvation comes through "knowing" the true nature of reality (and one's own being) as
taught by Christ, as being of an immaterial, spiritual origin, and living with an exclusive focus on the divine.

The representatives of "proto-orthodox" scriptural interpretation rejected all
of these variants of Christianity. As Ehrman clearly points out, modern efforts to
reconstruct the early history of Christianity always run the risk of interpreting the
strength and legitimacy of the immediate reception of Christ's teachings from the
vantage point of the "winning" side, i.e. from the orthodox understanding of what
the "correct" interpretation of those teachings was and is. This version insists
that all people start out as "true" believers, aligned with the "orthodox" (literally
straight/correct opinion) but over time may become corrupted with doubt or even
evil influences.[43] With that caveat in mind, it must be stressed that during the

early formative years of the Christian "church," there was no one "correct" interpretation of the Nazarene message. The three schools of thought just outlined (as
well as others) all believed to be correct in their understanding of Jesus Christ and
his mission on earth. Ehrman surmises[44] that competing theorists never knowingly adopt an incorrect stance on fundamentals (many could rightly maintain
however that exceptions are surely to be found in present-day politics), but rather
attempt to show why conflicting positions are wrong.

Copies Galore

Of the more than 5,000 Greek manuscripts in existence today, not one is identical to
another in every detail. This lack of homogeneity resulted in most cases not from
intentional manipulation but rather from the arduous process of copying the texts
in their entirety. With the exponential growth of Christianity in all parts of the Mediterranean in the first centuries of the Christian era, many versions of the Gospels,
Epistles, Acts, and other texts (including those of the Marcionites and Gnostics)
were in use in different regions. There was no such thing as a unified "canon" of
texts. With the expansion came an increased need for copies of the scriptures from
which sermons could be taught. The problem was that there just weren't enough
copies to go around, and so scribes were appointed to make exact copies of all the
texts that were available in the various communities of believers. It must be kept in
mind of course that this was long before the age of Xerox and high-resolution scan-
ners, so everything had to be done by hand, initially on papyrus scrolls, later on individual leaves or codices that could be bound up in book form.[45] There were many
advantages to reading texts in book form such as the ability to quickly locate a
needed passage without having to unroll endless yards of scroll.

The scribes entrusted with this horrendously tedious task were not necessarily the most highly educated theologians in the community, but rather men
who were fairly literate in Greek and probably eager to earn some money as well
as serve a good cause. Most of the time they were forced to write with the material
uncomfortably placed on their laps.[46] Anyone who has ever copied a lengthy text
by hand knows how easy it is to make different kinds of mistakes. If the language
is not one's native tongue, there's the additional problem of perhaps being inse-
cure about the spelling of a word, and in fact the vast majority of mistakes that occur in the scriptures are orthographical errata. But there are more serious
instances of not just words but indeed of lines and entire paragraphs being inad-
vertently omitted or added. Since the texts being copied were written with a cer-

tain number of lines on each page, it frequently occurred that two lines of text would end with the same phrase (*homoeoteleuton*) and the scribe who was copying would look back at the original text but his eyes would skip to the line below (*parablepsis*), thereby omitting everything that occurred in that line up to that phrase.[47] Metzger indicates that the entire verse of Luke 10:32 is missing in the *Codex Sinaiticus* because the previous line ends with the same verb.[48] In other instances the scribe would see the same word in a different place in the text before and duplicate unnecessarily an entire phrase or several sentences. In some cases, letters simply looked like others, either from the way they were written or because of their position in relation to other letters in the same word, often with complete shifts in meaning.

Scribes were probably even more prone to erroneous renderings when the original texts were dictated. Because of the dearth of primary texts, it was far easier and time-efficient for one person to read aloud the scripture to be copied with an entire room full of scribes taking down verbatim everything that was said. The results of this kind of effort can be both funny, and disastrous. Even for native speakers, it's very easy to replace a slightly unfamiliar phrase with one that sounds completely plausible. The phrase "I'll never be your beast of burden" in the lyrics of an old The Rolling Stones hit has been curiously rendered "I'll never be your pizza burning." "A girl with kaleidoscope eyes" from The Beatles' hit *Lucy in the Sky with Diamonds* became "A girl with colitis goes by."[49] An American husband was doing his best to be helpful by taking down a message from his wife's doctor regarding her Pap smear. Taped to the refrigerator door was a note that read: "Some lady from Guyna Colleges says the Pabst Beer is OK."

There was no shortage of this kind of blooper way back then either. Metzger has shown that a major source of error arising in the transcription of manuscripts from oral dictation resulted from the fact that in Koine (the blend of Greek dialects widely spoken in the Roman Empire), the three vowels *e*, *i*, and *u* as well as the diphthongs *eu*, *oi*, and *ui* gradually became essentially identical sounds,[50] much like the first vowels in the English words "merry" and "marry" or words containing the most frequent sound in the English language, the "schwa". This effect was particularly troublesome in the use of the personal pronouns *hymon* (your) and *hemon* (our). Metzger has found at least seven such confusing switches in I Peter alone. In some manuscripts the resultant renderings are unintelligible.[51] Complete shifts in meaning also occurred with various consonant sounds and added/omitted aspiration (cf. the difference between *ex ou* (from whom) and *ek sou* (from you): when spoken quickly, the two phrases sound exactly the same.) Inaccuracies in speech also effected changes in the grammatical structure of many sentences, resulting in significant changes in meaning. In other instances, homophones, synonyms, altered syntax, and even rearranged letters within words gave rise to numerous and significant variations in the final written product.

The demand for copies of the scriptures was so great that an entire enterprise of *scriptoria* sprang up, with each office employing sometimes dozens of scribes in one room. Many manuscripts contain brief commentaries written in the margins as a kind of reader's guide in accordance with a scheduled reading (*Lectionary*) of specific scriptures. Sometimes the scribe would add a personal (even comical) comment, which would then be integrated into the body of the text on the next go-around.[52] One of the most amusing errors, cited by Metzger as the "most atrocious," occurred when a scribe of *codex 109* got confused about the arrangement of the original text in Luke dealing with Jesus' family tree. The "original" text (i.e. the manuscript from which the copy was being made) consisted of two columns of twenty-eight lines each. Either as a result of carelessness or as an early version of employee sabotage, the scribe copied the text as if it had been written straight across the page. The result had God down as the son of Aram, and Phares as the creator of all.[53]

Far more serious are text variations that resulted from the scribes' theological convictions as to what the text should say. However well-intentioned, significant alterations and additions (statistically more likely than deletions) have cast doubt on the credibility of numerous passages, of which one of the most widely discussed is the Gospel of Mark. Many biblical authorities agree that the last twelve verses of this Gospel were added to the text by a different author. The oldest available manuscripts of the text end quite abruptly and despondently in verse 16:8 with the phrase *efobounto gar*. As Metzger has argued, it was exceedingly rare for any Greek text to end with the word *gar* (at times a kind of catch-word in Greek best rendered in conjunction with the participle in this phrase as "since" (King James reads "for"; the German text uses "denn".) In addition, the shortened text fills Mark's final statement with negativity and pessimism, completely lacking in the promise of salvation and eternal life central to the narration of the resurrection.[54] Theologians can only speculate as to why "Mark" never got to finish his Gospel; perhaps the last page of the text has simply been lost, or as was the case with several leaves from the Nag Hammadi texts, torn out and used as kindling by someone who had no idea what they were holding.

The source of the twelve-verse conclusion to Mark will likely remain a mystery, but the added text does go to show that there was certainly no lack of creativity when it came to amending scripture to a specific end. There was also no shortage of accusations that scriptures had been seriously manipulated and forged, always by the team on the opposite side of the theological divide of course, never by one's own scribes. The practice of forgery was certainly not uncommon. Frequently a scripture would be put in writing by an anonymous author (but not God), who then signed the name of an apostle to the text in order to make it seem trustworthy (as mentioned above, six of the New Testament's Pauline Epistles are deemed to be of dubious origin.)

Today we are confronted with copies of copies of copies of scripture which are identical only in part, but which differ from one another in many, many ways. These differences resulted frequently from honest mistakes such as those that might happen to anyone attempting manually to copy thousands of lines of text from sight or dictation. At the same time, one source of these errors was just as often (and more disturbingly) the outcome of a scribe's preconditioned interpretive understanding of what the text at hand had to mean.[55]

The Canon

The fate of the teachings of Jesus Christ and the interpretation of his mission on earth were decided with the acceptance and operationalization of the canon of New Testament scriptures. In a drawn-out struggle for dominance, proponents of the "proto orthodox" understanding of Christianity managed to exclude the entire array of scriptural texts used by competing religious factions, each of which had considered its own corpus of texts to reflect the "orthodox" (i.e. correct) interpretation of Christian teachings. It is often the right of might to create the "correct" version of history. The monopoly of truth claimed by the Inquisitors in one of Europe's less stellar eras and by the moral politics of America's Christian jihad are predicated on the orthodox interpretation of the genesis and evolution of Christianity in the first three centuries A.D.—an interpretation consolidated in Eusebius's seminal ten-volume historiography of the church, the *Ecclesiastical History.*

This orthodox tome relates a convenient story of renegade theological misfits hell-bent on corrupting the one, true understanding of Jesus Christ as the son of the one God, and of that son's ultimate sacrifice with his physical death on the cross as the final atonement for the sins of Fallen Man. This version of history generates a projected uninterrupted genealogy of body, mind, and intention through the lines of Adam and Abraham and culminating in Jesus Christ, the promised Messiah. Accordingly, conflicting views are portrayed as aberrant feral longings of misinformed and misguided deviants.

A startlingly different version of church history emerged through the meticulous work of Walter Bauer in his examination of early Christian communities in the Roman Empire. Bauer's thrilling account, which in places reads like a Dorothy Sayerskova Russian mystery novel, presents an abundance of historical evidence to substantiate his claim that in a great many communities prior to domination by the orthodox ecclesiastical hierarchy, "the heretics" enjoyed an already firmly established tradition as the Christians,[56] e.g. the Marcionites in Edessa (Macedonia), the Gnostics in Egypt (p. 48 and *passim*), Antioch (p. 66), and numerous communities in southeast Asia Minor (p. 82). Far from being representative of small groups of deviant theological weirdos, many of these non-Roman communities were very well established with entire sets of scriptures written and signed by apostles or men claiming apostolic authority by association. And far from being breakaway movements of any "orthodox" line of thought, many of these communities traced their claim to authenticity right back to the first years of the Christian era. Bauer's conclusion of course was that the view most Christians have always grown up with is ultimately based on mass deception and ignorance, written and propagated by the very same Church Fathers who just happened to win out in the bitter struggle for theological legitimacy. The battle, Bauer argued, was decided not on theological grounds or religious merits, but by the sheer power of the Church of Rome.

Like the smaller armies of regions that had dared to oppose Rome, these numerous and diverse communities of Christians who had blossomed within different sets of scripture and alternative interpretations of God, man, and Jesus Christ, were decimated by the dominant doctrine imposed by the hegemony of the Roman church as a doctrinal extension of the empire. Opposing views were not tolerated; scriptures that deviated from Rome's tenets were cast aside or burned as heretical. Sounds familiar. Is it any wonder then that the Nag Hammadi Gnostic Christians tried and luckily succeeded in protecting their most sacred scriptures from confiscation or destruction by burying them in the sands of Upper Egypt?

There was surely a growing uncertainty in the minds of many believers who saw the basis of their faith slipping into the status of hearsay based on hearsay. Parallels spring to mind of the fate of many languages pushed to the point of extinction. With every passing year there are fewer "originals" who know the given tongue, and hence fewer to pass on the tradition to future generations. Likewise, as the events surrounding the life of Jesus became ever more distant in the past, fewer "original witnesses" remained alive to pass on—by word of mouth—their "fresher" and "truer" recollections of what was already second-hand knowledge. It was only natural that believers would seek permanence in the form of written records of what was remembered. The oral tradition which had served as the sole basis for passing on the Christian message from one community and one generation to the next proved understandably quite unreliable in sorting out the authentic from the fabricated and altered. Old-timers at the time such as Bishop Papias of Hieropolis expressed preference for the oral manuscripts, but others saw the clear need for something tangible. As scholars like Ehrman and Metzger have repeatedly pointed out, all that the early Christians had had in the way of something rock-solid were the sacred texts of the Old Testament, hardly much good in propagating the good news of the Christian Gospels. Utter dissatisfaction with the Jewish texts had prompted Marcion to compound the first canon of texts in the first place. These had consisted of a de-Judaized version of Luke and ten Pauline Epistles, but had evoked the scorn of the entire "proto-orthodox" movement. In addition, the heresiologists found themselves repeatedly on the offensive against the teachings of Montanus (something of a cross between David Koresh and the Oracle of Delphi), who claimed for himself and his high priestesses direct oracular contact with the Holy Spirit, through which new and exciting heavenly messages were being revealed.

Part of the theological legitimization process itself demanded a corpus of texts to distinguish legitimate from illegitimate views, in other words an instrumental permanent record to allow defenders of the faith to cite chapter and verse. Historians of church doctrine agree that the finalized Canon of orthodox scriptures was a long time in the making[57] and to this day varies somewhat according to established doctrines of specific culturally defined regions. As with church history itself and the quest for universal legitimacy among competing doctrines, attempts to unite all "acceptable" scriptures into a universally valid ("catholic") corpus were wrought with debate and discord. With so many texts competing for a seat in the Canon and with so many vested interests arguing, Athanasius in A.D. 367 sent out his "Epistola Festalis" or "Festal Letter" to all the churches in his domain to notify them of the exact dates for Easter in the coming year. Picking up on the ongoing debates concerning the acceptance of particular scriptures within the proto-orthodox community at large, Athanasius decided to include a list of exactly those twenty-seven books of the New Testament found in use today, describing them as "springs of salvation." Based on criteria previously laid out by Origen, the list included the so-called *homologoumena* or texts on which there was for all practical purposes general consensus on their apostolic origin, as well as certain disputed texts, but not the Apocrypha. This list was subsequently reduplicated in the Latin Vulgate, which served as the official Canon of the Catholic Church for over a thousand years. It also functioned as the basis for translations into other languages.

Here again, the "proto-orthodox" movement won out over competing interpretations of the history and mission of Jesus Christ. Over time, the unrelenting onslaught of the heresiologists against all alternative understandings forced out these originally widespread groups of worshipers. Through the power of definition—by branding heterodox thinkers as heretics (one could perhaps propose "terrorists" in modern parlance)—the "proto orthodox" ideologues established themselves as a closed community that endured no opponents. The subsequent operationalization of a fixed Canon of texts was the final nail in the coffin of long-term influence within the ecclesiastical community—a fate that has endured until today.

Discrepancies

There are substantial numbers of seemingly irreconcilable differences in the reports and narratives in the Bible, both between Old and New Testaments, as well as in each set of scriptures considered separately. There are even self-contradictory accounts within individual books of each set of texts. An adequate discussion of such discrepancies would demand a lengthy volume devoted to that purpose; the discussion here has therefore been restricted to a few of the perhaps more important ones.

Both Matthew and Luke contain a delineation of Jesus' family tree with the former starting with Abraham and working forward, while the latter begins with Jesus and works its way back all the way to Adam. But the two versions are contradictory in terms of who was who. In Matthew, Jesus' father Joseph is listed as the son of Jacob, who was the son of Matthan, the son of Eleazar, the son of Eliud and so on. Luke lists Joseph as the son of Heli, who was the son of Metthat, the son of Levi, the son of Melchi and so forth. These two accounts are clearly irreconcilably different.

The texts of Matthew, Mark, and Luke note that Jesus was born in Bethlehem, but they differ in their accounts of the events and circumstances that surrounded his birth. In the Gospel according to Matthew, Joseph was worried that someone would find out that Mary was pregnant before he and she had even "gotten together," but an angel appeared to him to say that everything was going to be all right because the child was of the Holy Spirit. The text then describes how under the reign of King Herod, three wise men from the East had seen a star foretelling of the birth of the "King of the Jews" in Bethlehem and had sought out and found the family and promised child. When King Herod in Jerusalem got wind of the story, he sent out his soldiers to Bethlehem to kill every boy two years of age and under. An angel then appeared to Joseph in a dream to warn him of the impending disaster, urging the family to flee to safety in Egypt, which they did. They stayed in Egypt until after Herod had died and was succeeded by his son. Well aware that the son was as ruthless as the father had been, the family went back to Israel, but to Nazareth instead of Bethlehem. This version sounds remarkably similar to the narrative of Moses in Egypt.

In the version according to Luke, Joseph and Mary traveled from Nazareth to Bethlehem because of a census ordered by Caesar Augustus that required everyone to register in his city of origin. And it is Mary, not Joseph, to whom the angel appears to tell of the future birth of a child from God. Not a word about the murder of baby boys on the orders of Herod or of any lengthy sojourn in Egypt.

The texts also relate different stories of the prosecution's proceedings against Jesus. Luke states that Pontius Pilate sent Jesus to Herod, who had "jurisdiction" over the Galilean. The other three Gospels make no mention of Herod being called in as assistant prosecutor in the case against Jesus.

There are also contradictory accounts of the exact date on which Jesus was crucified. According to the text in John, Jesus was crucified on the day before Passover. But Matthew, Mark, and Luke inform us that the disciples are given instructions on how to find the appropriate room where they will all share the Last Supper—the Seder, or Passover meal—with Jesus. During this last Seder, Jesus tells the disciples that the unleavened bread is his body, the wine his blood, and they should all eat and drink. After dinner, in the Garden of Gethsemane, Judas betrays Jesus to the Roman guards who bring him to Pontius Pilate the next morning. After a dispute over the exact nature of Jesus' "crimes," Pilate allows the Jews to determine Jesus' fate. Jesus is then crucified later in the day, on Passover.

The Gospels note that Jesus was crucified in the midst of two thieves, but Matthew and Luke give us completely different accounts of what was being said while the three were hanging on the cross. In Matthew we read that even the robbers "reviled him" with taunts, but in Luke one of the men proposes that if Jesus really is the Christ, why not save himself and them at the same time. The other robber reminds his buddy in crime that unlike they, Jesus was wrongly accused and sentenced. Then he asks Jesus to remember him in heaven. Jesus promises: "Today you will be with me in paradise."

The scriptures appear to contradict each other's accounts of what Jesus' last words were on the cross. The Gospel of John relates a teleological last utterance: "It is finished" (in Greek: *tetelestai*). Matthew and Mark both quote Jesus' final words as "My God, My God, why have you forsaken me?" Luke offers yet a third version with Jesus' saying "Father, into Your hands I commit My spirit."

The accounts also differ in their narrations of how Jesus' loved ones discovered that he had risen from the dead. Matthew tells us that "as the first day of the week began to dawn, Mary Magdalene and the other Mary came to see the tomb." Immediately on their arrival apparently, "there was a great earthquake; for an angel of the Lord descended from heaven and came and rolled back the stone from the door and sat on it" (Matthew 28:1-2). In this version, even the guards become petrified. The angel then reassures everyone that there is no reason to be frightened, because the Lord has risen and is no longer in the tomb.

Luke's narration speaks of "they, and certain other women with them" coming to the tomb "bringing spices which they had prepared. But they found the stone rolled away from the tomb. Then they went in and did not find the body of the Lord Jesus. And it happened, as they were greatly perplexed about this, that behold, two men stood by them in shining garments. Then, as they were afraid and bowed their faces to the earth, they said to them, 'Why do you seek the living among the dead?'" (Luke 24:1-5).

John relates yet another version in which Mary Magdalene first goes to the tomb alone and, seeing that the stone has been removed from the tomb, runs back to Simon Peter and the other disciple to tell them that Jesus' body had been stolen. Peter and the "other disciple" both go to investigate. Arriving at the tomb after the other disciple, Peter goes into the tomb and finds the linens that had draped the body of Jesus lying on the floor, with the handkerchief that had been around his head, folded and placed to the side. The disciples then went home, presumably to tell everyone else what had happened, but still not realizing that Christ had risen. Mary Magdalene

> ... stood outside by the tomb weeping and as she wept she stopped
> down and looked into the tomb. And she saw two angels in white sit-

ting, one at the head and the other at the feet, where the body of Jesus had lain. Then they said to her, 'Woman, why are you weeping?' She said to them, 'Because they have taken away my Lord, and I do not know where they have laid him.' Now when she had said this, she turned around and saw Jesus standing there, and did not know that it was Jesus.

Jesus then asks her why she is crying. The text then explains that Mary thinks Jesus is the gardener (*ho kepouros*), suspects he has carried away the body, and asks him to show her where it is. Finally, "Jesus said to her, 'Mary!' She turned and said to Him 'Rabboni!' (which is to say, Teacher)" (John 20:1-16). Mary Magdalene then goes back to the other disciples and relates how she has seen and spoken with Jesus.

While the tenor of these narrations is the same, the accounts, as seen, do differ significantly in terms of the details they provide. The reader of the passages should bring to mind that they all have their origin in oral versions of the events. (The first written version of Mark did not come into being until some thirty-odd years after Jesus' death on the cross; John, presumably the last Gospel to be written down, wasn't transcribed until approximately ninety years after the resurrection.) All information about Christ and his teachings was spread by word of mouth from one person to the next, and when reporting any event orally over considerable variations in space, time, and language groups, it is only natural that certain details become changed in ways that best reflect the narrators' best recollections and intentions.

The differences among the Gospels are in some ways more striking than their similarities. In addition to the diverging and at times contradictory details offered of the accounts, there is the overall impression even a layperson cannot help but gain that each of the Gospels represents a different direction or even mindset in Christianity. The message in Luke lends itself perhaps to a universal humanistic reception of Christ's teachings, whereas Matthew and Mark seem more in line with the versions of Christianity most familiar to armchair worshipers tuned in at home to America's televangelist crowds.

What is believed to be the oldest fragment of any part of the New Testament has survived in the form of a piece of papyrus text from the Gospel of John. Found in Egypt in the 1920s, the isolated text was designated "P52" and was ostensibly part of the Gospel written in codex. Containing passages from John 18:31-33 and 18:37-38, the text is believed to have been written in the early to mid-second century. The Gospel of John presents a rather unorthodox view of God as a quasi-deistic universal principle of love not unlike that found today in Christian Science or even in the Apocryphon of John and the Gospel of Thomas.

God and Theodicy

With the triumph of the orthodox interpretation of Christianity, the Canon of acceptable scriptures was defined within the confines established by the Church of Rome. All scriptural exegeses necessarily had to conform to the established doctrine of the Church Fathers, who, as heresiologists par excellence, became successful at dispelling dissenting views. Only the human imagination can envision how different our world might be today had competing theologies (such as those of the Gnostics) become dominant.

Judged by the sheer volume and numbers of writings, the Apostle Paul shaped Christianity in ways that might have been unrecognizable to the founder of Christianity himself. The entire history of Christendom subsequent to the conversion of Constantine interprets its own premises and mission through the eyes, ears, words, and recorded deeds of the converted Pharisee. One cannot help but feel that the ideas, goals, beliefs, and values central to Jesus' teachings have been muted by the blare of do's and don'ts, right and wrong interpretations about Jesus. Dominant in Paul's binding commentaries about Christ is the Jewish (and pagan) notion of sacrifice as a form of appeasement for transgressions against God and the conviction that Jesus Christ was indeed the long-awaited Messiah of the Jews as promised in the Old Testament. (As a reminder, this interpretation stands in stark contrast to the understanding the Gnostics had of Christ.) Paul's lineage as a Pharisee is thus most transparent in his depiction of the all-important relationship from God to human beings through the mediation of Christ as the final sacrificial Lamb of God.

This concept of sacrifice lies at the heart of virtually all modern Christian notions of salvation. The human condition in this scenario is one defined by original sin as a direct outcome of the Fall of Man: "Therefore, just as through man sin entered the world, and death through sin, and thus death spread to all men, because all sinned" (Romans 5:12). The punishment for sin is death.

But the message of the evangelists is the promise of eternal life through Christ. How? By being "saved" or "born again." (This entails a couple of easy steps that can be carried out anywhere, anytime, in just a matter of minutes. *Nota bene!* The alternative—eternal damnation in the flames of hell—is the default setting.) All around the world, from the streets of Moscow to the Air Force Academy in Colorado Springs, every minute of every day, activists for Christ are diligently trying to save the world from damnation, by asking: *Have you been saved?*

The answer is just as simple as the question; it's either "yes" or "no". Salvation, according to evangelicals, is God's promise to all, irrespective of race, creed, age, income, looks, or even past deeds. By the same token, there are also no halfway houses on the road to perdition or paradise. Those who for whatever reason have not been saved, will burn forever, regardless of race, creed, age, income, looks, or even past deeds. Those with preferences for milder climates would do well to get with the program.

Christian broadcasting stations and Web sites all carry the easy-to-follow instructions for being saved. In brief, they contain these key talking points to God: One must first acknowledge that one has sinned and repent by asking God for forgiveness. Then one must acknowledge the belief that Christ died on the cross for our sins. This is God's ultimate gift to the world of human sinners. And, by continuing to have faith that Christ died for our sins, believers are guaranteed salvation. It should be noted, however, that this is clearly at odds with Jesus' own response to the question: *Teacher, what shall I do to inherit eternal life?* Christ's own answer, given back to the inquirer in the form of a rhetorical question, is reaffirmed on more than one occasion (in direct answer to the question above in Luke 10:27, as well as Matthew 22:37 and Mark 12:30): *You shall love the Lord your God with all your heart, with all your soul, with all your strength, and with all your mind, and your neighbor as yourself.* If the orthodox interpretation of scriptures were correct, shouldn't Jesus have given the poor man the "correct" answer right then and there?

What is most remarkable in the contrasting evangelical interpretation of Jesus Christ and his mission has nothing to do with Jesus himself but rather with the concept of God underlying those teachings. This is none other than the God of Genesis who spoke to Abraham, saying: "Take now your son, your only son Isaac, whom you love, and go to the land of Moriah, and offer him there as a burnt offering on one of the mountains of which I shall tell you" (Genesis 22:2). In the last minute, just before the diligent, faithful servant was ready to cut the throat of his own son, God called it off by saying "I now know that you fear God, since you have not withheld your son, your only son, from Me" (Genesis 22:12). This is the same God who "hardened Pharaoh's heart" so that he would show no compromise in dealing with the Jews being held captive in Egypt. God then sent down one curse after the next on the Egyptians, killing the first born of all living things in the country (even the animals), starving the people, killing their crops with swarms of locusts, so that his "wonders may be multiplied in the land of Egypt" (Exodus 11:9).

Considering the evidence, the answer to that age-old problem of theodicy: How can we reconcile the reality of evil with the existence of a benevolent God?[58] pretty much falls into place. Given the reality of evil in the world as we know it, these three statements cannot all be true: 1) God is good; 2) God is omnipotent; 3) God is omniscient.[59] Judging from the track record of the Old Testament deity, it's fairly clear which of these statements needs serious refinement.

Now the argument from evangelical theologians goes like this: Man is to blame for the evil in the world because God created Man in His image, with a free will either to do as told, or to disobey and suffer the consequences:

> Then the Lord God took the man and put him in the Garden of Eden to tend and keep it. And the Lord God commanded the man, saying, "Of every tree of the garden you may freely eat; but of the tree of the knowledge of good and evil you shall not eat, for in the day that you eat of it you shall surely die" (Genesis 2:15-17).

Every school child knows the rest of the story. The serpent, "more cunning than any beast of the field," came to Eve and explained that the information God had given her and Adam was incomplete,

> For God knows that in the day you eat of it your eyes will be opened, and you will be like God, knowing good and evil. So when the woman saw that the tree was good for food, that is was pleasant to the eyes, and a tree desirable to make one wise, she took of its fruit and ate. She also gave to her husband with her, and he ate.

And that was it! From that point on, the shit has been hitting the fan every minute of every day, all because the human species just couldn't get it right. Instead of following orders and leaving well enough alone, they had to go and tempt fate, spoiling paradise for all the rest of us ever since. God didn't force them to eat the forbidden fruit! They did it of their own God-given free will! The Creator has given us, so the argument goes, the capacity to choose right over wrong. God would have been pleased and everything on Earth would have been just peachy if we hadn't disobeyed the instructions we were given.

One central problem posed by the free will paradigm is raised in the question: *free will to do what?* A moment's thought about the underlying assumptions in this argument should make clear that any suspicion on the part of a perspicacious Eve of the snake's cunning motives *presupposes the very knowledge of good and evil* that allegedly came about as a result of acting in disobedience. The moment we include a negative as a potential act of evil, e.g. free to kill, we have assumed that the taking of a life is possible because that life is mortal. But mortality and the knowledge thereof are states created by God, not man. The scripture states quite clearly, "for in the day that you eat of it you shall surely die." If all life had really been immortal to begin with, how was anyone supposed to understand God's initial warning? If immortality was the initial state of things before the Fall, the very possibility of death should have been a non-issue, and the freedom to will death on another (when Cain killed Abel) would have been meaningless right from the start. The same argument holds true for any kind of determination or warning that presupposes even the possibility of a negative outcome. In other words, *why shouldn't Eve have believed the snake?!* Trusting and innocent as she was supposedly created to be, did she have any reason to think the snake was lying? The suspicion of a lie as a deliberate falsehood, or misrepresentation of the facts, in itself already assumes knowledge of good and evil.

Why did God put the tree of the knowledge of good and evil in the Garden of Eden in the first place? To test the creatures he had made in his own image? And what image was that? A character perhaps with the ability to distinguish between good and evil? If God put the tree there to test his subjects, being God, he must have known in advance what the outcome was going to be, so he should have left Eden alone without any such tree. At that point already, Adam and Eve presumably had the status of being the image of God, with a free will, so why tempt them? Especially if God already knew the outcome!

When tempted by the snake, what should Eve have given as the "correct" answer? When offered the fruit, should Eve have said, "No, God told me not to eat it and I'm not going to!" Ideally of course, that was the only correct response. Now if the purpose of the whole setup was to test Eve and her mate, what moral principle was being tested? Obedience and submission to authority? But there are and have been many situations in life in which disobeying is the only morally correct course of action to take.

Theologians have argued (Aquinas, St. Augustine[60]) that our earthly existence since the Fall has been one of continuous testing (as happened to Job) to determine who is worthy of entry into the final kingdom of God. The modified argument by analogy goes something like this: God's purpose ultimately is to allow humans to experience the grandeur and glory of nature and life by having them experience some of the hardship first. Without the trials of winter, we can't really appreciate the spring; without the experience of hardship, we can't properly value having all we need. But if there is an *endpoint of perfection* that contains the highest level and awareness of Good, Beauty, and Love, why not just create that state of being to begin with, without the necessity of intermediary steps or a path to get there?[61] All loving parents will confirm that they by no means need to see their child near death in order to appreciate the love they experience for their children.

But according to evangelical soteriology, works and deeds are not even the criteria for entry into heaven anyhow; faith alone and its proof through baptism and the acceptance of Jesus Christ as Lord, the Son of God, who died for our sins, are the open sesame. In other words, if Rudolf Höß, the infamous commander of Auschwitz, had been converted in the last minutes of his life before he was hanged in front of the entrance gates to terrestrial hell, if he had begged God for forgiveness and accepted Jesus Christ as his personal savior, he, too, so we are told, would have been guaranteed a seat next to our loved ones in heaven. *And the six million Jews? Oops, sorry. They're out of luck without conversion.*

This is an utterly unacceptable concept of justice and surely at odds with all the teachings lived and embodied by Christ.

This received interpretation of the life and teachings of Jesus Christ and his message of salvation are the product of an archaic belief system that emerged out of the practice of animal sacrifice; hence the idea that God offered his own son as the ultimate sacrifice on the cross for the sins of the human species. For the saved, there is always the happy end.

You can spin it, turn it, twist it, bend it, and shape it anyway you want, the fact is that the Judeo-Christian God as interpreted by our leading sects and denominations *lost all credibility in the Holocaust*. From the final viewpoint of the Absolute as Hegel promised in the *Phenomenology of Mind*, "The wounds of the Spirit heal and leave no scars behind." Hegel was wrong.

Auschwitz was not a detail in history, but the concretization of an absolute that demanded nothing short of the complete annihilation of all life forms of a given name, the total destruction of all that answered to a given description. The analytical imperative was carried out without recourse to any human experience. Nothing that life, the human individual in his or her heart, soul or mind could offer in defense; no tear an eye may have shed; no thought or feeling however loving and profound, came to the rescue of those slated for death *en masse*.

Luckily, few of us can grasp the horrors that defined the mundane death-as-life world of the camps. Jean Amery's earth-shattering account—*At the Mind's Limits: Contemplations By a Survivor on Auschwitz and Its Realities*—leaves the capable reader gasping for air.

No hidden agenda or plan; no "mysterious ways"; no ultimate purpose or goal could justify the infinite horror and grief that will remain for all eternity—and beyond—as a permanent, hideous stigma of all the human species is capable of, again and again. If God knew of the slaughter, he should have intervened right then and there. If he didn't, we need to find the higher-ups in charge of this place.

The whole setup from the initial days of the Fall until the moment of each individual's personal death is designed, so the story goes, to test our own behavior in exercise of our free will. But if God were God, that outcome is already known. God offers forgiveness and salvation for those like Job who continue to believe, in spite of the trials, tribulations, and utter horror that he allows to happen, just so that he can see confirmed what he in his omniscience already knows anyhow. And which he in his omnipotence could prevent! And at the end, he allows his only son to die a horrifying death on the cross as a sacrifice that he himself demands through the rules of the game he has designed and controls. Our whole miserable existence one big rigged game right from the start.

Even if the theological arguments for continued persistent faith in the face of opposing evidence were sound, thereby absolving God of man's responsibility for cruelty, the very idea that the supposedly "loving father" can be content in the role of passive by-stander, a callous voyeur to an endless tapestry of tragedy, is equally impossible to accept. What an undignified role for a universal deity.

There are indeed very few lessons to be gained from the Holocaust. But one thing is for certain: when hell does arrive at the hands of human evil with its limitless talent for cruelty, from whatever source, for whatever imaginable, banal purpose, don't look to heaven for help. In some countries (Germany, ironically, being one of them), failure to provide help to people in dire need is punishable by law ("unterlassene Hilfeleistung"). Where was the "Heavenly Father" in humankind's worst hours?

We could only hope that the Day of Final Judgment does come. There are many out there who would long to find themselves in the roles of cosmic D.A. and witness for the prosecution, to demand that the Creator himself account for the misdeeds he allowed to go unchecked. How ironic it is that even by the moral standards God's puny creations are capable of, the Divine plan is hideously flawed.

There is precious little in our world to protect us from the evil lurking within the human soul. As a system of morals, evangelical Christianity in its received form is bankrupt. It fails miserably to provide a moral codex of conduct that would, or could, allow humans to live peacefully with one another and in benevolent harmony with other forms of life in their natural environment. The exceptions are the so-called "Golden Rule" in Christ's Sermon on the Mount, sadly forgotten and neglected by those who identify themselves most militantly as his followers. It is astonishing that these profound imperatives are so conveniently ignored in the persistent fuss about that singly most important win-all/end-all obsession of evangelicals: sex.

Yes indeed, God created Man in his image and likeness. The spittin' image, one should add. One chip off the old block. And the proof is visible every day. Much like a father who sets his three-year-old son in a chair beside the freeway with the warning not to walk out into traffic. "The wages of sin is death," not to mention one hell of a tormented world full of all kinds of nasty, hideous surprises. The human and other species we share this planet with didn't ask to be born, and looking at the general scheme of things, we deserved a nicer creator. *Was he drunk or something?* And after all is said and done, we're expected to pretend that the whole show and game was just fine? After all the struggles on earth, after countless pleas for mercy at the hands of human beasts, the reward for the surviving Jews of the camps is one final slap in the face: Don't pass go! Don't collect $200. Go straight to hell.

America's advocates for school curricula dominated by hard science supporting evolution have the argument wrong. One should give the devil his dues and grant the creationists and proponents of "intelligent design" their day in court. There may indeed be evidence for "intelligence" in the grand scheme of things, but *this world* reeks of a Microsoft design. God snaps his fingers in so many sequences of evenings and mornings, breathes life into a mound of clay, creating a nice play thing, all while knowing full well, *a priori,* what the outcome is going to be. And when the damned favorite toy does make the wrong turn—*oops! This program has performed an illegal operation and will be shut down.* Should we "Retry, Cancel, Abort" perhaps?

Nature plays a cruel game. Life itself is a glorious promise persistently broken by death. The love that endures in our hearts and minds for the unique souls we wish close to us for all eternity, is scorned by the all-consuming bitterness of loss. This, too, is God's game. *Isn't life fun?*

History is played out as so many sequences of patches for the beta version, patches for the patches, *ad nauseum.* Wasn't that the whole point of the great flood? We've been damned, tortured, tormented, drowned, burned alive, smoked, glazed, and oven roasted; given abscessed teeth, cancer, Alzheimer's and AIDS; forced into helplessness as our only beloved child is ripped to shreds by bred-to-kill pit bulls. Old age, the crowning insult to a life worth living, denies us the dreams even nature itself has forced on us as an enduring promise. We cling to the insane notion that somehow, somewhere, someone out there might love and respect us despite the lines nature etches into every mirror. Only slowly to disappear into oblivion as the world laughs on. Indeed, all kinds of exciting things have been orchestrated on this world stage. And worst of all, our loved ones get to watch, *in grief*, the most dreadful of human emotions.

There can be no more poetry after Auschwitz, Theodor Adorno assessed. Not when every smile and every song are predefined by collective memories that cannot be stilled; memories that demand acknowledgement as the only fractured reality that will ever be. Barring a lobotomy for the species, there is no happy end. Whatever the message evangelicals scream throughout the heartland, the facts belie their faith.

No plan of a higher order; no hidden "divine agenda"; no form of punishment however conceived and implemented, could ever atone or compensate for the infinitude of memories of eternal evil, or for the endless grief smothering the minds and souls of the mothers who witnessed their little ones gassed, burned, and turned into human lasagna. The tortured screams from the ovens of the Holocaust and from the jungles of Rwanda will forever echo throughout the coldest regions of the cosmos, in this best of all possible worlds.

The God who was silent in the Death Camps of Europe and Rwanda should respectfully keep quiet about gay marriage and family values.

If there are elements of the Divine in our miserable, wonderful world, they're to be found in the child's love of its mother; in a mother's love of her children; in the lonely widow's love of her cat; in the most precious of life's mysteries—*empathy and mercy*. Judging from past experience, there's no use looking to heaven or the pulpits for God's mercy. In the worst events, God was a no-show, leaving behind neither an info notice nor a tracking number.

For the greatest part of America's brief history, public discourse and political action have been dominated by the hegemony of a Puritan tradition of Christianity. Carrying in its central dogma the doctrine of salvation *sola scriptura, sola fide,* this orthodox interpretation of Christian teachings has succeeded in defining the legacy of Jesus Christ in ways the originator himself may never have dreamed possible. It's highly doubtful he would have called them his own.

Notes

1 In the East Waynesville Baptist Church in North Carolina no fewer than nine regular members were reportedly forced out of the church by a young pastor who had called himself "the spokesperson for the most high." One of the excommunicated had been an upstanding member for forty-three years. The evicted had voted their conscience in support of John Kerry, against the warnings of the pastor that anyone who did so should repent or resign.

2 Quoted in Richard Hofstadter, *Anti-Intellectualism in American Life* (New York: Vintage Books, 1966) 66.

3 An in-depth analysis of the marketing strategies used by Whitefield and his followers can be found in Frank Lambert, *Pedlar Divinity: George Whitefield and the Transatlantic Revivals, 1737–1770* (Princeton: Princeton University Press, 2002).

4 Richard Hofstadter, *Anti-Intellectualism in American Life*, 67.

5 Cited in *ibid.*, p. 68.

6 See Charles Chauncy, *Seasonable Thoughts on the State of Religion in New England* (Boston, 1743).

7 Richard Hofstadter, *Anti-Intellectualism in American Life*, 69.

8 Mark A. Noll, *A History of Christianity in the United States and Canada* (Grand Rapids, Michigan: William B. Eerdmans Publishing Company, 2001) 98.

9 *Ibid.*

10 Cited in Mark A. Noll, *A History of Christianity in the United States and Canada*, p. 109.

11 Frank Lambert has written extensively on the role of religion in the formative years of the Republic and on the historical reception of the Great Awakening, which was not perceived or spoken of as such until after its occurrence. Lambert argues that the revivalist movement became nominalized as an extraordinary event by the very clergymen who had most to gain from its success. See Frank Lambert, *Inventing the Great Awakening* (Princeton: Princeton University Press, 2001); idem, *The Founding Fathers and the Place of Religion in America* (Princeton: Princeton University Press, 2003).

12 Mark A. Noll, *A History of Christianity in the United States and Canada*, 115.

13 See Ruth H. Bloch, *Visionary Republic: Millennial Themes in American Thought, 1756–1800* (New York: Cambridge University Press, 1985).

14 Sydney E. Ahlstrom, *A Religious History of the American People* (Garden City, New York: Image Books, 1975) 518.

15 *Ibid.*, 514.

16 See Albert J. Raboteau, *Slave Religion: The Invisible Institution in the Antebellum South* (Oxford: Oxford University Press, 2004) as well as Donald Mathews, *Religion in the Old South* (Chicago: University of Chicago Press, 1977). See also W.E.B. Du Bois, *The Souls of Black Folk* (1903) (New York: W.W. Norton, 1999).

17 See C. C. Goen, *Broken Churches, Broken Nation: Denominational Schisms and the Coming of the Civil War* (Macon, Georgia: Mercer University Press, 1985).

18 Cf. O. K. Armstrong and Marjorie Moore Armstrong, *The Indomitable Baptists* (Garden City: Doubleday Books, 1967).

19 See Mark A. Noll, *A History of Christianity in the United States and Canada*, 370.

20 Nancy Tatom Ammerman, *Bible Believers. Fundamentalists in the Modern World* (New Brunswick, New Jersey: Rutgers University Press, 1993) 23.

21 Nancy Tatom Ammerman offers detailed insight into these differences by reviewing certain theological distinctions as well as diverging demographic patterns; *ibid.*, 3–9.

22 The Texas state legislature drafted a bill requiring parental consent for teenage girls seeking an abortion. The original version of the bill provided for the publication of the names of judges active in juvenile abortion cases and how those judges had ruled, opening the possibility that judges whose rulings were at odds with the Christian right would be sitting ducks at the end of a shotgun. That provision was luckily removed in the final version.

23 See Jean Reith Schroedel, *Is the Fetus a Person? A Comparison of Policies across the Fifty States* (Ithaca, New York: Cornell University Press, 2000).

24 The entire text can be found at http://www.movieguide.org.

25 The WHO puts the figure at 288,000 deaths per year. See http://www.who.int.

26 For a complete rundown on why gays, Swedes, Thais, and Indonesians were to blame, visit the aforementioned Westboro Baptist Church's outline for eternal damnation at http://www.godhatesfags.com.

27 Of particular interest in this context is Jean L. Cohen's analysis of the role of the judiciary in the bedroom in *Regulating Intimacy: A New Legal Paradigm* (Princeton: Princeton University Press, 2002).

28 During a speech given in February 2006 to the Constitutional Court of South Africa, U.S. Supreme Court Justice Ruth Bader Ginsburg exposed one Internet-based attempt to silence liberal-leaning justices. Quoting from the explicit threat penned by the "irrational fringe" of critics, Bader Ginsburg said that the Internet posting had named her and Sandra Day O'Connor specifically: "Okay, commandoes, here is your first patriotic assignment...an easy one. Supreme Court Justices Ginsburg and O'Connor have publicly stated that they use [foreign] laws and rulings to decide how to rule on American cases. This is a huge threat to our Republic and Constitutional freedom...If you are what you say you are, and NOT armchair patriots, then these two justices will not live another week." Quoted in Charles Lane, "Ginsburg Faults GOP Critics, Cites a Threat from 'Fringe'," *Washington Post*, 17 March 2006, A03.

29 April 4, 2005, *Congressional Record*, 109th Cong., 1st sess., S3125–S3126.

30 James Dobson, *Marriage Under Fire: Why We Must Win This Battle* (Sisters, Oregon: Multnomah Publishers, 2004).

31 Excerpts from Dobson's book and further warnings of impending moral doom can be found at http://www.family.org.

32 Frank Rich, "Apres Janet, a Deluge," *New York Times*, 21 March 2004, 2.1.

33 Dennis Prager, "The (Culture) War of the Word," *Los Angeles Times*, 29 May 2005, M2.

34 See Walter Bauer's seminal study of the struggle for theological supremacy *Orthodoxy and Heresy in Earliest Christianity* tr. Robert Kraft et al., ed. Robert Kraft and Gerhard Krodel (Philadelphia: Fortress, 1971). Of equal importance in this context are Harry Gamble, *The New Testament Canon: Its Making and Meaning* (Philadelphia: Fortress, 1985) and Bruce M. Metzger, *The Canon of the New Testament* (Oxford: Clarendon, 1987).

35 Of particular note is the five-volume assault by Irenaeus entitled *Against Heresies*.

36 Cf. Bart D. Ehrman, *The Orthodox Corruption of Scripture. The Effect of Early Christological Controversies on the Text of the New Testament* (New York and Oxford: Oxford University Press, 1996) 13.

37 *Ibid.*, 51; cf. Eusebius, *Hist. Eccl.* III, xxvii.

38 Cf. Adolf von Harnack, *Marcion: The Gospel of the Alien God* , trans. John E.

Steely and Lyle D. Bierma (Durham, N. C.: Labyrinth Press, 1990).

39 Bauer, *Orthodoxy and Heresy in Earliest Christianity*, 22–43.

40 Of special note again are the multi-volume attacks launched by Irenaeus in *Adversus Haereses*, as well as Hippolyt's *Refutatio omnium haeresium* and Tertullian's *Adv. Marc.* and *Prescription*. Klaus Korschorke has examined Hippolyt's rhetorical arguments against Gnosticism in considerable detail in the German "Hippolyts Ketzerbekämpfung und Polemik gegen die Gnostiker. Eine tendenzkritische Untersuchung seiner 'Refutatio omnium haeresium'," *Göttinger Orientforschungen*, 4 (Wiesbaden: Otto Harrassowitz, 1975). See also the thorough analysis of proto-orthodox efforts to discredit Gnostic Christology in Bart D. Ehrman's *The Orthodox Corruption of Scripture*.

41 From among several particularly good texts: Elaine Pagels, *The Gnostic Gospels* (New York: Vintage Books, 1989); Hans Leisegang, *Die Gnosis* (Stuttgart: Kröner, 1985); Christoph Markschies, *Die Gnosis* (Munich, C.H. Beck, 2001); Boris Mouravieff, *Gnosis. Etudes et commentaires sur la tradition ésotérique de l'orthodoxie orientale* (Neuchâtel: La Baconniere, 2000).

42 James M. Robinson, ed., *The Nag Hammadi Library. The Definitive Translation of the Gnostic Scriptures Complete in One Volume* (San Francisco: Harper San Francisco, 1990).

43 To paraphrase Origen (omnes enim haeretici primo ad credulitatem veniunt, et post haec ab itinere fidei et dogmatum veritate declinant).

44 Cf. Bart D. Ehrman, *The Orthodox Corruption of Scripture*, 280.

45 The mechanics of early bookmaking are graphically explained in greater detail in Bruce M. Metzger's *The Text of the New Testament. Its Transmission, Corruption, and Restoration.* Ehrman plausibly explains how and why certain textual changes arose as a result of the scribes' active context-/content-based "reading" and interpreting of the manuscripts from which subsequent copies were made; see his *The Orthodox Corruption of Scripture*.

46 Cf. Bruce M. Metzger, *The Text of the New Testament*, 17.

47 Metzger points to this type of error in rendering the incomprehensible reading of John 17:15 in the *codex Vaticanus*: "I do not pray that thou shouldst take them from the [world, but that thou shouldst keep them from the] evil one." See *The Text of the New Testament*, p. 189.

48 *Ibid.*

49 Steven Pinker has analyzed constructions of this type from a linguist's perspective in *The Language Instinct: How the Mind Creates Language* (New York: HarperCollins Publishers, 2000).

50 Bruce M. Metzger, *The Text of the New Testament*, 191.

51 *Ibid.* He cites specifically Matthew 2:6 in the *codex Sinaiticus* as well as Matthew 21:19 and Mark 11:14.

52 *Ibid.*, 196–197.

53 *Ibid.*, 194–195.

54 There are other scholars who are quite willing to accept this shorter, downbeat version of the ending to the Gospel of Mark. In addition to those mentioned by Metzger there is the work of F.H.A. Scrivener, *A Plain Introduction to the Criticism of the New Testament* (London: George Bell and Sons, 1894).

55 This again is the subject of Ehrman's highly readable *The Orthodox Corruption of Scripture.*

56 Walter Bauer, *Orthodoxy and Heresy in Earliest Christianity*, 24.

57 Several authors provide detailed histories of the consolidation of scriptures into the New Testament Canon as we know it today: Bruce M. Metzger, *The Canon of the New Testament: Its Origin, Development, and Significance* (Oxford: Oxford University Press, 1997); Hans von Campenhausen, *The Formation of the Christian Bible*, translated by J.A. Baker (Mifflintown, PA: Sigler Press, 1997); Harry Y. Gamble, *The New Testament Canon: Its Making and Meaning* (Eugene, OR: Wipf & Stock Publishing, 2002).

58 By far the best discussion of this problem is found in Susan Neiman's *Evil in Modern Thought. An Alternative History of Philosophy* (Princeton: Princeton University Press, 2002). As in Neiman's extraordinary study, the term "evil" is understood here in the meaning it was given by Bayle as "crimes and misfortunes."

59 One of the more convincing discussions of this three-horned dilemma is that offered by Bayle in his entry under "Manicheans." See Pierre Bayle, *Historical and Critical Dictionary*, translated by Richard H. Popkin (Indianapolis and Cambridge: Hackett Publishing Company, Inc., 1991) 144–153.

60 Augustine, "The Free Choice of the Will," in *The Teacher, The Free Choice of the Will, Grace and Free Will*, trans. R. P. Russell (Washington, D.C.: Catholic University of America Press, 1968), III.

61 This argument is very nicely examined in Fred Berthold Jr., *Good, Evil, and Human Learning. A Critique and Revision of the Free Will Defense in Theodicy* (Albany, New York: State University of New York Press, 2004). See also N. Smart, "Omnipotence, Evil and Supermen," in *God and Evil*, ed. N. Pike (Englewood Cliffs, New Jersey: Prentice Hall, 1964); Antony Flew, "Divine Omnipotence and Human Freedom," in *New Essays in Philosophical Theology*, ed. A. Flew and A. Macintyre (London: SCM Press, 1955).

Chapter 4

America Means Business

Wall Street owns the country. It is no longer a government of the people, by the people, and for the people, but a government of Wall Street, by Wall Street, and for Wall Street. The great common people of this country are slaves, and monopoly is the master.
  —Mary Elizabeth, "Yellin' Ellen" Lease,
    Populist Leader, around 1890

JUST HOW MUCH RESPONSIBILITY DOES a government of, by, and for the people have vis-à-vis its citizens? Does the government have the social and moral responsibility to maintain a level playing field for competing commercial and public interests? Should it provide free schools and universities? Should it make health care universally available for all? Does the government have a moral obligation to see that its citizens don't become homeless and hungry? In turn, where do the rights and responsibilities of the citizenry lie? What are the limits of individual freedom? Should individuals be allowed to take their own lives if and when they please? Should individuals be free to behave in ways that might be harmful to other citizens? If General Motors or Ford put an engine in and wheels on an off-road vehicle the size of the Eiffel Tower with a fuel consumption rate of 125,000 gallons per mile, should they be allowed to mass produce it? Should interested parties be permitted to buy it?

The list of such questions could be extended *ad libitum*. What is important to remember is that these are not questions that people have always asked. Rather, the very possibility of thinking about and posing questions concerning the rights and limits of the individual vis-à-vis the state is predicated on the sixteenth-and seventeenth-century transformations of society into the economic-political constellations that actually generated for the first time the workable concepts of "individual" and the bourgeois "public." Prior to these fundamental changes in the economic structure of society, the human being was always conceptualized as a social entity, naturally embedded in the context and confines of the family, social class, the church, the city-state or *polis*. It would have been essentially meaningless to consider the individual per se outside these larger societal frames of reference prior to the genesis of the private individual and the freedom envisioned in modernity's emancipation process.

It was the development of the financially stable bourgeoisie with its mode of consent- or contract-based[1] market exchange that gave rise to the individual as an active agent, potentially independent of external authority. Seventeenth-century thought placed the individual at the center of deliberations concerning natural law and the structure and legitimacy of political entities. It is within this newly constituted paradigm of the bourgeois individual acting as an ostensibly autonomous agent within a defined social class vis-à-vis the state that the American experiment with government must be viewed. This, too, is the locus of decisions about human/individual rights and their preservation. Before even the first shots were fired in the American Revolution, the political form of the country-to-be had already begun to take shape in the ideas of Classical Liberalism.

Thomas Hobbes had examined the potential problems he saw brewing on the horizon as the individual became a distinct political entity. With the expansion of the exchange-based market economy, the emancipation process from the feudal society was generating an entirely new societal basis. Pessimist that he was, Hobbes saw the potential for absolute chaos. If left completely unrestrained to act out every whim and manifest every want and need, the human individual might soon fit the model of the rapacious super-brat Hobbes envisioned in *Leviathan* (1651) and later confirmed at Enron, Tyco, and WorldCom. Such a "solitary," "brutish," and "short" state of nature would be nothing short of mayhem, with the strongest annihilating the weakest in a winner-take-all battle for survival, surpassing even the situation defining America's inner cities and corporate boardrooms. Hobbes's solution was a social contract, agreed upon by all participants who valued their own survival, which stipulated that all citizens would cede *in toto* their individual urges and needs to an absolute sovereign, whose decisions on all issues would be final. By drastically restricting the freedom of all individuals within the society, the sovereign would guarantee the survival of each member and preserve the structure of the social contract.

Locke's "original position" (to borrow a phrase coined by John Rawls) started from the success he saw in bourgeois society after the Glorious Revolution. Like Hobbes before him, Locke, too, gave careful consideration to the role and responsibility of government for its citizens, but Locke's view of society was decidedly more upbeat. He saw the concrete creation of prosperity and opportunity where before there had been none. What's more, the newly structured system of exchanging manufactured goods for money opened up entirely new possibilities for investment, with the value of goods and property climbing in accordance with the labor needed to produce and enhance them.

Locke's model of civil society placed only a minimum of authority and power in the hands of the government. Citizens consented to abide by the laws written and agreed upon by the majority of educated people who owned property. The primary purpose of this legislature was to protect the interests common to all. Like Hobbes, Locke saw it as the responsibility of the government to defend the citizenry against foreign and domestic threats, and to preserve the natural rights of the governed to "life, liberty, and estate." Such protection was afforded in theory to all individuals in the society irrespective of class. Full active participation in drafting and enacting laws and in forming the body of the legislature was restricted to the bourgeois class of property owners, however, because of the commonality of their interests. In the same way that extremely wealthy families prefer their offspring to marry someone of similar wealth so as to preclude the possibility that the other is marrying for the money alone, the educated bourgeois merchant class recognized that those of similar station would necessarily support the same types of legislation and codes of ethical conduct.[2]

Such a separation of power according to means reflects a fundamental inequality in society, but Locke justified this breach in fairness by arguing that such imbalances were the result of God-given, innate differences in talent as well as of varying degrees of personal dedication and effort. Nature, Locke said, had simply bestowed upon some people a wee bit more wit and drive than it had others, and the naturally blessed tend to accomplish and hence acquire more. Locke thus saw it as a natural law of human nature that talented hard-working people wanted to accumulate as much wealth as possible. He went on to conclude that one of the few responsibilities of the legislature was to assure that this natural right was never infringed upon or curtailed by others. Locke did place certain moral limits on this "natural" propensity to acquire things by recognizing that it was wrong to amass so much that the excess would eventually go to waste. Locke saw the ideal solution to this problem in the monetary equivalent of the surplus. The hard-working individual should take the excess harvest amassed and sell it on the open market. The earnings could then be reinvested in more land or something else of value.

Reflected in this scenario is a context of harmonious interaction in which citizens live in agreement, as they so choose, without unnecessary or illegitimate interference from the government or from other citizens. Although all enjoy equal protection under the law, existing class differences are condoned as the result of both natural law and the unequal God-given distribution of intellect and drive. Locke defined the role of government in class-based economic terms, and his model of restricted government functioned as a superb ideological justification for the bourgeois-liberal, market-based political economy in full bloom at the end of the seventeenth century. Anti-absolutist to the core, the model opened the door for rational critical dissent to ultimately throw off the chains of despotism that shackled the American colonies. In drawing up the *Declaration of Independence* and the *Constitution*, the Founding Fathers relied heavily on Locke's theory of liberal democracy. Subsequent generations of ideologues have made extensive use of his reasoning in advocating a smaller role for government in favor of expanded opportunities for private enterprise.

The Republican Party of today represents a distinct trend in American history that has developed in response to and in tandem with the power of businesses to transform society and the natural environment. In order to shed light on this trend and to understand its origin, let us now look at a few key phases in that development.

A Government of the Propertied

From the outset, the centers of American political influence and power enjoyed a very cozy relationship with large sources of money. The Founding Fathers themselves derived from society's educated, propertied elite, and again, the threats to freedom and individual liberty swirling through their heads were always related to valid experiences with the type of monarchical absolutism that had defined most of European history. It is exceedingly doubtful, however, that any of these bourgeois participants in the social contract of civil society could ever have envisioned that the market forces "guaranteeing" a common purpose and the general acceptance of the foundations of the liberal state could become so lopsided as to afford a very small, select group of proprietors a ninety percent share of the country's assets and resources.

Right up to the present, American history reads like a mystery novel replete with plots and counter-plots, schemes and counter-schemes, disguised as public interest to support behind-the-scenes puppeteers of corporate bookkeeping, with government policies dancing to the tunes of Big Business. Periods of apparent pro-populist good heartedness are followed by gut-wrenching cutbacks in every conceivable publicly controlled function and by labor contracts that are scarcely worth the paper they're printed on. All in the name of what "the American people want": "personal freedom" and the "right to choose."

Statist and antistatist policies, which appear to follow each other in a caus-ally related cycle, are frequently two sides of the same concern for elitist monetary interests. One of the first expressions of statism came in response to Federalist Al-exander Hamilton's detailed plans to expand the role of the federal government in the regulation of commerce nationwide. Hamilton, who argued against allowing "the people" to have a greater voice in governing, supported giving "to the first class a distinct permanent share in the government." John Jay went even further: "Those who own the country ought to govern it." Hamilton also advocated the es-tablishment of a National Bank[3] (enacted by Congress and signed by Washington in 1791) that would assume the acquired debts of individual states, thereby fur-ther strengthening the centralized function of the federal government in its ability to pick and choose from the most powerful business and property interests, and to regulate the flow of money into the economy. Through the centralized regula-tion of lending schemes to select businesses, Hamilton also favored what today would be called "industrial policy," ostensibly to expand the nation's workforce and commercial potential to the fullest benefit of the owners.

Many of Hamilton's efforts were opposed by Jeffersonian republicans, who were leery of a strong central government in the hands of Federalist cronies. The Jeffersonians advocated autonomy for the individual states in determining eco-nomic policies and terms of commerce. Once in office, Jefferson tried to shift the balance of power back to the states. In part by repealing the federal excise tax and returning control of the banks to the states, Jefferson worked to restore individual state-based economic activity with a renewed focus on individual property own-ers and local merchants. As an avid supporter of the ideals of the French Revolu-tion, Jefferson detested the patterns of elitist government he had seen taking shape under Hamilton's pro-British baton. The Federalists were exceedingly powerful, with enough money to bribe and coerce at will.[4] It can be argued that the platform and practices of Jefferson's Democratic-Republicans developed in large measure out of economic (and constitutional) concerns about the potential consolidation of monetary policy in the hands of a select group of powerful merchants, as well as from the very real concern that a powerful, centralized authoritarian government of the type the colonies had fought to overthrow might gain an unshakable foothold.

The consolidation of republican political clout subsequent to the War of 1812 came amid a wave of nationalism as geographic expansion accompanied a sense of strength, pride, and geopolitical demarcation vis-à-vis "Old Europe" (Monroe Doctrine). At the same time, the country was experiencing growing pains with westward expansion, and already existing regional differences among the states became more pronounced. The Northeast experienced rapid economic growth with the development of new production techniques. Southern plantations, heavily reliant on slave labor, worked in high gear to harvest enough cotton to send to the bustling textile centers in New York. Once again a reminder that America's noble history would have been unthinkable without the spilled blood, endless sweat and tears, shackled bones, and broken hearts of the 4,000,000 slaves—the people who were not even counted as human. Supply-side economics at its ugliest extreme.

With the emergence of merchant capitalists, the entire realm of production and sales took on new dimensions. Merchant capitalists were not dependent on localized shops or specialized craftsmen; they had mastered the more important art of deal-making. By securing substantial sources of capital and credit, merchant capitalists were able to engage in large-scale sales across a potentially vast market by buying large amounts of raw material and having the work completed by a number of smaller shops. Unable to compete with these immense resources, the small shop owners and artisans gradually fell into the merchant capitalist network of production. The smaller businesses had to negotiate for as much as they could get from the merchant capitalists. They then used the money they received to pay their own employed craftsmen and kept as profit what was left.[5]

With the demand for increased worker productivity came physical exploitation and sheer exhaustion of workers toiling in miserable environments. Industrial states became increasingly protective of their own local interests and efforts were widespread to roll back federal influence on the issuance of loans. Hamilton's national bank had served one of its purposes well—that of restricting the amount of money created and flowing into the economy. But this inhibitory spigot function was gradually perceived at the state level to be a royal pain in the butt. This led some states to enact legislation to curtail the ability of the national bank to dictate terms of commerce on the state level. Maryland set an example in defense of its state banks by levying a tax on the Baltimore branch of the federal bank. When the national bank (then under its second twenty-year government charter) refused to pay, the case went to the Supreme Court. In *McCulloch v. Maryland*, the high court in a unanimous decision sided with the federal institution in upholding the national bank's *raison d' être* as originally authored by Hamilton. A virtually identical lawsuit was brought to the Court again just a few years later, this time involving a conflict of interest between a regional bank in Ohio and the federal financial institution. The high court handed down the same decision in *Osborn v. Bank of the United States*.

These decisions did not sit well with populist-tinged Jacksonian Democrats who supported smaller government, the sovereignty of the states, and the ideological sanctity of the "small man." What's more, thinkers of Jacksonian persuasion were convinced that the federal bank (the "monster") was instrumental in stuffing the coffers of a few at the expense of the rest. Jackson won hands-down in his 1832 presidential bid against Henry Clay, who during his tenure in the Senate had mustered up enough votes to get the national bank's charter renewed before it had even expired, eliciting of course a presidential veto. After reelection, Jackson was so incensed by the bank (and by implication by the Federalists pulling the strings behind the curtain) that he had federal funds taken out and put in small, private state banks. Here again, in the early years of the Republic the decisive issue at the heart of regulation concerned the best allocation of powers between the federal government ostensibly representing the interests of the nation as a whole, and individual states as localized divergent constituencies.

Another wave of fervent antistatism[6] came in reaction to a number of policies implemented by the Lincoln administration in its efforts to restore stability and unity to a nation ravaged and torn apart by the Civil War. Underlying these concerns were, of course, the same financial interests that were at the root of the conflict in the first place. As we know from his First Inaugural Address, Lincoln's concern (at least at the time) was no more for the welfare of the slaves than Bush 43's was for the Iraqi people:

> Apprehension seems to exist among the people of the Southern States, that by the accession of a Republican Administration, their property, and their peace, and personal security, are to be endangered. There has never been any reasonable cause for such apprehension. Indeed, the most am-

ple evidence to the contrary has all the while existed, and been open to their inspection. It is found in nearly all the published speeches of him who now addresses you. I do but quote from one of those speeches when I declare that "I have no purpose, directly or indirectly, to interfere with the institution of slavery in the States where it exists. I believe I have no lawful right to do so, and I have no inclination to do so." Those who nominated and elected me did so with full knowledge that I had made this, and many similar declarations, and had never recanted them.

The industrial North sought to expand its transportation networks to the large reserves of natural resources lying buried in the Southern hills and dales, and to enlarge its industrial base throughout the entire territorial area of the United States. Lincoln was firmly behind these efforts.[7] The conflict itself had led to general conscription and to taxes on income. To prevent an all-out nightmare from occurring, the federal government had to step in with relief efforts. Programs enacted to aid millions of freed slaves assisted in providing basic needs and in helping the desperate find some source of income. Pension funds were established to care for needy survivors of the war's battles. New literacy programs and general education classes were promoted to educate a population largely deprived of the privilege.[8]

A whitewashed historiography has all but obliterated from collective memory the "other civil war" as Howard Zinn called it,[9] in which the battles were carried out not at Antietam, Mobile Bay or Gettysburg, but on factory floors and at picket lines. The entire nineteenth century was rife with strikes and civil unrest of all flavors as workers struggled to stay alive and healthy despite fourteen- to sixteen-hour workdays and incomes that could barely keep onions on the table or a roof over their heads. The housing, too, often consisted of nothing more than dark holes-in-the-walls—unventilated, windowless, cold, dank, and mould-infested. Sickness was the chronic norm rather than the exception.

In 1839, the Hudson River Valley became the focus of an organized renters' movement to stop evictions orchestrated by the Rensselaer family who held quasi-feudal monopoly control over the land of more than 80,000 tenants.[10] Efforts by law enforcement officers sent in to collect back rent and evict were met with organized resistance. More than 25,000 tenants signed an anti-rent petition, but the renters' grievances were thrown out by the legislature. The Rensselaer family then allowed law enforcement agents to seize personal property and livestock from the tenants and sell it for rent. This, too, was met with resistance, but this time things got really nasty. State leaders in New York sent in several hundred state police to put down what the governor had described as "high treason" and an "armed insurrection" against the government.[11]

As defined in the constitutions of other states except Pennsylvania at the time, Rhode Island's voting rights were extended only to white men who owned property (land). This fact alone excluded thousands of otherwise eligible voters (and we thought Florida was bad) who had moved into urban centers seeking employment. In 1841, Thomas Dorr, a highly educated lawyer, took up the cause of the officially disfranchised and led a protest march of thousands in front of the capitol in Providence. The groups succeeded in drawing up a new state constitution that abolished land ownership as a suffrage requirement. They also managed to place their candidate Dorr on the "party" slate as governor. In a subsequent ersatz-election the unchallenged folk's hero was voted in as the next governor. Having been promised the aid of federal troops if bad came to worse, the sitting governor of the state issued a warrant for the arrest of Dorr, who wisely got out of Dodge just in time.

The Rhode Island legislature then set about revising its constitution to become more inclusive, but as Zinn notes, it still exhibited pronounced bias toward the landed gentry of rural estates.[12] When Dorr eventually returned to the state, authorities promptly nabbed him. He was then tried and convicted of treason and given a lifelong prison sentence. The subsequent governor showed mercy on the poor devil and ordered his release.

These were also the formative years of organized labor. Growing tensions between the rich and poor mounted as already deplorable living and working conditions were exacerbated by the economic crisis of 1837. Prices for everyday items as well as for rent were skyrocketing at the same time as real wages were being cut. According to Zinn, there were 50,000 unemployed just in New York City, with 200,000 living in squalor, while wealthier merchants, factory owners, and bankers sat back and pulled the strings. In the industrial urban strongholds, unions formed around the needs of workers from every trade. And for the first time, in 1825, women formed their own union; they even carried out their first organized strike against a mill in Dover, New Hampshire. A similar strike as Zinn notes was carried out on behalf of the female workers against a mill in Exeter, New Hampshire, in which the factory supervisor was caught setting back the clocks. The women were effectively being cheated out of hours of work per week, with nothing to show in return. Employers used every trick in the book to gain as much as humanly possible from man, woman, and child, while begrudgingly offering as little as humanly possible in compensation. A perennially familiar theme.

Class War in Perpetuity

The largest mass demonstration against unfair labor practices prior to the war was conducted by New England shoemakers. In addition to all the usual chicanery thrown their way by employers, the factory workers were putting in sixteen-hour days with less and less pay. Higher prices brought about by the 1857 crisis meant that most were simply no longer able to make ends meet. Many workers had already lost their jobs and some were being replaced by sewing machines, which substantially increased the number of finished shoes one worker could turn out. The initial strike of a few hundred workers in Lynn, Massachusetts, quickly encompassed the entire New England shoemaking enterprise with more than 20,000 on strike.[13]

Strikes for higher wages and shorter workdays were felt all across the country and in virtually every sector of the economy. In the northern states, Union troops were deployed against strikers to protect scabs. If there was ever any doubt (there wasn't) as to where the federal government stood on the issues of great divide between the haves and the nots, legislation enacted during and after the war served to set the records straight. In practices hauntingly familiar to those who found themselves at the losing end of legal battles against corporate giants during the Bush-Cheney era, pre-Civil War lawsuits against powerful businesses, as Morton Horwitz has shown,[14] were often turned over to single judges as opposed to jurors, who might have identified and empathized with the plaintiffs. Dependent on the generosity and good will of money's long-armed reach, judges became bosombuddies with the local tycoons who set the scenes and pulled the strings in county and state politics. Both Zinn and Horwitz cite one blatant example of the government bending over backwards to suit the whims and needs of the business community: Workers who signed contracts with the employer for a specified amount of time were not entitled to any monetary compensation if they decided to leave before the terms of the contract expired. A construction company, in contrast, was entitled to full compensation for any work accomplished, even if the contractor quit smack-dab in the middle of the job. Congress also came to the rescue of businesses suffering labor shortages due to the effects of the draft and persistent strikes.

From the vantage point of the country's newest version of *total business all the time*, many of the nineteenth century's pro-enterprise policies evoke the been-there done-that epiphany. So, too, the Contract Labor Law of 1864. Lacking millions of impoverished Oaxacans and Guatemalans streaming across the southern border, nineteenth-century lupine philanthropists received a godsend from Congress in

1864 with the passage of the Contract Labor Law. This handy piece of legislation —much like Bush 43's proposal for a Guest Worker Program (euphemisms have always been a hallmark of conservative compassion)—opened up the floodgates for businesses in need of the cheapest labor out there (China and India weren't yet on the CEO's horizon) and a virtually limitless supply of strikebreakers to boot. Dripping with benevolent goodwill, recruiting agencies such as the American Emigrant Company swung into high gear to lure desperate workers from Europe into promising positions of indentured servitude. The newcomers signed contracts with companies eagerly awaiting the arrival of new suckers who would work for literally nothing. The foreign laborers were to receive no pay in return for their labor until the cost of their transport and various fees were reimbursed—one year's worth of work in exchange for legal residence (had they only known about the Alvarado Street green card stores). The already dismal outlook for native-born wage earners suddenly looked and felt even bleaker. Indeed it was, and things only got worse.

In the post-Reconstruction Era, the waves of strikes only intensified. New methods of processing iron into steel and the development of new energy sources including electricity led to unprecedented structural changes in manufacturing and transportation. Factories gradually began to rely on the power of machines to complement and replace human labor. The real proof of what this country is all about under the stewardship of Classical Liberalism came with the rise to power of the so-called "robber barons," the moneyed magnates of limitless wealth and power—Jehovah's eighth curse on the new Egyptians. Several events of the subsequent decades testified to the grotesque partnership between the "rule of law" and the power of greed.

One of the broadest expressions of public solidarity for the new plight of the working class came out of the Pullman Strike of 1894. In several ways the problems that motivated the workers to put down their tools constituted a pattern typical of employer-employee relations at the time. George Pullman had constructed a neat little town on the outskirts of Chicago as a home for the more than 3,000 employees at the production site of his Pullman train cars. Since he had hoped to nip in the bud any problems associated with poor living conditions, he built the houses and indeed the entire town not only with appeasement in mind, but also with the purpose of getting the utmost from every worker. Houses were equipped with a number of conveniences normally lacking in similar company-owned facilities.[15] As elsewhere in comparable communities, however, prices for staples, daily consumer goods, and rent were much higher than anything the workers could afford on the meager wages Pullman was paying. Like the forty-seven million uninsured Americans today who are often forced to use their credit cards to pay for vital medical procedures, the inhabitants of the Chicago suburb fell deeper and deeper into debt as wages were cut five times, *while prices rose*. The money owed was then taken out of the paychecks so that there was always too much month left at the end of the money. The rail workers were effectively working just to pay off the debts, with no hope at all of ever being able to put anything aside. In a statement issued by the strikers on June 15, 1894, the workers complained that in the nearby community of Roseland, rents for better and more spacious accommodations were half the price of those paid by Pullman employees. The statement also pointed out that Pullman's refusal to increase wages enabled him consistently to underbid competitors, with the overall result that wages among workers in related industries were falling as well.[16]

Having reached the snapping point, the workers dropped their tools in a wildcat strike against the entire Pullman enterprise. With Eugene Debs at the helm, the American Railway Union (ARU) sent rail service in and around Chicago to a screeching halt. Every rail worker (some 50,000) in the region joined the strike in solidarity. The strikers' needs and concerns were twisted and changed by the press into acts of sabotage, with the *New York Times* describing ARU leader Debs as a "lawbreaker and an enemy to the human race." The *Chicago Times* spoke of the strikers' "work of destruction." Richard Olney, one of the directors of the Burlington and Santa Fe line, who by lucky coincidence just happened to be President Cleveland's attorney general at the time, got the chief executive of the nation to send in federal troops to put down the strike. With a force of some 14,000 armed men, federal intervention brought the conflict to a bloody end. Defamed by all the leading media as saboteurs, the angry workers rioted. Seeing no options left, many set fire to buildings and railroad cars. At least two dozen strikers lost their lives in the hailstorm of bullets that ensued; scores of others were injured. In the end, none of the demands was achieved, and Debs and three other ARU leaders sat in prison serving out sentences ranging up to three years (for Debs).[17]

Things were not much different in Chicago's sweatshops and rail and steel yards than they were in Pullman's workers' paradise or in any other of the country's thousands of examples of labor's relentless, merciless grind. Workers of all ages were broken down systematically. When the last vestige of individual property, the final tangible piece of personal furniture—the human body itself—is pushed to the brink of collapse, there's not much left in the way of relief or hope.

The promise of just fifteen minutes of rest can keep even the desperate going. It was only natural that the issue of single-most importance in the hearts and broken bodies of organized labor leaders was the eight-hour workday. And this was the demand shouted from the rooftops by the Federation of Organized Trades and Labor Unions of the United States and Canada. One anarchist-leaning labor organization that was very active in the Chicago area at the time was the International Working People's Association (IWPA), which counted among its ranks large numbers of German immigrants. The IWPA published several pamphlets in both German (*Freiheit* and *Arbeiter-Zeitung*) and English (*Alarm*), which kept members abreast of activities, meetings, and strike plans. But the IWPA also co ordinated to provide firearms to members for defense against attempts by company-hired thugs and pro-business militia known for their brutality. IWPA leaders also urged workers to defend themselves against assaults with weapons.

The IWPA initially opposed the eight-hour day on ideological grounds (believing it to be a half-hearted compromise on the real goal of a social revolution with subsequent labor-based ownership[18]), but later fell in line with mainstream thinking. On Saturday, May 1, 1886, more than 300,000 workers all across the country took to the streets demanding the official signum for the eight-hour limitation, and according to Paul Avrich, Chicago emerged as the hub of the drive. Things had already gotten underway the week before as tens of thousands demonstrated at the Lake Front with banners reading "Eight Hours—Working Time, May 1, 1886" and similar pro-labor slogans.[19]

Two prominent IWPA anarchist leaders, Albert Parsons and August Spies, were singled out in an editorial warning by the *Chicago Mail* with the headline "Brand the Curs". The incendiary anti-labor text spoke of the union's attempts "to bring about a series of strikes and to work injury to labor in every way." The pro-business magazine urged the police to "mark them for today. Keep them in view. Hold them personally responsible for any trouble that occurs. Make an example of them if trouble does occur!"[20] Despite the enormous tension felt on all sides leading up to May 1, nothing out of the ordinary happened.

On the following Monday, May 3, demonstrations and protests continued. In the afternoon, a farm machine factory owned by McCormick became the scene of a confrontation between strikers gathered to protest the company's long history of abusive anti-labor policies and to express their disgust at the scabs brought in to replace strikers. August Spies, who happened to be addressing an unrelated pro-labor crowd some distance away from the plant, was wrapping up his speech when a skirmish broke out between plant strikers and the scabs leaving the plant. In no time at all, police on alert to the possibility of violence rushed to the scene on behalf of McCormick. After wounding the resisting strikers with blows to the head and limbs with billy-clubs, the police then opened fire on the crowd, killing at least two of the strikers. Most labor historians agree that the total number of casualties may never be known.

This deadly attack on unarmed strikers prompted calls by the more militant factions of the IWPA for "revenge." Spies promptly wrote up a call-to-arms in English and German for the *Arbeiter-Zeitung* and urged workers all across the city to arm themselves for action. Some 2,500 copies of this "revenge circular" were quickly distributed among sympathizing activists as calls went out for a Monday night meeting.[21]

There, organizers called for a large gathering at 7:30 p.m. to be held at Haymarket. IWPA activist Adolph Fischer wrote up the circular advertising the event. At the bottom of the paper he added the phrase "Workingmen Arm Yourselves and Appear in Full Force!" and had some 25,000 copies printed. Spies strongly disapproved of the last line for fear that significant numbers would fail to appear.[22]

The meeting started more than ninety minutes late, and the turnout was much lower than the organizers had expected. Even the Democratic mayor of Chicago, Carter Harrison, showed up to make sure that the anarchist rabble-rousers didn't incite the audience to violent acts. The speeches themselves presented nothing out of the ordinary, offering little more than the usual phrases of a better future dominated by human concerns, not profit margins, and the need for labor to stand united in its demands for the eight-hour workday. One after the next, the orators urged the crowds to be strong, not to give up hope, but to continue in the struggle for humane working conditions. By 10 p.m., the mayor had seen enough to convince him that nothing eventful was going to happen, so he rode his horse home.

The last speaker, Fielden, was just making his closing remarks when the entire square was suddenly stormed by a surge of policemen who assembled in the middle of the crowd. The police captain demanded that the crowd disperse peacefully. Fielden expressed his astonishment that the police should have marched in and promptly asked for a plausible explanation. The warning to disperse was repeated. Suddenly, a bomb from somewhere flew into the middle of the police squadron. The explosion was so loud it could be heard for blocks. The windows in all the surrounding neighborhoods rattled in their frames. Without seeing much in the way of any clear target, the police started unloading their weapons into the crowd, killing and wounding untold numbers. Seven policemen were also killed, all but one (the only person killed by the bomb) shot by their own colleagues. Whether Chief of Police Bonfield was acting from a deep-seated antipathy towards organized labor or on command from invisible hands behind the curtains, may never be known. Most likely a good portion of both possibilities was involved. This was, however, the same police chief who on previous occasions had said that he wished he could get several thousand socialists together at one time without their women and children so he could "make short work of them."[23] Whatever the motive, the leaders and associates of the IWPA were all arrested on murder and conspiracy charges.

The prosecution was never able to identify the person who had actually constructed and then detonated the bomb. The D. A. displayed the incendiary texts of the IWPA's circulars in full spectacle, accompanied by menacing warnings of a plot of radical social violence to uproot the very foundations of good, honest, middle-class society. All sorts of containers and tubes were offered up as examples of bomb-making apparatus, none of which was even remotely connected to any of the defendants. Even many conservative observers of the trial including a few influential judges lamented that Judge Gary had not acted in accordance with any established legal procedures necessary to ensure a fair trial for defendants fighting for their lives. Avrich reports that female observers in the courtroom attracted Judge Gary so much that he often sat there drawing sketches and giggling with them flirtatiously instead of following the testimony of witnesses. Virtually all the decisions he made during the trial went against the defense team, which was especially crucial in light of the fact that all the men were being tried *en bloc* instead of in separate trials. Writer Carl Sandberg also later stated that every member of the public who followed the events before and during the trial was a priori convinced of the guilt of the men. The newspapers had all drawn sketches of them in such a way that they automatically looked devious and sinister.[24] The jurors, in contrast, were depicted as sincere, stable, highly rational, and nothing if not judicious. Right from the start, the defendants stood about as much chance at a fair trial as Scopes had at the "monkey trial." The jurors had been selected in a manner that was anything but fair: The bailiff was to choose from a pool the jurors best suited to the task. In an affidavit, one witness later revealed that the bailiff had told him that he was determined to select "such men as the prosecution wants."[25] Most of the jurors who were finally selected openly admitted to being convinced of the men's guilt from the outset. Perhaps the most damning feature of this corrupt process was the judge's acceptance of juror M. D. Flavin (directly related to one of the dead policemen) under complete admission by the juror that he was highly prejudiced against the defendants.

The verdict of course was evident before the gavel had even been touched. All the cards were stacked against the defendants: judge and jury, the press united under the continued assault of business against the labor movement, and the middle-class citizenry who dutifully believed all the press reported. The final *coup de main* came, as Avrich notes, with Judge Gary's charge to the jury in which completely new and easily fulfilled criteria were offered as grounds for conviction. If the men on trial for their lives had, whether by word of mouth or in writing,

> ... advised, or encouraged the commission of murder, without designating time, place or occasion at which it should be done, and in pursuance of, and induced by such advice and encouragement, murder was committed, then all such conspirators are guilty of such murder, whether the person who perpetrated such murder can be identified or not.[26]

The jury found all eight men including Spies, Parsons, and Fischer, guilty on all counts brought against them and recommended the death penalty for seven, life in prison for the eighth, Oscar Neebe.

The men were to be hanged on December 3, 1886. The verdict was promptly appealed and a stay of execution granted pending the outcome of the appeal. A massive drive to finance the appeal process was set in motion with fund-raising events staged in various places in Europe and the U.S. The Illinois supreme court unanimously denied the appeal in September 1887, stating that none of the errors recognized in the lower court's proceedings warranted a new trial or overthrowing the conviction. A final appeal to the U. S. Supreme Court was also unanimously rebuffed with the Court arguing that the case was not of a federal nature. As a last resort, thousands upon thousands of appeals from around the world landed on the desk of Illinois governor Oglesby, pleading for clemency for the prisoners. The convicted men wrote to the governor personally with requests for leniency. Spies asked that he alone be executed as a kind of sacrifice for the others, whom he knew to be innocent.

While awaiting the governor's decision, one of the convicted, Louis Lingg, put a stick of dynamite that had been smuggled into the prison in his mouth and blew his own face off. The governor was merciful with Fielden and Schwab, commuting their sentences to prison terms, but he upheld the sentences of the other men. Spies, Parsons, Fischer, and Engel were then hanged on November 11, 1887.

Three of the men who were serving out sentences were pardoned in 1893 by then-governor Altgeld.

Public sentiment at the time was whipped up into a frenzy feeding on the pro-business press's relentless attempts to vilify the leaders of the socialist/anarchist movement and to demonize their proposed solutions for a better world. The "red scare" that ensued helped pave the way for a century of ideology anathema to anything resembling socialism, with activist judges and complicit legislators fending off the perceived threat. With lots of help from deep-pocketed industrialists.

Shortly after the Haymarket tragedy, it was Louisiana's turn for bloodshed. This time it was southern Louisiana's sugar planters who had decided to make "short work" of strikers refusing to harvest the cane, one of the most important sources of income for the area. Virtually all of the enormously physically demanding labor was carried out by wretchedly poor blacks, earning pennies per endless day. They often had to accept scrip as pay, which as in other such arrangements, was valid only for items purchased at the stores owned by the planters themselves, with prices often double what they would have been elsewhere. In effect, the planters were sucking the blood out of the laborers trapped in this system of wage slavery.

The Knights of Labor had begun to organize railroad workers in the area in 1885 and gradually expanded to include the sugarcane workers. For all the brutal toil the cane field laborers put in, they had literally nothing to show for it. Now acting as one organized voice with the backing of the Knights of Labor, the men went on strike, demanding one dollar per day in additional wages, in real money, not scrip. At the request of the sugar plantation owners, foremost among them Judge Taylor Beattie, Louisiana Governor McEnery sent in troops to put an end to the situation. Many of the strikers were forced to leave the planter-owned shacks they had been living in, and assembled in Thibodaux with their wives, kids, and what few clothes they had. Estimates put the numbers of strikers at 10,000 blacks and 1,000 whites. As had been the case at the McCormick plant in Chicago and at dozens of other locales across the country, the militia was ready to use any means necessary to suppress the strikers and to protect the scabs sent in as replacements. Violence erupted apparently between strikers and scabs, at which point a melee ensued with white vigilantes killing "lame men and blind women...children and hoary-headed grandsires."[27] In the wake of the violence, more than thirty black men had been shot dead, and thousands were left homeless.

Unmitigated greed was also the ultimate cause of an especially gruesome tragedy in New York on March 25, 1911. As a result of the economic crisis afflicting the nation, employers were cooking up increasingly refined and wicked schemes to suck every last drop of energy out of the employees to cut costs and raise profits. The old trick of setting back the clocks an hour or two was in widespread use; intentional miscalculations on payroll—always to the benefit of the company—were commonplace, as were deliberate errors in counting finished piecework, the basis of pay. These tactics (and more) found their way into the mundane grind of the garment industry. The workers—the vast majority impoverished women from Eastern Europe and Italy—were routinely escorted to the toilets to make certain they hadn't pocketed any thread or slipped on one of the blouses they were making.[28]

Such were the conditions at the Triangle Waist Company, located at 27 Washington Place, near Washington Square in lower Manhattan. Owned and operated by Isaac Harris and Max Blanck, the factory occupied the top three floors of the ten-story Asch Building. To prevent workers from coming up with any fancy ideas about improving working conditions or getting better pay, the company had set up its own in-house version of a trade union and forbidden employees from organizing outside the company. At the time, there were approximately 500,000 garment workers employed in 500 factories in New York City alone, so finding suitable replacements for troublemakers was never a problem. Larger companies routinely hired tough-arms to track down unionizers and people attempting to rock the boat to beat the crap out of them on the way home from work. This, too, was the case at Triangle.

Descriptions of the deplorable working environment and backbreaking procedures could alone fill an entire volume. Many of the desperate women routinely put in fourteen- and fifteen-hour days, day in and day out, Monday through Monday. A warning sign visible for all employees to see reminded workers that those who failed to show up for work on Sundays didn't need to come back the next day. Desperate to survive, most followed suit. And at the end of the week, the employees had to pay for the use of the very sewing machines they had been "renting," as well as for the needles and thread. Accordingly, their pay was reduced by a set amount determined ad hoc by the managers, who kept track of every piece of lace and thread.

What they didn't give a damn about was worker safety. Instead of cumbersome requirements "hurting small businesses," they implemented their own homegrown deregulation policies. The rooms were covered in various kinds of cloth, mostly highly flammable cotton. Against the standard fire safety code, the doors opened towards the inside instead of outwards. Managers also kept the women locked in the factory space behind bolted doors to make sure that all the work got done and that no one made off with any thread. This, too, was in violation of safety regulations.

On that fateful day in March, fire broke out on the eighth floor where 200 workers were busy cutting and sewing. The fire had apparently started in one of the waste bins but spread quickly through the air ducts to the other side of the building near the fire escape. Some of the workers ran down the two sets of stairs on opposite sides of the structure; some took the fire escape while it was still possible. In just minutes, the fire escape collapsed from the weight of those fleeing in panic, sending at least twenty to their death below. Thousands of pieces of cloth used in the factory were a veritable fuse for the flames, which quickly filled the entire floor. Screaming for their lives, the women made a panicked run for the exit doors, but they were bolted shut. Some managed to get into the elevators while it was still possible; others took the stairs to the top of the building before these, too, were engulfed in flames.

Workers on the ninth floor had it the worst. Not only had they not been able to get out, they had not even been warned. Since the fire had started on the eighth floor, employees there had had a couple of minutes extra time to beat the flames. There was also sufficient time to call through to the tenth floor where a telephone operator received the incoming alert. But the ninth floor was without communication to the outside world. Witnesses described the unforgettable horror of the screams coming from all directions on the ninth floor. Onlookers from the streets below shuddered as one woman after the next made her way to the windowsills. With their clothes and hair ablaze, many jumped to their deaths. Some hugged each other in a pitiful embrace so as to ease the agony of death that awaited them. Others opened the doors to the elevators and jumped to the promise of a quicker death in the empty shaft. The fifty-four who died from the fall were among those whose remains could later be identified in the make shift morgues. The ninety-six others were largely burned beyond recognition.

In a tragic twist of fate, many of the corpses piled up on the sidewalk had become victims of the very conditions they had been fighting to change just a year earlier when strikes organized by Local 25 of the International Ladies' Garment Workers (ILGW) and the Women's Trade Union League (WTUL) stretched all across the garment district. A further sad irony, as David von Drehle notes, is the fact that the very policemen who had been there to harass these people during their protests, were now there to collect the bodies. Dozens of the primarily Jewish and Italian girls were only in their teens; one, Kate Leone, was only fourteen.

Each potentially liable party pointed the finger at someone else: the labor commissioner referred inquiries to the building commissioner, who in turned blamed the fire department.[29] In a manner so familiar to all Americans today, the owners of the Triangle fervently denied the charge that the doors in the factory had ever been locked. A subsequent investigation by the district attorney's office provided irrefutable evidence that the doors had been bolted shut. The *New York Times* concluded that blame was to be found on all sides, but that "no new laws are needed."

America's most horrendous work-related tragedy should never have happened, but the insatiable drive for more and more profit at the expense of all the expendable human life effected a callous disregard for these workers and the circumstances they were trapped in—a disregard as lethal as the Gattling gun, and definitely more painful. Von Drehle points to the literally daily toll such unsafe working conditions were taking on human lives all across the country. An average of one hundred workers each day lost their lives needlessly because employers refused to spend money to install safety equipment. Railroad workers were flattened as trains crushed them between or beneath thousands of tons of steel; iron workers were carbonized as seething cauldrons of liquid metal spilled onto them; miners were routinely buried alive as the flimsy supports in the shafts caved in.[30] Thousands per year succumbed to the callousness of management and owners who found their own homegrown or "voluntary" solutions (in consistent GOP parlance) to the fatal dangers facing working men and women.[31] With the rise in job-related injuries came an increase in lawsuits filed against company owners. The prevailing view had been that companies should not be held responsible for negligent worker behavior. But as Steven Diner noted, the sheer number of accidents occurring in clearly related patterns prompted in some instances changes in state legislation and the decisions handed down by the courts were not always in favor of the companies involved. Recognizing the advantage of having legal liability clearly defined, some business leaders actually began to support union demands for workmen's compensation, out of pure self-interest.[32]

Without exception, all the witnesses from the Triangle fire, who had barely escaped with their lives, testified that the doors of the ninth floor had been locked and that no amount of effort had been able to budge them.[33] As so often in American history, the best lawyers money can buy can also perform miracles. The Triangle owners hired Max Steuer, himself a former garment factory worker and reputedly the best lawyer in the country at the time. The men were acquitted of any wrongdoing. And in defiance of all claims to the contrary, *crime does indeed pay*. With the help of their savvy lawyer, owners Harris and Blanck raked in a substantial windfall from their insurance claim, which worked out to be $400.00 per corpse.[34] And judging from their actions later, they were not only completely remorseless, but also incorrigible. Max Blanck was caught locking in employees yet again in the new plant he had set up on Fifth Avenue. This time the judge fined him a grand total of $20.00 for the misdemeanor, but expressed his sorrow for having to charge him with anything. To rephrase von Clausewitz, *pecunia nervus belli et mortis*.

In 1913, yet another group of semi-slaves made headlines briefly in an event chronicled by Upton Sinclair in *The Coal War*. This time it was the miners in Ludlow, Colorado, site of a vast expanse of coal deposits of the Colorado Fuel & Iron Corporation, owned by the mega-rich and powerful Rockefeller family. The pattern of exploitation was a familiar one. Miners were forced to live in company-owned huts and a substantial part of their meager wages was paid in scrip, redeemable only at company stores. The families were hence forced to pay prices that were double those found in non-company stores. And here again, it was common practice for the miners to be cheated out of their income because the company would fix the weighing scales to register only a certain percentage of the actual weight of the coal mined by a given worker. The only reason the company didn't charge the miners for the filthy air they breathed was because management didn't think of it at the time.

By the autumn of 1913, the miners had had enough and decided to strike. As in Thibodaux, the management then kicked the miners out of the company-owned huts they were occupying. This forced the miners to string up tents in the valleys on the outskirts of the mines. In total, there were some 11,000 miners with their wives and kids sleeping in the tent-cities.

The Rockefellers responded by hiring professionals, the Baldwin-Felts Detective Agency, to go in and put an end to the trouble. The "Agency" brought in an entire arsenal of firepower including Gattling guns, but the miners, organized around the demands of the United Mine Workers of America, refused to budge from their make shift shelters. Colorado Governor Elias Ammons then upped the ante by sending in the National Guard to escort an assortment of scabs to secretly replace some of the miners—all at the request of the Rockefellers. Sporadic shooting took a life here, another there. The miners even sent in a representative, Louis Tikas, to discuss possible solutions to the standoff. The troops knocked the man to the ground and put three bullets through his back. The siege continued through the winter.

On April 20, 1914, things finally came to a showdown when the troops opened fire into the tents. To protect themselves and their families, the miners began a desperate struggle to dig trenches deep enough within the tents to escape the firestorm of incoming bullets. At night, the National Guard set fire to the tents and shot thirteen who were attempting to flee. Once day broke, the carnage was evident: two women and eleven children were found in one dugout, burned alive. And this at the hands of the noble National Guard. A detailed account of the events was given by Julia May Courtney ("Remember Ludlow") in May 1914 for Emma Goldman's *Mother Earth* magazine, and Woodie Guthrie committed the tragedy to verse and song in the 1946 title "Ludlow Massacre."

Protests formed all across the country as outraged citizens and unionists took to the streets to vent their anger. Workers from all walks of life declared their solidarity with the miners; socialists urged the downtrodden to take up arms to defend themselves against massacres of this type. In addition to the fifty-five miners and family members who died in vain, the collective was also ultimately abandoned by the political establishment, as not one of the demands was met.

Right through World War One, the battles carried out by labor for higher wages and humane working conditions were desperate and relentless; the coordinated responses by corporate capital backed by various types of militia, ruthless. With the outbreak of the war, Congress and President Wilson set about trying to raise enough money to fund the enormously expensive military undertaking. The strength of the Progressives and their legions of pro-labor activists and sympathizers was a force to be reckoned with, so part of the task was to mollycoddle labor union forces and their allies into keeping the rank and file at bay. Howard Zinn emphasizes that it was the wildcat strikes more than anything that struck fear into the hearts of company owners, who much preferred to go *mano a mano* in negotiations with union bigwigs. But workers knew that as far as negotiations or possible appeals to the legal system were concerned, their hands were tied. The Supreme Court had rejected every piece of legislation brought forth to raise the minimum wage, reduce the number of working hours per week or improve working conditions, arguing in each case that Congress had no mandate to dictate to individuals and companies what kinds of agreements they were allowed to adopt.

Sympathy in the general population was large and growing for the plight of workers as people everywhere—courtesy of the courageous muckrakers—became aware of the cold-blooded slash and burn tactics implemented by larger corporations such as Standard Oil of Rockefeller fame or Carnegie Steel. It must be noted however that with the growing differentiation in the workforce at the time, solidarity began to wane particularly among white-collar workers. Steven Diner provides a differentiated analysis of worker attitudes and behavioral patterns commensurate with the pecking order of American society during the Progressive Era. Various categories of white-collar workers, which included telephone opera-tors, sales clerks, and clerical workers, tended in general to oppose unionization and often sided with the positions taken by management in labor disputes.[35] Diner concluded that the failure of unions to organize the immense numbers of office staff during the era had little to do with employer opposition, but resulted rather from the simple "lack of enthusiasm" on the part of the employees them-selves.[36] With their jobs requiring a certain degree of flair, sophistication, man-ners, and higher than average math and language skills, white-collar workers invariably came to view themselves as superior to manual laborers. This posi-tioned them firmly among the petit bourgeois citizenry who admired the elite of society and tried to emulate the aristocratic mien and standards of dress flaunted by society's upper-crust starlets. At the same time, they often harbored a pro-nounced disdain for the work performed by the millions of unskilled sweaty min-ers and railroaders who were frequently immigrants with no mastery of English and little if any education. Part of the white-collar crowd's reluctance to side with the struggling manual laborers resulted from the fact that in many cases the em-ployer policies towards the higher rungs in the social order included "generous" bonuses, paid vacations, and added conveniences and incentives designed to make the job more rewarding. Many department store "sales professionals" took pride in the skills they were convinced set them apart from ordinary people. One notable exception as Diner comments was found among telephone operators, who proved more than willing to join some form of organized labor. As the vol-ume of calls rose exponentially, an abstracted form of Taylorization went into ef-fect, requiring the operators to suppress any natural inclination to tell the troublemaker off. Strict training procedures proscribed distinct pronunciation, in-tonation, and stress-timing patterns as well as head and body movements. Obser-vations and follow-up performance reviews were frequent.[37]

Back in the days when journalists actually worked to uncover things of real significance instead of sales pitching the glamour of Brad Pitt's hair styles or the agony experienced by an evicted Big Brother contestant, women such as Ida Tarbell took on the vilest and mightiest with the power of the pen. And, in those days, people actually read and listened. Her nineteen-part "History of the Standard Oil Company" exposed the Rockefeller empire's practice of what she termed "predatory competition": sell at a loss for as long as it takes to annihilate any remaining competitors, and once you've got them by the jugular, snap up the firm and raise the prices to your heart's content. People everywhere who followed Tarbell's series were enraged at the cutthroat practices. Henry Demarest Lloyd contributed with his articles and books (*A Strike of Millionaires Against Miners* (1890), *Wealth Against Commonwealth* (1894), *Labor Co-Partnerships* (1898) to the people's enlightenment with further tell-it-like-it-is expositions of money's powerful and merciless pull. And if it hadn't been for Upton Sinclair's *The Jungle*, rat-tail-'n'-turd sausage would still be the hotdog norm. In New York, Jacob Riis chronicled the lives and habitats of multi-ethnic paupers (*How the Other Half Lives* (1890))[38] packed into the city's rat-infested tenement hellholes. John Spargo laid bare the semi-slave status of children being worked to death in the hundreds of garment factories, mines, and steel mills around the country. Census data from 1900 put the total number of children in the U.S. workforce at around 1,250,000 —fully engaged in every sector of production. Historians believe the actual number could be significantly higher because households responding to the census questions listed their young employed daughters as "working women." Once again, the activist judges on the Supreme Court stepped in to declare the congressional attempt (Keating-Owen Act of 1916) to remedy this disgrace "unconstitutional." The legislation would have prohibited the sale of any products from factories or canneries employing children under sixteen, and commodities from coal or iron mines that hired kids under fourteen. Congress promptly revised the bill and passed the new version two years later, but the Supreme Court dealt the effort another lethal blow in *Hammer v. Dagenhart* by declaring that the "power of Congress to regulate interstate commerce does not extend to curbing the power of the states to regulate local trade." Congress subsequently sought to amend the Constitution to bar child labor altogether, but the proposed Child Labor Amendment failed the ratification process.

Opponents of the Child Labor Amendment included prominent politicians and socialites such as Anne Morgan, Elihu Root (Republican senator from 1909–1915), U.S. Representative Frederic R. Coudert (Republican from New York), Columbia University president Nicolas Murray Butler, and former president of Harvard University A. Lawrence Lowell. They all did their best to sully the arguments against the abhorrent practice of exploiting kids for profit. Most significantly, the list of naysayers also included the "preposterously named"[39] "National Committee for the Protection (sic) of the Child, Family, Home, and Church." *The Nation* concluded that beneath all the opponents' arguments that the amendment was basically "un-American" and would create a socialist, Bolshevist state with the police invading private homes to see if the young daughters in the family were doing the dishes—there were simply unadulterated economic interests at work to keep child labor intact.[40] (Somewhere out there in the wide wild hills of Idaho or Montana there must be a GOP-directed *madrasah* that teaches these people this spinning technique—a kind of cadre school for political hat tricks that takes what looks to be an obvious, prima facie valid fact or state of affairs and turns it into its opposite in such a way that everyone falls for it. The title of the organization set up with hefty financial backing to oppose the Child Labor Amendment was but one in a long series of designations consistently chosen by Republican administrations and their business partners to transform reality through language.[41])

There were a few flashes of light from the High Court, though, which appeared to rattle the sepulchers of big business. Acting perhaps out of personal spite, as Michael McGerr has suggested,[42] and a need to ally himself with grassroots progressives, Teddy Roosevelt turned federal watchdogs loose on John D. Rockefeller and the Standard Oil Company. In less than a year, an investigation concluded that the company was monopolizing the market from A to Z. The inquiry culminated in a suit filed against the company under the Sherman Anti-Trust Act, and the Supreme Court in 1911 upheld a federal district court's 1909 decision against the company.[43]

The High Court ordered the break-up of the behemoth into several regional companies, similar to the forced restructuring of telecommunications giant AT&T years later.

In general, the Sherman Act had functioned pretty much as a toothless tiger because of a palpable unwillingness of the government to take on the giants of industry and finance. This again put government practices and policies in the crosshairs of an increasingly dissatisfied public. Ultimately, Congress stepped in again in 1914 with the creation of the Federal Trade Commission and the Clayton Anti-Trust Act, both of which were designed to put some bite back into the Sherman tiger.

Much to the pleasure of the Progressives, in 1913 the government levied taxes on incomes greater than $100,000 and $500,000 per year at one percent and seven percent respectively. (The previous 1894 congressional measure to tax individual income was declared unconstitutional by the Supreme Court, fearing such measures would establish socialist precedents.) Wilson had also succeeded in lowering the tariffs placed on imported goods, giving many of the homegrown producers a run for their money and making the price of consumer goods a little cheaper for the poorer segments of the population. In its effort to curb employee dissatisfaction that might have led to strikes, the Wilson government worked more closely with plant owners, managers, and labor leaders. To help workers who were injured on the job, the Workingmen's Compensation Act of 1916 gave limited financial assistance at least to injured government workers (everyone else was left to hope for brighter days.) In the same year, Congress enacted the Adams Act, which put an eight-hour limit on the workdays of certain railroad employees. The presence of government in regulating trade and commerce was then strengthened with the outbreak of World War I and measures undertaken to support the economy in a time of crisis. Entire sections of commerce were suddenly under the auspices and control of the war cabinet management in Washington, as were the railroads. When the United States entered the war, these tax revenues increased precipitously, with the highest bracket for incomes over one million dollars shooting up to seventy-seven percent. But lower earners also felt the bite as taxes were collected on those making $4,000 or more at a rate of six percent. In 1917, the Food and Fuel Control Act was enacted to allow centralized government management of goods, services, and critical production facilities as needed. Many of these changes were coordinated through the newly established (1918) National War Labor Board, a precursor of sorts to the Labor Relations Board.

The measures undertaken by the Wilson administration to support the war effort were right up the alley of the country's Progressives. Corporate profit-making schemes at the expense of the country's millions of impoverished laborers took a back seat to the call for unity to overcome the common threat. Pulled together for the sake of the united whole, the Progressive dream of a society was founded not on class differences and the selfish individual quest for all that masses of ill-gotten money could buy, but rather as historian James Harvey Robinson saw it, on collective cooperation in the interest of the common good. Here, the common people found a meaning and a purpose higher than the enrichment of a rich person's pockets. Grosvenor Clarkson of the War Industries Board spoke of an unprecedented "industrial dictatorship" forged "of necessity and common consent" that united the nation into an organic whole.[44] While not creating a socialist's paradise by any means, the nationalization of leading segments of industry coupled with centralized control of food and fuel to make sure all got through the trying times, allowed the inner-most longings of the anti-capitalist reformers to flourish in the hope and belief that the path to a utopian future had finally been opened. Some of the dreamy-eyed went so far as to proclaim that laissez-faire was dead.[45] In *The Promise of American Life* (1909), Herbert Croly praised the insight garnered by many during the Progressive Era that the future had "to be planned and constructed rather than fulfilled of its own momentum."

As the war ended, the state-run programs were dismantled and hopes began to fade—but they didn't die completely. There was no denying the facts though: the country was back to business as usual, with the no-frills gold-diggers in charge. Wilson could see the writing on the wall as a backlash set in against the "Bolshevist" destruction of enterprise and the American spirit of individualism.[46] The tactic was most convenient. By constructing a new external foe (along the lines envisioned by Carl Schmitt) in the form of Bolshevik ideas and their manifestation in violent upheaval, industrialists and their governmental representatives could successfully link labor union strikes and demands for higher wages and better working conditions to the hyped, marketed, and subsequently perceived threat of a violent takeover of the United States by powers opposed to American ideals of individualism and freedom. During his campaign for president in August 1920, then-Senator Warren Harding warned:

> It would be the blindness of folly to ignore the activities in our own country which are aimed to destroy our economic system and to commit us to the colossal tragedy which has both destroyed all freedom and made Russia impotent…We do hold to the right to crush sedition, to stifle a menacing contempt for law, to stamp out the perils to the safety of the republic or its people when emergency calls, because security and the majesty of the law are the first essentials of liberty…The group must not endanger the individual… .

Once he took the reins in the Oval Office, Harding wasted no time letting the shit hit the fan.

West Virginia's coal miners had been struggling for livable wages and safe working conditions for years. The same patterns of exploitation as those now so familiar existed throughout the region. Workers were trapped in conditions tantamount to bondage, with little hope of ever working their way out.[47] In September of 1921, the United Mine Workers set out to bring many of the as yet unorganized coal miners of Mingo and Logan Counties into the safer network of organized labor. Bought and borrowed by the corporate hotshots of the region, the county officials and peacekeeping forces had routinely harassed and intimidated local union activists.[48] But things turned really nasty when C.E. Lively, a hired assassin, opened fire on two union activists, Sid Hatfield and Ed Chambers, as they were standing in front of the courthouse in McDowell County. Both men died. In response to the completely unprovoked attack the union appealed for a general mobilization of all workers statewide for a march on Logan County. Shortly after one contingent of miners arrived at Blair Mountain, fighting erupted between county militiamen and the miners, who had been smart enough to arm themselves. Worried about a possible escalation of the violence, the state governor asked President Harding for armed federal support to counter the unrest. Harding complied, sending in armed militia to support the mine owners. Someone up through the chains of command even ordered airplanes to bomb the miners into submission. This was ostensibly the only incident of bombs ever being dropped on American civilians within the United States. The miners eventually acquiesced.

The Republicans painted a picture of a nation in turmoil under the autocratic rule of big government. They sought to retake the nation in the name of unbridled individual freedom. And it is here that we see a pattern emerge in the American political landscape, one that has been with us ever since.

Nice Republican Phrases—Harsh Republican Reality

Among the most effective instruments routinely put to use by GOP strategists on the voting public is the technique of political spin mentioned above, now commonly referred to as "bait and switch," i.e. completely switching the population's conventional perceptions of people, places, procedures, and events, and replacing them with "new and improved" versions of reality, designed to reflect the party's core ideas. One hallmark of switch language is the "corporate euphemism" familiar to the business world. Human resource specialists for instance are aware of many types of code routinely used in letters of reference for former employees. Phrases such as "gets along especially well with his colleagues" might mean that the employee had the habit of sleeping around with other staff members. "Works well without supervision" could be taken to mean that the employee is capable of staying busy on her own, or that she won't do anything she's told.[49] In the hands and power networks of the Republican Party, demo-linguistic programming effectively creates an alternative "take" on reality to replace the commonplace view of things, and then in a second phase drafts legislation to secure the legitimacy of the new definitions and premises at work in the political discourse being created.

A case in point can be found in one of the clearest formulations of Republican ideals ever committed to public record: Herbert Hoover's "Rugged Individualism" speech given in 1928 in New York during his run for the White House. The suggested premises and carefully drawn arguments set forth in this pre-election appeal to voters laid the groundwork for generations of Stalwarts right up to the present day.

Hoover defined the issues at stake in the election about to be held as two competing and contradictory notions of how the United States should be governed. The principles unwaveringly adhered to by the Republican Party, he explained, are "deeply rooted in the foundations of our national life, and the solutions which it [the party] proposed are based on experience with government and a consciousness that it may have the responsibility for placing solutions into action."

Hoover asked voters to look at the party's track record after seven years of continued economic growth and widespread prosperity. Household savings had grown; there were far more cars for families to flit around town in; people had "more to eat, better things to wear, and better homes." What's more, he contended, there was greater job security for both men and women, and there was less fear of the horrors routinely accompanying old age. He praised the multitude of modern electrical conveniences that made life more enjoyable by taking the sting out of once time-consuming chores. More people had access to an improved system of education, and scientific research was world-class. In short, America had become the envy of the world and a powerhouse of human potential. But, he concluded, the wealth, stability, and technical marvels of modernity would have been impossible "without the wise policies which the Republican Party has brought into action in this period... ." And foremost among these policies, he maintained, was "the resistance of the Republican Party to every attempt to inject the government into business in competition with its citizens... ."

Cast your eyes back to Europe, he warned his listeners, and you will discover the "stifling of private initiative on the one hand, and overloading the government with business on the other." The "American system," he insisted, stands for "the spirit of adventure of individual initiative and of individual enterprise." This is Classical Liberalism at its best.

Hoover warned that government regulation of free enterprise would inevitably "destroy political equality," "cramp and cripple mental energies of our people," and "dry up the spirit of liberty and progress." The speech warned of those who would turn back the clock to Wilsonian wartime statist policies, while at the same time rejecting the results experienced in the Gilded Age of extreme laissez-faire: "The very essence of equality of opportunity is that there shall be no dominations by any group or trust or combination in this republic, whether it be business or political."

Given the level playing field of equal opportunity, the argument goes, anybody can come to America and make it big. Progressive ideals and the measures the reformers proposed to achieve them rested in Hoover's view on a mistaken notion of

> ...liberalism that interprets itself into the government operation of business. The bureaucratization of our country would poison the very roots of liberalism that is free speech, free assembly, free press, political equality, and equality of opportunity. Liberalism should be found not striving to spread bureaucracy, but striving to set bounds to it. True liberalism seeks freedom first in the confident belief that without freedom the pursuit of all other blessings and benefits is vain. That belief is the foundation of all American progress, political as well as economic.

One can only speculate as to whether Hoover was completely aware of the full import of his statement that economic freedom must be preserved if political freedom is to remain intact. Politically the speech appealed foremost to business leaders of every economic tier. A governmental creed of non-intervention spoke to and from the savvy businessman's inner soul. Furthermore, the promise that powerful monopolies would not be tolerated reassured the owners, managers, and white-collar staff of smaller companies that the American dream of successful enterprise based on talent and hard work was still alive, kicking, and waiting to be fulfilled. But Hoover also spoke to the new arrivals, the immigrants primarily from Europe, who for whatever reason had felt the need to break with a stifling, hopeless, or perhaps torturous past and to seek happiness and fortune on American shores.

What is remarkable is that even today in this opening phase of the new millennium, the substance of Republican rhetoric has remained unchanged. There are the old familiar phrases about freedom to be who and what you want; freedom from the dictates of tyrannical autocrats; freedom to speak your mind without fear of arrest. These were issues that surely resonated with the large numbers of immigrants who had found their way into New York at the time. Valid as the points may be, in the Republican version of reality liberalism's natural laws of human rights are carefully woven into a causal network of economic freedoms, upon which, Hoover insisted, personal freedom ultimately rests: "... economic freedom cannot be sacrificed if political freedom is to be preserved."

Where does this then leave the seamstresses of the Triangle Waist Factory? the coal miners of Ludlow? the cane harvesters of Louisiana? With no economic freedom—none whatever—*where is their political freedom?* On paper only. Nicely packaged in the pretty little Cinderella tales of working through the coal dust and 200,000 yards of cotton fabric until one day the sun comes shining through the bedroom window and the dream of being a whole person comes true. The quasi-religious message mastered by every teacher and preacher in America sounds so lovely on paper, but *it just ain't so*. And in answer to the thought just muttered by the opposition: there are also lottery winners.

The fires that keep this flame of hope burning from sea to shining sea are re-kindled with every generation. And luckily for the country as a whole, there has been genuine progress on many fronts, thanks to the hard-fought efforts of organized labor. But with that hope comes the evil twin of Republican political rhetoric, warning of "frivolous lawsuits" that destroy businesses; minimum wage demands that "will lead to unemployment"; workers' compensation and healthcare costs that "stifle small business owners." With so many years safely between us and the poor women who perished in the Triangle tragedy, one would think that those oh-so woe-is-me business owners would have learned a thing or two about humanity and the frailty of our bodies, minds, and spirits. Not a chance. The American worker will be "nickel and dimed" (as Barbara Ehrenreich convincingly showed[50]) as long as there is a scaffold to climb, a brick to lay, a load to haul, or a table to serve. And had it not been for the bloody, hard-fought battles of wildcat strikers and the political power of labor, women would still be locked inside sweatshops and men would still be dying from limbs being ripped into taco meat by unsafe machinery. Without child labor laws, tots of ten and eleven would start every day with a smile and *Welcome to MacStingy's, may I take your order?*

Despite the progress made, the overall war between business and labor has been lost, with the winners flaunting a permanent, globalized victory pose. True, there are corporations and even smaller companies today that do provide "generous" "benefits packages" for their employees, but they are the exceptions. A clearer picture of the business community's wants and needs can be found at the Web site (http://www.nfib.com) of the National Federation of Independent Businesses (NFIB). An action alert posted in July of 2005 urged all members to contact their congressional representatives and senators to demand defeat of Senator

Ted Kennedy's proposal to raise the federal minimum wage from $5.15 to $7.25 per hour.[51] This was of course nothing new, as every proposed raise in the minimum wage is met with the same argument by Republicans, that smaller companies will be put out of business and unemployment will rise. It is ironic that those same business owners who are always on the verge of bankruptcy and the poor house, tend to drive the newest and largest model Mercedes, live in the classiest gated communities of seven- and eight-figure homes, have time and money for vacations three or four times per year, are treated by the best doctors in the top hospitals, and send their kids to the swankiest Ivy League schools. Even in the 1930s, that same complaint was stale. Franklin D. Roosevelt told it like it was in his fireside address on May 24, 1938, the evening before he signed in legislation to establish a federal minimum wage:

> Do not let any calamity-howling executive with an income of $1,000.00 a day, who has been turning his employees over to the Government relief rolls in order to preserve his company's undistributed reserves, tell you—using his stockholders' money to pay the postage for his personal opinions—tell you that a wage of $11.00 a week is going to have a disastrous effect on all American industry.

The numbers have changed, but the same tired old line never gives up. Given the math, their generosity just doesn't add up to much but slave wages. At the given minimum wage of $5.85 per hour, even a full month's worth of work adds up to a mere $936.00 based on a five-day workweek. In cities like Los Angeles, with one of the largest concentrations of impoverished people in the industrialized world, even the smallest studio apartment rents for more than $500.00 per month. That doesn't leave much left for rice, beans, and kids' shoes, not to mention transportation.

As far as laws are concerned that might protect the safety of workers or prohibit managers and owners from locking their employees inside the plants, they're there on paper, but all too often willingly violated by the companies themselves. The *New York Times* reported on January 18, 2004, that Wal-Mart routinely locked many of its employees inside some 350 of its stores across the country. In one instance, heavy machinery crushed the ankle of a Wal-Mart employee in Corpus Christi, Texas, but the worker was locked in. The only option would have been through the fire exit, but all employees were told if they ever used that door except in a fire, they would automatically be fired.

The situation for janitors hasn't been any better. In a July 13, 2005, report by the *Los Angeles Times*, staff writer Steven Greenhouse revealed that among the nation's 2.3 million employed janitors, gross violations of labor and safety laws were routine. In many cases, the workers had become the unsuspecting victims of well-organized schemes involving outright criminal fraud. With no telltale paper trail to leave behind, the predominantly illegal immigrant workers received orders from their contractors to work the first two weeks without pay as a trial period; they willingly complied. The contractors prefer to hire unauthorized/undocumented laborers, making it easier for them to get the most for their money. With the GOP in power, labor authorities usually look the other way. The men and women sometimes put in an eighty-hour week spread out over sixteen hours a day, 364 days a year (they thank God for Christmas.) Many of the contractors whose identities surfaced in Greenhouse's investigation were unwilling to pay extra for overtime. To circumvent anything that might have added an extra penny to their overall costs, they came up with the clever idea of using the names of former janitors and booked any time in excess of forty hours in the ex-employees' files. Eager to earn as much as possible to make ends meet, the workers complied, at $3.50 per hour, all under-the-table. That was a full $1.65 below the federal minimum wage at the time. None of the men and women interviewed for the report ever received any overtime pay, and in fact they were warned that if they complained they would be fired on the spot. The shady hiring companies often tell the janitors that the quickest and best way to make it big is to buy into a franchise scheme. Believing the saga of the American dream, the hopeful scrape together all they can from friends and family back home, usually amounting to around $10,000.00. They never see the money again. Instead, the "franchise" (often nothing more than a mailbox name) takes the loot and does an Enron.

Even in the case of giant conglomerates, employees are routinely put into working conditions that injure and kill. British Petroleum's oil refineries in Texas City, Texas, were so poorly maintained and equipped that on two separate occasions in 2005 alone, fires broke out when metal pipes normally found between the heat exchanger and the compressor of the Resid Hydrotreatment unit failed. A total of sixteen men died in the explosions and fires that resulted; another 170 people were injured. The Chemical Safety and Hazard Investigation Board informed BP of a number of serious issues it had found at the Texas refinery that urgently needed to be resolved. The company had already aroused the suspicion of the Occupational Safety and Health Administration in April of 2005 for violating a number of safety measures. At the company's Indiana plant an employee suffered a cracked skull after a wooden guardrail broke off; the shoddy piece of lumber hadn't been replaced in over sixty years. And that from one of the world's largest corporations with a net profit of $16.2 billion in 2004 alone.

Investigations of arbitration procedures between disciplined or terminated workers and their employers have uncovered widespread cases of forced overtime. All too often, employees of little means and no savings must juggle jobs as full-time care-givers for parents in need of urgent care while bowing to the overtime demands of employers who won't take "No" for an answer. Single women and mothers are especially vulnerable to the practice and are often forced to choose between rushing home to give their mother an insulin shot and keeping their job. The no-brainer then forces them into deeper economic strains and straits as they struggle to recover on unemployment benefits. The Labor Project for Working Families has estimated that worldwide "more than 930 million children under fifteen are being raised alone in households in which all of the adults work."[52]

When it comes to human life, businesses have exhibited the most callous, cold bloodedly calculating behavior imaginable. Indeed, the preference of profit over life has been the norm throughout history and should serve as a tactical lesson about the pitfalls of entrusting our survival to free enterprise.

Two more recent cases in point: In 1971, Ford Motor began selling its popular Pinto, a subcompact car. The affordable car appealed to average commuters with its relatively good gas mileage and svelte appearance. Ford had spent a great deal of money on designing the car and getting the assembly lines set up for its production. During the pre-sale crash tests, however, several of Ford's engineers noticed that there were serious problems with the fuel tank design. When they requested and scheduled a meeting with other Pinto team leaders to present the findings and attempt to come up with possible solutions, a grand total of two people came.[53]

The tests had shown that because of a serious structural flaw, if the Pinto was rear-ended even at a moderate thirty miles per hour, the connecting pipe to the fuel tank would likely break off, spilling gasoline all over the road. The fuel tanks themselves were then prone to ramming up against the differential casing, from which four sharp bolts could punch holes in the tank. Even the slightest spark from metal grinding across asphalt was more than enough to set the car and the surrounding area on fire. If the crash were serious enough to compromise the structural integrity of the doors, the driver and passengers would likely burn to death.

And that's exactly what happened. Dozens of Pinto drivers each year were rear-ended, with the horrible result that many passengers burned alive. Many lost their limbs to the flames. Others were burned over their entire bodies, reduced to unrecognizable flesh forms. Instead of offering any kind of sincere expression of grief and ordering an immediate recall of all the vehicles on the road (which in their heyday were coming off the assembly lines at the rate of about 500,000 per year[54]), the concerned folks at Ford sat down and looked at the problem from the only perspective that has ever seemed to matter in America. They conducted a cost-benefit analysis. Their reasoning went like this: If we assume an average of 180 people burning to death each year at a cost of $200,000 (government figures) per person in out-of-court settlements, plus another 180 being seriously but not fatally burned at a cost of $67,000, plus another 2,100 totaled cars valued at $700 each, we get a composite cost of $49.5 million dollars for a year's worth of accidents. But, if we recall all the eleven million cars and 1.5 million small trucks known to have the same kind of defect, the costs of repairing all these vehicles at $11 each works out to $137 million. Clearly it's cheaper to let the drivers and passengers burn and die. And that they did.

Ford fought against the implementation of governmental safety standards designed to force manufacturers to correct such design flaws in order to save lives; the necessary repairs just weren't profitable. Mark Dowie noted that the conservative figure for Pinto deaths was 500 by 1977, but many think the actual numbers were much closer to 900. And the numbers have a very real meaning—one that can never be weighed or felt on paper. For behind each one is a story of shattered lives and untold suffering—all for $11 per vehicle.

Not to be outdone, Ford's bigger brother of "so goes America" fame ran up against an almost identical conundrum at about the same time. Not surprisingly, the problem plagued several different models, all equipped with fuel tanks that burst into flames when the cars were hit from behind.

In July of 1991, the McGee family of Florida was driving through Virginia in their 1983 Oldsmobile Cutlass station wagon.[55] Unfortunately for the family, a trailer that had become unhitched from a car bumped into the rear end of the station wagon, rupturing the gas tank and wrapping the family in flames within seconds. The teenage son, who was slower in exiting the vehicle, was completely engulfed in flames and died within hours; a cousin who had been along on the trip succumbed several weeks later. The mother suffered burns over forty-eight percent of her body and required extensive skin grafts over a period of months. In response to their tragic loss, the family filed suit against General Motors in the state of Florida.

According to studies conducted on identical models of the family car, the weight of five or six occupants plus luggage pushed the vehicle so low to the ground that clearance for the fuel tank in the rear was only six and a half inches. The walls of the gas tank were only one-eighth of an inch thick, making it particularly susceptible to any kind of structural damage. The tanks were also placed dangerously close to the rear bumpers of the car, making them especially vulnerable to rear-end collisions. Investigations also revealed that lawsuits based on similar accidents in GM vehicles produced over a ten-year period from 1973 to 1983 had begun piling up, with more than one hundred filed against the company on related charges. The lawyers for the corporation tried to shrug off the McGee collision as a "freak accident" that would most likely occur only once in every twenty-four billion miles driven. But the Center for Auto Safety soon discovered that GM had conducted its own tests on the construction of the car and had determined that by adding a protective cover or "bladder" over the fuel tank, ruptures and hence deaths by fire could have been prevented. The approximate cost for the modification: $10.00 per vehicle.

More disturbing for GM was a secret memo written by one of the corporation's own engineers, Edward C. Ivey. The memo text, prepared as a "value analysis," laid out in black and white the cost calculations for the deaths that likely were going to occur. "Each fatality has a value of $200,000.00," the memo said, and there could be as many as "500 fatalities" in GM cars per year. The director of the Center for Auto Safety, Clarence Ditlow, stated on a CBS *60 Minutes* segment that the cost of the necessary safety modification would have been in the range of $10 per car, but the company had taken a strictly profit-oriented approach to the problem and concluded that "if the government doesn't mandate it and [it] costs more than $2.20, don't do it."

Subsequent developments in the trial showed that lawyers for GM had encouraged Edward Ivey to state that he couldn't remember why he had written the memo or for whom. The goal of the strategy they were pursuing was to have the memo declared inadmissible because he had written it out of personal interest only. The legal team for the McGee family obtained contradictory evidence from former GM engineer Ron Elwell, who testified that he had received a copy of the Ivey calculation, together with a cover page identifying the highest levels of the Oldsmobile management group as recipients. The deposition of another GM employee of twenty-six years revealed that company lawyers had been to his office to examine all the files he had related to fuel-fed fires in GM vehicles. Some of the files were promptly shredded outside his office; others were taken by the legal team. The Florida court later obtained confidential GM documents containing details of conversations that had transpired in 1981 between company lawyers and Edward Ivey in which he clarified that he had prepared the cost calculation for the higher-ups at Oldsmobile and that the company had then adopted a very guarded approach to the substance of the documents for fear that the content might one day be exposed. The court documents further revealed that one of GM's lawyers on realizing that Ivey was a potential walking time-bomb for the company, had written:

"Obviously Ivey is not an individual whom we would ever, in any situation, want to be identified to (plaintiffs) ... and the documents he generated are undoubtedly some of the potentially most harmful and most damaging were they ever to be produced."

GM had managed to keep the content of the Ivey memo secret for a long time. But the company lawyers were still doing their utmost to see that the documents would not be allowed as evidence in the trial. Florida judge Arthur Franza found the documents to be admissible. With the help of a sympathetic jury, the family won the battle and was awarded $33 million for their pain and suffering. GM took its appeals all the way to the Federal Appeals Court. Ironically, one of the leading attorneys representing GM was none other than independent council Kenneth Starr, star of the impeachment proceedings brought against Bill Clinton. Mr. Starr's arguments before the appeals court—that admitting the documents detailing conversations between Edward Ivey and GM lawyers would violate attorney-client privileges—proved successful. Attorney Kendal Few, who argued against GM in the South Carolina court, maintained that because of the documents Kenneth Starr had in his possession about the Ivey memo and his allegedly perjured statements in sworn depositions, Starr himself was legally and ethically obliged to inform the court that Ivey's statements were perjured. Starr's failure to do so, in Few's assessment, constituted obstruction of justice. American history might have taken a different course had his argument fallen on favorable ears.

The McGee family and the hundreds of other GM car owners who were injured or killed because of the company's willful and continued production of a vehicle proven to be a death trap in the event of rear-end collisions, were ideal plaintiffs for class action lawsuits. The same could be said for the 3,000 Navajo uranium miners who during their employment with Union Carbide (source of the Bhopal methyl isocyanate spill that killed between 3,000 and 6,000) and Kerr McGee (of Karen Silkwood fame) were never told by the company that they were working with and constantly exposed to a highly toxic substance. Now, years later, the men are dropping dead like flies from lung cancer and leukemia. Or of the thousands of predominantly African-American residents of "cancer alley" in southern Louisiana, home to dozens of chemical processing plants, whose fumes and leaks contain an entire cocktail of known carcinogens. The low-income inhabitants of communities such as Convent, Norco, East Baton Rouge, and Alsen display a medical reference book's worth of symptoms and illnesses, with staggeringly high cancer rates. Desperate residents in Alsen tried their luck with a class action suit in 1981 seeking $3 billion from local chemical giants. They settled for much less and ultimately agreed never to sue again.

By definition, class action lawsuits seek to redress the harm inflicted on larger numbers of people. This fact alone sets them apart from cases involving single individuals as litigants who may have suffered unfair treatment, personal injury or harm, but for whom no widespread pattern of abuse, neglect or harm is evident. By their very nature, class action suits present a preponderance of evidence indicative of large-scale wrongdoing. Litigation of this type also goes to the heart of critical problems inherent in the implementation of Classical Liberalism as a normative construct. Leaving the fate of earth's intricate biological-ecological network to "market forces" is a recipe for disaster—a fact that is painfully evident in Texas along the Rio Grande. To avoid costly environmental measures enacted under administrations less friendly to corporate wherewithal, many American chemical companies chose to relocate their processing facilities just across the Rio Grande in Mexico, where a few dollars here and there will get you anything you want. A number of these companies established *maquiladoras* employing Mexican nationals as the cheapest sources of labor available. Subsequent to the passage of the North American Free Trade Agreement literally thousands of such operations including corporate giants like GM and AT&T sprang up in the border areas separating the two countries. In the immediate vicinity of some plants, water concentrations of xylene rose to 50,000 times the level acceptable by U.S. standards. Other tests taken of water directly from the Rio Grande revealed an entire laboratory of chemicals, many at thousands of times the level considered toxic. The health and birth statistics of the area reflect as much, with exceptionally high rates of birth defects, particularly anencephaly, common on both sides of the river.

If one single reason could be extracted from the many motivating factors the cabal of business leaders had to prohibit the election of Al Gore in 2000, it would be the Clinton/Gore administration's refusal to let industry pollute at will. Carol Browner, who headed the Environmental Protection Agency for eight years in the Clinton administration, took the unprecedented step in 1997 of revoking the permission granted to Shintech by the state of Louisiana to set up a polyvinyl chloride plant in Convent, one of the communities in "cancer alley" already plagued by dozens of chemical processing facilities. In the same year, the Nuclear Regulatory Commission refused to allow the construction of uranium enrichment facilities in that state. The Republicans nationwide were beside themselves with rage at measures designed to protect people and the environment over business interests. Writing for *The Weekly Standard* in 1998, pro-business author Henry Payne criticized these decisions as examples of "environmental justice" from the desk of Al Gore. One Louisiana official referred to EPA activists as "little Hitlers."

During his 2004 campaign for "re"-election, Mr. Bush went to great lengths to promise the corporate world an end to "junk lawsuits," meaning of course civil action taken by groups of people all across the country who have suffered or died from design flaws in automobiles, toxic waste dumped into the environment or similar hazards. The traditional view of the American court systems was that juries, not the president, are empowered with the right to decide who is right and who is wrong, but that appears to be falling by the wayside as well. The Republican march in defense of business rights took a giant leap forward in 2005 with passage of the Class Action Fairness Act. Judging from the wording with "fairness" in the title, one would normally be led to think that the legislation would somehow benefit the victims of unfair conduct. But this was Republican-sponsored/written language designed to benefit the pro-Republican base of businesses and corporations in their desperate struggle against "junk lawsuits" filed by litigants with a common grievance. In a classical Republican spin on the law, Mr. Bush went on to say that

> ... when used properly, class actions make the legal system more efficient and help guarantee that injured people receive proper compensation ... That is an important principle of justice. So the bill I sign today maintains every victim's right to seek justice, and ensures that wrongdoers are held to account.

Enacted with the support of a large number of wilting Democrats, the bill made it extremely difficult for victims of corporate malfeasance to file class action suits by transferring the locus of litigation into the federal court system. In sharp contrast to state courts, federal judges have been much less receptive to plaintiffs in class action suits, and perhaps more importantly, the Bush administration took great strides to put as many of its own select (i.e. pro-business) judges as possible on federal court benches.

To whom but government can the people turn to enact fundamental changes in the way America's profit-addicts run their businesses? Changes necessary to protect the lives and limbs of millions of potential victims. Historically, talks and pleas to management have rarely proved successful. In fact, "troublemakers" were often beaten to pulp by management's hired hands. To whom but government could America's workers turn when every hour dredged out in cruel sweat got them only less than the month before, as they fell ever further into debt?

The stern warning of Hoover's message not to allow government to interfere in business rings as hollow as today's identical Republican ploys. The trick is always the same: the carefully constructed boogey-man of governmental totalitarianism will steal your freedom, force you into a socialist gulag, burn down your church, permit sex with children, rob you of the "freedom to choose" a pension or medical plan, and stifle business, putting you out of a job. In reality, the whole spiel is nothing more than a memorized script of fanciful spin, all cleverly wrapped up in the guise of protecting freedom. All that's being protected are the bigger and bigger profits.

Instead of becoming an active player in the world of business, the government's role should be that of umpire, Hoover insisted. The same line of argument has been resurrected by every Republican administration since. The fallacy of the analogy lies in the underlying assumption that the players themselves stand on equal footing and that the rules of "the game" (i.e. business interests versus labor rights and the public good) have been fairly drawn up to allow for a match among equals. This has never been the case. Without extensive intervention from a necessary higher order of reason, heavy-handed business interests will always have the deck stacked in their favor.

Classical Liberalism defined the threat to individual freedom and to the social contract in terms of the autocratic regimes common to the period in which liberalism was born; it did not and could not recognize the potential danger arising from the community of property owners or capitalists themselves. In the period in which this model of society germinated, capitalism had not yet achieved the capacity to transform an individual bourgeois merchant or land proprietor into a power magnate whose influence could rival that of nations, or, as we shall presently see, destroy the entire planet.

Notes

1 For clarification of the concept of social contract in use at the time, see the *Blackstone Commentaries on the Laws of England*, Introduction § 2, pp. 47–48. Available online from the Avalon Project at Yale Law School at http://www.yale.edu/lawweb/avalon/blackstone/introa.htm#2.

2 Reinhart Koselleck has analyzed the historical transformation of private thoughts in content-based discourse into public opinion and published writ. See *Critique and Crisis. Enlightenment and the Pathogenesis of Modern Society* (Cambridge, Massachusetts: MIT Press, 1988) 53–76.

3 Hamilton's concepts are most clearly laid out in his reports to Congress (1790–1791). His proposal for a national "Bank of the United States" ("Report on a National Bank") is articulated in the third of these, whereas the second ("Report on the Public Credit") takes on the issue of a debt consolidation scheme by the national treasury. The fourth ("Report on Manufactures") spells out his plans to promote individual segments of manufacturing (read: to cozy up to particular interests) to further the overall stability and status of the country.

4 Cf. Philip S. Foner, *From Colonial Times to the Founding of The American Federation of Labor*, vol. 1 of *History of the Labor Movement in the United States* (New York: International Publishers Company, 1998) 82–96.

5 *Ibid.*, 67–68.

6 Historian Mary O. Furner has identified five distinct cycles of antistatism. See in particular her "Antistatism and Government Downsizing. An Historical Perspective," in *Policy Briefs/ Future of the Public Sector* (Urban Institute, December 1, 1996).

7 Howard Zinn cites a telling speech about Lincoln ("a first-rate second-rate man") delivered by Wendell Phillips at the Tremont Temple in Boston the day after Lincoln's successful bid for the White House: "Not an Abolitionist, hardly an antislavery man, Mr. Lincoln consents to represent an antislavery idea. A pawn on the political chessboard, his value is in his position; with fair effort, we may soon change him for knight, bishop or queen, and sweep the board." Quoted in Howard Zinn, *A People's History of the United States–1492–Present* (New York: HarperCollins Publishers, 2003) 190.

8 For a decidedly antistatist take on these efforts, see Thomas DiLorenzo, "Birth of an Empire," *The Free Market* 15, no. 7 (July 1997).

9 Howard Zinn, *A People's History of the United States–1492 –Present*, 211–251.

10 A thorough account of the rent-wars and their long-term effects on antebellum society can be found in Reeve Huston, *Land and Freedom. Rural Society, Popular Protest, and Party Politics in Antebellum New York* (New York and Oxford: Oxford University Press, 2000).

11 Cf. Howard Zinn, *A People's History of the United States*, 211–213.

12 *Ibid.*, 215.

13 These strikes were also characterized by a greatly increased political consciousness among members of the organized movement. They set out to debunk the brainwashing techniques and myths of success so often propagated by the ideologues of entrepreneurialism. With the harsh and immediate reality of the Civil War setting in, the process of intensified politicization

was brought to a halt. For an in-depth analysis of the events and their implications in labor historiography, see Alan Dawley, *Class and Community: The Industrial Revolution in Lynn* (Cambridge, Massachusetts: Harvard University Press, 2000).

14 Morton Horwitz, *The Transformation of American Law–1780–1860* (Cambridge, Massachusetts: Harvard University Press, 1977) 186–188.

15 Details of both the model town and the paternal system operated by Pullman as well as an analysis of the strike itself are given in Almont Lindsey, *The Pullman Strike: The Story of a Unique Experiment and of a Great Labor Upheaval* (Chicago: University of Chicago Press, 1994).

16 United States Strike Commission, *Report on the Chicago Strike of June–July, 1894, by the United States Strike Commission* (Washington, D. C.: Government Printing Office, 1895), 87–88.

17 For an extensive first-hand account of the strike from someone who observed the events as they were unfolding, see William H. Carwardine, *Pullman Strike* (Chicago: Charles H. Kerr Publishers Company, 1994).

18 Cf. Paul Avrich, *The Haymarket Tragedy* (Princeton, New Jersey: Princeton University Press, 1984) 181 and *passim*.

19 *Ibid.*, 184.

20 *Chicago Mail*, 1 May 1886, and quoted in Avrich, *The Haykmarket Tragedy*, 186–187. Avrich also notes that the *Chicago Mail* article was reprinted in the December 31 1887 issue of the IWPA paper *The Alarm*.

21 Avrich points out that this meeting had in fact already been planned prior to the incident at the McCormick plant. Cf. Avrich, *The Haymarket Tragedy*, 191.

22 *Ibid.*, 193.

23 *Ibid.*, 212.

24 *Ibid.*, 262.

25 *Ibid.*, 264.

26 *Ibid.*, 277. Original source: *Abstract of Record I*, 7.

27 Anonymous, "Red-Handed Murder: Negroes Wantonly Killed at Thibodaux, La." (November 26, 1887), in *The Weekly Pelican* (New Orleans, Louisiana), vol. 1, no. 52 (November 26, 1887), reprinted in Howard Zinn and Anthony Arnove, *Voices of a People's History of the United States* (New York: Seven Stories Press) 223.

28 Details of the frightening working conditions in the garment industry are found in David von Drehle's remarkable book *Triangle: The Fire That Changed America* (New York: Grove Press, 2003). For this reference cf. page 7.

29 *Ibid.*, 184–185.

30 *Ibid.*, 3.

31 Howard Zinn cites the truly shocking figures released by the Commission on Industrial Relations that put the number of job-site injuries for 1914 at 700,000 and work-related deaths at 35,000. There was no compensation for anything. At the turn of the century (around 1900) there were some 280,000 children as young as ten fully working every-

where a buck could be made for management. Mother Jones reported seeing dozens of children who had lost their fingers and hands in some kind of factory machine. Many of the child laborers in Philadelphia went on strike in 1903, demanding that their hours in the textile mills be reduced from 60 to 55 per week so that they could attend school. See Howard Zinn, *A People's History of the United States*, 329.

32 Steven J. Diner, *A Very Different Age. Americans of the Progressive Era* (New York: Hill and Wang, 1998) 47.

33 David von Drehle, *Triangle—The Fire That Changed America*, 219.

34 *Ibid.*, 264.

35 Steven J. Diner, *A Very Different Age*, 155–175.

36 *Ibid.*, 162.

37 *Ibid.*, 171–175.

38 This book can be read in its entirety online at http://www.cis.yale.edu/amstud/inforev/riis.

39 "Exploiting the Child," *The Nation*, vol. 138, no. 3593 (May 1934): 551.

40 See also Beulah Amidon, "Children Wanted," in *Survey Graphic*, vol. 26, no. 1 (January 1937): 16.

41 No sane person could seriously conclude that child labor practices such as those already described could "protect" children as the title wants to suggest. Likewise, no right-minded person could possibly imagine that the way to cleaner air is to promote industrial gaseous emissions and SUV fumes, or that we can better protect the forests and clean water by chopping down millions of trees and releasing arsenic into the drinking water. But these and more preposterous instances of deliberately altered reality have come to light in recent years.

42 Michael McGerr, *A Fierce Discontent. The Rise and Fall of the Progressive Movement in America* (Oxford: Oxford University Press, 2003) 158.

43 *Ibid.*

44 Grosvenor B. Clarkson, *Industrial America in the World War: The Strategy Behind the Line, 1917–1918* (Boston: Houghton Mifflin, 1923) 9. See also Michael McGerr, *A Fierce Discontent*, 284–285.

45 Michael McGerr, *A Fierce Discontent*, 282.

46 Historian Robert K. Murray provides an account of corporate America's "red scare" campaign during the period. Particularly interesting are the cartoons and chants that made their way into public discourse at the time. See his *Red Scare: A Study of National Hysteria, 1919–1920* (Westport, Connecticut: Greenwood Publishing Group, 1980).

47 A detailed description of the miners' struggles in the coal fields of West Virginia is given in David Corbin's *Life, Work, and Rebellion in the Coal Fields: The Southern West Virginia Miners, 1880–1922* (Urbana, Illinois: University of Illinois Press, 1981).

48 Howard Burton Lee has written a straightforward eye-witness account of the violent conflicts dubbed the "West Virginia Coal Wars" in the appropriately titled book *Bloodletting in*

Appalachia: The Story of West Virginia's Four Major Mine Wars and Other Thrilling Incidents of Its Coal Fields (Parsons, West Virginia: McClain Printing Company, 1969).

49 Robert J. Thornton has even written a book on the subject: *L.I.A.R. The Lexicon of Intentionally Ambiguous Recommendations. Positive-sounding references for people who can't manage their own sock drawers* (Naperville, Illinois: Sourcebooks, 2003).

50 Barbara Ehrenreich, *Nickel and Dimed: On (Not) Getting By in America* (New York: Owl Books, 2002).

51 As a number of labor rights activists and economists have repeatedly argued, the federal minimum wage in no way represents an income potential that would allow an individual to survive, much less a family. Holly Sklar noted, "It would take more then $9 in 2006 to match the federal minimum wage peak reached in 1968, adjusting for inflation. At today's $5.15 an hour, it takes two minimum wage workers to earn what one made 38 years ago." Holly Sklar, "Wanted: A High-Road Economy," 17 March 2006, TomPaine.com. See also ead.: *Raise the Floor: Wages and Policies That Work for All Of Us* (Cambridge, Massachusetts: South End Press, 2002).

52 Figures tallied by the Labor Project for Working Families can be found at http://www.laborproject.org.

53 For a detailed account of the Pinto problem from an automotive engineering perspective, see the Web site http://www.engineering.com/content/ContentDisplay?contentId=41009014.

54 Cf. Mark Dowie, "Pinto Madness" (1977, The Foundation for National Progress), retrievable at http://www.motherjones.com.

55 The family's account of the accident and subsequent details of the lawsuit were the subject of a CBS *60 Minutes* segment by Steve Kroft, Leslie Cockburn, Don Hewitt, Philip Scheffler, Josh Howard, and Merri Lieberthal, "Perjury and Obstruction of Justice?" (February 7, 1999) *60 Minutes*.

Chapter 5

God's Own People: The GOP

IN SO MANY WAYS, AMERICA'S REPUBLICANS—the Grand Old Party—embody all that is healthy, wholesome, powerful, and patriotic in the country's short history. This is the party of the good old days when mom and pop showed their compassion by hiring the kid from the other side of the tracks for a summer job; the tradition of good clean fun, sock-hops and campfires; Christian fellowship, candles, carols, and mistletoe at Christmas; homemade cookies and cupcakes; solid family values, firmly rooted in white middle-class courage to defend the laws of the land.

Their would-be opponents can also pride themselves on family values of sorts, but Democrats have been left the spoils of war, the hand-me-downs of dishwasher day jobs, empty beer cans, screaming kids, shitty diapers, and past-due car payments. They've had their share of fun in sex, with more than just the high school sweetheart. They're hard workers, but not the greatest talents at making ends meet, with the heart (at times) to stand up for what's right by saying "kiss-my-ass" to higher authority.

Rigid distinctions between traditionally liberal Democrats and conservative Republicans cannot always be easily drawn, and cross-party voting patterns by region and by issue have become common. The generally acknowledged divisions extant in party politics today range from the left-wing liberal Democrat to the right-wing conservative Republican, with the center of gravity ostensibly falling in the much-ballyhooed political middle road. The initial division of liberal or conservative is more precisely defined by social and fiscal distinctions. "Ideal-typical" social liberals on the left end of the spectrum hold that governments should stay out of a person's private life completely; that what two people irrespective of gender do in intimacy with each other is (barring murder or serious injury) of no one else's concern. They generally oppose the death penalty as well as legislation restricting pornography, the use of soft drugs such as marijuana, or a woman's right to an abortion. Fiscally, this demographic group supports increased government spending (generally through higher taxes levied on the wealthy) to support the needy, to provide free education and public health care, while cutting public funds for the military. At the other extreme are the Christian conservative Republicans whose values were examined in Chapter 3. With zero tolerance for sex outside marriage strictly defined as the traditional Judeo-Christian bond between a man and a woman, they are vehemently opposed to abortion and pornography and advocate the return of prayer to public school. Their fiscal motto is *God helps those who help themselves*. What's more, the Bible clearly states that man would have to earn his livelihood by "the sweat of [his] brow." *People who want to work will find it, but people who don't have the ambition or the will should either be forced to learn life's hard little lessons, or just do without. It shouldn't be the responsibility of decent hard-working citizens to pay for someone else's free ride.*

Looking at the Republicans and Democrats sparring over issues whose fundamentals will likely never change is a bit like viewing a World Wrestling Championship—it's all show, for reasons that will later become clear. The jumps and kicks, the hard slams on the mat, the jabs and the pokes, are the media-ready version of a political Jerry Springer sling-out. And every four years the two "combating" parties present the same schlock. The party in power reads off a list of accomplishments with delegate applause punctuating the commas and periods in the accolades. If they're Democrats: the jobs that were created; the economic growth that brought thousands out of poverty; the higher standards of education that were achieved; the programs that helped people get back on their feet; the safer streets and neighborhoods. Admittedly, not bad. If they're Republicans: the economic growth that was attained; the unrivaled status of America's armed services; the greater security against the country's enemies; the return of God to the homeland. And every four years the "opposition" recants the same central theme: *"America, it's time for a change in the White House. Let us mark a new beginning! Let us restore the glory and honor that was once America!"* If they're Democrats, the litany of complaints encompasses: the rise in corporate greed and corruption; the cuts in spending for the needy; the perks given to businesses at the expense of labor and the environment; the growing gap between rich and poor. If they're Republicans: the wasteful spending by a welfare state; the loss of competitiveness among businesses; the harm inflicted on the business community by tax increases, worker compensation, and unemployment benefits; the stifling of free enterprise by environmental regulations; the decay in traditional moral values.

In the campaign run-up to the Iowa caucuses on January 3, 2008, many Americans across the country had pinned their dreams and internet donations on the great non-white hope, Mr. Obama. His skin color, exuberant youth, the fact that he'd actually inhaled, and his backing by none other than the grand dame of daytime TV, Oprah Winfrey, all lent credence and big bucks to his campaign as the un-Republican (un-Bush) candidate. His banner carried one single word in super-size letters: CHANGE. Never mind the absence of any outspoken commitment to a radical restructuring of the grotesquely imbalanced foundations of "super capitalism" (as Robert Reich aptly referred to the dominant existing forms of U.S. economic policies); *change* was what the people wanted, no matter what the outcome. All part and parcel of the *American-Idol* style personality contests and surrounding hype that the people have been told constitute the democratic process.

The extent to which the political parties and their representatives will go to muster up enough votes for the slide into elected office can be seen in the comic pandering techniques that have developed over the years. With the growth in the Hispanic population rising exponentially, candidates from both parties have hit the airwaves speaking Spanish with gringo accents thick enough to be taken for an oil spill. The condescending, underlying assumption being of course that Hispanics are just not really bright enough to learn English and can be reached only in the one language they understand.

When seen from the outside, American politics is decidedly lopsided. John Micklethwait and Adrian Wooldridge (authors of *The Right Nation. Conservative Power in America*) correctly observed that even the most right-wing conservative governments in Europe are still further to the left of the American mainstream. The crucial political center in the United States is in fact comparatively quite conservative. This fact alone has given the GOP the needed critical mass to transform its ideology into the single most dominant and enduring force in American politics, despite a never-ending series of Republican-led economic downturns. With its uncontested control of the middle, the party has rarely been forced to backtrack on important platform issues or to dilute policies it has upheld as banner-slogans for conservatives. This certainly cannot be said of the Democratic opponents who repeatedly find themselves in a tug-of-war for swing-voters from the center. (As the German left once described the SPD (Social Democratic Party), the Democratic Party is what one might call the "foreskin of the working class" —when things get serious, it pulls back.)

In the last forty years alone, the GOP has produced three presidents (Nixon, Reagan, and Bush Forty-Three) who have left permanent etchings on the social, economic, and political fabric of the United States. And for better or worse (history will side with the latter), the GOP has done more to shape American foreign policy in the eyes of the rest of the world than have perhaps all the corporate images of America combined. There were interludes of other Republican presidents, but they will be relegated (perhaps luckily) to the back burner of historical memory.

The strategies and efficacy of the Republican Party follow historically mediated developmental patterns in three interlinked realms: the ideological, the political, and the implementation of both in economic policy. Republicans are living documents attesting to American success: *from rags to riches in ten easy steps, through nobody's efforts but "my own."* (In real life of course, the rags are usually there only on paper, but it's a nice bedtime story for the kids.) These home-front models of success serve to establish what is legitimate, and not, in the expectations citizens might have of the state. As a consequence, Republican politics is firmly based in the healthy/wealthy sectors of the business community, encompassing demographic strata as diverse as corporate boardroom bigwigs and family-based retail stores. At the same time, the party has traditionally held a stranglehold grip on social conservatives and the religious right. By default, what is left of the opposition is relegated to the "losers of society" (i.e. the intelligentsia, environmentalists, and certain minorities) with little financial backing except from the dwindling likes of trade and professional unions and grassroots associations attempting to gain a voice through the Internet.

The mindset we associate with the ideals of the Republican Party has been a potent force in shaping political discourse and in setting domestic policy since before the Republic came into being. This mindset and its ideals are an integral part of the American character and the guiding vision of the writers of the Constitution. *The question is: is this vision adequate for the survival of our life-world in the twenty-first century?*

Two features distinguish the policies of the Republican Party from competing political ideals (foremost being those of a socialist agenda): the isolation of the individual as an independent agent abstracted from a larger framework of social/biological relationships and the responsibility to maintain the underlying conditions that make the larger life-world possible; the integration/implementation of individualism as an ideology into a coherent economic strategy. The first relies on the concept of natural law and individual rights as expounded by philosophers and theorists of Classical Liberalism; the second is an adaptation of theories of political economy in the line of Adam Smith, Alfred Marshall, F. A. Hayek, and Milton Friedman. Consistently linked in theory, the historical practice has shown that different eras have experienced different political struggles in which one or the other theme becomes dominant in the arena of ideas. The first component is derived in relation to governmental authority and is expressed as "freedom from." The second component is predicated on the validity and general acceptance of the first.

It is one thing to extol universal human rights and the freedom to follow one's dreams without external repression; it is quite another, however, to fill those rights with predefined, ready-made content. What began as a theoretical construct in defense of individual rights vis-à-vis the state was quickly followed by the logical extension of that apology in the form of laissez-faire economic doctrine. Initially defined negatively as a lack of governmental interference, the doctrine has metamorphosed into positive, pro-business governmental bias. The power of corporate interests to determine both domestic and foreign policy has resulted in a polity-state relation in which the people are largely absent from the equation. This new form of statism is business-oriented precisely because business has become the state. Non-corporate elements become crucial only with the threat of civil unrest or with wages and salaries dropping so far below the radar screen that they threaten sales in a chain reaction, with potential massive disruptions in the electorate.

The GOP has been remarkably successful in centering its political agenda on a two-pronged platform of combating perceived social ills associated with anti religious liberalism and educational elitism, while at the same time freeing businesses and entrepreneurs from the constraints of "anti-growth" regulations (related to the dumping of toxins into the environment, fair wages, worker's compensation, health care, paid sick leave) and taxation. Since not all the ballot boxes or voting machines can be rigged, nor the precincts controlled by family members and allies, there is this gnawing need to pull off a good showing of support for the official party platform. Lower taxes, the perennial favorite, are a no-brainer when the Republicans strut before the masses of conservatives glued to the event. The social ills propagated by party ideologues are defined through the Judeo-Christian model of righteousness as outlined here in the third chapter. Church-based community services, Christian youth associations, pro-Bible school curricula, religious out reach programs, and faith-based civic involvement are seen as instrumental in keeping

rejoiced. A great schism opened between those who knew the memorized official answer to why we were there, and those who dreamed of a better world.

The classrooms' pledges of allegiance to freedom and the spread of democracy were tearing at the seams. Regimes once granted America's unwavering support lost their aura of innocence too, as societies divided along class lines crumbled. Armed with the omnipotent words of a foreign god and his earthly representative, multitudes of dissenters took revenge in an overwhelming show of force, inflicting once again lethal wounds on a trusted American appendage, and one of the Military Industrial Complex's most prized customers. In daily parades before the eyes of the watching world, America's unwilling symbols of weakness were once again the taunted proof that a giant could be brought to its knees. Adding insult to injury, even the desperate attempt to rescue the country's sons and daughters from the fangs of a people's wrath died in the anonymous sands of No-man's Land. Shamed and rebuked in the eyes of the world, America was a land shackled in self-doubt.

And so, on that day in January 1981, on the West Front of the Capitol, stood Ronald Reagan, a tall and valiant symbol of a new life, cleansed of impotence and deceit, strengthened by a newly-found vision of the future and the confidence that, once again, it was morning in America. The people had found a new unity in the consciousness that, like Phoenix from the ashes, the country has always been able to remake itself. As Reagan put it: "America is back."

And as if ordained by God Himself, the American hostages held in Iranian captivity for 444 days were "magically" released from custody and on their way home, confirming in the eyes of the credulous millions that they had indeed made the right choice in Ronnie. (Only later would they find out what kinds of—shall we say "back-stabbing"?—wheeling and dealing were involved between Reagan's trustees and the Mullahs, and at what price. But the throngs of adorers wouldn't have cared; he was their man.) And then there was the troublesome economy. With inflation rates at the time near thirteen percent and public debt approaching twenty-seven percent of the GDP, something was needed to turn the ship around. Before the eager eyes of millions, Reagan addressed the problem and his intended solution directly: "In this present crisis, government is not the solution to our problem; government is the problem." Allow individual freedom to thrive, foster American ingenuity and can-do-ism, encourage the entrepreneurial spirit to reshape reality according to the law of supply and demand, and everything else will automatically fall into place—the persistent axiom of Republican

ideology. As he gazed out over the throngs gathered for the signs of collective re-
newal, Reagan declared: "The business of our nation goes forward." Few realized
at the time just how literally he meant it.

His mission was two-fold: First, to restore America's confidence in herself at
home and her image abroad by catapulting the country into an exalted position of
unrivaled military superiority; second, to put the country on solid economic footing with widespread prosperity derived from expanded economic growth. The
two strands of policy were of course connected.[2]

Reagan's 1981 Economic Recovery Tax Act (ERTA) laid the groundwork for
what Jim Hightower called "one of the quickest and most regressive redistributions
of wealth" ever. The legislation contained key elements of the 1978 Kemp-Roth Bill,
with massive reductions in both corporate and individual marginal tax rates. Of
particular importance was the fact that the reductions applied also to unearned income (i.e. money made from the ownership of property or from savings accounts).
In less than two years after Reagan took office, corporate contributions to total federal revenue amounted to little more than a miserly six percent, the lowest percentage ever.[3] The other big winners were the jet-setting high-rollers who saw their
marginal tax rates fall from seventy percent in 1979 to just twenty-eight percent in
1988.[4] Reagan's ideologues justified these moves with the supply-side theory that
cutting taxes from the upper income groups would encourage tax payers to actually
pay their fair share instead of having their accountants find every loophole available, thereby increasing total federal revenue.[5] A second advantage (so the supply-side belief) was that big-earners would give the economy a huge boost by
reinvesting the extra cash on hand in new equipment and by hiring new employees. Conservative economists never tire of repeating the select figure that during the
Reagan era the overall share of taxes paid into federal coffers by the wealthiest five
percent was close to forty-six percent. True as that may be, it is equally important to
note that during the period in question the net earnings of America's upper income
groups reached astronomical heights. At the same time, there was tight control over
the money supply. Appointed by Jimmy Carter to chair the Federal Reserve, Paul
Volcker concluded early in his tenure that inflation was wreaking havoc on the
economy, so he set out to combat it by raising interest rates eventually to a staggering twenty percent. The effect on investment borrowing and personal credit was
strangling. On the brighter side, though, as William Greider[6] correctly analyzed, was
the pleasantly "unexpected" outcome for the rich: with hundreds of millions of dollars in bonds and interest-earning accounts, America's upper class suddenly found

itself swimming in more money than it knew what to do with (a persistent problem it seems).

True to the antistatist ideology Reagan professed, the administration intensified the campaign already set in motion by Jimmy Carter to "deregulate" important sectors of business and finance from governmental control, including the nation's airlines, the banking system, and the oil, transportation, and telecommunications industries (this led among other things to the breakup of AT&T.)[7] The Carter administration had acted in 1978 to release the airlines from the governmental controls established during the New Deal through the creation of the Civil Aeronautics Board. In addition to controlling virtually every aspect of the airline industry from take-off times and carrier destinations to the size of vomit bags, the market was basically closed to hopeful start ups. By freeing the airlines from these controls, the government reasoned that increased competition would stoke better service and create a wider expanse of more flexible flight schedules, all while offering the public much cheaper fares and a comfier ride. The number of routes and carriers predictably shot up at the bat of an eyelash and the carriers sought to lure in customers with an increasingly appealing array of services, perks, and enhanced comfort. Domestic fares plummeted from an average of $140.00 in 1975 (in 1983 dollars) to around $60.00 in 2000,[8] and the total number of domestic passengers rose from 200 million in 1975 to more than 650 million in 2000.[9]

The airlines suddenly found themselves in a survival-of-the-fittest struggle to attract and keep customers without falling into red ink. The increased competition began to take its toll not only on service with luggage being lost or sent to wrong destinations, planes arriving late, and onboard snacks being eliminated or reduced to a bag of peanuts; the far more worrisome sides of the cutthroat survival throes began to manifest themselves in more frequent crashes, killing hundreds in the process. A number of airlines resorted to flying older planes that should have been taken out of service. At the same time, many carriers were cheating on their maintenance schedules and necessary repairs. Others resorted to overloading the cargo area with more than the allowed weight.

In January of 2000, Alaska Airlines Flight 261 was flying north along the California coast on a return trip from Mexico. The plane (an MD-80) had just reached the northern perimeter of Los Angeles when the pilots reported problems with the horizontal stabilizer. The plane suddenly went into a nosedive position and plunged into the Pacific. All eighty-eight passengers and crew died in the crash. Search and recovery missions were able to locate important pieces of the body of the aircraft including the horizontal stabilizer. Analysis of both the plane's movement and the conversations between the pilot and the control tower led investigators to suspect that this crucial component of the plane's tail assembly was responsible for the severe angle of descent.

The National Transportation Safety Board (NTSB) investigated the crash using all available resources and it presented its draft report in an open-door "sunshine" session. Disturbingly, the agency noted that

> ...during the initial fleet survey required by the AD [Airworthiness Directive AD-2000-0351], two additional MD-80s in the Alaska Airlines fleet...were found to have jackscrews worn beyond limits. The wear rate on these two aircraft was over four times the wear rate anticipated by the manufacturer.

With the aid of an extensive, carefully designed test program, investigators examined in minute detail the components of the horizontal stabilizer assembly and the chemical breakdown of the lubricants used. They determined that "the only factor found to explain this level of severe wear is a lack of lubrication."

The panel also focused on Alaska Airlines' extension of the time period between professional lubrication procedures (which it found to be very inadequately performed) and concluded:

> A review of records indicates that the interval for jackscrew lubrication was extended four times with no objection from the FAA between March 1987 and July 1996...Additionally, in the wake of the most recent extension there in 1996, in '97, Alaska Airlines replaced Mobilgrease 28 with Aeroshell 33 for jackscrew lubrication without following appropriate internal and standard industry practice procedures which dictate that the intervals should actually be decreased when a grease change is made until data shows its successful service history has been achieved. In sum, Alaska Airlines (sic) extended lubrication intervals increased the likelihood that a missed or inadequate lubrication would result in excessive wear.

The report went on to chide the carrier's delay in having its planes regularly inspected for "end-play" of the assembly components:

> Because the Alaska Airlines increased fleet utilization at that time, the interval between end-play checks occurred approximately every 9,550 flight hours. By contrast, the manufacturer's recommended interval at that time...was every 30 months or 7,200 flight hours, whichever comes first.

Moreover, the panel discovered that Alaska Airlines had used its own in-house version of a critical restraining fixture that "did not conform to Boeing specifications and the Systems Group documented several differences between the two." Extensive tests determined "low reliability" for the homegrown version.

NTSB investigators went to the carrier's service and maintenance facility in San Francisco to look at the circumstances surrounding the last lubrication of Flight 261's MD-80 and determined that the company's mechanic who had done the last lube job on the plane "didn't appear to have a solid knowledge on the actual lubrication procedure." Boeing experts estimate the minimum time required to complete such a procedure to be three and a half to four hours, but the mechanic questioned admitted he had spent roughly an hour doing the work.

When the investigators looked at the maintenance records submitted by Alaska Airlines, they found a number of very serious concerns. Some of the people at the airline who were conducting the end-play inspections had had virtually no previous experience. Even "as recently as Spring 2002," i.e. two full years after the fatal crash of Flight 261, inspections of the Alaska Airlines' jackscrew assemblies found "inadequate lubrication...on rudder control tab bearings on two separate aircraft...One bearing fell apart when removed."

The list and discussion of egregious errors and inadequacies goes on, a full 292 pages.[10] Almost as serious as problems related to Alaska Airlines itself were the questions of why the Federal Aviation Administration (FAA) had not bothered to follow up on the extended maintenance intervals to determine, as it should have, that they were completely inadequate. Was the FAA not even aware of the problem, or had it just simply chosen to look the other way? According to the NTSB report, at the time of investigation, one airline in particular, Delta, exceeded even Alaska Airlines' interval of end-play inspections.

One final point in the report is worthy of attention:

With respect to FAA oversight, we found in our investigation that FAA surveillance of Alaska Maintenance Program in general and the Oakland facility in particular had been deficient for several years prior to the accident. The principal maintenance inspector...stated that they were too busy with administration to do any surveillance. The chief of the Seattle Certificate Management Office stated in a formal memorandum to the Director, Flight Standards Service, November 12th, 1999, that the staffing had reached a critical point. Alaska was in a state of aggressive growth and expansion and the FAA staff was not able to meet the work demands. He concluded that, "The risk of incidents or accidents at Alaska Airlines is heightened."[11]

The parallels to the Triangle fire are unmistakable. Why did Alaska Airlines choose to forgo scheduled maintenance for a later day and to use in-house versions of critical replacement parts without following regulations to report and receive clearance for such substitutions? Why was the carrier employing mechanics with a sub-par performance record and inadequate specialized training? As in so many other instances of death and serious injury at the hands of businesses, common sense tells us that the carrier was trying to save money—at the expense of eighty-eight people who lost their lives in a few minutes of horror. The death toll could have been much higher. And once again, behind the numbers and details were people with families, all left behind to grieve and wonder why it had to happen to them. Future travelers should be pleased to know that much of the airline maintenance and inspection work these days is being done for even less overall cost, in El Salvador.

This case says a great deal about the need for regulation and unconditional, impartial, incorruptible supervision by higher authorities. It may of course be extremely cost-saving for an airline, a dental clinic, a hospital, or a nuclear power station to hire unlicensed, undocumented, cheap labor to do the work of professionals, but the long-term costs to the public are enormous. According to a PBS report that aired in November of 2004,[12] Los Angeles County's H.A.L.T. team (Health Authority Law Enforcement Taskforce) had more than 900 cases of illicit medical practice under investigation, some of which have led to patient deaths. Many of these cases revolved around ordinary men and women with no medical training or license who suddenly decided that they could do what they'd seen the pharmacist, internist, dentist or ER docs do, and they went at it. One of the supervising investigators with the California State Dental Board stated that she had even found a dental operating room in a private garage—full of filth, with the motorcycle standing near the patients' chair. The irrigation tubes leading into the patients' mouths were hooked up in the toilet. But dental clinics are only one of the many issues the team investigates. Pharmaceuticals of every kind and strength are being sold at swap meets and in department stores; children are receiving the wrong kinds of injections in the back rooms of toy stores. The ultimate in deregulation.

The Carter-Reagan initiative to return control of business and finance over to the free market forces didn't stop with the airlines. In what ultimately worked out to be a major cost for taxpayers, Congress was forced to bail out the bankrupt savings and loan associations after a string of deregulated failures. The savings and loan institutes were originally conceived as a simple way in which members of a given community could deposit money and then later participate in the S&L's mortgage lending plan. During the Great Depression Congress had restricted the amount of interest the savings and loan associations could charge to five percent, and this figure had not been tweaked to fit changing circumstances. Given the very high interest rates that banks were offering thanks to Volcker's tight money policy at the beginning of the Reagan era, the savings and loan associations soon found themselves in a real financial crunch as customers naturally began withdrawing their savings from the five percent limit and placing it in higher-rate investment schemes. The writing was on the wall: in a very short time, the S&L's would have no funds whatsoever and would have to declare bankruptcy, in which case the federal government would have had to pay back any money lost to S&L investors. Congress decided the best course of action would be simply to annul the limitations originally placed on the savings and loan associations during the depression era by letting them (through the Garn—St. Germain Depository Institutions Act of 1982) offer interest rates comparable to those of leading investment institutions.

As with the airlines, an all-out struggle broke out among a number of the savings and loan associations to offer the most competitive rates of investment. This served the purpose of luring back attractive sums of money, but by offering substantially higher interest rates to attract money in, the S&L would not be able to pay the money back without breaking the bank. Various internal schemes were devised (a few fraudulent) to raise money. According to a 1988 report by the Federal Home Loan Bank Board, these schemes were a major contributor to the ultimate series of bankruptcies that subsequently occurred. The most notorious (and costly) of these failures involved the Lincoln Savings of Irvine, California. In 1993, the director of the institution, Charles Keating, was ultimately convicted of racketeering and fraud and sentenced to prison. The final cost to taxpayers was in excess of $150 billion.

The Reagan Revolution also involved a truly dramatic shift in the way federal money was used, and it is this change of heart in public sentiment accompanied by ruthless downsizing in social programs that arguably had the most enduring effects on American society. For those born with silver spoons on their platinum platters, the Reagan era meant much more of the same. "Flaunting" the wealth one "had earned" was a popular pastime among the truffles and caviar crowds, who were certainly not losing any sleep over the fate of the cardboard-box people sleeping in the streets of America's inner cities. At the time Reagan was elected into office, the nation was abuzz in supply-side theory and the type of monetarism promoted by Milton Friedman.[13] Both approaches to political economy entail implications for a radical societal overhaul; both share the conviction that government (as Reagan never tired of saying) is the problem, not the solution. This was of course only a convenient descriptor, a handy hook Reagan insouciantly tossed into public discourse in his characteristic *ah-shucks* manner to pitch the real content, which lay elsewhere, and was far more insidious. The more genuine aim behind the ideology came to light in the wizard communicator's favorite anecdote (which he may have truly believed) of the "Cadillac Queen" from Chicago. The real case in question involved a woman who was charged and convicted of collecting approximately $8,000 in welfare payments by using two bogus case names. Each time Mr. Reagan told the story, he was able to embellish it with his own take on welfare recipients so that by the time someone finally, thankfully, insisted that he stifle it, the woman had collected in excess of $150,000.00, went by close to a hundred different names, and was registered with the welfare offices under a whole slew of different social security numbers and benefits payments going to scores of different addresses. The Republican Gipper-loyalists bought it each time, with anger spewing from their nostrils like steam from a smoldering volcano.

Ronnie and Nancy became gracious role models in the nation's revolt against liberal paternalism, purging the collective consciousness of any forms of guilt that might have prompted a donation here or an additional assistance program there. Even as governor Mr. Reagan had touted California's Welfare Reform Act of 1971 as a sure fire way to get all the freeloaders off their lazy asses. The actor's contempt for the destitute was assuaged by the euphemistic sales pitch designed to sugarcoat the dismantlement of Aid To Families With Dependent Children (AFDC). In classical Spencer-Hayek-Friedman-Gilder-Wanniski manner, Reagan argued that public assistance did little more than keep able-bodied people in bondage, hooked in a dependent relationship with the generous hands of big government. So he set out to "help" them by cutting off their money supply.

Reagan also had "the theory" ready and waiting to support him in all 1,077 pages of the Heritage Foundation's *Mandate for Leadership*; in George Gilder's *Wealth and Power*; in Charles Murray's *Losing Ground*; in F. A. Hayek's *The Road to Serfdom*; and in Jude Wanniski's *The Way the World Works*. (And people thought Hillary had lost it when she spoke of a "vast right-wing conspiracy.") What's more, Reagan actually enjoyed reading, so he may very well have found the Oval

Office's own version of Potter magic in the best the conservative mind has to offer. (With George W. Bush's talents lying clearly elsewhere, he's likely to have relied on the 90-second sound-clip version of the texts.)

However well intended (so the theory goes), welfare ultimately leads recipients into a permanent state of dependence on governmental handouts and robs them of any inner initiative to go out and look for a job that will allow them to stand on their own two feet. Now of course it goes without saying that what these nice compassionate Republicans have in their hearts and minds is only the well-being of all the poor folks in the country, so it's easy to understand the policy that naturally segues from the theory: cut off their money supply, come what may.

In stark contrast to other cultures and lifestyles, WASPs have always felt a deep disdain at the idea of grown men and women living off the costs of others, family or not. Italian *mamone* may find it appropriate to live with their mamas and exploit the maternal instinct and willingness to clean and cook until the sons are at retirement home age, but white Protestants will have none of it. By the time the kids—and by extension, the needier elements of society—are old enough to have sex and vote, they should be out on their own, earning their own money with no favors from anyone. The "school of hard knocks" teaches America's future generations of WASPs that life isn't always a bed of roses. And when the going gets rough, accept your individual responsibility! Bite your lip, grin and bear it, reach down and pull yourself up by your bootstraps! *It's not society's responsibility to rescue you from that freefall you're in! It'll make a man out of you!* Ronnie did, time and time again, in all his best movies. But for the millions who had to choose between a sack of potatoes and the next bus fare, the reality of Reagan's eight percent cut in assistance looked a lot less promising than the hype about opportunity. And that was just part of the story. The graduation ceremony in Draconian fiscal policy came with the cruel seventy-six percent reduction in housing assistance for the poor. This prime example of responsible Republican social policy left more than two million Americans homeless, with an official number of 32.5 million subsisting below the poverty line. In truth, the numbers were much, much higher because the poverty level has consistently been defined according to a figure worked out by Mollie Orshansky of the Social Security Administration in 1964.[14] Federal subsidies for low-income housing projects fell from $74 billion in 1980 to a paltry $19 billion eight years later.[15] Reagan's cuts were death sentences for many homeless who succumbed to hypothermia in inner-city streets. Those that were lucky enough somehow made it to Los Angeles or Miami to avoid the terror of sub-zero winter temperatures. The streets of Los Angeles were packed with thousands of men, women, and small children, lying side by side in any cardboard boxes they could find to protect themselves from the elements and hungry rats. In New York City, reports emerged of the estimated 100,000 "mole people" who sought protection from the cold (and the steely-eyed Very Important People of passing limousines) in the tunnels below Gotham's extensive subway system. There, mothers delivered and reared their infants, many of whom rarely glimpsed the light of day. Here, there was no "morning in America," only perpetual darkness in a twilight world on the cusp of life and death. The *Los Angeles Times* received the anonymous report of a woman who was forced to survive by living in her car. Because Diane's (as she called herself) job didn't pay enough for her to afford the security deposit on an apartment, much less the monthly rent, she had no option but to work during the day and sleep in the back seat of her car at night. And contrary to the many conscience-comforting myths popularized about the homeless in America, Diane was neither mentally ill, nor addicted to anything other than good food. And it sure as hell was not her "choice" to live in her car.

The ugly doctrine of Social Darwinism (a latent golden oldie among high-class conservatives) accompanied Reagan and his protégés in spirit, if not in name, every step of the way. The boundless pride of the nation's growing stock of self-made millionaires and billionaires had obliterated the sentimental kitsch of natural empathy for the dispossessed. Had it been legal, some clever Wall Street go-getter would no doubt have found a lucrative final solution to the homeless problem by turning all the good for-nothings into freshly ground diet dog food at a gourmet price. And the Brioni-clad cronies would not have said a word.

At the same time that the Reagan administration was slashing discretionary social programs by a full thirty percent, it was pampering the Bohemian Grove's dealers in death with a forty percent increase over the already exorbitant sums meted out during the Carter administration as a response to the Soviet invasion of Afghanistan. The laissez faire ideology underpinning administration policies had suddenly become remarkably Keynesian in its treatment of the military-industrial complex.[16] This redistribution of public funds to the benefit of the defense industries with their hundreds of subsidiaries and contractors mirrored the shift in the tax structure to favor the wealthy.

Reagan's ambitious plans for the Pentagon were based in part on perceived threats particularly of Soviet expansion. But behind the magic curtain was the Hollywood "reality" created by the defense industry with the sole purpose of raking in that additional $330 billion up for grabs—thanks to their man in the White House.

The factual list of characters appointed to key positions and plots hatched out during the twenty years spanning the Reagan-Bush-Bush administrations read like a conspiracy novel. It was, without the fictional elements.

The first official confirmation that U.S. intelligence had (intentionally) exaggerated both the extent and speed of the USSR's expansion and modernization of its nuclear arsenal came in the form of CIA documents ("Intelligence Forecasts of Soviet Intercontinental Attack Forces: An Evaluation of the Record") declassified on March 9, 2001. As New York Senator Daniel Patrick Moynihan noted at the time, the documents revealed seven years of "consistent overestimates" of the actual threat posed by the Soviet military arsenal.[17] Writing for the Cato Institute's *Policy Analysis*, former staff official at the Office of the Secretary of Defense Earl C. Ravenal called Reagan's imbalanced budget "the most provocative in living memory," and warned of the serious long-term effects the enormous deficit-spending program could have on future generations.[18]

Even Hollywood did its part to make sure the nicely marketed threat made its way into the family living room. *The Day After* (1983) was a made-for-TV movie designed with one purpose in mind: to scare the dickens out of Joe and Flo Blow right in the American heartland by proving once and for all how real and menacing the Russian threat really was. The media event was a true spectacle—American infotainment at its best. What's more, the movie event of the decade was preceded by weeks of theme-based discussion rounds and talk shows that went all out in their effort to pitch the movie as the cinematic version of the fate awaiting America unless the country committed itself to a new and massive deterrent system. On November 20, 1983, half of all adult Americans[19] sat glued to the scenes of Apocalypse (always a front-runner among the perpetually bored suburbanites with little but Armageddon to look forward to) streaking across the sky toward reality's own *Pleasantville*: Lawrence, Kansas. Yes, the inevitable conclusion followed: *If it can happen in Lawrence, it can happen anywhere.*

As Vandenberg had warned Truman, where there is no actual war, the threat of one has to be conjured up. And since there was not yet any 9/11 style event to lend credence to the threat pitch, nor any "aluminum tubes" as "proof" of impending doom, Washington made do with general anxiety and cinematic kitsch. Combined with the intelligence hype about the growing Soviet threat and its intentions to conquer the Oakville Mall, the movie's message got through to the American people loud and clear. Something had to be done.

As in all happy ends courtesy of Hollywood, the fearless hero came to the rescue of a nation on the brink. This time it was Ronald Reagan himself, right off the big screen. Ronnie would show those evil Russians who the toughest kid on the block was. And he carried with him a whole bunch of exciting new schemes to flex America's armed abs and biceps. It was by all appearances to this end that the Reagan administration introduced its ambitious "Star Wars" plan, a.k.a. the "Strategic Defense Initiative (SDI)". Destined for revival under every Republican administration until for some reason it is no longer needed, this system would allow the U.S. to station laser beams and ultra-fast missiles in space that would intercept any incoming warheads from hostile forces and knock them out before they had a chance to annihilate any local Wal-Mart—*and that from a "superpower" that sent ice trucks destined for Katrina victims on a wild goose chase in half a dozen states, all trying to find Louisiana.* As humans rely more and more on the mystique of technology, ever-nuttier ideas abound. Of course no one really believed the system would work, but it contributed nicely to stuffing the pockets and coffers of defense-related industries.

Ronald Reagan had wisely chosen his cabinet from an arena of candidates intimately connected with large defense-related corporations, many of whom (both men and companies) resurfaced under the Bushes. But perhaps the phrasing is misleading in its assumption that Reagan acted in a sovereign manner to select his circle of advisers; it would likely be more accurate to say that these men were selected for various governmental posts based on their affiliation (in the original Latin sense) with people in just the right places.

The Bechtel Corporation, one of the chief recipients of post-Saddam Iraq contracts handed out by the Pentagon, was able to place one of its "former" employees right at the head of the trough in the person of Caspar Weinberger, Reagan's secretary of defense. Mr. Weinberger knew the ropes as few others did, but his eagerness to transform the world to Bechtel's advantage ultimately led to his involvement in the so-called "Iran-Contra" scandal, in which the U.S. secretly sold arms (e.g. TOW anti-tank and HAWK surface-to-air missiles) to Iran in exchange for the American hostages taken shortly after the overthrow of Reza Pahlavi. Deals subsequently negotiated between members of the Reagan administration and the Iranian government involved the sale of more weapons systems, but the proceeds were used in defiance of the 1982 Boland Amendment to supply the Nicaraguan right-wing Contras with arms. Mr. Weinberger was indicted on felony charges related to his perjurious testimony before the congressional committee investigating the details of the Iran-Contra affair, but he predictably received a presidential pardon from his good friend George H. W. Bush. Blame for the covert, illegal activity reached all the way to the top, but the Great Communicator delivered a touching father-knows-best Checkers moment on national TV to say he firmly believed the actions he had taken were morally the right thing to do in defense of freedom. As always, the country's vocal majority could see no evil from the Right. With goose bumps of pride and swelled breasts, the teary-eyed defenders-of-freedom simpletons bought the gimmick. All was forgiven, and life went back to normal.

Caspar Weinberger was succeeded by none other than "Spooky" Frank Carlucci,[20] a former wrestling partner of Donald Rumsfeld from their bunk bed days together at Princeton. Carlucci was a long-time foreign-service official who had seen his fair share of controversial activity, beginning in the 1950s with his questionable involvement in the CIA's attempts to oust Patrice Lumumba as prime minister of the Congo. Like Salvador Allende a decade later, Lumumba mysteriously but quite conveniently wound up dead in January 1961.[21] The circumstances surrounding Lumumba's assassination were also depicted in the prize-winning film *Lumumba* by renowned Haitian director Raoul Peck. In the cinematic version of events, Carlucci is seen conversing with men holding the prime minister prior to the leader's murder. Carlucci is asked his opinion on what to do with the man. Lawyers for Carlucci were able to have the scene cut from the HBO version shown on American TV in 2002.[22]

Following his assignment in the Congo, Carlucci was sent to Brazil, where the CIA was involved in yet another attempt to oust a pro-Castro/pro-socialist government, this time that of Joao Goulart. In previously secret documents declassified and released by the National Security Archive in 2004, the public learned of the extent of U.S. involvement in the 1964 coup d'état. Among the declassified documents were recordings of President Johnson, pressing U.S. representatives and attaches in Brazil to "take every step" to see that the socialist regime came to an end. Lincoln Gordon, the U.S. ambassador to Brazil at the time, demanded Washington do everything in its power to support the overthrow being hatched out by General Humberto Branco—to prevent Brazil from becoming "the China of the 1960s." In early April 1964, the plan succeeded, with Goulart taking refuge in neighboring Uruguay.

Following an assignment to Portugal as the U.S. ambassador, Carlucci returned to Washington as deputy director of the CIA during the lackluster Carter presidency. From there it was on to the Pentagon as deputy secretary of defense until Weinberger resigned, leaving Carlucci to fill the vacancy. His vast experience with covert elements in the government and with key players in the Department of Defense made him a walking Google of military contacts, who somehow always managed to pull the right strings and triggers. This expertise later put him in good stead as president of the enormously powerful, influential, and enigmatic Carlyle Group. This private investment consortium has been linked to a number of deep-pocketed Republican bigwigs, with ties not only to all facets of the defense industry, but also to investment funds from the Bin Laden family of Saudi Arabia. Key players in the international web of Carlyle associates are men such as former president George H. W. Bush, James Baker III, and former British Prime Minister John Major. Among the many interesting investments linked to the Carlyle Group is MedPointe, a New Jersey-based pharmaceutical company. As David Lazarus of the *San Francisco Chronicle* pointed out,[23] the company is one of three nationwide that produces potassium iodide tablets, critical in the event of a nuclear attack. The tablets are taken to saturate the thyroid with iodine to prevent the absorption of harmful radioactive substances that could lead to a much higher incidence of thyroid cancer in certain individuals. Should Osama and Co. ever fulfill their dream of nuking four or five major metropolitan areas, there's a handsome profit waiting for the tablet makers. (Of course no right-minded person would ever think that the lure of big money might prompt certain groups of individuals to take events into their own hands and hasten destiny, would she?)

Because of the company's vast holdings in military-related industries, it has become one of the country's premier defense contractors, with lots to gain from the fallout of a nice little war in Iraq or the threat of a terrorist attack here and there.[24] The Corporation Board Room/Reagan Cabinet combo was further complemented by James A. Baker III, chief of staff during Reagan's first term in office, but secretary of the treasury during the second term. Mr. Baker went on to become George H. W. Bush's secretary of state. He played a major role in the election campaign of George W. Bush, and as if no conflict of interest could possibly have come to mind, Baker was on the oversight committee to ensure a fair and accurate recount of the bitterly contested 2000 vote in Florida.

Corporate reins on governmental programs seemed to tighten under the George H.W. Bush administration. When in 1990 Mr. Bush first began to inject the phrase "new world order" into his speeches, so-called "conspiracy theorists" began an immediate rundown of political and industrial puppet masters lurking behind the scenes with plans for global control: the Bilderberg elites and the Bohemian Club, coupled with Skull & Bones or Masonic Lodge insiders, were seen as the most likely candidates. Dominionist Christians saw the book of Revelation prophecy confirmed of a single world government in cahoots with the Anti-Christ.

Verbal coherence has never been the most prominent trait among Bush family members, so when the president was finally asked to explain the term during the weeks preceding Operation Desert Storm, none of the reporters privy to the president's answer was able to decipher the content. Bush did speak of stability in the Persian Gulf and of "arrangements…set in place." He also alluded to projects for a lasting peace between Israelis and Palestinians, and to "evolving democracies" elsewhere in the world for which the U.S. had "a program" in mind. Little imagination is required to realize that this "program" was not about teaching new techniques in flower arranging. In fact, the world had been given a hands-on preview of the New World Order in 1989 when George H.W. Bush ordered some 26,000 U.S. troops to invade Panama with the explicit purpose of kidnapping the country's acting CEO, General Manuel Noriega, and bringing him back to the U.S. to stand trial on charges of drug trafficking.

Irrespective of any validity the charges against Noriega may have had, the move itself was unprecedented. Father Bush justified the blatant violation of all accepted international legal codes by claiming that "General Noriega's reckless threats and attacks upon Americans in Panama created an imminent danger to the 35,000 American citizens in Panama. As President, I have no higher obligation than to safeguard the lives of American citizens."

Within days U.S. forces tracked down and captured the general, who had sought refuge at the Vatican embassy. Noriega was then brought to Florida where he stood trial. In his place, the U.S. installed the government of Guillermo Endara, the victor of the May 1988 national election that Noriega had subsequently nullified. Noriega's tenure as regent was thoroughly tainted with corruption, violent repression of opponents, fraud, and trade in contraband. He had publicly stated just months before the U.S. intervention that Panama was "in a state of war with the United States." The United States had felt justified in bringing a formal indictment against the general in 1988, the same year that Panamanian President Delvalle attempted to remove Noriega from the positions he held in the Ministry of Defense. The move backfired when the National Assembly chose to remove the president instead.

In justifying the American intervention and abduction of Noriega before the United Nations Security Council, U.S. ambassador Thomas Pickering invoked Article 51 of the United Nations Charter upholding "the inherent right of individual or collective self-defence if an armed attack occurs against a Member of the United Nations ... ." The "attack" underlying the argumentation referred not only to the murder of an American soldier, but ostensibly also to the onslaught of illicit drugs finding their way into America's inner cities.

The international community was quick to condemn the U.S. invasion as a willful violation of international law, despite the *New York Times* editorial with claims to the contrary.[25] With a vote of seventy-five in favor (twenty opposed, thirty-nine abstentions), the U.N. General Assembly passed Resolution A/RES/44 /240, deploring the U.S. action against Panama as a "flagrant violation of international law and of the independence, sovereignty and territorial integrity of States." The resolution also called for the "immediate cessation of the intervention and the withdrawal from Panama of the armed invasion forces of the United States."

Whether a continuation of the Noriega-dominated regime in Panama would or could have posed any real political or strategic threats to U.S. interests in the Canal Zone, which by many accounts were waning anyhow, is a matter of speculation, despite clear indications of growing anti-gringo/pro-nationalist sentiments in the Panamanian population at the time. The Torrijos-Carter Treaties had opened the path for complete Panamanian control over the Canal Zone on December 31, 1999. As a Panamanian political power figure, Colonel Omar Torrijos had implemented a number of changes to Panamanian infrastructure during the 1970s that quite possibly aroused Pentagon/CIA suspicion. His fatal plane crash in 1981 led many, including Colones Roberto Diaz Herrera, a high-ranking officer in the Panamanian military, to point the finger at Noriega and his American protectors at the time. It was also widely believed that Noriega and his CIA friends had had a hand in the assassination of Dr. Hugo Spadafora, a Noriega opponent in the Torrijo administration.[26] One sobering facet of U.S. involvement with Noriega is the fact that the Reagan-Bush team, who had ridden into Dodge on a high horse of moral rectitude, law and order, was not only well aware of all of Noriega's evil deeds, they were actually actively employing him on CIA pay rolls, just as they did Osama and his Freedom Fighters.

Coup de Tête

In 1993, the world was granted a temporary reprieve from the state-sponsored redistribution of wealth and power into the hands of society's cream. Had Americans finally had their fill of the war of the rich and famous being fought on the backs and coffins of those trapped at the bottom? Had they finally seen that the

Alger myths rang hollow? Had they finally grasped that drastic reductions in taxes meant no services except for those in the arms and oil business?

Whatever else may have come out of the Clinton-Gore administration, the two politically savvy sunny boys took the arena of public sentiment with a message of hope by and for the common, working people who'd been left behind during the seemingly endless years of Republican reign. Clinton's 1992 acceptance speech at the Democratic National Convention in New York put the men and women of the forgotten middle class in front with an emphasis on "centrist" politics. Whereas the Republicans had vented off their steam about taxes squandered on pork barrel public programs (always to be interpreted as welfare and benefits programs for working people and the poor), the Democrats called for mechanisms to put people back to work. With millions of Americans homeless and countless others barely eking out an existence if they were lucky enough to have a job at all, the realization came that it was indeed "the economy, stupid," which was galvanizing potential across the country to challenge head-on the callously pro-business, anti-working class cabal dominating the political landscape. Fleetwood Mac's folksy "Don't Stop Thinking About Tomorrow" was piped in for the audiences around the country, mimed by smiles of what appeared to be a genuine conviction that the people mattered, not as pawns in a vicious circle of wage cuts and threats of closures if wages rose, but as ends in themselves, with lives and goals worth pursuing:

> Tonight ten million of our fellow Americans are out of work, tens of millions more work harder for lower pay…This election is about putting power back in your hands and putting government back on your side. It's about putting people first.

Clinton's message relied heavily on the widespread discontent and anxiety palpable throughout the middle and working classes. He directly addressed the "forces of greed and the defenders of the status quo," warning that "your time has come and gone. It's time for a change in America."

The program itself was ambitious by American standards, aiming at nothing short of "health care for every American" and "equal justice under the law." Clinton's speech reminded the country that during the twelve years of continuous Republican practice the United States had "gone from first to thirteenth in the world in wages," and had "wasted billions and reduced…investments in education and jobs," all while accruing a national debt more than double that of the previous Carter administration. "We can do better," Clinton thundered.

But the platform of the newly formed Democratic Party was by no means socialism in-the-making. In fact, Clinton warned the left not to expect government to provide all the answers:

> There is not a program in government for every problem, and if we want to use government to help people, we have got to make it work again... That's why we need a new approach to government, a government that offers more empowerment and less entitlement...A government that is leaner, not meaner; a government that expands opportunity, not bureaucracy; a government that understands that jobs must come from growth in a vibrant and vital system of free enterprise.

Despite the centrist approach to problem-solving, the programs in the Clinton agenda encountered an uphill battle from the start. Ms. Clinton's proposals for universal healthcare were essentially dead on arrival, as lobbyists for the country's leagues of health insurance providers and profit-oriented health maintenance organizations pulled all the stops to annihilate the perceived threat to their guaranteed comfy money wells.

Republican opposition to the Democratic model of a "people first" government gained momentum in 1994 with the so-called "Contract with America," authored by then House Speaker Newt Gingrich and leaders of the Republican National Committee. In November of that year, the GOP swept both houses of Congress, dramatically limiting the Democrats' efforts to put a more social face on federal policies. The "contract" contained among other things important recommendations for welfare reform. By linking the issue of continued benefits with the aversion cultured, stirred, shaken, and shared by Reagan ideologues to the idea of lazy freeloaders thriving off of the taxes of hardworking Americans, the Republican spin on welfare took hold and became the socially presentable view. Congressional Republicans viewed the "Contract with America" as a popular mandate as far-reaching as the "Reagan Revolution" had been. The GOP's attack was more notable for the control it gained over the terms of public discourse than for the brakes it actually put on legislation. Republican leaders became experts at hogging the mikes in front of assembled media reps as they unleashed a relentless barrage of lingual programming with every thought and counter-thought beginning with "The American people..." The blanks in each case were completed with Republican ideas that had been temporarily mothballed during the period of initial enthusiasm for the Clinton programs. What is astonishing in light of such partisan rancor is that no one ever bothered to call them on the carpet for this mother of all generalizations, as Saddam might have put it.

Just as they had done in the build-up to the "Contract with America" revolution, the moneyed sources bloating the coffers of the Republican action committee (GOPAC) wasted no time in launching a full-scale attack behind the scenes of the centrist "liberals" in the White House. No pages, panties or dollars were left unturned as the pro-industry profiteers hooked up with guiltless evangelicals to send the "leftist" pack packing. And as if the Good Lord himself had suddenly answered their prayers, lo and behold back in the sticks of Arkansas was a feeding frenzy in the making. Republicans en bloc began licking their chops as "Whitewater" started to dominate media headlines. But unlike later schemes devised to demonstrate the existence of weapons of mass destruction on foreign soil, there was no easy hat trick to produce documents that would not readily be identified as fraudulent.

At the center of the Whitewater investigation were financial transactions related to the purchase of 220 acres of prime Ozark Mountain land in Northwest Arkansas, Wal-Mart territory. In 1978, while he was still attorney general of the state and she was a partner in the Rose Law Firm, Bill and Hillary Clinton teamed up with James and Susan McDougal to form the Whitewater Development Corporation. James McDougal then later became Arkansas director of economic development for a short while under the reins of Governor Bill Clinton in 1980. The partnership obtained loans for a little over $200,000 for the declared purpose of constructing tracts of vacation homes on the Ozark property, but the plans were ill conceived and the project ultimately floundered.

The McDougals went on to buy a small savings and loan called "Madison Guaranty" and hired the services of the Rose Law Firm to take care of the legal troubles brewing on the horizon as investigators examined financial contributions to Clinton's campaign for governor. Portions of these contributions had allegedly been taken from funds deposited by customers of Madison Guaranty. Like many other savings and loans at the time, the McDougal venture in lending was driven out of business by a series of bad investments, including the Whitewater land development project.

Shortly before Bill Clinton became president in 1993, the Federal Resolution Trust Corporation (RTC), ostensibly set up as a federal regulatory agency with oversight over S&L investment schemes, began investigating the financial records of Madison Guaranty on suspicion of fraudulent activity. During Clinton's campaign for the White House, the RTC, then headed by Republican Jay Stephens, forwarded a criminal referral implicating the Clintons in wrongdoing to the offices of the U.S. Attorney General. In 1994, the justice department's special counsel investigating Whitewater/Madison Guaranty, Robert Fiske, Jr., was replaced by none other than Kenneth Starr, the lawyer who had so gallantly defended General Motors in the lawsuits brought against the behemoth by the families of drivers and passengers who had burned in the crashes involving poorly designed GM cars. As discussed earlier in the previous chapter, GM had willingly concluded that it would be cheaper to pay off the death claims than to recall the cars in order to fix the design flaw. Kenneth Starr had done his dead-level best to prevent all the damaging documents against GM from ever seeing the light of day.

After years of intensive investigation costing in excess of $30 million in taxpayer money, the Republican inquisition against the Clintons had produced zilch. All arms of the investigation had turned up nothing in any way incriminating. That was all about to change, however, and Republican prayers were soon to be answered again as Mother Nature herself reminded the world of biology's most fundamental tenet: It's the testosterone, stupid!

With a total price tag of $47 million plus, the epochal tête-à-penis between Monica Lewinsky and Bill Clinton will likely go down in human annals as the most expensive and talked-about blow job ever. Whatever truths may ultimately be learned from the ins and outs of Ms. Lewinsky's comings and goings in the Oval Office, by the spring of 1999 the American public had overdosed on media coverage orchestrated to the fullest, courtesy of the moral vanguard of the GOP.

Who could forget the barrage of TV images of Monica? Her brunette mane had more bounce than a waterbed in a Bangkok brothel, virtually assuring her a career as a Clairol girl once her sure-to-be-in-the-making tell-all book sales dropped below profitability levels. And completely in sync: that unmistakable 1-800-dietplan buoyancy which overnight must have doubled the Dramamine sales among the nation's TV viewers following the endless replays of Monica's walks to and from waiting limos.

What does it say about any government agency—the White House in particular —which promotes young charmeurs of any sex into intimate accessibility to the most powerful, horniest people in the world with the ease with which Monica was able to bring the nation's hormonally challenged CEO to the brink of persona non grata? One can easily imagine the damage an entire harem of Al Qaeda-trained mouse-pad Mata Haris might inflict without ever firing a shot. Driven by a getting-to-the-top identity search and an age-old urge to wipe out the competition, this puppy of the Reagan years had reached the age of Machiavellian maturity, sexual and otherwise. Monica was basically following the tricks of the trade.

In the December 1998 issue of *George*, Gretchen Craft Rubin recommended what she had identified as the "Top Ten Ways To Win Power in D.C." The first rule advised lots and lots of social networking. No faulting Monica there. In the bat of an eye, this girl had managed to pick up the "buzz" (Rule 3) on all the major players in the White House, possibly some from the Pentagon as well. She was unfortunately sabotaged with Rule 4, which advised "working the phones":

"Hello, this is Linda Tripp speaking."

"Hi, Linda. It's Monica. Did you just hear something clicking?"

And one must fear that she must have taken Rule 6 (staying near to sources of power) and Rule 7 ("pucker up") somewhat too literally. It took Kenneth W. Starr's gentle encouragement and a few subpoenas to get her to follow the advice of Rule 9 to keep a sharp memory. And one wishes an act of God had prevented her from ever hearing those Nike commercial slogans (Rule 10): "Just do it!"

For his part, President William Jefferson Clinton was prost(r)ate proof of humanity's vulnerability to the irrational and erratic striking zone of testosterone. If a Yale graduate and Rhodes scholar can so easily and consistently give in to pangs of the groins, contrary to all prudence and logic, what hope is there of saving us from the whims of nuclear-armed Al Qaeda campers? When in the final analysis even the highest levels of power are contingent on a rationality that so easily succumbs to the edicts of the same drives that make the birds, bees, rats, and stray dogs so pitifully predictable, how dire is the human predicament? Where does it leave the fate of our planet, pray tell, when the omega question is decided by a long-term plan that keels over in the face of kneeling temptation?

What was the real essence of Monica's attraction to Bill? Surely not the person, but the Office and the accompanying keys to success, power, and fame ("I'm going to live forever..."). And what young girl would not feel flattered at being called into mandibular service by the Commander-in-Chief, for whom all rise? Even in the midst of smut, any common slut (male or female) must feel honored at the thought of going down in history as a pivotal focal point in the affairs of the most powerful nation in human history. After all, it wasn't as if Monica was caught performing fellatio on the Taco Bell Chihuahua. No, the setting was none other than the sitting president in the nation's First Address, and this was no anonymous surfer dude to be swallowed up in the jaws of a southern California siren, but the subject of "Hail to the Chief."

What is surprising is the fatal tactical move that ultimately brought Monica with impunity to her knees before the grand jury. Was it perhaps nothing but pride in her role as the ultimate seductress that made her blab to the mother of all confession booths, Linda Tripp? Had she really been in love with Bill and simultaneously equipped with all the necessary smarts to land her where she was, why risk it all in a telltale confession to a woman she could hardly consider her closest confidante? Was it simply a schoolgirl's infatuation with the number one jock that just had to be bragged about to the cheerleader on a summer camp outing? Or was it a calculated claim to fame as the First Temptress?

Taking into account the notoriety surrounding Monica and the extent to which her liaisons with Bill affected the wheels of government in general and the office of the president in particular, not to mention the millions in tax payers' money, we can well imagine that Monica will be given a unique place in American history, with stylish insets adorning the pages of high school history books for as long as books survive.

And then there was Bill. He will surely best be remembered for those famous lines uttered on national television on January 16, 1998. Not since the reign of the infamously maniacal Tricky Dick had conservative Americans witnessed anything so ignominious as the ceaseless accusations of improper affaires d'amour on the part of William Jefferson Clinton. From the revelations of intimate details regarding the unusual shape of his penis (perhaps the result of overuse?), to the highly partisan impeachment in the House of Representatives, the presidency of Bill Clinton was beset from the start with a certain horny-boy-from-Arkansas aura. Coupled with a down to-earth biscuits-'n'-gravy grin, Bill won over the hearts of many fine Americans, as evidenced by polls taken prior to presidential elections and subsequent to impeachment. Even moderate true-to-the-party-line Republican DARs caved in when it came to casting their votes for either a Dana Carvey look-alike or southern-fried-catfish tenderness. In more ways than one, Bill Clinton served to bring America's amusingly disturbed relationship to human sexuality to a head, so to speak. The boxer-shorts style openness with which Clinton transformed the traditionally stuffy Oval Office into a much-delayed playground of a sixties-style hippster's love pad could only have come from one who had been tempted but did not inhale (and Pascal talked about the course of historical contingencies in relation to Cleopatra's nose). The years of wanting to but abstaining suddenly erupted in scenes of midlife-critical hanky-panky fit for a *Forest Gump* sequel.

It could come as no surprise that this white-boy Othello should find himself on the receiving end of so many vilifying efforts by the more erotically challenged members of the conservative Christian militia, armed with chapter and verse. Enter: the prurient doyens of morality, special prosecutor Kenneth W. Starr, as the Hermes of debauchery in slow motion, aided by the most photogenic of the GOP's slew of moral apostles from both houses of Congress. Day by day, hour by hour, they filled the airwaves with expressions of "justified anger," contempt, disgust; this "vast right-wing conspiracy" invested ceaseless energy and money into the outrage campaign of lectures in morality, carefully orchestrated to get the balls rolling against the libertine liberals in government. Their masterpiece "father-knows-best" theater of carefully choreographed psychological warfare presented to the public a pious picture of wholesomeness in a Manichean struggle against evil personified. The hypnotically repetitive testimony of Washington's ethical pit bulls became such a pervasive part of mundane American experience that the nation's TV audience collectively switched over to a year-end *Best of Richard Simmon's Upper Thigh Workout Session* for relief.

On December 19, 1998, Bill Clinton became only the second president in American history to be impeached by the House for "crimes" committed while in office. In total, four articles of impeachment were brought against Mr. Clinton. According to Article 1, the president was said to have "willfully provided perjurious, false and misleading testimony" on August 17, 1998, in testifying before the grand jury presided over by Kenneth Starr, and to have lied about his prior false testimony in the Paula Corbin Jones sexual harassment lawsuit against him. This was originally the case involving Ms. Jones's charges of sexual harassment against Mr. Clinton as the then-governor of Arkansas. Article 2 charged that Mr. Clinton had "provided perjurious, false and mis leading testimony" in his written responses in December 1997 and during his taped testimony in January 1998 in the same case. Article 3 held that the president had "prevented, obstructed and impeded the administration of justice" in an attempt to "delay, impede, cover up and conceal the existence" of pertinent statements and testimony in the Paula Jones case. The last article of impeachment maintained that the president had willfully engaged in the "misuse and abuse" of the presidential office inasmuch as he had "refused and failed to respond to certain requests for admission" and deliberately gave "perjurious, false and misleading sworn" testimony in the impeachment inquiry.

Only Articles 1 and 3 were passed in an extremely partisan vote with 228 voting YES, 206 voting NO on Article 1, and with 221 YES as opposed to 212 NO votes on Article 3. Article 2 failed with a majority of 24 NO votes; Article 4 overwhelmingly went down to defeat with a majority of 137 NO votes.

At first glance it would seem to common sense that the president was guilty as charged, given the premises of impeachment and the evidence presented. Were his statements to the grand jury not the same car mechanic tactics he had used in his unforgettable January 26, 1998, nationally televised denial of sexual relations "with that woman, Ms. Lewinsky"? And how he had prepared for that denial: He had visibly rehearsed those clinched jaws of bitterness and that Rock-of-Gibraltar firmness to his countenance. His taut lips were practice-perfect for the role of victim; that scolding index finger cast in the role of baton as he hammered home his how-dare-you innocence. But then he had been caught and had had to come crawling back, sheepishly, to the American public in a televised mea culpa that enjoyed the same degree of success as the dinner party fart blamed on the dog.

And then came the granddaddy of them all: the televised grand jury testimony which only served to open up the scarred wounds that had hardly begun to heal with the American public. Who could forget the semantically slimy define-your-terms approach ("again, it's how you define 'alone'") to slipping out of the special prosecutor's below-the-belt questions? To the general public, it was deception flagrante delicto. Coupled with the cowardly semantic quibbling over the verb "be" in the third person singular and wrangling over body parts and the things that can be done with them (and people thought the blood drop count in the O.J. trial was hairsplitting.) Millions of the president's hard-boiled fans felt betrayed and disgusted. John McLaughlin of *The McLaughlin Group* called it "the lie of the decade, maybe the lie of the century." Clinton-friend and former White House Counsel Lanny Davis echoed those sentiments in his book, *Truth To Tell*, in which he related how perturbed and disappointed he had been at the president's reference to his answers in the Paula Jones deposition as "legally accurate." "That is talking like a lawyer, not like a president," Davis said in a televised interview.

Based on Mr. Clinton's past efforts and obvious success as a playboy, it would have been a no-brainer to side with Paula Jones in her civil suit against Mr. Clinton. At the time, few Americans would even have trusted the man to baby-sit the family Rottweiler. But there were far more complex issues involved at the heart of the entire impeachment process. According to Mr. Clinton's lawyers, his misleading or allegedly perjurious statements before the grand jury were given in response to questions that were not of a "material nature" in the Paula Jones case and therefore by definition not perjurious. With respect to the statements he made in his January 17, 1998, deposition concerning his relationships with Ms. Lewinsky, the president had had this to say: "These encounters [i.e., those that produced the famous stains on Monica's blue dress] did not consist of sexual intercourse. They did not constitute sexual relations as I understood that term to be defined at my January 17, 1998, deposition."

And how indeed had the president understood "sexual relations" to be defined? The actual definition used in the deposition read like this: "A person engages in sexual relations when the person knowingly engages in or causes contact with the genitalia, anus, groin, breast, inner thigh or buttocks of any person with an intent to arouse or gratify the sexual desire of any person."

The president's peculiarly literal interpretation of this definition of sexual relations is not that uncommon. Case in point: Many sexually active men from various Arab traditions would consider it the gravest affront to assume that they had had sex with a man, even if and when in the eyes of a European or American sexual intercourse had actually occurred. The respective vulgar words in Iraqi dialect for example connote the sexual behavior of each partner: *doudeki* signifies the passive (anal or oral) recipient (i.e. the homosexual), whereas the complementary *farakchi* is assumed to be a sexually active non-homosexual man who is not particularly fussy about where he sticks his penis, but who would never in his wildest dreams consider touching the pride and joy of the other man. And barring any shame these two might feel, both would admit that the passive partner had had sexual relations with the active partner, but not vice versa.[27] From the grand jury's view, however, it was Mr. Clinton's insistence that, given the definition of sexual relations used in the deposition, he had not in fact had sexual relations with Ms. Lewinsky, but she had had sexual relations with him, which drew a blank. From their perspective, the explanation ranked about as high on the credibility scale as stumper Hillary oy-vay Rodham's belated *bat mitzvah*. The definition cited was in fact the definition proposed, clarified, and agreed upon in the grand jury.

Who knows what went on behind those allegedly open doors in the Oval Office? Were the president's statements in his testimony evasive, incomplete, misleading? Definitely. That said, however, this was a legal battle in which legal technicalities were essential to winning, as is the case in a great many lawsuits around the country, and no separate special sets of laws could or should have been concocted for the particular fact that it was the President of the United States himself who was on trial. As many Washington Democrats chimed in: *Yes, the president is not above the law, but neither is he beneath the law.*

How did the nation arrive at this sad state of affairs that nearly brought the government to a halt? In a roundtable discussion on *Larry King Live*, Bob Woodward pretty well summed up the thoughts of the rest of the world: "This is going to go down in the history archives and people in a hundred years are going to look at it and they're going to say, 'What in the hell was going on in America? What were we doing? And why were we focusing on this?' It makes absolutely no sense."

The American people were surely not to be envied, having to make such a grandiose decision about the future of their most powerful and exceptionally popular chief executive based solely on the dearth of prose from *The Federalist Papers* concerning "treason, bribery and other high crimes and misdemeanors." In an inquiry of such magnitude the question necessarily forced itself on the investigative mind: Was the subject about which perjury was committed of any consequence legally, or pertinent to the issue of moral rectitude? Or is strict and unswerving adherence to truth under oath in a Kantian sense a conditio sine qua non for holding public office? Would lying about reasons for going to war against another country, costing thousands of innocent lives, be as egregious and impeachable as lying about sex with an office aide?

Speaking in a discussion round on CNN's *Larry King Live*, James Carville (the better half of D.C.'s most famous polit-commentary duo) had the best summary yet of the events surrounding the impeachment debacle: "This is nothing more than a grown man acting stupid with a young woman and not wanting anybody to find out about it. You can't elevate it to nothing above that. You can huff and puff and pontificate and everything else, but that's all it is." Sadly, the families of soldiers dropped in the dust of Iraq cannot say the same.

It was no accident that the Republican members of the House Impeachment Hearings came across as so many convened responses to a casting call for the leading role in *The Stepfather* sequels IV, V, and VI. So soft-spoken and concerned; so detailed; so orderly; so clean as to come naturally equipped with a Teflon-coated digestive tract. It is surely no accident that film and television have so often cast the ever-wholesome, mild-mannered do-gooder as the exemplary villain in documentaries profiling serial murderers. (The in-court confessions of the BTK killer—a long-time elder in his local church—fit right in with the pattern.) There is something quite chilling about the thought of checking into a Dobson-Starr Motel and finding a pleasantly mild-mannered human connoisseur of Fancy Feast at the reception. Lurking beneath the veils of piety are often the darkest of secrets. (And what self-respecting gay man would not have immediately identified Tom DeLay, Gary Bauer, and Trent Lott as, alas, "one of us"? And who except good old Larry Flynnt knew the real nature of Bob Livingsston's extramarital encounters?)

Of course the cunning of historical reason reached its ironic high point in none other than the *Republican* administration of George W. Bush. In 2006 and 2007, many of the GOP's own darkest skeletons started popping out of the closets faster than prisoners on fresh young flesh—all to the deep embarrassment of God's Own People. Florida Representative Mark Foley, deeply-good Christian Republican and former co-chair of the Congressional Caucus for Missing and Exploited Children, had been forced to resign as news of his history of penning sexually explicit emails to young *male* congressional pages became public. Another Republican senatorial do-gooder from Louisiana surfaced on the "escort service" client list of Ms. Deborah Jeane Palfrey. In a statement released to the Associated Press, the nice family father described his actions as "a very serious sin in my past for which I am, of course, completely responsible." Of course all's well that end's well as the Senator had "asked for and received forgiveness from God and [his] wife in confession and marriage counseling."

There was also the case of Representative Bob Allen, Republican of Merritt Island, Florida, who was charged with a second-degree misdemeanor for kindly offering to perform oral sex on an undercover *male* police officer for $20.00 (even in cases of illicit sex, Republicans tend to be outright tightwads.) And then of course there was the case of *I'm-not-gay!* Larry Craig, the nice Republican Senator from Idaho, who had pleaded guilty to disorderly conduct (*it all depends on how you define "disorderly"*) after his arrest in the toilet of the Minneapolis-St. Paul airport. Mr. Craig, too, was accused of soliciting sex from an undercover *male* police officer. (The devil must have made him do it.) And we haven't even touched on the whole slew of corruption scandals and lobbying misdeeds plaguing the Republican benches of both houses of Congress.

The moral of history's lessons: Beware of those that promise a return to moral integrity and vow to clean up the "filth" in society/politics. The louder the moral chants and rants against gays and lesbians, the deeper and darker the secrets they hide. But with Republicans monopolizing "morality" and the "Laws of God," all alternative interpretations of reality find themselves in the impossible position of opposing the Almighty. Sweating like a pew of small-town whores at mass, Democrats are perpetually caught with their pants down, forced to fess up to teaching the birds and the bees at Sunday school as it were, while publicly pressed to *say it ain't so*.

Whatever else may be said in superlative terms—and that is no small amount—about the most powerful and indeed most contradictory empire the world has ever known, it is a nation obsessed with a perceived link between sex and sin beyond any degree of normality. That an entire country could so consistently entertain such an adolescent preoccupation for over two hundred years is as astonishing as the orgasmic frenzy displayed by American boys when downing their first bottle of booze.

When a nation's laws and cultural climate provide for the expulsion of a six-year old from school because he kissed a classmate (who was even of the opposite sex) and for the arrest of an eleven-year-old Swiss boy on charges of attempted molestation because he helped his little sister pee, it becomes clear that the human forces upholding that status quo are purple-ripe for the Heaven's Gate crowd. With chaperones from the religious right leading the way, *quis custodiet custodes?*

Given the past (and present) history of Republican antics, it's safe to assume that in reality the forces instigating the first phase of America's own regime change had far more mundane things in mind that are best expressed in simple dollars and cents. The religious zealots from all the church pews were putty in the hands of those really pulling the strings. And pull they did.

By the late 1990s, even "the American people" had had enough of the relentless campaign by the GOP to inflict as much damage as possible on the Democratic base with *sex!* mud-slinging campaigns. Republican moderates feared losing momentum as the impeachment debacle began to wane. A number of pundits contended that the Republican Party, though fairly united in its fiscal conservative platform, was being torn apart at the seams on social issues such as abortion and gay rights (enlightenment is possible now and then even among Republicans). Sensing a shift in public sentiment, the party power apparatus came up with an entirely new hat trick to win back support: "Compassionate Conservatism"—one of the wiliest ploys ever crafted in modern political weaponry.

With the sympathy-evoking imagery of Bambi at the slaughterhouse, then-governor of New Jersey Christine Todd-Whitman and John Rowland of Connecticut humbled themselves before the eyes of the cameras, confessing that "many Americans right now have an impression of the Republican Party that's mean-spirited, vindictive." (*Whatever gave them that idea?*) John Rowland added that GOP leaders had "done terrible damage, because ... we've developed a laundry list of people that we're against"—including, as he failed to add, anyone in a sub-million income bracket and all those who still believe Jesus was sober and serious when he delivered the "Sermon on the Mount."

Quite a confession coming from card-carrying members of a group that still expects to see the countenance of Ronnie chiseled into Mt. Rushmore. Even the dourest and direst of Republican big shots joined the extreme makeover of the party's public image, reaching at times climactic peaks. On July 24, 1998, Capitol police officers Jacob J. Chestnut and John Gibson were fatally shot in the line of duty by a deranged mental patient from Montana. Expressions of sympathy for the families went out from all branches of government and from the general populace. For GOP leaders, this was a camera-ready moment that lent itself as the perfect backdrop to reinforce the message of Republican compassion. Dick Armey and Newt Gingrich, visibly ravaged by studied grief, took the lead in front of assembled cameras. With quivering chins and touching sobs of photogenic sorrow (one wonders how long they practiced), they hardly looked the part of the legislators who had hammered through the Scrooge laws designed to reduce benefits to the poor.

No moment of national concern was left un-grieved by the Republican spin machine as the party focused on regaining the hearts and minds it had lost through what the public had begun to perceive as "mean-spiritedness." The GOP response to Clinton's State of the Union message of January 20, 1999, provided as yet another wonderful photo-op to spin the record straight. Unlike the master curmudgeons of the House Impeachment Hearings, new, younger, dynamic PR reps took the stage as veritable geysers of positive self-reliance. On this particular evening it was House members Jennifer Dunn of Washington, accompanied by Steve Largent (Oklahoma), an imposingly positive All-American jock who had won the trust of his constituents through his tackle and touchdown prowess. Carefully silhouetted against the pearlescent Capitol dome, they beamed with pristine WASPy purity and sanctity. Not since the tandem Gerber-Baby duo of Affleck and Damon on Oscar night had the country experienced this kind of double-dosed preppy peppiness. Alas, hidden beneath the layers of compassion and all the catchy feel-good phrases ("I'm a gardener ...") was the heart of the message: *tax cuts*—the universal mantra of the Grand Old Party. A clear case of wolverine intentions clothed in sheep's innocence. With so many taxpayer dollars at stake and corporate interests standing to reap untold rewards in the next election, the Republican power brokers set to work on retaking government by hook and by crook. The outcome is known to all.

Notes

1 Immigration became a heatedly debated issue in the House in December of 2005, with the two factions of Republicans described here opposing each other over the issue of border security and a Bush-backed guest worker program. See Jeffrey H. Birnbaum's article "Immigration Pushes Apart GOP, Chamber," in the *Washington Post*, 14 December 2005, A01.

2 Two of the most informative books on the political-economic forces at work during the Reagan era are: Kevin Phillips, *The Politics of Rich and Poor. Wealth and the American Electorate in the Reagan Aftermath* (New York: Random House, 1990) and Michel Albert, *Capitalism vs. Capitalism. How America's Obsession with Individual Achievement and Short-Term Profit Has Led It to the Brink of Collapse* (New York: Four Walls Eight Windows, 1993). An important contribution that addresses the continuation of these policies in subsequent Republican administrations is found in Robert Reich, *Supercapitalism: The Transformation of Business, Democracy, and Everyday Life* (New York: Alfred A. Knopf, 2007).

3 Kevin Phillips, *The Politics of Rich and Poor*, 78 and *passim*.

4 By comparison, from 1979 to 1990 Sweden's marginal individual tax rates went from 87 to 65 percent, France's from 60 to 53 percent, Japan's from 75 to 50 percent, and Germany's from 56 to 53 percent.

5 Several books on supply-side theory and implied public policy attained near-cult status within the Reagan administration and its associated conservative think tanks. See in particular the highly influential work of Jude Wanniski, *The Way the World Works* (1978) (Washington, DC.: Regnery Publishing, Inc., 1998), acclaimed by arch-conservative Robert Novak as one of the two most important political tracts to appear after World War II. See also George Gilder, *Wealth and Poverty* (1981) (Oakland, California: ICS Press, 1993) and Charles Murray, *Losing Ground* (1986) (New York: Perseus Publishing, 1995).

6 William Greider, *Secrets of the Temple* (New York: Simon & Schuster, 1987) 401.

7 An extensive analysis of the pros and cons of forced deregulation in telecommunications was conducted by Richard S. Higgins and Paul H. Rubin, *Deregulating Telecommunication* (West Sussex, England: John Wiley & Sons Ltd., 1995). See also the account of AT&T's battles through the court system and its struggles against antitrust accusations by rivals such as MCI in Alan Stone, *Wrong Number: The Breakup of AT&T* (New York: Basic Books, 1989).

8 Source: *Economic Research and Data*, Federal Reserve Board of San Francisco Economic Letter 2002-01; January 18, 2002.

9 *Ibid*.

10 All findings cited are taken from the NTSB report: *Aircraft Accident Report*. Loss of Control and Impact with Pacific Ocean Alaska Airlines Flight 261 McDonnell Douglas MD-83, N963AS About 2.7 Miles North of Anacapa Island, California, January 31, 2000. NTSB Number AAR-02/01; NTIS Number PB2002-910402. The full report is available at: http://www.ntsb.gov/publictn/2002/AAR0201.htm.

11 *Ibid*.

12 Val Zavala, "Life and Times," (November 4, 2004) KCET Los Angeles.

13 Of particular interest in this context is Friedman's *Capitalism and Freedom* (1962) (Chicago: University of Chicago Press, 2002).

14 See Gordon M. Fisher, "The Development and History of the Poverty Thresholds," *Social Security Bulletin*, vol. 55, no. 4, Winter 1992, pp. 3–14. Only slight changes have been made over the years, with adjustments calculated in accordance with the increases in the Consumer Price Index. In 1981 the government even reduced the 124 types of thresholds considered under the original poverty calculation scheme to just forty-eight. During the Reagan administration, however, the definition of what constituted poverty retained the most conservative figures in use. Ms. Orshansky had based her original calculations on a low-cost food plan for a family of four, which at the time was a major cost factor (roughly thirty-three percent) of a lower-income household budget. Over the decades, cost ratios have shifted dramatically so that transportation, medical treatment, and rent now constitute the bulk of the financial burden on low-income families. This would in turn necessitate an entirely new cost-poverty threshold analysis. Needless to say, Republicans have often claimed that such a necessary revision is nothing but an attempt by "bleeding-heart liberals" to raise the actual official federal figures for the poverty threshold. The 2003 official level for a family of four was merely $18,660. Accordingly, a four-member family earning $19,000 would not have fallen under the poverty line.

15 Peter Dreier, "Urban Suffering Grew Under Reagan," *Newsday*, 10 June 2004.

16 Cf. Richard Stubbing, "The Defense Program: Buildup or Binge?" *Foreign Affairs*, Spring 1985, and idem with Richard A. Mendel, *The Defense Game* (New York: Bessie/Harper & Row, 1986).

17 See "New Doubts and Cast on CIA's Soviet Analyses," *Philadelphia Inquirer*, 10 March 2001, A01.

18 Earl C. Ravenal, "Reagan's 1983 Defense Budget: An Analysis and an Alternative," *Policy Analysis*, no. 10, April 30, 1982.

19 This was reportedly the largest viewing audience for any TV-movie up to that time.

20 Several sources offer intriguing portraits of Mr. Carlucci and his pull among global bigwigs. See in particular Dan Briody, *The Iron Triangle. Inside the Secret World of the Carlyle Group* (Hoboken, New Jersey: John Wiley & Sons, Inc., 2003) 22–30; Tim Shorrock, "Company Man," *The Nation*, 14 March 2002.

21 Stephen R. Weissman's research into U.S. involvement in the assassination concludes that at the least the U. S. government was a willing by-stander. Under Eisenhower's directive and the CIA's "Project Wizard," plans were drawn up to have Lumumba forcibly removed from office and replaced with pro-Western Mobutu Sese Seko. According to Weissman, because the U.S. was afraid of Lumumba's possible return to power, the National Security Council's Special Group authorized CIA intervention through arms provisions to anti Lumumba/pro-Mobutu forces. See Stephen R. Weissman, "Opening the Secret Files on Lumumba's Murder," *Washington Post*, 21 July 2002, B03, and id., *American Foreign Policy in the Congo, 1960–1964* (Ithaca, New York: Cornell University Press, 1974).

22 See Joanne Laurier, "'Carlucci' bleeped from HBO version of Lumumba," World Socialist Web Site, http://www.wsws.org/articles/2002/mar2002/carl m15_prn.shtml.

23 David Lazarus, "A Firm in Position to Profit," *San Francisco Chronicle*, 21 March 2004, J-1.

24 See in particular, Dan Briody, *The Iron Triangle. Inside the Secret World of the Carlyle Group, supra*, as well as Greg Palast, *The Best Democracy Money Can Buy* (New York and London: Plume/The Penguin Group, 2002) 104–105.

25 "Why the Invasion Was Justified," *New York Times*, 12 December 1989, A3.

26 For a closer look at the history of the U.S.–Panama conflict see Eytan Gilboa, "The Panama Invasion Revisited: Lessons for the Use of Force in the Post Cold War Era," *Political Science Quarterly*, vol. 110, no. 4 (Winter 1995/1996): 539 – 564. See also "Democratic Peace and Covert War: A Case Study of the U.S. Covert War in Chile," *Journal of International and Area Studies*, Seoul National University, vol. 12, no. 1 (June 2005): 25–48.

27 In January 1999 none other than the *Journal of the American Medical Association* revealed that research conducted in 1991 by the Kinsey Institute for Research in Sex, Gender and Reproduction had shown that 60 percent of the 599 students interviewed at a university in the Midwest believed, like the president, that engaging in oral sex was not considered "having sex." The American Medical Association, not renowned as a cabal of the left, promptly fired the seventeen-year veteran editor of *JAMA*, Dr. George Lundberg, in a coup de grace. The publication of the research had coincided with the Senate impeachment trial against the president.

Chapter 6

The Evil of Banality:
Corporate Greed And Bush Forty-Three

> The magnetic power exerted by patently threadbare ideologies is to be
> explained, beyond psychology, by the objectively determined decay of
> logical evidence as such. Things have come to a pass where lying
> sounds like truth, truth like lying. Each statement, each piece of news,
> each thought has been preformed by the centers of the culture industry.
> —Theodor W. Adorno, *Minima Moralia*

HISTORY'S TURNING POINTS ARE ROUTINELY judged more severely by those
who live through them than by those privileged to read about the gulps and chokes
from a distance. Only posterity will know whether this tendency will also apply to
the "presidency" of George W. Bush. To be sure, few leaders in world history have
elicited such obsequious adulation on the one hand, utter loathing on the other.

To anyone paying halfway decent attention to the news and commentaries
toward the end of 1999 and throughout much of campaign year 2000, it should
have become readily apparent that for some odd reason George W. Bush was the
media sweetheart who could do no wrong. It was as if the public was being "out-
foxed" by a massive PR machine that had taken control of news anchors' faces,
gestures, word choice, and sentence intonation. Had the invisible hands of campaign support given behind-the-scenes instructions on how to make George W
look good, plausible, trustworthy, and electable? While portraying rival Al Goré as
a special breed of tree-hugging liberal who was at best out of touch with "the
American people," at worst a continuation of the "immoral" policies of the previous occupant of the Oval Office. The daily rounds of political punditry allowed anchors visibly to perk up with interest when discussing the sundry "solutions"

being proffered by the Rove campaign. At the same time, many of Gore's speeches and proposals were accompanied with subtle but effective glances of boredom, bewilderment, and skepticism, segued with suggestive questions such as, *Will the American people be able to 'warm up' to Mr. Gore, who has often been criticized as wooden and boring?* To be sure, to the astute observer the message should have been clear that by the summer of 2000, George W. Bush had already been appointed to the White House, long before the actual election in November.

Those lucky enough to have been observing the spectacle secondhand from abroad found themselves merely having to cope with the unseemly physiognomy and gestures of the nation's chosen *primus inter pares*. Mr. Bush stepped onto the global political scene with a practiced swagger and a smirk befitting the proud victor of a late-night frat-house masturbation contest, completely devoid of the *gravitas* of a world leader. And as is typical of mainstream American political discourse, media pundits collectively caught on to a working byline that seemed to become more popular (and hence "truer") every time it was uttered: *Mr. Bush was just the kind of guy you'd wanna go out and have a beer with*, meaning in the land of Disneyland governors and pink taffeta Eiffel Towers that he was just right for the job. The simple-minded, straight-shootin', kick-back, down-home kind of a guy.

The Republican 2000 sweep of both the executive and legislative branches of government sent a shock wave around the world. From the outset the pro-business/anti labor/anti-intellectual agenda of the Bush team proceeded to dismantle the scarcely existing social safety net, restrict regulatory measures designed to keep in check industry's inner urge to "dump" on the environment, and deal out a governmental carte blanche to the energy sector's efforts to redefine profit on its own unregulated terms, while opening up sources previously dreamed of but declared "off base" thanks to geopolitical *realpolitik*.

What ultimately ensued was a debacle destined to rob the United States of America—that self-proclaimed beacon of divine providence and champion of democracy and human rights on foreign shores—of virtually all credibility and dignity on the global stage. If history has looked on the plots and crimes of Republican Richard Nixon as the "dirty tricks" of a semi-demented, paranoid mind, what would it call the cleanly planned and purposefully executed usurpation of governmental power by the concerted efforts of a cabal of Republican insider boys with rich and powerful friends (not to forget family), in all the right places? The "election" of November 2000 was no mere glitch, but rather the appointment into power of a thoroughly pro-business regime hell-bent on rewriting the geopolitical landscape. Much points to the same being true in a repeat performance in 2004.

How convenient it was for front-running media darling George W. Bush to have his blood brother Jeb calling all the shots from his "Flamingo Road" governor's office in Tallahassee, Florida. Did the people seriously expect "fair and balanced" treatment of the opponents? To the millions of innocent TV viewers around the world who had an unsettling inkling of just how much was riding on the outcome of this election, the events unfolding across America on that fateful day in November of 2000 seemed to show a neck-and-neck race to the finish. Audiences around the world had learned of the deep divisions rupturing beneath the surface of hushed income disparity in the wealthiest of nations. As was the case throughout much of the country's history from the time of the Second Great Awakening, a religious/cultural schism pitted enlightened urban cosmopolitanism against the self-proclaimed servants of God called out by the pulpits to appoint the Anointed One to the helm. From the religious perspective, this election was nothing short of a showdown between Good and Evil, a Manichean war whose first battle was determined at the ballot box.

Little did anyone suspect that the terms of this decision had already been tilted way to the Right months before the candidates had paid off their final stumpers. Thanks to the dedicated persistent work of Greg Palast, the world learned a number of deeply disturbing facts surrounding Mr. Bush's "triumph" at the polls—facts that should (and in lesser respected countries perhaps would) have annulled the results.

The scheme to assure a "fair and balanced" election was brilliantly conceived and executed. Florida Secretary of State and Bush-family faun Katherine Harris negotiated a clever contract with Database Technologies, now a subdivision of ChoicePoint of Atlanta, Georgia. The $4 million no-bid contract (a *de rigueur* practice in the Bush "presidency") handed Database Technologies the responsibility for "cleaning up" the pool of potential registered voters in Florida by "scrubbing" all felons (and former felons) from the lists of eligible voters. It should be noted that there were other companies equally capable of completing "the task" at far less expense to taxpayers,[1] but as ChoicePoint's continued cozy history with the Bush government has shown, there was a—shall we say "very special"—relationship at work here. The significantly higher fee was allegedly required to ensure that all the names ultimately scrubbed from the voter lists were indeed ineligible to vote. In April of 2001, Cynthia McKinney (Congresswoman from Georgia) convened a special hearing to investigate the allegations that Database Technologies on orders from the state of Florida had purged the voter rolls of thousands of legitimate—and "coincidentally" Democratic—voters. Company testimony before the hearing pointed the finger directly at Florida state officials who at one time had insisted that Database Technologies eliminate voters whose names were an eighty percent match with those of convicted felons. The company reasoned that thousands of eligible voters would needlessly and illegally be eliminated in the process. According to Palast's account of the proceedings, ChoicePoint vice president James Lee testified

> ...that the rules for creating the [purge] list would mean a significant number of people who were not deceased, not registered in more than one county or not a felon would be included on the list. Likewise, DTB made suggestions to reduce the numbers of eligible voters included on the list.[2]

Faced with the legal and moral dilemma, DBT apparently pondered different solutions to fix the conundrum. But Florida, "says DBT, told the company, *Forget about it.*"[3]

Truly outrageous are the types of concrete examples Greg Palast and his team of investigative journalists uncovered. Not only were potential voters eliminated whose names were similar, read in either direction (i.e. both "John Paul" and "Paul John"), but also voters whose "crimes" *had not even been committed yet.* Such was the case with Thomas Cooper, black male, age twenty-eight, who "was" convicted of a felony in the state of Ohio in 2007, in other words six years into the future.[4] Moreover, at variance with Florida state law as clarified by the state supreme court, Jeb Bush's office was requiring all voters who had ever been convicted of felonies in other states, even if their voting rights had been restored, to maneuver their way through an impossible Kafkaesque maze of request forms and verification documents to prove their renewed eligibility to vote in Florida.

One might rightly ask: *How could the state of Florida know which voters to eliminate in order to ensure that the final tally went in favor of brother George W?* This was the easiest obstacle of all to surmount. Just get rid of as many African-American voters as possible. Historically, blacks vote overwhelmingly for the Democratic Party candidates. And here the procedure was made all the easier by the fact that Florida identified all voters by race. By virtue of the authority vested in her as Secretary of State, Ms. Harris proudly declared George W. Bush the take-all winner of the 2000 presidential election in the state of Florida. By a whopping 537 votes.

The Democrats, in what appeared to be a half-hearted effort to salvage what they could, seemed publicly bewildered by the cards stacked against them. They began an arduous process of recounting the votes while at the same time seeking court injunctions to force manual examinations of the chads and otherwise questionable ballots. From the viewpoint of Bush supporters, the choice of James Baker III (of the Carlyle Group) for the task of overseeing the vote recount was a wise one. His grandfatherly serene demeanor; his smooth bedside voice and manner; the appearance of unflappable fairness, all coalesced to create the media-savvy persona of an honest, impartial, do-gooder everyone implicitly trusted. Baker's painful projection of "fairness" was backed up by a tactic that proved incredibly successful as he hammered home the message of "concern" in front of the nation's TV audiences:

> Let me begin by repeating what I said yesterday: The vote in Florida has been counted, and the vote in Florida has been recounted. Governor George W. Bush was the winner of the vote, and he was also the winner of the recount. Based on these results, we urge the Gore campaign to accept the finality of the election, subject, of course, to the counting of the absentee, the overseas absentee, ballots, in accordance with the law. They obviously have decided instead to proceed with yet a third count of votes in a number of prominently Democratic counties. This course of action is regrettable. Moreover, in recent days, supporters of our opponents have filed a number of lawsuits—at least eight, by last count—challenging, in different ways, the results of the election.
>
> I said yesterday that we would vigorously oppose the Gore campaign's efforts to keep recounting until it likes the result. And therefore, this morning we have asked the United States District Court for the Southern District of Florida to preserve the integrity and the consistency and the equality and finality of the most important civic action that Americans take: their votes in an election for president of the United States. We feel we have no other choice...
>
> Machines are neither Republicans nor Democrats, and therefore can be neither consciously nor unconsciously biased...Therefore, we ask that there be no further recounts of already recounted ballots...At some point...Florida's voters, and indeed all Americans, are entitled to some finality in the election process...We urge our opponents to join us, join with us in accepting the recounted vote of the people of Florida.

The real truth was left to investigators to determine once the black-robed justices of the Supreme Court had "examined" the case, coming down unsurprisingly (and along predictable lines) in a five—four ruling on the side of George W. Bush. Of course no one would ever think that any closer ties between a justice or two on the bench, who may just have happened to be a hunting buddy of one of the candidates in the contested election could possibly have had any impact on the decision. *Heavens no! This isn't Cuba, Russia, or Venezuela!*

Florida's purge of eligible voters had indeed paid off in the most blatant and far-reaching example of manipulation in American history. The Database Technology programs alone had ousted 94,000 Florida voters—nearly all of them African-American Democrats—from the political process. Not even 3,000 of these were in fact ineligible. Voting machines in predominantly black counties swallowed up incorrectly completed ballots without notifying the voter that the ballot would not register properly. In upper-middle-class white strongholds, heavily Republican by bank account, erroneously completed ballots were ejected automatically, thereby signaling to the voter to do it again correctly. Another staggering 179,855 votes —the vast majority of which yet again were located in Democratic-heavy constituencies—were simply not counted. One can only guess how many more were flushed down the sewers or conveniently thrown in with the swamp gators. *And the USA assumes for itself the "right" to "monitor" elections in other so-called "banana republics"?*

The newly *appointed* "president" had a clear and simple agenda: turn the responsibilities of government over to corporations; let "the markets" take care of everything by both setting short- and long-term objectives and choosing the easiest, most cost-effective means of accomplishing those goals.

Now the primary purpose of any American-style corporation is to earn profit —fill the coffers of the shareholders by increasing the market value of the company and its assets, and the happy campers will reward the CEO and his/her entourage with impressive bonuses, perks, compensation and retirement packages. "Oilman" that he was, George W. Bush had developed a special fondness for the "concerns" and "needs" of the energy sector, and they gladly reciprocated by giving generously not only to the president's election campaign, but to every Republican (and many Democrats) in any way connected to Washington. Of particular concern to the oil and energy giants was that they not be hampered by vexing regulations related to exploration to discover new deposits of oil and natural gas, and that they not be encumbered by environmental laws requiring caution about what they release into the environment.

Even if candidate G. W. Bush had been as mum about his true intentions as "President" Bush proved to be about revealing the factors and interests influencing his administration's policies (and those of his VP), the list of campaign donors (i.e. the business interests) who appointed the nation's drinking-buddy poster boy into the highchair of power could have given a fairly accurate assessment of where the country was headed. Compiled from data released by the Federal Election Commission, the list of top contributors was published by the non-partisan Center for Responsive Politics and by the Center for Public Integrity.[5] The list of contributors reads like a *Who's Who* in class warfare, with labor unions and associations such as the American Federation of State, Country, Municipal Employees (biggest contributor to the Democrats); the International Brotherhood of Electrical Workers; the Communication Workers of America; the Service Employees International Union; the Carpenters & Joiners Union; the American Federation of Teachers; the National Education Association; United Auto Workers; the Machinists/Aerospace Workers Union; and the Teamsters Union, all solidly behind Democratic Party candidate Al Gore. (In spite of themselves, people often do recognize which side their bread is buttered on.) The total tally from these millions of nickels and dimes in tips and minimum wage jobs worked out to be $132,804,039.

Concentrated in the highest echelons of American society were the forces of Big Money, flicked over to the Bush team on behalf of petroleum/energy giants ($1,889,206); financial institutions ($1,327,131); insurance corporations ($1,644,662); and health "professionals" ($2,813,933). All told, Big Business put together the stately sum of $185,921,855 in support of the GOP's bring-'em-on top gun.

Not surprisingly, with so much to gain in profit from an administration averse to government interference in price controls (and cheap imports from neighboring countries), the pharmaceutical industries contributed the bulk of their funds to the Republicans as well (Pfizer gave eighty-five percent of its $2,472,166 in contributions and Bristal-Myers Squibb donated eighty-seven percent of its $2,364,412 to the GOP.) GlaxoSmith-Kline and Eli Lilly & Co. were also "blinded by the right" with eighty-six and eighty percent respectively of their contributions channeled into the GOP pot.[6]

Quite interesting from the environmental angle as well as from the geopolitical perspective is the influence exerted by the oil and energy industry. According to figures released by the Center for Public Integrity, oil and energy corporations spent a staggering $381,228,935 on lobbying activities from 1998 through 2003, all with the explicit purpose of seeing legislation passed that would deal the best monetary hand to the corporations behind the numbers, which when broken down into a "top ten" list looks like this: 1. ExxonMobil Corp: $55,897,742; 2. Chevron Texaco Corp: $32,465,770; 3. Marathon Oil Corp: $29,154,000; 4. BP Plc: $28,414,646; 5. Royal Dutch Petroleum Co: $26,770,768; 6. American Petroleum Institute: $20,120,630; 7. Entergy Corp: $15,757,504; 8. Enron Corp: $15,615,000; 9. Occidental Petroleum Corp: $12,647,436; 10. Unocal Corp: $10,810,000.

One important energy giant strategically missing from this list of ghostwriters of American law is Koch Industries, "the biggest company you've never heard of—and their owners like it that way."[7] The company's recent history also offers a textbook lesson on how Big Business runs the country. With yearly earnings routinely exceeding those of Microsoft, this quiet little family-owned company based in Wichita, Kansas, is a high-rolling power player in global politics, and a substantial contributor to Republican coffers. But its "chief political influence tool is a web of interconnected, right-wing think tanks and advocacy groups" such as the Cato Institute (co-founded by Charles Koch), the Federalist Society (newly-appointed Supreme Court Chief Justice John Roberts is a member), Citizens for a Sound Economy, and the Reason Foundation. Common to all are Koch family values: laissez-faire economics with an absolute minimum of public oversight.

All the King's Horses

As former CEO of Halliburton, now infamous for the $1.7 billion no-bid contracts it was awarded in Iraq (to the—shall we say "less than complete satisfaction"—of the Iraqi people), Dick Cheney was basically a petroleum industry insider metamorphosed into the role of Vice President and dangerous part-time duck hunter. Just days after taking the reins in Washington, Cheney convened an "energy task force" (officially known as the "National Energy Policy Development Group") to map out the country's energy policies for the next century. The semantics of the phrase surely led unsuspecting readers at the time to imagine all kinds of sensible, responsible activities taking place in a serious effort to solve the country's mounting energy needs without killing beast, fish, and fowl in the process.

Not so. In fact, the "task force" was essentially charged with crafting a sound energy policy to fulfill the wish lists of industry giants themselves. As revealed in an energy department email obtained by Judicial Watch, the Bush administration was in effect sending out open invitations to industry lobbyists.[8] With the subject heading "national energy policy," the email from the desk of senior department adviser Joseph Kelliher to industry rep Dana Contratto asked point blank: "If you were King, or Il Duce, what would you include in a national policy, especially with respect to natural gas issues?"[9] Conservative lobbyists and corporate CEOs were ecstatic at the prospect of finally being able to write legislation that would put billions into the pockets of shareholders.[10] They could also make sure that past crimes against nature were justly punished with a nice little slap on the wrist.

The *Wall Street Journal* had commented several months prior to the 2000 election that all the big oil companies generously funding the Bush campaign would indeed expect a type of *quid pro quo* from a Bush presidency. The paper also noted that Enron, "whose executives have been Mr. Bush's most reliable supporters throughout his political career, will have a special pull on a President Bush's affections."[11] Indeed they did. As outlined by Carl Pope and Paul Rauber,[12] Enron's efforts to manipulate the price and availability of electricity in California—a move that brought the nation's largest state to its knees in terms of both lost production and net financial loss—had relied on the corporation's successful strategy within the Cheney task force of blocking proposals for the modernization of transmission lines. The Bush-Cheney scheme sided with Enron's carefully crafted design to delay implementation of digital switches in the power grid structure. Even after the most widespread total power outage in American history, the Bush administration chose to make grid modernization contingent on passage of legislative provisions favorable to the petroleum and energy conglomerates.

And the energy/petroleum sectors had far more irons in the fire than just Dick Cheney. Another key player in industry's first line of offense within the Bush administration was John Graham, famous for his cost-benefit algorithms to determine whether it was worth it for companies to install this or that safety measure to protect public health and safety. Graham's calculations logically became the bible of big polluters. During his tenure as head of the Harvard Center for Risk Analysis, Graham's name became associated with studies funded by such corporate giants as General Electric, Exxon, Monsanto, and Union Carbide (a name that still strikes fear in the residents of Bhopal, India, because of the 1984 dioxin catastrophe there). One such Graham study was produced at a time when various states and municipalities[13] across the country were considering bans on the use of cell phones by drivers. Generously funded by none other than AT&T Wireless Communications, Graham's study predictably concluded that the estimated increase in fatal accidents resulting from drivers' use of phones behind the wheel was conveniently offset by the productivity gains achieved through staying connected.[14]

During nomination hearings before the House Subcommittee on Energy Policy, Natural Resources, and Regulatory Affairs/Committee on Government Reform (March 12, 2002), Professor Lisa Heinzerling exposed many of the serious statistical anomalies and methodological flaws found in Graham's work. In Heinzerling's view, Graham had been using "his research on life-saving costs in arguing for a major restructuring of our regulatory system. And he has reserved a special disfavor for environmentally protective programs."[15] As other leading critics have pointed out, the types of cost-benefit analyses used by Graham and his team consistently over-inflated the "estimated costs" of implementing certain types of safety measures for the protection of workers or clean-up procedures to decontaminate a toxic site. Heinzerling cited Graham's use of a cost estimate of $99 billion "per year of life saved" to control chloroform released from paper mills. This enormous sum was included in Graham's list of expensive life-saving interventions for its shock effect, i.e., to cast a prohibitive shadow of economic infeasibility on environmental regulatory intervention per se. The problem with Graham's example of chloroform control at paper mills is that the intervention had never even been proposed by anyone.[16] Graham had also come out against government regulation of dioxin emissions since statistical analyses had put the risk of developing cancer from dioxin exposure at one person per one hundred, or at about the same risk of dying in a car accident, "and was thus 'normal'."[17]

The Republicans (with no large protest from the "opposition") ushered John Graham through the confirmation hearings into his new position as director of the Office of Information and Regulatory Affairs (OIRA), a department within the Office of Management and Budget. Robert F. Kennedy, Jr., described the office as perhaps the "most antidemocratic institution in government."[18] Though somewhat obscured from public view, the control exerted by OIRA "can profoundly affect the nation's health, safety, and environmental safeguards—unimpeded by public debate or accountability," as Kennedy put it.[19] From the economic standpoint of the petroleum, chemical, and energy industries, the Bush administration couldn't have chosen a more anti-environment, pro-business advocate to lead the office.

Other industry team leaders included property rights zealot Gale Norton, Secretary of the Interior at the time, who publicly dreamed of one day establishing a "home steading right to pollute."[20] Norton's partner in watching out for the state of our public lands and treasured wilderness reserves was J. Steven Griles, a former major lobbyist for petroleum and energy companies.[21] According to Kennedy, Bush's baby-faced "boyhood genius" campaign manager, who knew precisely when and how to dig up Texas dung and spread it, was still invested in Enron stock to the tune of $250,000 at the very same time the administration was working on its new energy policy.[22] Lewis Libby, later indicted and convicted for the less than truthful statements he made in the investigation of events surrounding the disclosure of Valerie Plame as a CIA operative, was Dick Cheney's chief of staff and privy to virtually all the ins and out's at energy task force meetings. During his tenure as lawyer, Libby "sold tens of thousands of dollars' worth of stocks in Enron, ExxonMobil, Texaco, and Chesapeake Energy."[23] George W. Bush's number two woman, Condoleeza Rice, who became national security adviser and subsequently secretary of state, had served on the board of directors at Chevron for years. Former chief economist at ExxonMobil, Kathleen Cooper, was chosen by the Bush team as undersecretary of commerce for economic affairs.

With all the king's horses in office, one piece of the energy policy puzzle after the next began falling into place—to the full satisfaction of the coal, oil, gas, chemical, and pharmaceutical industries.[24] After months of secret bargaining the Report of the National Energy Policy Development Group was finally released in May 2001. It was nothing more than "an orgy of industry plunder, transferring billions of dollars of public wealth to the oil, coal, and nuclear industries, which were already swimming in record revenues."[25] The *quid pro quo* legislation was so blatantly pro-industry that environmentalists sounded the alarm. Joining in on the alert was none other than the independent General Accounting Office, which sued the Department of Energy to force open the task force's secret files. On similar grounds, both the Sierra Club and Judicial Watch litigated against Cheney's group through the Federal Advisory Committee Act (FACA), which had stipulated that governmental bodies that make use of officials outside of government must allow full public access to all their transactions.

The first court ruling came from the gavel of U.S. District Court Judge John Bates, who sided with Cheney's separation of powers argument and concluded that the GAO did not have sufficient reason to force the Cheney task force to open up their records. It should be noted that Judge Bates had diligently served the interests of Independent Counsel Kenneth Starr's investigation of the Clintons and was himself a Bush judicial appointee—not that anyone would ever suspect bias of course. Media reports hinted that the GOP-dominated Appropriations Committee had threatened to hack off substantial amounts of the GAO budget if it insisted on pursuing the case. Whatever the truth may have been, the GAO fell in line with Republican wishes, with a few demonstrative whimpers from the "opposition." Judicial Watch and the Sierra Club were successful in their suits in the U.S. District Court (the presiding judge was the Reagan appointee Emmet Sullivan.) The Cheney forces appealed the decision, forcing the issue into the U.S. Court of Appeals. There, too, Cheney drew the shorter stick, forcing the executive-industrial alliance to appeal to the U.S. Supreme Court. Despite widespread pleas and commentaries from many of the country's leading intellectuals and political strategists (including some from the GOP itself), Cheney hunting buddy Justice Antonin Scalia categorically refused to recuse himself from the case. Writing for *Slate.com*, Dahlia Lithwick described (March 14, 2004) Scalia's twenty-one-page "Je refuse!" memorandum as "a shabby, echoey voice emerging from behind the wizard of Oz's curtain."[26] The refusal sadly lent further substance to the widespread perception among the politically discontented that the United States was slowly but surely moving in the direction of all the totalitarian regimes the country has so consistently publicly disdained.

With the two consistent voices of sanity (Bader Ginsburg and Souter) dissenting, the High Court in effect sent the suit back to the lower appeals court. Commenting for the World Socialist Web Site, John Andrews accurately noted "the brazen double standard" visible in Justice Kennedy's majority argument that the executive branch of government be protected "from vexatious litigation that might distract it from the energetic performance of its constitutional duties." The court had certainly spoken with a different tongue in *Clinton v. Jones*, but of course *there* sex had been at issue.

What is indeed most perplexing about the case is why Cheney and Co. were so desperate to keep the minutes of the task force meetings from ever seeing the light of day. With characteristic acuity Paul Krugman openly contemplated a thought experiment of several possible scenarios. One could easily imagine that Cheney's energy policy records may have contained "incriminating evidence" of sorts, perhaps with plans for "divvying up Iraq's oil fields in 2001,"[27] in which case the paper trail would remove all doubt about the real reasons why Bush took the country on an extended Middle-East Easter egg hunt. A further possibility is that the written records of task force proceedings might have detailed for example the full extent of Enron's profitable manipulation of California's energy supply, which sent the state through wave after wave of rolling blackouts and added untold millions to Enron's executive suites. A third possibility (viewed by Krugman as the most disturbing) is that Cheney and his crew were defending the secrecy of the task force documents as a matter of "doctrine that makes the United States a sort of elected dictatorship: a system in which the president, once in office, can do whatever he likes, and isn't obliged to consult or inform either Congress or the public."[28]

Until the documents are published in their full, uncensored form, the public can only speculate about the details. Judging the Bush/Cheney administration from its unmistakable track record, we'll say the most likely answer is *All of the above.*

One of the immediate beneficiaries of the change in mindset accompanying Bush into power was Koch Industries. During the last months of the Clinton administration, a ninety-seven-count indictment was leveled against Koch Industries, Inc., Koch Petroleum Group, L. P., and four employees for alleged crimes against the environment in accordance with standards defined under the Clean Air Act. As explained in the Department of Justice press release, the indictment also charged the named parties "with conspiracy and making false statements to Texas environmental officials."[29]

Details of the case obtained by the justice department revealed that Koch managers had been notified by an employee that the company's West Plant refinery outside Corpus Christi "had at least 91 metric tons of uncontrolled benzene in its liquid waste streams, some 15 times greater than the 6 metric ton limit that applied to the refinery." Benzene, a known carcinogen linked to the development of both lymphoma and leukemia, had been added by the EPA in 1977 to its list of toxic pollutants. The Department of Justice report also revealed that despite persistent and un-remedied shutdowns in the operation of a control device (Thermatrix Thermal Oxidizer) designed to destroy benzene,

> Koch Industries and Koch Petroleum Group intentionally vented large amounts of untreated benzene fumes directly to the atmosphere through a bypass stack. The benzene released through the bypass stack exceeded 10 pounds per 24-hour period on several occasions, and Koch Industries and Koch Petroleum Group did not report these releases to the National Response Center as required by the provisions of the Clean Air Act.

Lois Schiffer, assistant attorney general for environmental issues at the DOJ, courageously warned that "companies that produce dangerous pollutants simply cannot focus on profit and efficiency at the expense of a community's health."[30] (Epidemiological data available for the area around Corpus Christi and other petroleum-based communities of the Gulf Coast show a significantly greater incidence of various types of cancer linked to environmental pollutants as well as highly elevated rates of asthma and other respiratory diseases among children and adults.[31])

According to a profile of Koch industries written by Bob Williams and Kevin Bogardus, the four Koch Industry employees named in the indictment faced prison sentences of up to thirty-five years for their alleged involvement in the toxic dump and its cover-up. The company itself could have been hit with fines totaling more than $350 million.[32] No sooner had the Bush team taken control of the centers of government than as if by command from a magic wand the justice department agreed to a settlement of a "whopping" $20 million in fines in exchange for a "guilty" plea on one "single count of concealment of information." The company and its trustworthy employees were then basically free to go. Similar outcomes awaited the other eight corporations charged with willful or negligent contamination of the environment at the end of the Clinton administration. How does corporate America spell "relief"?

One nagging problem that obviously vexed industry/administration insiders was the Environmental Protection Agency and its watchdogs of concerned citizens groups who felt it worthwhile to keep as many poisons as possible out of the water we drink, the air we breathe, and the food we eat—public concerns dismissed by John Graham as a "syndrome of paranoia and neglect." The final strategy adopted by the administration consisted of two carefully planned and executed lines of attack. First, *challenge the scientific data itself by all means necessary* (with the populations of pro-Bush states convinced that global warming is "a hoax" (so the public record of Republican Senator James Inhofe of Oklahoma) and that the earth as created by God is 6,000 years old, a "slam-dunk" as George Tenet might have put it). Second, *change the language and the message* of the sales pitch to hit all the chords Americans have been trained and processed to love and look for. *They bought the victory of the Florida follies, why wouldn't they fall for this?*

Cheating in Science

For the right amount of money, people will do and say just about anything. "Scientists" are no exception. When a company wants to embellish its corporate image and hide the little loss here and the big loss there, what better way to achieve this aim than by hiring a renowned accounting firm to cook the books? And when a factory or power plant can save money by disposing of poisonous by-products such as mercury, arsenic, dioxin or benzene in the cheapest way possible, what better way than hiring "experts" to agree that just dumping all the stuff is not only not that bad, it can even be downright good for you. Behold the right-wing think tank.

As the brainchildren of conservative foundations, right-wing think tanks are instrumental in steering public policy across a broad range of issues—from the tax code and school choice, to gay rights and foreign policy. As laid out in the Tax Reform Act of 1969, foundations are prohibited from direct lobbying activities. Moreover, they cannot support the lobbying efforts of institutions that have received grants from the foundations. As the National Committee for Responsive Philanthropy has noted, because

> ... the term "lobbying" was narrowly defined—as communicating with legislators about specific pieces of legislation—and did not prohibit other strategies that can influence legislation, foundations are able to fund organizations working on public policy without fear of government reprimand.[33]

In cahoots with its mega-rich friends in all the right foundations, the Bush administration began "calling for papers" out of the magic drawing rooms of think tanks, all ready and willing to obfuscate numbers, delete crucial data, drop a couple of numerical orders, reinterpret data, and lie.

Through virtually every layer of the legislative process and its eventual implementation by the executive, the Republican power bloc had woven an intricate mesh of deception, with the nation's most egregious polluters calling the shots. Kennedy reported details of a meeting between executives of various coal and utility companies and a favored lobbyist for Edison Electric Institute, Quin Shea, in April of 2001. According to the transcript of the meeting (closed to outside scrutiny), Shea assured the energy leaders in attendance of an enjoyable ride thanks to Bush's plan to do away with the New Source Review standards regulating power plant emissions: "We're taking steps right now to reverse every piece of paper that EPA has put together where they could call CO_2 a pollutant under the Clean Air Act."[34]

As to the future of the Kyoto Protocol in the hands of the Republicans ("our party"), Shea was euphoric: "Kyoto is absolutely dead...For those of you...who want to continue to beat a dead horse, let me tell you right now, there will be no equine resurrection here."[35]

How right he was. The dealers in death began a promotional campaign for the "Clear Skies Initiative" (yet another of those wonderfully creative GOP euphemisms) designed to roll back most of the environmental clean-up features contained in the Clean Air Act. Under the Republican/industry's catchy Newspeak version of the law, energy companies would be allowed to increase their total emission of mercury into the environment by 520 percent per year (and educators worry *now* about a dumbed-down population) through a "cap-and-trade" system. Pre-Bush pollution control measures had aimed at a reduction of sulfur dioxide emissions to two million tons by 2012; Bush-initiative backers thought that a 225 percent increase was perfectly acceptable. Whereas levels of nitrogen oxide would be cut back to about 1.25 million tons by 2010 under terms of the already established Clean Air Act, the GOP's industry-friendly version of breathable air was to let nitrogen oxide emissions rise by sixty-eight percent by 2008.

Another major source of grievance for many industries including energy companies, paper mills, and chemical plants around the country was a 1977 amendment to the Clean Air Act known as the New Source Review. At issue were older power and production plants that could not possibly have complied with any of the pollution reduction measures mandated by the Clean Air Act. Under the terms of the New Source Review, any increase in output at the older plants would require retrofitting the plant with the best available technology.

There wasn't a polluter in the country not thanking his lucky stars that God had put George W. Bush and Friends in the seats of power. As Public Citizen and the Environmental Integrity Project clarified, Bush and the GOP also had a little help—$6.6 million worth from the "30 biggest utility companies owning most of the 89 dirtiest power plants."[36]

Consistently hovering near the top of the list of "generous donors" supporting Republican pro-industry/anti-environment foundations is the Koch family. The Charles G. Koch Foundation, the David H. Koch Foundation, and the Claude R. Lambe Charitable Foundation, all rely on funding from Koch Industries and related companies. The foundations give vast sums of money "to nonprofit organizations that do research and advocacy on issues that impact the profit margin of Koch Industries."[37] Among the organizations supported by Koch money: the Competitive Enterprise Institute, the libertarian Cato Institute, and the Foundation for Research on Economics and the Environment. As noted by the authors of the *Axis of Ideology*, Citizens for a Sound Economy (also Koch-funded) falls under the ranks of a 501(C)(4) organization, prohibiting it from receiving foundation funding, but its subsidiary, the CSE Foundation, is classified as a 501(C)(3) and is thus exempted from such tax law restrictions. (Also of interest is the fact that Republican "Contract with America" co-author and former House majority leader Dick Armey is co-chairman of CSE. The perfect marriage of ideas, interests, and position.)

Figures released by the Center for Public Integrity and the National Committee for Responsive Philanthropy reveal that one of the top recipients of Koch foundation funds ($23 million from 1985—2002) has been George Mason University with its Mercatus Center. The right-wing, free-market madrasah has become somewhat specialized in churning out studies and research reports that are consistently right in line with corporate interests and are designed to punch holes in the attempts by environmentalists and labor advocates to hold industries accountable for toxic waste and occupational safety.

Careful reading of Mercatus Center publications provides a clear picture of the group's ideological bent. Of particular note are the series of research papers and public commentaries contributed by authors of the "Regulatory Studies Program" under the directorship of Susan E. Dudley, former EPA employee. Ms. Dudley has articulated the goals and concerns (particularly about government interference in the free market process) in her *Primer on Regulation*.[38] The paper contains a brief historical overview as well as an analysis of various types of regulation as seen from the public choice perspective. At the discourse level, the paper contains much of the antistatist GOP jargon the country has grown accustomed to during decades of screams for lower taxes and the tear-sac tugs about the need to allow businesses to do their thing. Dudley speaks of the "regulatory burden" placed on American employers and workers alike and the daunting task of understanding the material even for those who've written it. She references among others the work of libertarian/pro public choice economists W. Mark Crain (of the Center for Study of Public Choice, also at George Mason University), James Ralph Edwards, Gordon Tullock, Arthur Seldon, and Gordon L. Brady.[39] Not surprisingly, Dudley echoes the tenor of John Graham's research at the Harvard Center for Risk Analysis, in which the cost-benefit algorithm described earlier is critical in deciding if, what, and how to regulate.

A similar line of argument was taken in a public interest comment written by Daniel R. Simmons, a research fellow at the Mercatus Center. At issue were arguments concerning the efficacy of the Environmental Protection Agency's Proposed National Emission Standards for Mercury. The wording of the first sentence of the introduction to the paper is in itself quite revealing: "In high doses, there is little doubt that mercury is toxic to humans."[40] The implied subtext is of course that in doses below that upper (perhaps "exaggerated?") threshold, there's really nothing to worry about. (With the Koch Foundations as the largest single donor group to the Mercatus Center, it is easy to understand why Koch Industries would have a vested interest in the validity of such arguments. Mercury is one of the toxic substances routinely emitted into the atmosphere and streams by coal-burning power plants and by a number of other industrial processes.)

In the main, the commentary presented the following arguments against the EPA's proposed rule change under consideration at the time.[41] First, the EPA's benchmark reference dose (RfD) for mercury assumes as harmful to humans a much lower concentration (5.8 parts per billion) by accepting the results of studies conducted in the Faroe Islands and adjusting downward the RfD obtained there to account for uncertainties. The thus obtained RfD, Simmons contended,[42] was not substantiated by results obtained in the Seychelles Islands, which found no link between a wide range of possible health issues and methylmercury.[43]

Secondly, Simmons maintained that the exact pathway by which mercury emitted from power plants winds up in the human body is not completely understood. To support this contention he quoted from the EPA's own "1997 Mercury Study RTC" [Report to Congress], in which the agency "supports a plausible link between anthropogenic releases of Hg from industrial and combustion sources in the U.S. and methylmercury in fish." At the same time, the EPA acknowledged that its study

> ...relied heavily on computer modeling to describe the environmental fate of emitted mercury because no monitoring data have been identified that conclusively demonstrate or refute a relationship between any of the individual anthropogenic sources in the emissions inventory and increased mercury concentrations in environmental media or biota.[44]

Thus, Simmons concluded, "EPA has no actual data that support such a link."[45] Simmons insisted that in terms of cost effectiveness the EPA study and subsequent proposed rule change relied on accompanying reductions of other targeted gases such as nitrogen oxide and sulfur dioxide. In other words, in terms of significant emission reductions for mercury alone, the EPA was unable to make its case.

He also contended that "various recent rulings" by the EPA relied heavily on an alleged link between human illness and concentrations of particulate matter, as examined in the Harvard Six Cities study and in similar research conducted by the American Cancer Society. Simmons said that the results of both of these studies, however, inasmuch as they address such a link, were "spurious and not representative of a cause-effect relationship" because of associated methodological "problems of uncontrolled confounding, latency time for disease development, and biologically implausible variations in the apparent PM2.5-mortality rate association."[46]

In a maneuver worthy of John Graham himself, Simmons argued that the EPA's proposed rule change to reduce mercury in the environment could actually lead to more deaths per year. His reasoning went like this: According to the EPA's own estimates, the proposed improvements in power plants would cost around $1.6 billion per year to implement section 112 MACT (maximum achievable control technology). Costs for the implementation of section III with a simultaneous reduction in sulfur dioxide and nitrogen oxide would require "between $2.9 billion and over $4.5 billion per year" plus an expected additional "$8.2 billion in capital costs."[47] Simmons went on to say that the only acceptable basis of determining the cost : benefit ratio was to use the concept of "opportunity cost" as defined by the Office of Management and Budget in Circular A4 in conjunction with Executive Order 12866: "Opportunity cost of an alternative includes the value of the benefits forgone as a result of choosing that alternative."[48]

But, Simmons pointed out that the costs of improvements to power plants would ultimately be passed on to consumers in the form of higher bills, and studies have shown[49] that a $15 million-dollar income reduction is statistically associated with the loss of one human life. Therefore, given the total estimated costs of the EPA's proposed changes to power plant technologies, an additional 545 people would have to die. In other words, additional regulation designed to clean up the environment actually kills people because it is expensive.

Finally, Simmons believed that the EPA had failed to show that people would actually derive a positive health benefit (a further OMB requirement) from not having mercury with their hamburgers.

There was clearly too much fish in this man's diet. The arguments presented are problematic for a number of reasons. To maintain, firstly, that because the exact mechanism is not fully understood by which mercury released from power plants winds up on the dinner plate, that therefore no link exists and hence nothing need be done about it, offers up a false conclusion predicated on generalizations of ambiguous terms. The "exact link" cannot in any sensible discourse imply that individual molecules of methylmercury be traced from their point of origin in the smoke stacks at a power plant through the atmospheric complex of clouds, dust, water vapor etc., then via rain into the first levels of the food chain etc. This is not the burden of proof. In like manner, we do not need to know the exact manner in which the driver or passenger in an SUV rollover sustains fatal injuries. It suffices to know that injuries normally occur in such single-vehicle accidents and that the consequences have to be improved safety standards in the design of those vehicles. But the argument is also factually wrong. Biologists understand quite well how the heavy metal compounds wind up in our organisms and it most certainly isn't because the fish in lakes and streams engage in collective midnight runs on the local 7-Eleven. We are equally all too familiar with the long-term effects of mercury poisoning.

Similarly fallacious is the spurious false-cause claim that expenditures required to modernize power plants to cut emissions would necessitate an increase in utility prices, which would then reduce the overall take-home pay of low-wage earners and ultimately lead to their death. Such fanciful concoctions out of the confines of right-wing "think" tanks generalize from an observable link between poverty and mortality rate statistics, both of which are unspecified in terms of agent/cause to a conclusion that posits a specific cause. It is one thing to establish a link between the overall health of low-income families as a result of poor nutrition and living conditions associated with a lack of finances; it is quite another to then say that because power plants A, B, and C have modernized their facilities and the costs will eventually be passed on to consumers, that therefore more poor people will die this year as a result of the extra $18.00. The "concern" proudly championed for the poor is also the only instance in which the proponents of pro-business rules have ever even thought about society's impoverished.

Simmons took the OMB guideline requiring that proposed rule changes "explain how the actions required by the rule are linked to the expected benefit" and used it to a purpose it must not be allowed to serve. Analogously, safety regulations requiring bicyclists and motorcyclists to wear helmets have resulted in lives being saved in accidents that otherwise might have resulted in the death of the cyclist due to head trauma. Now the authors of this regulation cannot expect the public to show that the wearing of a helmet while sitting at the dinner table or lying in the bathtub will prove beneficial to the person wearing it. And yet this is exactly what Simmons argued should be shown in the case of mercury emissions.

Even more worrying than the weird science cooked up in right-wing think tanks is the conscious falsification of data, procedures, and findings. This widespread practice through all ranks of pro-industry bureaucrats and decision-makers has become such common practice that it can be compared to the state-controlled censorship common among "totalitarian" regimes. In February 2004, the Union of Concerned Scientists released the results of its first of two extensive investigations "of many of the allegations made in the mainstream media, in scientific journals, and in overview reports issued from within the federal government[50] and by non governmental organizations" that the Bush administration was executing "a well-established pattern of suppression and distortion of scientific findings … across numerous federal agencies."[51]

The findings expose shockingly egregious patterns of deception throughout many branches of Republican/industry-dominated federal agencies. The UCS reports provide the most credible proof yet of the "unprecedented" "scope and scale of the manipulation, suppression, and misrepresentation of science by the Bush administration."[52]

Case in point: In the spring of 2002, the EPA had completed a study of mercury emissions from power plants and detailed the potential neurotoxic effects exposure to the heavy metal would have in the population. Among its findings was the unsettling statistic that eight percent of women from sixteen to forty-nine had blood mercury levels so high that their offspring might suffer from impaired cognitive and motor-sensory development. The EPA findings were not what the White House and its corporate directors in the energy industries wanted to hear. According to documents obtained by the UCS, the administration went out of its way to keep the EPA findings under wraps and where necessary to alter the data to conform to the whitewashed version of reality favored by the White House. The EPA report was thus held in limbo for nine months by the White House Office of Management and Budget and the Office of Science and Technology Policy (OSTP). Thanks to someone with a conscience at the EPA, the report was finally leaked to the *Wall Street Journal*.[53]

The UCS investigation also confirmed a report released by Eric Pianin of the *Washington Post* of yet another instance of industries making the rules. Thanks to the GOP's cozy relationship with all the big polluters, twelve entire paragraphs were copied "from a legal document prepared by industry lawyers" for inclusion into the EPA's lubricated guidelines on mercury emissions.[54]

Lisa Heinzerling and Rena Steinzor reported a whole slew of errors, deletions, and blatantly altered data within the doctored EPA report. Their examination of the findings revealed a persistent attempt by the OMB censors to trivialize the toxic effects of mercury exposure. Evidence widely held to be incontrovertible among real scientists was called into doubt through carefully executed changes in the language of the text, in one instance as Heinzerling and Steinzor note, through the targeted omission of the adjective "confirmed" in a phrase such as "the confirmed health risks of mercury."[55] As they also pointed out, documented evidence substantiating mercury's damaging effects on the cardiovascular system was replaced

...with the considerably more mealy-mouthed, "It has been hypothesized that there is an association between methylmercury exposure and
an increased risk of coronary disease; however this warrants further
study as the new studies currently available present conflicting results."[56]

Other creative changes in the original EPA report on mercury were carried out by
Elizabeth Stolpe, a former employee for the good old friends at Koch Industries.
Ms. Stolpe had been strategically repositioned in the White House Council on Environmental Quality (CEQ). (Not quite as appropriate as appointing Kim Jong Il
to head Human Rights Watch, but getting there.) According to Heinzerling and
Steinzor, Ms. Stolpe simply removed a phrase linked to statements by the National Academy of Sciences describing the earlier reference dose for mercury (5.8
parts per billions) adopted by the EPA as "scientifically justifiable."[57]

The EPA was apparently pressured into "revising" its data in another case
involving Halliburton's (Dick Cheney's old stomping grounds) newly developed
technique of getting oil and gas out of ground deposits. Commonly known as
"hydraulic fracturing," the technique pumps highly toxic benzene into the areas
containing fuel deposits. According to Kennedy, the EPA had discovered in 2002
that the technique could lead to ground water contamination. Members of Congress were notified of the findings. Just days later, however, the agency magically
readjusted the results of its report, as it said "based on 'industry feedback'."[58]

The Republican-led corporate sanitizing coup of scientific data by no means
restricted itself to merely rewriting science. Through the careful study of interviews with government officials and analyses of internal documents and public
records, the Union of Concerned Scientists uncovered a clearly widespread pattern of intimidation directed at administration employees who failed to toe the
pro-industry party line.

Many of the hundreds of expert committees and commissions charged with
advising the various branches of government not in political but rather professional capacities have undergone significant top-down structural changes at the
behest of the Bush administration. In the October 25, 2002, edition of *Science*, ten
highly acclaimed research scientists from leading universities published a scathing commentary on the Bush administration's well-established practice of under-
mining "the process by which scientists provide advice to the U.S. government."[59]
As reported in the *Washington Post*, Tommy Thompson (then-secretary of the Department of Health and Human Services (DHHS)) had summarily disbanded two
entire panels (the National Human Research Protections Advisory Committee

and the Advisory Committee on Genetic Testing within DHHS), because many of the solutions being considered to address ethical issues of genetic research and testing "conflicted with the religious views of certain political constituencies."[60] The commentary also expressed disdain at Secretary Thompson's replacement of fifteen research scientists in the Advisory Committee to the Director of the National Center for Environmental Health with "scientists that have long been associated with the chemical or petroleum industries, often in leadership positions of organizations opposing public health and environmental regulation."[61]

In addressing the my-way-or-the-highway approach heavy-handedly implemented by the Bush administration, the commentary warned that "scientific advisory committees do not exist to tell the secretary what he wants to hear but to help the secretary, and the nation, address complex issues."[62]

The outcome of several of Thompson's decisions will likely be seen and felt in families all across the country for years to come. Like most heavy metals, lead ingested through air, food or water even in relatively small amounts can lead to serious developmental problems, mental retardation, kidney failure, and liver and brain damage. The problem of lead poisoning in children has been thoroughly documented and most leading experts agree that previously established reference limits of amounts considered dangerous to a child's health (ten micrograms per deciliter) were too high. The Centers for Disease Control were therefore considering (in 2002) lowering the standard reference dose for lead poisoning. According to statements given by Dr. Susan Cummins (former director of the lead advisory committee from 1995—2000) in interviews with the Union of Concerned Scientists, DHHS Secretary Thompson made the unprecedented move of rejecting people nominated by the staff scientists in favor of "five individuals who were all distinguished by the likelihood that they would oppose tightening the federal lead poisoning standard."[63]

As it turned out, one of the replacements chosen by Thompson was none other than Dr. William Banner, a toxicologist who had previously testified in a civil case for the paint company Sherwin-Williams. As cited in the UCS report, the text of Banner's deposition shows him testifying that in his view no clear link had ever been established between developmental problems in children and lead exposure at levels below seventy micrograms per deciliter.[64]

Decisions equally stunning became the norm rather than the exception. A former supervisor for the Fish and Wildlife Service in North Dakota related how his entire team of biologists was fired because it had dared to report violations of the Endangered Species Act by the Army Corps of Engineers in its attempts to divert the current of the Missouri River.[65] As Kennedy explained, the Office of Management and Budget's decision to outsource 425,000 federal jobs had a deep impact on the way environmental oversight was conducted. Thousands of positions previously occupied by environmental research scientists were "contracted out to industry consultants already in the habit of massaging data to support corporate profit taking."[66] The Public Employees for Environmental Responsibility and the Union of Concerned Scientists conducted a survey among the 1,400 scientists employed at the U.S. Fish and Wildlife Service to assess the concerns the service members had about their contribution to the preservation of endangered species. According to an NRDC commentary on the results of the survey,[67] the majority of the respondents expressed their dismay that decisions taken by the agency had often been overturned or revised at the request of industries whose activities might otherwise have been curtailed as a result of agency actions. The overwhelming majority believed that the agency's involvement in species protection was inadequate. One respondent from California was quoted as saying that "science was ignored—and worse, manipulated."

Another especially disturbing example of the effects of government and industry teaming up can be seen in the oversight decisions involving the pesticide atrazine. Under the terms of a settlement reached in a lawsuit filed by the United Farm Workers of America and the National Resources Defense Council against the EPA for its failure to protect the public from the harmful effects of atrazine, the government was supposed to establish a monitoring program to keep track of the chemical's increased spread into rivers, lakes, streams, and ground water supplies. The Bush administration turned right around and gave control of the monitoring process to the very company that manufactures the pesticide.[68]

Against a mountain of evidence implicating atrazine in a wide range of health problems, specifically prostate cancer and lymphoma (the incidence of which has now reached frightening levels), the EPA made the decision in October 2003 not to limit the use of the pesticide. Environmental organizations immediately became suspicious that something was afoul in the decision. Under the Freedom of Information Act, the NRDC filed several requests for documents pertaining to EPA deliberations and its decision on atrazine. Neither the White House nor the agency itself was forthcoming. To press the issue, the NRDC then filed a follow-up suit accusing the White House and the EPA of violating the Freedom of Information Act. Begrudgingly, the White House handed over twenty-two documents consisting largely of black stripes to cover up "secret" information. (Of course in the "War on Terror" even grandma's recipe for tapioca pudding has been a potential enemy of the state, but especially dangerous apparently are those who have a bone to pick with corporate America.) In total, eighty other documents deemed material and germane to the investigation remained firmly in the grips of the White House.

As difficult as the road was intentionally made, the NRDC did manage to uncover secret negotiations and agreements reached between the EPA and the manufacturers of atrazine. As reported on the NRDC Web site, the private agreement would allow for the unrestricted continued use of atrazine, and the manufacturer (Syngenta)

> …will only be required to take additional steps, such as increased monitoring, when a stream exceeds a "level of concern"—apparently a range from 10 to 20 ppb—over a vaguely defined "prolonged period," and only then for the most contaminated of the 40 monitored streams.[69]

It should be noted that by the EPA's own determination, some species will suffer severe bodily harm from exposure to atrazine at only 2.16 ppb.

As bad as the government's pro-industry bias in dealing with environmental poisons was, it paled in comparison to the administration's ability to twist the facts to fit in with its own agenda on global warming (now officially known in Bush/industry parlance as "climate change"). Robert F. Kennedy, Jr., appropriately commented that the Bush administration's efforts to discredit the scientific data on global warming were "arguably unmatched in the western world since the Inquisition."[70] No serious scientist outside the labs directly funded by Baptists for Bush and the American Petroleum, Coal, and Energy Association 1-800 School for Climate Study has any doubt that human activity—specifically the burning of fossil fuels—is directly linked to the full 1.8-degree increase in average global temperature over the last century. Five of the last fifteen years have been the hottest on record in the Northern Hemisphere, with dramatic shifts in precipitation patterns; 2005 was cited as the overall hottest year on record. Regions in the oceans north of the Arctic Circle that just decades ago froze into solid sheets of ice, remain today passable only by boat, resulting in a dramatic loss of life in the polar bear population (the animals either drown or starve because of their reliance on the ice pack for hunting.) In the summer of 2007, *for the first time in recorded history*, the long-sought Northwest Passage linking Europe and Asia via the North Pole was ice-free—clear and open for sailing. (Of course commercial interests from a wide group of countries jumped to the front of the line with wild dreams of yet new ways to exploit nature's demise—with the promise of increased profits and savings in shipping costs.)

Calculations obtained from a supercomputer in December 2005 revealed that by the year 2100 the top eleven feet of the permafrost will have melted in most of the Northern Hemisphere. David Lawrence of the National Center for Atmospheric Research was quoted by the *Los Angeles Times* as saying that the meltdown of that much ice near the surface "could release considerable amounts of greenhouse gases into the atmosphere, and that could amplify global warming." He also warned that climate research "could be underestimating the rate of global temperature increase."[71]

Scientists attending the American Geophysical Union conference in San Francisco in 2002 reported the largest ice and glacier loss in Greenland's recorded history. In just ten years, the area of ice melt in Greenland had doubled to 685,000 square kilometers. Measurements taken in the area in 2004 and 2005 showed that the melting process was occurring at rates scientists familiar with shifting climate patterns had never dreamed possible. Stanford University's Terry L. Root analyzed data collected on 1,473 species and concluded that global warming is already having an impact on the habitats and the adaptive behavior of many of the species. This was especially evident in plant and animal populations in higher latitudes, where the effects of global warming are much more pronounced.

Extensive Antarctic studies conducted by Isabella Velicogna and John Wahr revealed that in particular the West Antarctic Ice Sheet has lost massive amounts of ice.

Based on data obtained from the Gravity Recovery and Climate Experiment (GRACE) satellites, the team's measurements indicated an alarming loss rate of approximately "152 ±80 km^3" of ice per year.[72]

In December 2003, the American Geophysical Union released a joint statement on the *Human Impacts on Climate*. As adopted by the AGU council, the statement points unequivocally to the overwhelming evidence that

> ... human activities are increasingly altering the Earth's climate. These effects add to natural influences that have been present over Earth's history. Scientific evidence strongly indicates that natural influences cannot explain the rapid increase in global near-surface temperatures observed during the second half of the 20th century.[73]

The declaration also points out that actual shifts in atmospheric and ocean surface temperatures as well as patterns of precipitation rely on processes so complex that concrete predictions are exceedingly difficult. Nevertheless, the paper states,

> AGU believes that no single threshold level of greenhouse gas concentrations in the atmosphere exists at which the beginning of dangerous anthropogenic interference with the climate system can be defined. Some impacts have already occurred, and for increasing concentrations there will be increasing impacts. The unprecedented increases in greenhouse gas concentrations, together with other human influences on climate over the past century and those anticipated for the future, constitute a real basis for concern.[74]

Warnings of this type received international backing by the UN-sponsored Intergovernmental Panel on Climate Change (IPCC), which was awarded the Nobel Peace Prize in October of 2007 for its long-range studies of global warming. The IPCC's "Synthesis Report," approved by scientists and experts from 130 countries, was released in Valencia, Spain, prior to the global conference on climate change held at the end of 2007 in Bali, Indonesia. Rajendra Pachauri, who served as director of the IPCC, warned that concrete steps had to be taken immediately if global catastrophe was to be avoided: "If there's no action before 2012, that's too late."

These are not the warnings of a group of $4.95-per-minute-call-now TV psychics but the sound predictions of the world's largest group of physical scientists. But, there were powerful financial interests hell-bent on making a joke out of the findings and systematically downplaying the severity of the crisis. In January 2006, long-time director of the Goddard Institute for Space Studies at NASA, James E. Hansen, finally went public to expose the intimidation tactics used by the Republican administration in its efforts to silence scientists' uncomfortable findings. As one of the country's leading climate experts, Hansen has warned of the dire consequences facing the planet if greenhouse gas emissions are not dramatically curbed. In a speech given in December 2005, Hansen essentially challenged the U.S. to acknowledge the extent of the problem and to take an active role in trying to solve it. He also cited the importance of using existing technology to transform the automobile industry into a maker of environmentally friendly vehicles.

During the course of several interviews conducted with the *New York Times*, Hansen described detailed measures taken by leading government officials to keep him quiet. One senior public affairs official at NASA reportedly declined requests by

National Public Radio for interviews with Dr. Hansen about his findings and his conflicts with the Bush administration. In denying the request, the official was quoted as saying that it was important "to make the president look good"—a task that might not have been so easily accomplished on "the most liberal" radio station.[75]

In a sweeping censorship move, the public affairs office also ordered a complete review of all of Hansen's outgoing publications and lectures to make certain they were favorable to the Bush administration's party line. Hansen commented that the Bush-friendly officials at NASA felt it was "their job to be this censor of information going out to the public," but at the same time he warned that he did not accept such censorship as part of normal procedures at NASA.

Now it's one thing to change the rules of the game to suit the home team, but it's quite another to sell the program to the public; someone just might be paying attention. And this is where the cadre School for Republican Spin and Reality Distortion comes in.

According to the institute's description of itself, *The Luntz Research Companies* are the only firm in the nation's capital focused on language. The company is specialized in development and implementation of words and phrases that effect real changes in the way people perceive and react to events and policies. Thanks to the now infamous sixteen-page insider memo forwarded by the Environmental Working Group to *New York Times* staff writer Jennifer 8. Lee and published in the March 2, 2003, edition of the paper, the reading public is now onto where the GOP comes up with its fanciful take on reality. It would seem that today's immoderate Republicans have all mastered the lingo.

Cases in point: In June 2005, it was revealed that Philip Cooney, chief of staff at the White House Council on Environmental Quality, had doctored a federal report on global warming to make the results sound completely tenuous. Cooney was yet another of the many eagle scouts for industrial polluters who had been strategically placed into a commanding position within a Bush/industry-led decision-making body following years of service as a hustling lobbyist for the American Petroleum Institute (in the words of David Michaels, "one of the nation's leading manufacturers of scientific uncertainty"[76]). Michaels hit the bull's eye when he likened the Bush administration's policy of "manufacturing uncertainty" to the "science" of the tobacco companies whose "expert witnesses" repeatedly testified under oath that there was no evidence linking cigarette smoking to lung cancer, and that there was no proof that smoking was addictive. As Michaels correctly commented, creating this element of uncertainty is "a business itself,"[77] with doubt being created about the dangers of practically every chemical used in all the manufacturing industries—despite the thousands who have died or are now suffering through terminal illnesses.

Dozens of pro-business think tanks spew out the bogus numbers and manufactured doubt in catchy phrases with advice to memorize the lines and throw them back at those who see the growing dangers around them. Some are so far-fetched in their efforts that the message would be cause for laughter were the consequences not so dire and real. Under the banner "FreedomWorks—Citizens for a Sound Economy & Empower America" posted as an "open letter to ExxonMobil Shareholders," the Director of CSE [the Koch Foundation brainchild] in Texas sent out a plea to put a halt to the "extremists on global warming." And taken right out of the industry's school prayer book was the phony-baloney of there being "no proof that human activity contributes significantly to greenhouse gasses!!!"[78] The paper had also dealt in twenty-first century alchemy of sorts: while admitting that the use of fossil fuels has indeed contributed to emissions of greenhouse gases, the flyer maintained that this contribution was actually quite minimal. In fact the increase in carbon dioxide so often lamented by environmentalists "is only one of several greenhouse gases and the most prevalent—water vapor—is by far the most prevalent greenhouse gas, responsible for 95 percent of the greenhouse effect (sic!)."[79] For those who just may have forgotten, water vapor is *not a cumulative/forcing* greenhouse gas but the molecular component of the hydrologic cycle that gives us life on earth. But with backers like ExxonMobil and its $5.7 million in efforts in 2001 alone to prove that global warming is a hoax, some seem to be selling housing developments on Neptune.

In August of 2002 Friends of the Earth received a letter addressed to George W. Bush himself. The authors were various individuals and a total of thirty-one groups of like ilk calling on the "president" to boycott the Earth Summit being held in Johannesburg, South Africa, that year. The letter was explicit in its demands and warnings:

> Even more than the Earth Summit in Rio in 1992, the Johannesburg Summit will provide a global media stage for many of the most irresponsible and destructive elements involved in critical international economic and environmental issues. Your presence would only help to publicize and make more credible various anti-freedom, anti-people, anti-globalization, and anti-Western agendas.

The letter went on to state that "the least important global environmental issue is potential global warming, and we hope that your negotiators in Johannesburg can keep it off the table and out of the spotlight."

What words do reveal. The statement directly contradicts the warnings given by Britain's prime minister (finance minister at the time) Gordon Brown: "We have sufficient evidence that human-made climate change is the most far-reaching and almost certainly the most threatening of all the environmental challenges facing us."[80]

The uniform response of the Bush/industry administration to the mounds of evidence linking human activity to global warming was proffered by the former CEO and chairman of ExxonMobil himself: "If the data were compelling, I would change my view. But the data is not compelling."[81]

These are the same lines spewed by all members of the Bush/industry administration, their secretaries, aunts, cousins, and talking parrots; they have not only learned the speech by heart, they've also been trained in using it effectively in public. All thanks to The Luntz Research Companies.

The company's lingual re-programming guidelines were first drawn up by Frank Luntz, one of the architects (along with Newt Gingrich, Dick Armey et al.) of the ("the American people want") "Contract with America" that swept the country in 1994 with the same public enthusiasm as that once bestowed on pet rocks and Tickle Me-Elmo. The principles of the positive message were laid out in Luntz's 222-page guide, "The Language of the 21st Century." It's all there—everything we've heard about the keys to winning the war on terror, the necessities for tax cuts, the privatization (no, "personalization") of social security, and the administration's "concern" for the environment (described by the master in one of his rare candid moments as the Achilles heel of the Republican Party platform).

The leaked memo from The Luntz Research Companies contained a telling passage, noting "how often Republicans are depicted as cold, uncaring, ruthless, even downright anti-social."[82] (No one could have said it better.) The author does not mince words. In the struggle to control the public's perceptions on global warming, Luntz issued this decisive advice on tilting the discourse toward the Republican version of reality:

> *The scientific debate remains open.* Voters believe that there is no consensus about global warming within the scientific community. Should the public come to believe that the scientific issues are settled, their views about global warming will change accordingly. Therefore, you need to

continue to make the lack of scientific certainty a primary issue in the debate, and defer to scientists and other experts in the field.[83]

As a matter of course every elected GOP official and candidate for dogcatcher then spouted off the same learned lines, with industry leaders leading them by the hand. Even the think tanks couldn't manage to come up with a better line as evidenced by the official statement from the Koch-affiliated Citizens for a Sound Economy: "…the theory of climate change is far from settled, and there is not a consensus in the scientific community on the issue."

Frank Luntz has studied the American psyche, and he knows what makes it tick. Whereas the Athenian Academy proudly displayed above its portals the importance of mathematics for all who would understand the nature of reality, The Luntz Research Companies live by the motto that facts don't really matter—*it's how you tell the story that counts.*[84]

It would admittedly take a lot of smooth-talking salesmanship to convince anyone that the Republican Party is pro-environment, but Frank Luntz is a miracle propagandist. In its eight easy-to-follow talking points, the Luntz memo cum elaborations unwrapped the keys to winning over the millions of malleable Americans who will believe just about anything you throw at them, provided it gels with what they've been trained to want to hear. Luntz's first tactical rule to win over the voters: *you've got to connect with the people; show them you're a real person with normal human interests; a person who cares about those around him* (admittedly, not the easiest task for Republican clients). Luntz's advice: "Tell them a story from your life."

Right on cue, Republicans from all ranks started bringing out the family photo albums and doctoring up cute little stories of "Back on our little prairie farm in Nebraska." Tender, touching moments, every one of them. Fortunately for the world, there are people out there who are still awake and alert to the clever tactics of used-car sales pitchers in state power. One such group (http://www.luntz speak.com) has been successful at exposing this brain washing program for what it is. They've also managed to collect and analyze some of the more memorable gems of Applied Luntzspeak nicely juxtaposed next to the Luntz memo points to which the comments adhere.

Case in point: the Senate confirmation hearing of Bush-appointee Mike Leavitt for the post of EPA Administrator on September 17, 2003: "When President Bush announced my nomination, I described an experience I had at the Grand Canyon at age eight. My family arrived at the south rim at twilight, just in time to see a giant shadow creep across the canyon."[85]

There it was—a made-for-TV Luntz-moment. All that was missing was the giant hand-painted backdrop of the setting sun and the triumphant chords of the theme music from *Gone with the Wind*. Tomorrow is another day! (And all that in a little tot of eight. *Golldarn, ain't he somethin'!*)

The near-perfect interview candidate went on to fill in all the Luntz blanks to create one hell of a sellable picture—a collage of all the little tidbits that Americans have been trained to listen for and cherish. There was the important "leaning experience," coupled with victory in the face of defeat during his term in office at the Grand Canyon Visibility Transport Commission (*what the hell?*). As the "teamwork" solidified and his knowledge of the problems expanded, his group made good use of the "local" (*Hello friendly neighbor*) gimmick to better relate to the family-oriented listeners (and to prove what a "good guy" and "team player" he was). (The phrase also helped to fulfill Luntz requirement number 7: "Describe the limited role for Washington.") Leavitt's statement:

> Serious problem solving and collaboration began to occur, and, ultimately, a twenty-year plan was developed. We developed a way for every state to design its own plan that met national standards...This experience taught me that enforceable national standards can be a catalyst to bring parties together, but national standards work best if participants are allowed to use innovative neighborhood strategies.[86]

A never-fail line that has popped up time and again in Republican comments about the environment is derived from Luntz rule number 6: "...stress that you are seeking 'a fair balance' between the environment and the economy." And true to form, Republican Leavitt obliged in full armor:

> The two of us [the reference is to former governor of Oregon John Kitzhaber] were joined by another dozen governors and invited hundreds of environmental practitioners of every persuasion to help capture the principles that lead to balance: balance between this generation and the next, balance between sustainable environments and sustainable economies and balance among regions.

Republican statements on the environment nearly always reflect one or more of the techniques developed by the Luntz school of rhetoric, and they have been remarkably effective. And this is precisely where the beauty of this new school of brainwashing through language lies—it can be (and has been) applied to almost any aspect of public policy. Political pundits have marveled at the campaign genius of Karl Rove as the man behind the curtain; they have dramatically underrated Frank Luntz in his ability to manipulate public discourse. The man has captured the mindset of all those who have fallen for the American dream but haven't yet awoken to the reality. He knows what the still-dominant public—all the variations of clean, wholesome families from *Pleasantville, USA*—wants and needs to hear, and has instructed Republicans on how to say it. Some 59,000,000 fell for it in 2004.

In truth, the Bush/industry decision to tell the rest of the planet to take the Kyoto accord and shove it was never about science and numbers at all. They knew all along that their "data," "projections," "research results" were for the birds. As was apparent from the struggle (described in Chapter 4) of the miners, farmers, garment and industrial workers against the hunger-wages and inhumane working conditions dictated by industry, it's always been about money—only money. The Triangle Waist Company "couldn't afford" to allow its hundreds of young women to work in an unlocked factory from which they might have walked off with a spool of thread. It "wasn't worth it" for Ford to recall the thousands of Pintos and make the repairs for a couple of bucks. It "wasn't profitable" for GM to fix the faulty design in its cars, which engineers clearly knew posed a serious fire hazard. In all these instances, it was never anything but pure and simple greed that allowed thousands to burn alive or be crushed, scalded, and torn apart at the body's own seams. There is no collective class memory, only collective suffering.

For modern industries, it's "too costly" to install equipment to curtail the emissions of mercury, nitrogen oxide, carbon dioxide, and particulate matter. In this case, though, it's the fate of the entire planet that's at stake.

There is of course an added bonus rarely mentioned in public. The good born-again Christian that he is, Mr. George W. Bush was actually hastening the Second Coming. The Bible speaks of floods, famines, earthquakes, pestilence, wars and rumors of wars—all necessary events in the "natural" unfolding of apocalyptic prophecy portending the end of time. With swarms of Dominionists behind him, speeding up the destruction of the planet was perhaps just "fulfilling the Lord's will." As for all the other living beings destined for doom? *Get over it!*

Cui Bono?

September 11, 2001, ceased being a calendar date to become a watershed event in American and ultimately in global political history. All around the world, everyone with access to TV or the Internet looked on in horror as events unfolded that fateful day. With the first plane striking the North Tower of the World Trade Center in lower Manhattan, a sense of tragic fate enveloped viewers. Ceaseless thoughts and questions flooded the minds of onlookers who were overcome with sadness and sympathy. But minutes later when the scene was repeated, an abyss of fear and helplessness opened up, swallowing the suddenly unified American psyche. For this was no mere fluke; no longer the work of a subdued, blinded, or dead pilot; no longer the outcome of a machine out of control, but something sinister and deliberate. The production of evil from the minds of hidden monsters.

Two of America's greatest symbols stood mortally wounded, like a popular idol desperately trying to stop the blood gushing forth from her slashed throat. Cameras from every perspective followed the death throes of the dying giants. Suddenly the human capacity to conceive of horror found itself trumped by reality. For dozens in the loftiest tiers, despair from the pain of flames searing through eyes and skin found the last relief of choice in that one final leap out of earthly existence. Within minutes, the towering symbols of modernity collapsed on themselves in scattered piles of toxic soot and ashes. It takes a lot to leave Americans speechless, but 9/11 did.

No one at the time knew that within hours of the first plane hitting its intended target, plans started to unravel for counter-attacks as the highest civilian and military elements in government opened their dossiers marked "Iraq". Notes taken by aides to Donald Rumsfeld in a secret briefing held within hours after American Airlines Flight 77 had crashed into the Pentagon revealed that the secretary of defense was asking aides to develop launch plans for an attack on Iraq. He demanded to have the "best info fast. Judge whether good enough hit S.H. [Saddam Hussein] at same time. Not only UBL. Go massive...Sweep it all up. Things related and not."[87]

Over the following four days debates and discussions were held at Camp David on appropriate U.S. response strategies. The consensus was that Iraq would have to be put on the back burner until Afghanistan and the Taliban were taken care of.[88] But the agenda persistently put forward by Dick Cheney, Donald Rumsfeld, and Paul Wolfowitz focused from the outset on regime change in Iraq. According to Bob Woodward, Colin Powell (secretary of state at the time) was especially irritated with the talk centered on invading Iraq. In a meeting with General Hugh Sheldon, Powell is said to have openly expressed his bewilderment and disdain at Rumsfeld's comment that there was now an "opportunity" to address the issue of regime change in Baghdad.[89]

In an interview conducted June 15, 2003, on NBC's *Meet the Press*, retired General Wesley Clark confirmed the flurry of activity in the executive branch to put part of the blame for 9/11 on Saddam's palace doorstep: "There was a concerted effort during the fall of 2001, starting immediately after 9/11, to pin 9/11 and the terrorism problem on Saddam Hussein."

Moderator Tim Russert wanted to know "by who?" Clark then clarified:

Well, it came from the White House, it came from people around the White House. It came from all over. I got a call on 9/11. I was on CNN, and I got a call at my home saying, "You got to say this is connected. This is state-sponsored terrorism. This has to be connected to Saddam Hussein." I said, "But—I'm willing to say it, but what's your evidence?" And I never got any evidence.

The sources "from all over" that Clark was referring to consisted primarily of the men, women, foundations, and think tanks affiliated with the so-called "Neo-Cons" (neo-conservatives) and their top organization: Project for the New American Century. Representing the vanguard of free market-oriented enterprise (many members maintain close ties with the American Enterprise Institute) and its underpinnings in the American concept of individual freedom, the ideological apparatus is heavily biased toward policies of aggressive intervention on a global scale to promote governments and societal changes that best serve American ideals and corporate interests. The group had even authored a somewhat startling piece of work in September 2000, exactly one year before the cataclysmic events in New York. In a white paper entitled "Rebuilding America's Defenses—Strategy, Forces and Resources for a New Century," the project cryptically augured: "Further, the process of transformation, even if it brings revolutionary change, is likely to be a long one, absent some catastrophic and catalyzing event—like a new Pearl Harbor."[90]

The Neo-cons went on a PR offensive with ready-made punch lines claiming that the attacks of 9/11 couldn't possibly have been carried out by a group of renegades alone, but must have been planned at the state level. As neo-con Richard Perle told the *Washington Post* just hours after the attacks, "Someone taught these suicide bombers how to fly large airplanes. I don't think that can be done without the assistance of large governments." Other neo-con ideologues—Bill Kristol (chairman of PNAC and writer/editor for the *Weekly Standard*), former CIA director James Woolsey, Undersecretary of Defense (and former World Bank president) Paul Wolfowitz, and John Bolton (later appointed as U.S. ambassador to the United Nations)—echoed the refrain, each time publicly naming Iraq as the culprit of choice.

Washington went into anti-Iraq high gear with plans being secretly drawn up to take over Baghdad once decisive demonstration of force had reorganized Afghanistan. The plan to take Iraq developed around interrelated steps: First, the United States began to define Iraq as the central pillar of an "axis of evil." In speech after speech, Bush executive staff members began to identify Iraq as a sponsor of terrorists (i.e. Hezbollah and now Al Qaeda), and as a rogue regime in potential possession of weapons of mass destruction. The message consistently conveyed to the American people was this: *We saw on 9/11 what evil these bastards are capable of; we can't wait until they're equipped with weapons of mass destruction.* Saddam Hussein has used such weapons in the past on his own people. He is now our sworn enemy and if given the chance, he'll use them against us as well.

Secondly, once the public was convinced of the need to act on Iraq, the plan could proceed to isolate the Baghdad regime through calls for immediate and unconditional surrender of all weapons of mass destruction it was hiding or developing. Failure to do so—already a given premise within the calculation—would force the U.S.'s hand, either to "lead a coalition of the willing" to force Saddam out, or to "go it alone."

In a secret and personal memo written on March 25, 2002, by Britain's foreign secretary, Jack Straw, to Prime Minister Tony Blair on the eve of the latter's meeting with George W. Bush in Crawford, Texas, Straw laid out the case for military intervention against Iraq. The memo is significant in that it anticipates the opposition the British government would surely face from both the public and the prime minister's Parliamentary Labour Party (PLP). The memo also provides selling points on how best to counter such opposition:

> The rewards from your [i.e., Tony Blair's] visit to Crawford will be few. The risks are high, both for you and for the Government. I judge that there is at present no majority inside the PLP for any military action against Iraq, (alongside a greater readiness in the PLP to surface their concerns). Colleagues know that Saddam and the Iraqi regime are bad. Making that case is easy. But we have a long way to go to convince them as to:
> - the scale of the threat from Iraq and why this has got worse recently;
> - what distinguishes the Iraqi threat from that of eg Iran and North Korea so as to justify military action;
> - the justification for any military action in terms of international law;
> - And, whether the consequence of military action really would be a compliant, law abiding replacement government.

In each case, Straw points to lack of real evidence that could stand the test of public scrutiny, but suggests an approach that might get around the pitfalls of having to prove each element of the case:

> If 11 September had not happened, it is doubtful that the US would now be considering military action against Iraq. In addition, there has been no credible evidence to link Iraq with UBL and Al Qaida. Objectively, the threat from Iraq has not worsened as a result of 11 September.

Straw firmly believed at the time the memo was written that the government's best bet to convince the PLP of the need for military action was to emphasize

> ...that Iraq poses a unique and present danger...that it:
> * invaded a neighbour;
> * has used WMD and would use them again;
> * is in breach of nine UNSCRS.

The memo goes on to acknowledge (obviously in reference to Bush, Cheney, Rumsfeld et al.) that "there are those who say that an attack on Iraq would be justified whether or not weapons inspectors were readmitted." Against this view, Straw expressed his firm belief "that a demand for the unfettered readmission of weapons inspectors [is] essential, in terms of public explanation, and in terms of legal sanction for any subsequent military action."

Any unbiased reader proficient in English would walk away from the content of the Straw memo with the distinct impression that military action against Iraq was essentially a done deal. Every effort had to be made, however, to ensure that the ensuing attack would stand the test of international law and could be endorsed by sitting members of parliament and by public opinion. This interpretation of the memo is corroborated by two subsequent developments.

The Bush administration's plans on Iraq developed in large measure along the outline sketched in the Straw memo. In August 2002, Vice President Cheney declared with unerring conviction: "There is no doubt that Saddam now has weapons of mass destruction; there is no doubt that he's amassing them to use against our friends, against our allies, and against us."

The administration argued that the United Nations Security Council Resolutions obtained in 1991, 1993, and 1998, allowing the use of force against Iraq, were still in place so that an additional resolution was in fact unnecessary. Under pressure from the British prime minister, Colin Powell and scores of international scholars, the Bush team was eventually persuaded to go back to the U.N. to seek an additional resolution stating that Iraq was in continued material breach of the terms of Resolution 687 (reached at the end of the first Gulf war), and if it did not immediately comply by turning over all weapons of mass destruction, serious consequences could follow. The administration had also begun to feel the heat building in every country around the world. In protest marches of a magnitude unseen in modern history, the populations of entire cities all across Europe, Asia, and the Americas took to the streets, demanding that Bush & Co. rescind their war plans.

The Bush administration countered with arguments repeated in endless series of quips, pics, and sound bites month after month; they were the same ones used by Colin Powell (accompanied by George Tenet and John Negroponte) in his extraordinary appearance before the U.N. Security Council. As Powell reportedly later acknowledged, this was not one of the more stellar moments in his long career. The U.S. team pulled out all the stops for its February 5, 2003, show and tell display of all the "intelligence evidence" collected against Iraq. The presentation included taped phone conversations between Iraqi government officials, statements made by Iraqi defectors, satellite still photos, satellite video footage of what were allegedly mobile biological labs and chemical weapons depots, as well as detailed information on Iraq's attempts to reconstitute its nuclear weapons program.

Among the biological warfare agents the U.S. claimed Iraq was producing were highly lethal toxins such as anthrax, botulinum, aflatoxin, typhus, tetanus, and ricin. Powell and his team cited numerous first-hand sources who claimed to have detailed knowledge of the true extent of Iraq's germ warfare arsenal. The U.S. also claimed that Iraq had

> ...embedded key portions of its illicit chemical weapons infrastructure within its legitimate civilian industry. To all outward appearances, even to experts, the infrastructure looks like an ordinary civilian operation... Under the guise of dual-use infrastructure, Iraq has undertaken an effort to reconstitute facilities that were closely associated with its past program to develop and produce chemical weapons.[91]

The U.S. further claimed that Iraq's attempts to purchase "high-specification aluminum tubes from 11 different countries" were clear evidence of a "massive clandestine nuclear weapons program."

With the devil painted on the wall, Powell's U.S. team then depicted what was surely for all Americans the ultimate horror scenario as a very real and present danger: "...the potentially much more sinister nexus between Iraq and the Al-Qaida terrorist network, a nexus that combines classic terrorist organizations and modern methods of murder."[92]

All roads to Baghdad originated ultimately in the ruins of the World Trade Center. Colin Powell was adamant in claiming that "every statement I make today is backed up by sources, solid sources. These are not assertions. What we're giving you are facts and conclusions based on solid intelligence."

Following this masterful presentation of all the rock-solid evidence at the U.N., the Bush White House went into what could be described as a collective Helen Mirren pout: stoic determination to prevail and fully aware of the pain that duty would demand. In a press conference on March 6, 2003, just days before the U.S. all-out attack on Iraq, Bush stood fully enveloped in feigned solemnity before the world's cameras and querying journalists:

> I, eh, wish Saddam Hussein had listened to the demands of the world and disarmed. That was my hope. That's why I first went to the United Nations to begin with on September 12, 2002, to address those issues as forthrightly as I knew how. That's why months later we went to the Security Council to get another resolution called 1441, which was unanimously approved by the Security Council, demanding that Saddam Hussein disarm. I...am hopeful that he does disarm. If he won't do so voluntarily, we will disarm him.

Powell's U.N. presentation was based on the October 2002 National Intelligence Estimate (NIE), Iraq's Continuing Programs for Weapons of Mass Destruction, prepared by the CIA under acting director George "slam-dunk" Tenet. It was "a pure coincidence" that the NIE contained all that the Bush White House, the PNAC strategy group, and the oil conglomerates wanted to hear. This was the same information given to Congress when George W. Bush asked for a green light for war. Mr. Bush continued to accuse the Baghdad regime of "engaging in a willful charade with inspectors." "He has used weapons of mass destruction on his own people; he's invaded countries in his own neighborhood. He's trained and financed Al Qaeda-type organizations before."

On March 20, 2003, Bush Forty-Three made good on his threats to overthrow Saddam. Once U.S. troops were on the ground in Iraq, many good, trusting Americans were convinced that WMDs would be popping up everywhere, adding to the list of incentives to make those *we-told-you-so!* phone calls to the Elysee Palace and the Kanzleramt. And search they did—with every man, woman, child, rabbit, and cockroach brought into the hunt. The Iraq Survey Group scoured the land far and wide; they searched high and low; they climbed every mountain and opened every pickle jar—all to no avail. Even the most ardent Bible & Bush believers began to have their secret moments of doubt. Democratic lambs, not normally wanting to stir up any kind of fuss, picked up on calls for an official explanation of what had gone wrong with the intelligence. In a loud domino effect, the political sentiment eventually swung in favor of a full congressional investigation into how the country could have been duped into going to war based on all the "solid facts" furnished by the intelligence community.

More than a year later, on July 9, 2004, the full results of the Senate Select Committee's "Report on the U.S. Intelligence Community's Prewar Intelligence on Iraq" were released. In substance the report confirmed what the rest of the world (i.e., the people, not governmental partners in crime) had known from the start. Among the numerous key findings of the committee:

> Conclusion 1. Most of the major key judgments in the Intelligence Community's October 2002 National Intelligence Estimate (NIE)...either overstated, or were not supported by, the underlying intelligence reporting. A series of failures, particularly in analytic trade craft, led to the mischaracterization of the intelligence. The major key judgments in the NIE, particularly that Iraq "is reconstituting its nuclear program," "has chemical and biological weapons," was developing an unmanned aerial vehicle (UAV) "probably intended to deliver biological warfare agents," and that "all key aspects—research & development (R&D), production, and weaponization—of Iraq's offensive biological weapons (BW) program are active and that most elements are larger and more advanced than they were before the Gulf War," either overstated, or were not supported by, the underlying intelligence reporting provided to the Committee...
>
> The assessment that Iraq "is reconstituting its nuclear program" was not supported by the intelligence provided to the Committee...
>
> The statement in the key judgments of the NIE that "Baghdad has chemical and biological weapons" overstated both what was known and what intelligence analysts judged about Iraq's chemical and biological weapons holdings...
>
> Similarly, the assessment that "all key aspects—R&D, production, and weaponization—of Iraq's offensive BW program are active and that most elements are larger and more advanced than they were before the Gulf War" was not supported by the underlying intelligence provided to the Committee.

In its second conclusion the committee also chided the intelligence community both for the egregious failure to communicate the thoroughly uncertain reliability status of its "assessments" and for its failure to "explain to policymakers the uncertainties behind the judgments in the October 2002 National Intelligence Estimate."[93]

The intelligence community was also sharply criticized for failure to achieve effective interdepartmental communication and feedback, and for its lack of reliable human intelligence sources. In addition, the committee took the analysts to task for the readiness of all involved to assume as legitimate and given the very evidence being sought. This tendency to "group think" precluded legitimate challenges to assumptions, which should have been, but were not, an integral component of analysis procedures. Moreover, as later confirmed by former U.N. weapons inspector David Kay, what information the CIA did have was largely being rewritten based on old data obtained from the early 1990s, prior to the outbreak of Operation Desert Storm.

In an interview conducted with Jim Lehrer on PBS's *The Newshour* the day the Senate report was released, committee chairman Pat Roberts and vice-chairman Jay Rockefeller elaborated extensively on the findings. Roberts stated bluntly that "in the end, what the president and the Congress used to send the country to war, was information provided by the intelligence community, and that information was flawed."

In response to a question posed by Lehrer, Rockefeller added that "we had flawed intelligence on enough, I think, to cause us not to go to war...We went in under false pretenses. We did not have the reason to do it, and my judgment is the president wanted to do it."[94]

The question of White House involvement in pressuring the intelligence community to arrive at specific results was answered for the most part along party lines. The majority Republicans in the Committee concluded that there was no evidence to suggest that any undue pressure had come from the Bush administration to prejudice the findings. Speaking perhaps for the minority opinion, Jay Rockefeller had this to say:

> There are various ways of doing pressure. What we focused on in the report was, you know, if we interviewed an analyst and we're putting pressure on that analyst, did any of them complain that our staff was putting pressure on them. The answer is, "No, they didn't." But there are all kinds of other pressures. Mr. Kerr, who is deputy director of the Central Intelligence Agency, did a study on this and came out with the

view that there was a lot of pressure. George Tenet himself was visited by analysts who complained of being pressured, and he used the phrase, "if you want to relieve the pressure," thus justifying the fact that there was pressure on these folks, "then don't tell them anything if there isn't new information." But most importantly, the ombudsman of the CIA, whose job it is to listen to people's complaints said that in his thirty-two years of work in the CIA, he had never seen so much hammering, i.e. pressure, on the intelligence community.

Plus the fact that all during this time in advance of the intelligence that he was getting, the president and his top administrators—the top folks—you know, Cheney, Rice, Rumsfeld, Wolfowitz, etc.—they were putting out these hair-raising, paralyzing, horrifying statements about what was going to happen, was about to come back to the homeland, the mushroom cloud. This is pressure, folks. This is pressure.[95]

Lawrence Wilkerson, who served as Colin Powell's own chief of staff, had helped prepare the report that the former secretary of state gave to the United Nations on February 5, 2003. In an interview with *NOW*'s David Broncaccio, Wilkerson stated categorically: "I participated in a hoax on the American people, the international community, and the United Nations Security Council."[96]

Wilkerson, who has been a Republican all his life, also explained that Vice President Dick Cheney was the driving force behind the pro-war movement to remove Saddam Hussein from power. In a follow-up to Wilkerson's revelations, Broncaccio asked: "Is it reasonable to think the administration knew about this skepticism?" [The reference was to the serious doubts expressed within the intelligence community concerning the "evidence" Powell was presenting against Iraq.]

Wilkerson replied: "Six months ago, I would have said 'No.' Em, eh, since that time, however, there have been some revelations."

At least one of the "revelations" Wilkerson may have been referring to was a whopper: On May 1, 2005, the world finally learned the real story. The *Sunday Times* (London) obtained a top secret memo dated July 23, 2002, which had been sent to the most senior British cabinet members who were in charge of working out a cogent Iraq policy with the United States. The memo was written in the form of minutes summarizing all the talking points of Prime Minister Tony Blair's July 23, 2002, meeting with these cabinet members. The "Downing Street Memo" (as it has come to be known) gives decisive insight into the Bush/neo-con administration's strategy, motives, and publicly touted rationale for invading Iraq.

("C" refers to Sir Richard Dearlove, director of Britain's foreign intelligence service MI6):

SECRET AND STRICTLY PERSONAL – UK EYES ONLY

DAVID MANNING

FROM: MATTHEW RYCROST

DATE: 23 JULY 2002

S 195/02

CC: Defence Secretary, Foreign Secretary, Attorney-General, Sir Richard Wilson, John Scarlett, Francis Richards, CDS, C, Jonathan Powell, Sally Morgan, Alastair Campbell IRAQ: PRIME MINISTER'S MEETING, 23 JULY Copy addressees and you met the Prime Minister on 23 July to discuss Iraq. *This record is extremely sensitive. No further copies should be made. It should be shown only to those with a genuine need to know its contents* [emphasis in the original text]. John Scarlett summarized the intelligence and latest JIC assessment. Saddam's regime was tough and based on extreme fear. The only way to overthrow it was likely to be by massive military action. Saddam was worried and expected an attack, probably by air and land, but he was not convinced that it would be immediate or overwhelming. His regime expected their neighbours to line up with the U.S. Saddam knew that regular army morale was poor. Real support for Saddam among the public was probably narrowly based.

C reported on his recent talks in Washington. There was a perceptible shift in attitude. Military action was now seen as inevitable. Bush wanted to remove Saddam, through military action, justified by the conjunction of terrorism and WMD. But the intelligence and facts were being fixed around the policy. The NSC had no patience with the UN route, and no enthusiasm for publishing material on the Iraqi regime's record. There was little discussion in Washington of the aftermath after military action... .

It doesn't get any more damning than this. Not only was the Bush team hell-bent on going into Iraq regardless of the results obtained by U.N. weapons inspectors on frequent visits to the country, but the evidence itself was "being fixed"—in other words trumped up, fabricated, to justify the invasion. Like dirty cops who plant evidence against non-compliant bad guys in order to secure a conviction, Bush & Co. set about constructing the *mise en scène* of war in Iraq long before the world had a clue as to what was happening.

Under Bush Forty-Three, the neo-con wing of the GOP and its blood brothers in the petroleum and energy industries were able to lend entirely new dimensions and depth to the Republican promise popularized during the Harding campaign to have "less government in business and more business in government." The Bush administration was even able to mimic history, with Halliburton easily outdoing Harry F. Sinclair's Mammoth Oil Company (of Harding era Teapot Dome fame) in its ability to secure zero-bid government contracts in support of its desperate attempts to secure Iraqi *Oil!* (Where, oh where is Upton Sinclair?)

In spite of all evidence to the contrary, former Halliburton CEO and US VP Dick Cheney stepped before an audience at the American Enterprise Institute and declared unwaveringly: "Any suggestion that pre-war information was distorted, hyped or fabricated by the leader of the nation, is utterly false."[97] But according to information declassified in 2005, the Bush administration had even been warned that claims Iraq had sought to buy large quantities of uranium in Africa were most likely false. And yet in his State of the Union speech in January of 2003, the president stood before the nation and asserted that Iraq had indeed attempted to make such a purchase.

The purpose of knowingly and deliberately making such dubious accusations? To frighten the American people into supporting the build-up to war. Senator Carl Levin put it this way: "The only possible purpose of telling the American people that the British had learned that Saddam was seeking uranium in Africa was to create the impression that we believed it. But we didn't believe it! The intelligence community did not believe it!"

Lawrence Wilkerson assessed the pre-war efforts of Cheney and Rumsfeld in now familiarly grim terms: "What I saw was a cabal between the vice president of the United States, Richard Cheney, and the secretary of defense, Donald Rumsfeld."

Paul R. Pillar, former national intelligence official responsible for the Middle East sector from 2000—2005 was equally forthright in his indictment. Pillar's scathing critique of the Bush team's Iraq policy cited in particular the enormous disparity between the administration's pre-war pro-war propaganda and the real facts established by the intelligence community itself. In no uncertain terms, Pillar concluded that official intelligence analysis was not relied on in making even the most significant national security decisions, that intelligence was misused publicly to justify decisions already made, that damaging ill will developed between policymakers and intelligence officers, and that the intelligence community's own work was politicized.[98]

Former UN chief weapons inspector Hans Blix described a revealing encounter he had personally had with Dick Cheney in 2002 in which the vice president was quite candid about his and the administration's plans: "Vice President Cheney said that 'I want to...tell you that we will not hesitate to discredit you in favor of disarmament.' That's what he said. I was a little taken aback."[99]

In truth, no one had been fooled by the propaganda trail except the screaming goons who filled Madison Square Garden in 2004 with their silly foam thongs: *Flip-flop! Flip-flop!* (in reference to John Kerry's justified retake on the build-up to war).[100] Those who had kept apace with the administration's tricks knew exactly what it was all about and they carried placards saying so: "No blood for oil!" The *Moscow Times* had been right all along with its insight into where the Project for the New American Century was leading: "Not since 'Mein Kampf' has a geopolitical punch been so blatantly telegraphed, years ahead of the blow."[101]

Like John Gotti at the confession booth, George W. Bush came forward in January 2006 in a nationally televised mea culpa: "It is true that much of the intelligence turned out to be wrong. As president I am responsible for the decision to go into Iraq...My decision to remove Saddam Hussein was the right decision."

As much as the Big Business White House must be faulted for catastrophic environmental policies and its implementation of fiscal policies that were nothing short of declarations of class war, the decision to remove Saddam Hussein was justified, but not for any of the reasons concocted by the Bush team. There was only one legitimate reason to invade Iraq and that was to do the morally right thing. The Left objected, but had failed to do its homework. No self-respecting humanist should ever befriend the devil.

Prior to the invasion, Western Europe was full of exiled Iraqis who had left their beloved home by any means available, risking not only their own lives and limbs, but also those of their families left behind. Many were first-hand witnesses of the unspeakable brutality of Saddam's henchmen. Thousands of others suffered in hell on earth. Iraqi parents had been forced to watch as brutes gouged out the eyes of their children; men and women were put feet first through power-driven tree shredders; others had their legs twisted around until bones snapped and sockets shattered; some were thrown into baths of acid. Given the existing options, all but the truly insane would have preferred even the Republic of Exxon to the ceaseless, senseless horrors that defined Saddam's regime. The tragedies of Iraq, Rwanda, and Darfur attest to the impotence of moral reason and to the failure of the "global community" at large to do what is right. Why did Colin Powell's

U.N. presentation not put the human tragedy at the forefront of the only argument that mattered? In the era of globalized wants and needs, it was surely deemed of least importance. There were other, far more pressing forces driving the show, and thanks to 9/11 the chosen strategy stood a far better chance of being accepted by the American public.

Aside from offering a sanctioned cover for armed efforts to reshape the global petro-political landscape, the attacks of 9/11 were enormously beneficial to the Bush/industry administration in yet other important and potentially far-reaching ways. The United States Constitution places the burden of declaring war in the seats of Congress. However, with passage of the National Security Act in 1947 the president's power was greatly expanded to include an entire network of executive instruments such as the Department of Defense, the Central Intelligence Agency, the National Security Council, and later the ultra-secretive and high-tech National Security Agency. In more recent history most instances of US military intervention have proceeded on an ad hoc basis, circumventing the need for a formal declaration of war.

What sets the "war on terror" apart from all previous instances of military conflict is the fact that the enemy is postulated and hence potentially eternal. By declaring "We are at war!" as an expected response to the attacks, the president invoked all the special privileges that Congress has historically granted a wartime president. The post 9/11 "forces of terror" are real jihaddists on fast-tracks to paradise, but at the same time they are projected enemy combatants whose existence begins and ends as an operationalized abstract *definiendum* within the executive branch of the American government. While the former can be curtailed and even eradicated, the latter, as an ideal, is potentially immortal, limited only by the political will and tactical necessity to maintain its existence. Since there is no centralized enemy authority capable of final, formal surrender under contractually verifiable terms, the only conceivable termination of the conflict becomes the sole prerogative of the party under attack. In other words, the war on terror is over when the president says it is.

Several important policy shifts have been implemented as a result of this open-ended conflict. The office of the executive has assumed for itself the enormously powerful role of defining who and what the enemy is, while at the same time declaring all evidence that might invalidate the designation as both inadmissible and potentially damaging to national security. By declaring (as Lincoln had done with his "doctrine of necessity" and the ensuing suspension of the writ of *habeas corpus*) national security to be the ultimate goal under which all others must be subordinated, the president further assumed for the executive office the unitary power of deciding the fate of all those it defined as "enemy combatants."

The extent to which the Bush administration was willing to use "the terror card" in fulfilling its quest for unchecked power became apparent throughout the pre-election period in 2004. With Democrats branded as sissified intellectuals incapable of hitting 'em hard (a characterization appropriate in domestic but not foreign affairs), the Rove-Luntz strategists hammered home the message that in order to keep the country safe, the American people needed to put that straight-shootin', kick-ass Texas farm boy back in the White House for four more years. As a presentable, effective political tool in the hands and mouths of Republican strategists, the "war against terror" became a linguistic conjuring trick claiming legitimately to invoke the same rights and privileges as those accorded the executive in real instances of congressionally declared "war."

The shock of 9/11 and the horror of the carnage left in its wake would seem to legitimize the use of "all means necessary" to defeat the enemy that inflicted the wounds. When the *New York Times* revealed in December 2005 that shortly after 9/11 George W. Bush himself had authorized the National Security Agency to tape the phone calls of thousands of American citizens, much of the country was aghast at the prospect that Big Government was listening in on their most banal chats and intimate secrets. The president used a nationally televised news conference to defend his decision—with the now universally valid one-size-fits-all excuse: *We are at war!*

In an essay published on Slate.com, Walter Shapiro accurately commented on Karl Rove's "plan for GOP victory" in 2006: "War, war, and more war."[102] Referring to a speech Rove had given earlier to a few hundred fans at the Republican National Committee, Shapiro emphasized that

> …what Rove underscored in his…presentation was the degree to which the White House [is] gearing up for another "He protected Us Against Osama bin Laden Even If We Can't Find Him" election. For terrorism remains the most potent political argument for reelecting a Republican Congress. Iraq may be a quagmire, but Rove and Co. are stuck with it. That is why Democratic critics will constantly hear variants of Rove's assertion, "To retreat before victory has been won would be a reckless act —and the president and our party will not allow it."[103]

With the ever-ready specter of bombs exploding on Main Street, *Yourtown, USA*, what red-blooded American patriot or politician would dare oppose anything the president deemed necessary in the war on terror? At the going rate, the menace of Al Qaeda as a political operative has worked every time and will likely continue to do so as long as the threat "exists." To be sure, the success rate has been so impressive that if one didn't know better, one could almost suspect that Osama was on the payroll of some hidden Washington lobbyist or think tank. With the events of 9/11 gradually fading in public memory, one can only hope that some sharp-minded Republican strategist doesn't come up with a plan to "re-enact" things to stoke the embers of fear.

In its efforts to consolidate power, the Bush/industry administration was executing yet another coup. With Federalist Society member John Roberts already confirmed as the new chief justice of the Supreme Court, the administration was pulling all the stops to get Bush-nominee Samuel Alito (a.k.a. "Scalito") successfully through the arduous Senate confirmation hearings. They needn't have worried. In one of the best political commentaries ever penned, the otherwise modestly reserved editorial board of the *New York Times* warned of the long-term consequences of a Roberts-Thomas-Scalia-Alito Court. Aptly titled "Senators in Need of a Spine," the editorial chided Senate Democrats in particular for their apparent willingness "to cooperate" with White House plans to staff the Court in the president's image "by rolling over and playing dead."[104]

Among bloggers and pundits nationwide who had grasped the significance of allowing the mild-mannered proponent of the unitary executive doctrine ("The president has not just some executive powers, but the executive power—the whole thing"[105]) into the highest chambers of the judiciary, fear and disgust were palpable. Author Paul Rogat Loeb referred to the Alito nomination as "a clear and present danger that can only be stopped by our Senators finding the courage to challenge an administration that respects only power."[106] Echoing the sentiments of "rank-and-file Democrats across the country," Robert Parry insisted that "Democratic leaders, for once, set aside political gamesmanship and recognize that Alito and his radical theories of an all-powerful executive are a serious threat to the future of the American democratic Republic."[107]

Various civil rights groups, the National Organization for Women, and Senators Kennedy and Kerry of Massachusetts called for a filibuster to at least grab public attention to the dangers of an imperial presidency sanctioned by a quintet of pro-industrial judicial pit bulls. With Democrats ever fearful of their own shadows cast in the bright light of Republican paternal rectitude, religious self-righteousness and self-proclaimed monopoly on patriotism, the weak-kneed "opposition" caved in to the red flags being raised by GOP ideologues warning of the "radical" nature of the filibuster. The *New York Times* had the clinching response: "It's easy to see why Democrats are frightened of it [a filibuster]. But from our perspective, there are some things far more frightening. One of them is Samuel Alito on the Supreme Court."[108]

As predicted, the Democratic swing votes were more concerned about the campaign after-effects that party-pooping on the shoo-in nominee might have had. In an act of chivalrous gallantry worthy of medieval knights, the guiltless father-knows-best contingent of the Republican wing had already chided the unwieldy troublemakers Kennedy and Biden for making poor Ms. Alito cry in public. The strategically wounded and camera-ready spouse hadn't expected people to be so mean to her sweet hubby during the confirmation hearings. *The very idea!* of actually pressing Sam on important issues like the legality of federal wiretapping of private citizens, the unlimited detention of defined enemy combatants, or the use of extraordinary rendition (and torture) to make uncooperative detainees more pliable. Not that the misguided questions of fractious senators mattered much anyhow. Answering out of a closet so deep not even Houdini could have escaped, Mr. Alito tefloned his way out of any answers that might later have stuck.

In the end, the conscience of the nation rested on the courage of Senator Kennedy to piss on Mr. Specter's pious pouts by holding out the judicial can of worms for the world to smell. In a speech given January 19, 2006, to the Center for American Progress, Senator Kennedy again warned the nation that, if confirmed, Alito would "have an enormous impact on our basic rights and liberties for years and even decades to come."[109] Though vast numbers of soccer moms and Nascar dads took no notice of the hearings or their outcome (how could Alito compete with the yearly countdown to the Superbowl?), handing over the Supreme Court to pro-industry, anti-civil-liberty ideologues of the Bush/Cheney imprimatur was nothing short of the American version of the Enabling Act. For as Kennedy clearly spelled out, much, indeed the future of American civil society was at a turning point. At stake, as leading proponents of expanded executive power have reasoned,[110] is the constitutionality of a number of federal agencies and commissions charged with important oversight functions. One can only imagine the outcome of future U.S. "elections" (already a disgrace among nations) if the Federal Election Commission were placed in the sole domain of the president: Republican powerhouse incumbents would routinely garner enough votes to break the ninety percentile barrier. Ditto for the Federal Communications Commission in its capacity to shape the definition of "acceptable" content on radio, television, and the Internet. The outrage conjured up over Janet Jackson's boob blitz hints at the family-value future in store. Republican-controlled databases replete with information collected on every Google search keyed in by uncomfortable political opponents could be used for everything from simple blackmail (*How do you think your family is going to feel when they find out you spent forty minutes watching two men getting it on?*) to search, seizure, and indefinite detention at an undisclosed location.

With such critical agencies in the hands of an absolute executive, it's difficult to imagine that any of the big players like Enron, Koch Industries, Global Crossing, Ford, and GM would ever be called to task for transgressions of any kind. How many thousands would have to die before public sentiment stirred revolt? How many Erin Brokovitch causes would have to emerge before "the people" exercised their Second Amendment right. All in the name of national security—a scenario all-too familiar in the deadliest versions of twentieth-century political systems.

Mr. Bush succeeded, quite surreptitiously as many constitutional scholars would argue, in implementing the alleged power of the unitary executive by either nullifying or completely circumventing with the stroke of his pen more than 750 pieces of legislation through "presidential signing statements". Among the most notable and egregious of these edicts was his de facto annulment of the ban on torture throughout both the U.S. military and the intelligence services. Bush declared: "The president, as commander in chief, can waive the torture ban if he decides the harsh interrogation techniques will assist in preventing terrorist attacks."

Conveniently for the party in power, the ill-defined "terror" parameter becomes universally applicable. At the same time, potential dissent can be effectively curtailed by the general alert warning of potential "accomplices," signaling the need for extended surveillance of the legal defenders of constitutional and human rights. All opposition thus becomes a potential enemy of the state, which in turn sets in motion all means necessary to assure that both the adopted New Speak as well as a constant state of fear and loathing of the executive-defined "enemy" remain operationally viable.

Washington Post staff writer Dan Eggen described in March of 2006 how the Bush administration had "launched initiatives targeting journalists and their possible government sources. The efforts included several FBI probes, a polygraph investigation inside the CIA and a warning from the Justice Department that reporters could be prosecuted under espionage laws." The *Post* also quoted the concern expressed by Bill Keller, executive editor of the *New York Times*, that "some days it sounds like the administration is declaring war at home on the values it professes to be promoting abroad."[111] Totalitarianism can be rooted even in the exceptionally banal: *Flip-flop! Flip-flop!*

The military/industrial administration has had a remarkable record of consistency. Just as they systematically positioned all the right people in the most strategically leveraged positions; just as they succeeded in rewriting important regulations on toxic emissions into air, water, and soil for the benefit of industrial polluters; just as they rolled back the irksome executive orders signed by Clinton to protect key elements of the environment; just as they rewrote science on the most important issues affecting us all, so, too, they set out to lock in the biggest prize of all: Iraq's vast supplies of oil. And not to be forgotten: the Centgas/Unocal dreams from the Reagan years of oil and gas pipelines from Central Asia through Afghanistan and Pakistan to waiting American tankers in the Indian Ocean. Two pearls in this world's oyster were ripe for the taking.

But how? Not even the mumbo-jumbo gurus of Washington's best think tanks would be able to justify to the world *just doing it*. Lo and behold, just like the thousands of missing votes in Florida, fate had a way of making all things work together for the good of those lying in wait.

The official version is that Lee Harvey Al Qaeda acted alone in masterminding the events that changed American history. From the psychotic fringe convinced the earth rests firmly within the nightmares of Charles Manson, to the left wing boudoirs of intellectual Europe, theories of who was really behind 9/11 popped up everywhere, with many Muslims immediately pointing the fingers at a US/Zionist conspiracy. In the more staidly cynical bohemian enclaves of Europe, quiet suspicions looked back across the Atlantic itself, murmuring queries no one was allowed to hear. And so, forced to reflect on "the unthinkable" itself and to ponder the one question few have dared to ask...

Would they? *Hahahahahahahahaha!*
Did they? *"The science is still out."*

Ample anomalous peculiarities in the Bush/Cheney story of hijacked planes warrant an altogether new—and this time truly *independent* investigation of the events. The "official" script, directed by Philip Zelikow (just one of many hand-select luminaries of the Bush administration), concealed or willingly ignored more than 120 aspects of the tragedy, according to David Ray Griffin's *The 9/11 Commission Report: Omissions and Distortions*. Had the nation's journalists been doing their jobs instead of beating the drums and blowing the whistles of teary-eyed patriots, the world could have heard the first-hand testimony of William Rodriguez, janitor of twenty years in the North Tower. According to Rodriguez's sworn account, corroborated by fourteen of the janitorial staff near him at the time, the very first explosion came from the sub-basement levels of the building *before* the planes ever struck the higher floors. One man working in the sub-basement level at the time received life-threatening third-degree burns from the explosions that went off where he was, *before* the planes struck the upper floors hundreds of yards away.

One of the many courageous New York City firefighters who risked his life to save those trapped in the buildings, stated in an interview immediately after the events that he had distinctly heard a "Boom! Boom! Boom!—all the way down—as if they had planted detonations." Of course with George W. Bush's own younger brother and cousin at the helm of the company in charge of security at the World Trade Center, one would have to wonder how explosives could ever have found their way into the buildings.

What most definitely will *not* remain anomalous are the long-term after-effects of the collapse of World Trade Centers 1, 2, and 7. Instead of duly warning and evacuating the residents of affected boroughs in New York City and neighboring New Jersey, the Bush-led Environmental Protection Agency, with Christie Todd-Whitman still at the megaphone, went public just days after the events with this pacifying message: "I am glad to reassure the people of New York and Washington, D.C., that their air is safe to breathe and their water is safe to drink."

It was of course yet another of the Bush administration's many bizarre renditions of facts. In the Deutsche Bank building across from World Trade Centers 1 and 2, the amount of the potent carcinogen asbestos measured in the air exceeded the recognized safety limits by 112,000 times—virtually guaranteeing the later development of asbestosis or lung cancer for those who breathed it. The toxic cloud that spread out over the surrounding areas contained an entire assortment of poisons besides asbestos, including radioactive Americium, the heavy metals lead, mercury, chromium, and many polycyclic aromatic hydrocarbons, PCBs, and dioxins—thousands and thousands of tons of poisons, whose synergistic effects are completely unknown. The air conditioning system of the South Tower alone contained some 90,000 pounds of freon. When incinerated, this gaseous fluorocarbon is transformed into phosgene, the same chemical warfare agent that killed untold numbers of soldiers in World War I. Many of the poisons still linger silently in the offices, stores, schools, hospitals, and apartments in the affected areas.

Experts agree that in the coming years there will be a mass epidemic of all kinds of nasty illnesses, many of them incurable and fatal, stemming from these toxins. When interviewed for director Penry Little's documentary film *911—Dust and Deceit at the World Trade Center*, New York Congresswoman Carolyn Maloney emphasized that the people who are now beginning to die are all "in the prime of their lives." Jeffrey Smith, a worker at ground zero, added the ominous prediction that "the death toll from 9/11 is going to be astronomically higher than 3,000. Who knows how many thousands are going to die beyond that because of exposure?"

Mortgaging What Future?

Even in the one area long touted as the Party's home turf—a sound fiscus—the GOP has failed miserably. The hopelessly imbalanced budget at the end of the Reagan-Bush I era and its astronomic accumulation of debt taught the post-Clinton administrations nothing. In fact, they succeeded in taking a budget surplus and turning it into the largest heap of red ink the world had ever seen through an entire series of tax cuts worth more than $850 billion, and that in the midst of two armed conflicts and a net loss of close to three million jobs, vast numbers of which were in important manufacturing sectors. In the aftermath of 9/11, Alan Greenspan and the Federal Reserve adopted an "accommodative" monetary policy, which not only encouraged Americans to go out and shop (not that it took much prodding), but also pumped in excess of $3 trillion in credit into the economy. Personal debt skyrocketed to summits unseen while the overall savings rate of the nation as a whole dropped to a negative sum.

Americans then discovered a very clever way of making money out of nowhere by inflating the value of the houses they owned. On both coasts in particular, real estate experienced double-digit price increases. By 2004 sellers were routinely receiving hundreds of offers for what just a few years before might have been considered junk. One interested buyer in Los Angeles told of visiting a run-down shack-like two-story in a gang-infested barrio in which drive-by shootings had become a regular form of neighborhood entertainment, only to find a line of other interested parties stretching around the block. New Yorkers told of the cut-throat race to land property, with each potential buyer offering thousands more than the last. Mortgage lenders did their part to add to the mess by offering interest-only payment plans.

Convinced that long-term interest rates would stay low and that the value of their houses would continue to climb forever, many smart shoppers began to see buying and selling houses or "flipping" as it came to be known, as the get-rich-quick scheme made in Fed heaven. Suddenly home equity loans were there for the taking. Swarms of homeowners grabbed at the chance to be millionaires overnight by borrowing against the value of their homes, perceived to be doubling by the minute. And banks everywhere were all too eager to oblige. With so much cash in their pockets, the new rich went on an extended shopping spree, totaling up more personal debt than the world had ever seen. One more red stain added to the catastrophic current account deficit of $750 billion for the fiscal year 2005 alone.[112] Even outgoing Fed Chairman Alan Greenspan eventually saw the writing on the wall and began to warn in his humblest of ways of the dangers of inflated assets.

As U.S. interest rates began to rise, so too did the lack of liquidity especially among homeowners who had acquired so-called "sub-prime" mortgages. By the summer of 2007, the Ponzi scheme had completely collapsed, threatening to hurl the nation into a full-scale recession. Foreclosures and defaults reached an all-time high in December of 2007. The lack of transparency in the vast mortgage market added to the general volatility, jeopardizing many of the largest financial institutions. By some estimates, write-offs by both domestic and foreign banks could easily have exceeded half a trillion dollars. The dollar nose-dived on world markets, threatening the exalted status of the greenback as the world's reserve currency and robbing Americans and the government of what little buying power they had left.

This all had a tremendously negative impact on U.S. solvency as a whole. According to a report released by OMB Watch in 2004, federal revenue for that year was at its lowest (15.7 percent of GDP) in fifty-four years. As a percentage of GDP, tax revenues dropped by 5.2 percent in the first three years of the G. W. Bush presidency in large measure because of the massive tax cuts hammered through Congress by the Republican power brokers as favors for their wealthy sugar daddies. To make matters even worse, the president planned to increase the national debt by $1.9 trillion from 2004 to 2009, while continuing to reduce taxes.[113] In March of 2005, OMB Watch concluded that "if current tax policies are made permanent without revenue offsets, as the president and many Republicans in Congress would like, the debt held by the public will explode to well more than 100 percent of the total economic output of the country before 2050."[114]

Figures drawn up by the Congressional Budget Office in 2005 at the request of Nancy Pelosi, House minority leader at the time, indicated that under the Bush plan to make permanent the tax cuts enacted in 2001 and 2003, the national debt would suddenly skyrocket after 2010. It was for that reason that the Republican administration drew up a five-year plan with a 2009 cut-off date. "By doing so," OMB Watch warned, "they are intentionally misleading the American public about the true cost of their current tax and budget policies."[115]

In February 2006, George W. Bush submitted his proposed 2007 budget to Congress. Like a chip off the old Reagan chopping block, the budget called for all the predictable slashes in social programs (28 percent in education, 30 percent in housing and urban development) plus $36 billion in Medicare reductions over five years, and all the equally predictable increases in defense (7 percent) and homeland security (9.8 percent). As North Dakota Democratic Senator Kent Conrad assessed it: "This budget is utterly detached from any financial reality— first keep running up the debt; just keep adding up to the charge card; just keep mortgaging the future."

White House Press Secretary Scott McClellan countered in typical Republican spin: "We are a nation at war. We're going to fund our troops."

By March 2006, for the first time in history, the U.S. government was on the verge of defaulting on its treasury notes. Without the additional shot in the arm, the U.S. government would not even have been able to pay the interest on the colossal debts to its many foreign creditors. Both houses of Congress jumped in to allow the government to borrow an additional $781 billion. During the first five years of the G. W. Bush administration, Congress was forced to raise the debt ceiling on four different occasions. The financial tax-cut wunderkinder of the Bush administration had managed to bring the national debt ceiling to a staggering $9 trillion—the largest in human history. Worked out on a person-to-person basis, that was $30,000 for every man, woman, and child in the country. Add to these already breath-taking numbers future entitlement liabilities in social security and Medicare and the mounds of red ink climb to an incomprehensible $41 trillion. The only thing keeping the banana republic afloat is the willingness of foreign governments to buy up U.S. treasuries to the tune of $3 billion per day! If the central banks of China and Japan ever decided that it was time to invest more wisely, the U.S. would be sunk. The debts stretch as far as the eyes can or will ever see, from now until kingdom come. With all manufacturing done in China and the greatest number of jobs created to make you smile, how could the country ever hope to pay it off? In all likelihood, they can't. And the situation is likely to look even bleaker once the Gulf Arab states introduce the ultimate challenge to the greenback in the form of a unified currency in 2010. These deep-pocketed money-pits will then be accepting their own bank notes in payment for oil and will no longer be required to hold dollars in reserve, ending the global dominance of the U.S. currency. Realizing the dire straits the U.S. economy was in—yet again under a Republican administration—Senate Minority Leader Harry Reid of Nevada was quoted as saying George W. Bush "will go down as the worst president this country has ever had."[116] (Mr. Reid echoed the sentiments of much of the human race.)

But the substance of Republican funny math was known long before Mr. Bush was ever appointed to office.

The Means Justify the End

The patterns described in the chapters on America's dominant public ideology are unmistakable and systemic; the lessons to be learned no less so. The Republican Party reflects an outdated ideology rooted in an eighteenth-century model of the individual/society complex that is no longer adequate to the world of the twenty-first century. Supported by a distinctly narrow interpretation of Christianity, the party presents to the world a dysfunctional model of the perfect society, free of any control that is not derived from the party's own cadre schools of industrial psychologists. This "plan" for economic and social progress allows crimes against humanity and the environment to flourish while millions fall through the cracks of a "safety net" being dismantled by relentless privatization. The great tragedy is that Americans—even would-be opponents—have swallowed the pitch by promising to "heal the nation" by "uniting us as a people and getting beyond our differences," as if economic and social disparity were based on conflicting answers to the question *Paper or plastic?* And the entire world suffers.

One persistent problem in American politics is the blatant attempt by both parties to hide explicit class allegiance. *Class war* is a key term whose legitimacy the Democrats refuse to acknowledge. The rationale behind such futile efforts becomes clear, however, when the link between class-consciousness and political affiliation is more closely examined. The paradigm of *What's the Matter with Kansas?*[117] articulates in part the breakdown in the theorized correspondent relationship, long touted as a staple by orthodox Marxists, between social class and political affiliation. As the analyses of Herbert Marcuse et al. clearly showed, there is often a perplexing asymmetry between the social reality predicated on class defined by income levels and discernible trends in political affiliation. To date, vast numbers of working class Americans, many barely able to eke out an existence, are staunch Republicans, with absolutely nothing to gain from GOP victories, but everything to lose.

Given these historical premises, what can a "Democratic Party" be? In its efforts to establish itself as both a kinder, gentler "party of the common people" and a viable alternative to all-business-all-the-time Republicans, the Democratic Party is forced into a constant catch-up game of piecemeal engineering, attempting to reverse the damage done by the government of Big Corporations, while forced to fight with the artillery meted out by the other side.

History speaks against a future radical departure from the underlying premises: the country was founded on the belief in the unlimited expansion of private enterprise. Expressed in positive terms, the Republican political-economic ideology liberates the human individual entrepreneurial spirit from the constraints of societal obligations to a "common good," while replacing the general will with personal freedom and self-reliance. In this antistatist doctrine, the potential for individual freedom codified within liberal democracies recognizes the possibility for complete emancipation from the contexts of society per se, with no one else to answer to except one's own conscience and bank account.

One further fundamental flaw in the plan to allow "market forces" to sort out our problems is the underlying and deeply erroneous assumption that all problems are economic in nature. They aren't.

Economic policies must be critically examined with respect to their legitimacy. What role should we allow for the human community? What importance should we attach to the biological survival of the planetary ecosystem? When does the widening gap between rich and poor become irreversibly unstable and self-destructive? Whose responsibility are social justice and individual survival? Surely any economic model or system of government that denies adequate health care[118] to more than forty-seven million and forces countless others to sleep in cardboard boxes in the dead of winter, scraping through garbage cans for nourishment, cannot be worthy of emulation by anyone. Instead of screaming *flip-flop!* as their slogans of choice, Americans nationwide should have been yelling *Been there, done that, hated it!* But the deception is so thorough and the spin on reality so depravedly unique that no other answers come to the public mind except the parroted party lines.

Over and over again, throughout much of American history, Republican administrations have pushed through fiscal policies that have benefited the wealthy to the detriment of the middle and working classes. Coupled with globalization and dramatic shifts into information-based economies, imbalanced tax cuts and their concomitant patterns of wealth redistribution have effected many of the deeply-disturbing trends described in this book.

Republican ideology as manifested in quasi laissez-faire social, economic, and public policies threatens far more than the survival of millions at home between the Atlantic and the Pacific. The need to regulate the energy sectors, the transportation industry, the use of natural resources, and all economic activity whatsoever in accordance with the potential impact of industry and consumption on the biosphere as a whole arises from the simple fact that the damage being done to every niche of our ecosystem is so overwhelming in its long-term impact, so complex in the synergistic effects of changes to just one component, that nothing short of a global consortium of ecologists and the readiness of human power players to look beyond the short-sighted interests of their individual nation-states and constituencies can have any hope of saving us from destruction. Specific industries and industrial practices need to be stopped dead in their tracks, while others need to be promoted if research and development aims contribute to potential solutions rather than add to the problems.

The GOP's free market-based solutions for every problem from constipation to Al Qaeda arise in the heads of people who have lost touch with reality. All the years spent jiggling and rigging the figures for profit margins and asset values have blinded their minds to the fact that there is a non-economic reality out there of a dying planet, with the potential for catastrophes far surpassing the great flood. Corporations operate solely for profit. Unless there is substantial money involved, there is no corporate interest in de-toxifying the oceans and atmosphere, not at least before the Atlantic has reached the 52nd floor of the Empire State Building. *But hey, dude, you gotta look on the bright side. Just think of how many new business opportunities rising ocean levels will bring! The right idea put into practice could make us millions with new housing construction projects in the middle of the oceans over Kansas and Nebraska. And we haven't even mentioned the new sporting challenges that will open up. How about diving tours to former offices in Dallas or the Chicago Loop? And hey, surf's up!*

Marking a ballot for the Republican Party is not the political equivalent to choosing vanilla over chocolate ice cream; it is the moral equivalent to driving drunk. The premises of laissez-faire lead to a state in which human reason relinquishes its claim on setting priorities and policies for the good of all life to the profit-driven dictates of business interests. The American model of free-market society allows the haphazard, short-term concerns of corporations to take precedence over the life-world essential to all. In a reversal of the classical equation of instrumental reason, such a model implies that the means (free market privatization) justify the end (whatever the bank account can deliver). Given the extension of Classical Liberalism to its current historical fulfillment in globalization with a potential reversal in the roles of developed and developing, rich and poor nations, the ultimate goal of the best life for the greatest number has been assigned to the accidental unfolding of the means—"market forces." By unanimous consent the corporate world of mega-dollars and super-egos has been declared the universal victor in the battle of ideas. The stakes are high—nothing less than the survival of our planet.

The same men who didn't give a damn how many thousands of pension funds they destroyed or how many thousands of investors' lives they ruined with their willfully, maliciously fraudulent schemes to stuff their own bank accounts, are the same men who are equally indifferent to the fate of every plant and animal on the only biological habitat we have. It should not shock us when men schooled in a different world of faith and values see nothing worth redeeming in ours. *Is one any less evil than the other?*

Notes

1 The investigative research conducted by Greg Palast points to previous, ostensibly legitimate supervision of voter registration conducted in 1998 by Professional Service Inc., which charged the state of Florida a total of $5,700 for the task. The fee promised Database Technologies was $2,317,800 for the first year alone. Cf. Greg Palast, *The Best Democracy Money Can Buy* (London: Plume, 2003) 44.

2 *Ibid.* 59.

3 *Ibid.*

4 *Ibid.*, 54–55.

5 The Websites for both contain detailed lists of campaign financing figures. See http://www.opensecrets.org and http://www.publicintegrity.org.

6 Source: Center for Responsive Politics.

7 Greg Palast, *The Best Democracy Money Can Buy*, 111.

8 Several studies have examined in great detail how money controls legislation. See in particular Elizabeth Drew, *The Corruption of American Politics* (New York: Overlook Press, 2000); Jeffrey Birnbaum, *The Lobbyists. How Influence Peddlars Work Their Way in Washington* (New York: Random House, 1992); Elizabeth Drew, *Politics and Money: The New Road to Corruption* (New York: Macmillan, 1983); Philip Stern, *The Best Congress Money Can Buy* (New York: Pantheon Books, 1988). Of older date but no less important is Karl Schriftgiesser, *The Lobbyists: The Art and Business of Influencing Lawmakers* (Boston: Little, Brown & Co., 1951).

9 See http://www.judicialwatch.org/1770.shtml.

10 Judy Pasternak, "Bush's Energy Plan Bares Industry Clout," *Los Angeles Times*, 26 August 2001, A2. See also Jim VandeHei, "Cheney Sees Little Role for Conservation in Energy Plan Aimed at Boosting Supply," *Wall Street Journal*, 1 May 2001, A12.

11 Greg Hitt, "Bush's Donors Have a Long Wish-List and Expect Results," *Wall Street Journal*, 31 July 2000, A1.

12 Carl Pope and Paul Rauber, *Strategic Ignorance. Why the Bush Administration Is Recklessly Destroying a Century of Environmental Progress* (San Francisco: Sierra Club Books, 2004) 102–111.

13 Public Citizen mentions the communities of Marlboro, New Jersey, as well as twenty-two states that were reportedly considering bans in July of 2000. The first law prohibiting cell phone use while driving was enacted in Brooklyn, Ohio, in 1999. See Public Citizen's full report: *Safeguards at Risk: John Graham and Corporate America's Back Door to the Bush White House* (March 2001), available at: http://www.citizen.org/congress/regulations/graham.html.

14 Mary O'Brien, "Natural Resistance," *Eugene Weekly*, 5 April 2001.

15 The complete text of Heinzerling's testimony is available at: http://www.citizen.org/congress/regulations/graham/heinzerling_testimony.html.

16 See Lisa Heinzerling's testimony as well as Ralph A. Luken, *Efficiency in Environmental Regulation: A Benefit-Cost Analysis of Alternative Approaches* (Boston: Kluwer Academic Publications, 1990).

17 Carl Pope and Paul Rauber, *Strategic Ignorance*, 52.

18 Robert F. Kennedy, Jr., *Crimes Against Nature. How George W. Bush and His Corporate Pals Are Plundering the Country and Hijacking Our Democracy* (New York: HarperCollins Publishers, 2004) 59.

19 *Ibid.*

20 *Ibid.*, 54; see also David Helvarg, "Unwise Use: Gale Norton's New Environmentalism; Secretary of the Interior Gale Norton," *The Progressive*, 1 June 2003.

21 For a closer look at Griles's connections to all the right people, see Michael Shnayerson, "Sale of the Wild," *Vanity Fair* (September 2003).

22 Robert F. Kennedy, Jr., *Crimes Against Nature*, 97.

23 *Ibid.*

24 *Ibid.*, 99. See also "The Cheney Energy Task Force: How NRDC Brought the Records to Light," NRDC, accessed at: http://www.nrdc.org/air/energy/taskforce/bkgrd.asp; "Heavily Censored Papers Show Industry Writes Energy Report," viewed at: http://www.nrdc.org/media/pressreleases/020327.asp.

25 Robert F. Kennedy, Jr., *Crimes Against Nature*, 99.

26 Dahlia Lithwick, "Je Refuse!" Slate.com, 14 March 2004. The full text is available at http://www.slate.com/id/2097350/.

27 Paul Krugman, "A Vision of Power," *New York Times*, 27 April 2004, A25.

28 *Ibid.*

29 Department of Justice press release "Koch Industries Indicted for Environmental Crimes at Refinery." The full text of the press statement can be found at http://www.usdoj.gov /opa/pr/2000/September/573enrd.htm.

30 *Ibid.*

31 Beth O'Brien, "Industrial Upset Pollution: Who Pays the Price? An Analysis of the Health and Financial Impacts of Unpermitted Industrial Emissions," (8 August 2005) published by Public Citizen and accessible at: http://www.citizen.org/documents.

32 Bob Williams and Kevin Bogardus, "Koch's Low Profile Belies Political Power. Private oil company does both business and politics with the shades drawn," Center for Public Integrity, (15 July 2004), available at: http://www.publicintegrity.org/oil.

33 Jeff Krehely, Meaghan House and Emily Kernan, "Axis of Ideology. Conservative Foundations and Public Policy," National Committee for Responsive Philanthropy (2 March 2004) 10.

34 Cited in Robert F. Kennedy, Jr., *Crimes Against Nature*, 119.

35 *Ibid.*

36 Michael Collins, "Bush Easy on Utilities, Group Says," *Cincinnati Post*, 6 May 2004.

37 *Ibid.*, 40.

38 Susan E. Dudley, "Primer on Regulation," (*Policy Resource* No. 1, Mercatus Policy Series, November 2005).

39 See W. Mark Crain, "The Impact of Regulatory Costs on Small Firms," (U.S. Small Business Administration's Office of Advocacy, 2005); James Ralph Edwards, *Regulation, the Constitution, and the Economy: The Regulatory Road to Serfdom* (Lanham, Maryland: University of America, 1998); Gordon Tullock, Arthur Seldon and Gordon L. Brady, "Government Failure: A Primer in Public Choice," (Cato Institute, 2000).

40 Daniel R. Simmons, "Public Interest Comment on EPA's Proposed National Emissions Standards for Mercury," (Regulatory Studies Program, George Mason University, June 28, 2004).

41 Notice for the Proposed National Emission Standards for Hazardous Air Pollutants; and, in the Alternative, Proposed Standards of Performance for New and Existing Stationary Sources: Electric Utility Steam Generating Units; Proposed Rule, 69 Fed. Reg. 20, p. 4652 (January 20, 2004) and 69 Fed. Reg. 87, p. 25052 (May 5, 2004). Docket ID No. OAR-2002-0056; FRL-7658-4.

42 *Ibid.*, 6–7.

43 Simmons cites the work of K. Crump et al., "Benchmark Concentrations for MeHg Obtained from the Seychelles Child Development Study," *Environmental Health Perspectives* 108, no. 3 (2000): 257–263; G. Myers et al., "Secondary Analysis from the Seychelles Child Development Study: The Child Behavior Checklist," *Environmental Research* 84, no. 1 (2000): 12–19; and C. Axtell et al., "Association between MeHg Exposure from Fish Con-

sumption and Child Development at Five and a Half Years of Age in the Seychelles Child Development Study: An Evaluation of Nonlinear Relationships," *Environmental Research* 84, no. 2 (2000): 71–80.

44 Notice for the Proposed National Emission Standards for Hazardous Air Pollutants; and, in the Alternative, Proposed Standards of Performance for New and Existing Stationary Sources: Electric Utility Steam Generating Units; Proposed Rule, 69 Fed. Reg. At 4658.

45 Daniel R. Simmons, *Public Interest Comment*, 8.

46 *Ibid.*, 12.

47 *Ibid.*, 13.

48 The text of the circular can be obtained from http://www.whitehouse.gov/emb/circulars/a004/a-4.pdf.

49 He cites the estimate arrived at by Randall Lutter, John F. Morrall, W. Kip Viscusi, "The Cost-per-Life-Saved Cutoff for Safety-Enhancing Regulations," *Economic Inquiry* 37, no. 599 (1999).

50 The report mentions the House Committee on Government Reform, Minority Staff, Special Investigations Division, "Politics and Science in the Bush Administration," August 2003.

51 Union of Concerned Scientists, *Scientific Integrity in Policymaking. An Investigation into the Bush Administration's Misuse of Science*, March 2004, 1–2. The full text of both reports is available at http://www.ucsusa.org.

52 *Ibid.*, 2.

53 J. J. Fialka, "Mercury Threat to Children Rising, Says Unreleased EPA Report Warns," *Wall Street Journal*, 20 February 2003, A1.

54 E. Pianin, "Proposed Mercury Rules Bear Industry Mark," *Washington Post*, 31 January 2004, A04. See also the editorial "Mercurial Rulemaking," *Washington Post*, 19 March 2005, B06.

55 Lisa Heinzerling and Rena Steinzor, "Political Intervention: The White House Doctors Mercury Conclusions," (Center for American Progress, 16 April 2004).

56 *Ibid.*

57 *Ibid.*

58 Robert F. Kennedy, Jr., *Crimes Against Nature*, 85.

59 David Michaels et al., "Advice without Dissent," *Science*, vol. 298, 25 October 2005.

60 *Ibid.*

61 *Ibid.*

62 *Ibid.*

63 Union of Concerned Scientists, *Scientific Integrity in Policymaking*, 22. The UCS investigation also cites a report from the Office of Representative Edward J. Markey, "Turning Lead Into Gold: How the Bush Administration is Poisoning the Lead Advisory Committee at the CDC," 8 October 2002. This report is available online at http://www.house.gov/markey/Issues/iss_environment_rpt021008.pdf.

64 Union of Concerned Scientists, *Integrity in Policymaking*, 22. The figures cited refer to those the UCS says were contained in the deposition of Dr. William Banner, Jr., June 13, 2002, in *State of Rhode Island v. Lead Industries Association*, C.A. No. 99-5526 (Superior Court of RI, April 2, 2003).

65 See Robert F. Kennedy, Jr., *Crimes Against Nature*, 88.

66 *Ibid.*, 91.

67 The brief commentary on the survey is available at: http://www.nrdc.org/bushrecord /printArcicles/2005_02.asp.

68 For a brief history of the government's track record on dealing with atrazine and related chemicals, see the NRDC Web site at http://www.nrdc.org. See also Kennedy's brief summary in *Crimes Against Nature*, 91–92.

69 "EPA Cut Private Deal with Manufacturers," National Resources Defense Council. The texts of this and related NRDC documents can be obtained from http://www.nrdc.org.

70 Robert F. Kennedy, Jr., *Crimes Against Nature*, 77.

71 "Permafrost Thaw Might Speed Global Warming," *Los Angeles Times*, 31 December 2005, A9.

72 Isabella Velicogna and John Wahr, "Measurements of Time-Variable Gravity Show Mass Loss in Antarctica," *Science online*, 2 March 2006.

73 "Human Impacts on Climate," American Geophysical Union, December 2003. The text of the joint statement can be read at: http://www.agu.org/sci_soc/policy/sci_pol.html.

74 *Ibid.*

75 Andrew C. Revkin, "Climate Expert Says NASA Tried to Silence Him," *New York Times*, 29 January 2006, 1.1.

76 David Michaels, "The Art of 'Manufacturing Uncertainty,'" *Los Angeles Times*, 24 June 2005, B11.

77 *Ibid.*

78 Other samples of catachrestic right-wingisms can be found in the text of the open letter at http://www.freedomworks.org/processor/printer.php?issue_id1393.

79 *Ibid.*

80 Heather Timmons, "Climate Change Is Called Economic Threat at Talks," *New York Times*, 16 March 2005, A6.

81 Lee Raymond, CEO and Chairman of ExxonMobil on *Charlie Rose* (PBS) 8 November 2005.

82 "The Environment: A Cleaner, Safer, Healthier America," The Luntz Research Companies–Straight Talk, 132. The full text of the document can be viewed at http://www. luntzspeak.com.

83 *Ibid.*, 137.

84 *Ibid.*, 132: "A compelling story, even if factually inaccurate, can be more emotionally compelling than a dry recitation of the truth."

85 Testimony of Governor Mike Leavitt, Senate confirmation hearings September 17, 2003.

86 *Ibid.*

87 David Martin, "Plans for Iraq Attack Began On 9/11," *CBS News*. For the full text of the report see http://www.cbsnews.com/stories/2002/09/04/september11.

88 Bob Woodward, *Plan of Attack* (New York: Simon & Schuster, 2004) 24–26.

89 *Ibid.*, 25.

90 Thomas Donnelly, Donald Kagan, Gary Schmitt, "Rebuilding America's Defenses–Strategy, Forces and Resources for a New Century," (Project for the New American Century, 2000) 51.

91 Remarks by U.S. Secretary of State Colin L. Powell to the United Nations Security Council, 5 February 2003.

92 *Ibid.*

93 Source: United States Senate Report on the U.S. Intelligence Community's Prewar Intelligence Assessments on Iraq.

94 Pat Roberts and Jay Rockefeller in conversation with Jim Lehrer, *The News Hour* (PBS) 9 July 2004.

95 Jay Rockefeller in conversation with Tim Russert, *Meet the Press* (NBC) 11 July 2004.

96 Lawrence Wilkerson in an interview with David Broncaccio, *NOW* (PBS) 3 February 2006.

97 Dick Cheney in a speech given November 21 2005, to the American Enterprise Institute.

98 Paul R. Pillar, "Intelligence, Policy, and the War in Iraq," *Foreign Affairs*, vol. 85, no. 2 (March/April 2006): 15.

99 Hans Blix, quoted on *NOW* (PBS) 3 February 2006.

100 Kansas being what it is, a full disclosure of the Bush push to war at the time of the Republican National Convention would likely even have strengthened these Christian jihadis in their conviction that Bush was the strong man for the job.

101 Chris Floyd, "Global Eye–Dark Passage," *Moscow Times*, 20 September 2002.

102 Walter Shapiro, "Rove: It's the (eternal) war stupid!" Slate.com, 21 January 2006.

103 *Ibid.*

104 "Senators in Need of a Spine," *New York Times* (editorial), 26 January 2006, A22.

105 Samuel Alito in a speech given in November 2000 to the Federalist Society.

106 Paul Rogat Loeb, "Alito's Clear and Present Danger," Tompaine.com, 24 January 2006, http://www.Tompaine.com.

107 Robert Parry, "Blocking Alito," Tompaine.com, 30 January 2006, http://www.Tompaine.com.

108 "Senators in Need of a Spine," *New York Times, supra,* at note 104.

109 Senator Ted Kennedy on the nomination of Samuel Alito, *Congressional Quarterly Transcriptions* 19 January 2006.

110 See in particular Steven G. Calabresi, "The Structural Constitution: Unitary Executive, Plural Judiciary," *Harvard Law Review*, vol. 105, no. 6 (1992): 1153; Steven G. Calabresi and Christopher S. Yoo, "The UnitaryExecutive during the second half-century," *Harvard*

Journal of Law & Public Policy, vol. 26, issue 3 (2003): 667; Steven G. Calabresi and Saikrishna B. Prakash, "The President's power to execute the Laws (Response to Lawrence Lessig and Cass A. Sunstein, *Columbia Law Review*, vol. 104, no. 3 (1994): 1)," *Yale Law Review*, vol. 104, no. 3 (1994); Cass Sunstein, "The Rehnquist Revolution," *The New Republic*, 27 December 2004.

111 Dan Eggen, "White House Trains Efforts on Media Leaks," *Washington Post*, 5 March 2006, A01.

112 See in particular Paul Krugman, *Fuzzy Math: The Essential Guide to the Bush Tax Plan* (New York: W. W. Norton & Company, 2001); Peter G. Peterson, *Running on Empty: How the Democratic and Republican Parties Are Bankrupting Our Future and What Americans Can Do About It* (New York: Farrar, Straus and Giroux, 2004); Paul Krugman, *The Great Unraveling: Losing Our Way in the New Century* (New York: W. W. Norton & Company, 2004) 443–466; William Bonner and Addison Wiggin, *Empire of Debt. The Rise of an Epic Financial Crisis* (Hoboken, New Jersey: John Wiley & Sons, 2006) 191–296.

113 Source: *2005 Federal Budget Continues Fiscal Decline* (4 February2004), OMB Watch; available at http://www.ombwatch.org/article/articleview/2028/1/2.

114 *Bush, Congress Hide True Costs of Permanent Tax Cuts* (21 March 2005),OMB Watch, available at: http://www.ombwatch.org/article/articleview/2740/1/92.

115 *Ibid.*

116 Carl Hulse, "Senate Approves Budget, Breaking Spending Limits," *New York Times*, 17 March 2006, A22.

117 See Thomas Frank, *What's the Matter with Kansas?* (New York: Henry Holt & Company, 2004).

118 The U.S. obsession with making health care dependent on employment makes about as much sense as making menu choices in a restaurant dependent on patrons' shoe sizes. Thanks to the lobbying power of the lucrative health insurance corporations, realistic alternatives that work in other countries are automatically labeled "unworkable" because they "limit" patients' options—as if having no health care at all were a viable choice.

Chapter 7

The Fading American Empire

No nation is permitted to live in ignorance with impunity.
—Thomas Jefferson, 1821, Virginia Board of Visitors

ALL AROUND THE WORLD, FIRST-HAND reports by people who've been to the United States for varying lengths of stay testify to the (were it not so alarming) almost comical depth of ignorance rampant among even so-called "educated" Americans. A young woman from Sao Paolo who had decided to brush up on her English by attending intensive classes while living with native speakers in a "home-stay" arrangement expressed her utter bewilderment at the question posed to her by the mother of the family: *Did you vote for Clinton in Brazil?*

Russian and Armenian students at a community college in California were told by their instructor to print instead of using longhand. The explanation: *Cursive writing is British; printing is American.*

A young man from Tokyo was astonished to learn that the two teenage children in his home-stay family (one in the ninth, the other in the eleventh grade) were unable to name the months of the year in their correct sequence.

A middle-aged woman from Eastern Europe who had been a devoted teacher all her life applied for a position with the Los Angeles Unified School District in the hope of being able to teach elementary students again. On her resume she naturally included the teaching experience she had gained with young Palestinians in the Gaza Strip. The LAUSD interviewer in charge of assessing the woman's credentials queried quite incredulously: *Now what could you possibly have been teaching in a strip club?*

Two young Swiss men on a trek around the world found themselves on the last leg of their journey in the United States. With their accents giving them away as "not from around these parts," they were politely asked by a group of young American teenagers where they were from. When they identified their country of origin as Switzerland, one of the Americans politely asked: *Which freeway do you take to get there?*

A young American college graduate from a world-renowned public university on the West Coast had decided to explore the world by teaching English abroad. Upon completion of the teacher-training program in Los Angeles, she decided to gather some specifics about potential target countries by calling the program coordinator. She was told that the best-paying jobs were likely to be in the United Arab Emirates and a few other countries in the Persian Gulf. About three weeks after this inquiry the young woman rang up the teacher training department yet again to vent her frustration: *I've been trying to find the contact information for that school you told me about in L.A. called "United Arab Emirates" but it's not listed in any phone book or school directory.*

A young woman from the north of England was dumbfounded by the Americans she'd become acquainted with on an outing to Las Vegas. Having clarified the origin of her accent—*I'm from England*—the young woman was suddenly at her wits' end with the follow-up question posed by her American admirers: *So did you like have to learn English in school and stuff? Cause you like hardly make any mistakes.*

The responses elicited by Jay Leno of NBC's *Tonight Show* while "Jay-Walking" are not, the program asserts, staged. As hard as it is to believe and as bitter as the truth is to swallow, the answers to some of the most basic questions about facts, figures, people, and places, reflect levels of ignorance few would believe possible. The participants, supposedly selected at random, derive from a wide spectrum of professions, ethnic and religious backgrounds, and income brackets. They have little in common except for being adult Americans who should know better. Here the tenor of some of the most astonishing samples:

Question: *What was the significance of Hiroshima?*
Answer: *Wasn't there some kind of poison gas attack there?*

Question: *What language do they speak in Great Britain?*
Answer: *British.*

Question: *Have you ever met anyone who speaks British?*
Answer: *No.*

Question: *When did man first land on the moon?*
Answer: *1920.*

Question: *If you met someone from Amsterdam, what nationality would they be?*
Answer: *I have no idea—Amsterdanian?*

Question: *What is the capital of the United States?*

Answer: *Las Vegas?*

Question: *When was World War III?*

Answer: *After World War II.*

College administrators and university professors have repeatedly expressed their exasperation at the deplorable writing and reading skills of American undergrads who are unable to correctly complete required assignments. Year after year, the results of international assessments in math and science routinely put U.S. students at levels far below those of students from even much poorer developing countries. In 2002, RoperASW prepared a survey for the National Geographic Education Foundation to obtain a broad measure of geographic literacy among young people (ages eighteen to twenty-four) in nine countries: Canada, France, Germany, Great Britain, Italy, Japan, Mexico, Sweden, and the United States. Although the United States had already bombed and invaded Afghanistan, only seventeen percent of the American youth could locate Afghanistan on a map. Only forty-two percent of the Americans knew that Al Qaeda and the Taliban were actually based in Afghanistan—the smallest percentage of correct answers of any national group represented in the survey. The Americans also ranked last on the question about the population size of the United States itself, with an astonishing thirty percent believing it to be between one and two billion! Many Americans had no clue where the Pacific Ocean was and when asked to identify the state of New York on a map, every single state west of the Mississippi River was identified at least once as New York. The highest number of total correct answers (seventy percent) on the survey was submitted by young people from Germany, Italy, and Sweden. U.S. youth scored next to last with fewer than fifty percent correct responses.[1]

The 2006 results of the Organisation for Economic Co-Operation and Development's Programme for International Student Assessment (PISA) were similarly discouraging. The survey is conducted triennially among fifteen-year-olds from fifty-seven participating countries to assess science, reading, and math skills. More than 400,000 students took part. In the science category, Finland attained first rank with a total of 563 points, followed by Hong Kong-China, Canada, and "Chinese Taipei". The United States came in twenty-ninth in rank with a total score of only 489, below countries with incomparably smaller per capita incomes. The assessment of student math performance was even worse, with the U.S. falling into thirty-fifth place (score: 474) behind Azerbaijan and the Russian Federation (both 476). Students from Taipei schools in contrast obtained the highest rank with a total score of 549.

These troubling displays of ignorance and sub-average aptitude are by no means restricted to the young or the trivial. Approximately 100,000 Americans die each year as a result of someone's inability to read, fill, or administer prescription medicine correctly. Patients have entered hospitals with gangrene on one foot only to have the healthy foot removed and the toxic appendage left intact. Women have gone into surgery for a mastectomy only to make the horrifying post-operative discovery that the healthy breast had been removed instead of the cancerous one. Patients have discovered weeks after surgery that they weren't improving because tools, pieces of rubber, cloth, metal or plastic had been left inside them during the operation.

On the battlefield, allied troops often have more to fear from American soldiers engaging in "friendly fire" (mistaking the Union Jack for a Swastika perhaps) than from the official enemies themselves. Failure to use or correctly read updated maps of specific target areas have resulted in tragic mishaps such as the May 8, 1999, bombing of the Chinese embassy in Belgrade. When Chinese President Hu visited Washington on April 20, 2006, the Americans committed an embarrassing diplomatic faux pas on the White House lawn by introducing the national anthem of the guest as being that of the "Republic of China" (a.k.a. Taiwan). Even NASA's Climate Orbiter went bye-bye at a cost of no less than $125 million because of "a failure to recognize and correct an error in a transfer of information between the Mars Climate Orbiter spacecraft team in Colorado and the Mission Navigation Team in California..." In simple English, the one team "used English units (e.g. inches, feet and pounds) while the other used metric units for a key spacecraft operation."[2]

Most public discussions and debates about sub-par student performance are linked to the failing school syndrome. Critique routinely evolves into a mud-slinging blame-game fought out among teachers, parents, students, and elected office holders responsible for churning out the money, or not. Teachers across the country rank among the most poorly paid and least respected (both elements go hand-in-hand) "white-collar" employees. Their jobs are also among the most dangerous.

A young man from New York had longed to be a teacher for many years. After less than three years on the job in the local public high school of a mid-sized community, he quit to go teach in the prison system, where it was safer. A similarly inspired educator from the South left his job after a brief stint of being threatened and abused with every pejorative in the book. "Not even for $250,000 a year could you get me to go through that again," he commented.

Huseyin, a young man from Istanbul, Turkey, was recruited into the Los Angeles Unified School District with imaginative positive ideas about educating young people and starting a new life in America. After less than six months on the job he was ready to leave. In reflecting back on the lessons he had learned before heading back home to Turkey, he described the period as "probably the worst experience of my life." The details of his encounter with America's brightest read like a film script. Students come to class consistently late and have often forgotten their books, paper, and pens. With the largest teenage pregnancy rates in the industrialized world—thanks both to the Vatican and to a proof-of-potency masculine mystique—Los Angeles County also has the highest high school dropout rates. Huseyin reported that several of the girls in his class were juggling roles of being both full-time middle school students and mothers. Most chose the dropout route.

Equally disheartened were two third-grade teachers who had been recruited from Spain. The female instructor had the "pleasure" of having to deal with a nine-year-old boy who had suddenly decided the classroom was the best place to masturbate. More commonplace frustrations arise from parents and older gang-banging siblings who threaten the instructors if "Junior" is given a bad grade or reprimanded for anything.

A young female instructor in an urban school witnessed first-hand the potential outcome of giving an honest grade. Knife scratches circumnavigated her car which rested helplessly on its four slashed tires. She was greeted in the hall the next day by the "C" student who smirkingly fired off the quick question: *How's your car?* As the smile inverted, he added: *The next time it's you, bitch!*

A teenage boy of Japanese descent was so desperate to find a school in which students were actually learning that he enrolled in a rather expensive program designed predominately for European and Japanese students of English as a Foreign Language. When the instructor realized the boy was a native speaker of English, the boy was told he had enrolled in the wrong program. "No," he explained, "I want to stay here because I'd like to learn something. At my school the teacher just reads the newspaper and all I can do is to try to memorize formulas or read."

Aghast at the very idea of the teacher reading the paper in class, the EFL instructor remarked that the teacher should be fired for being lazy and incompetent.

"Oh, no," the boy insisted. "It's not his fault. He doesn't really have a chance to teach because the students turn up their music so loud while they're dancing and no one would pay any attention anyhow. The teacher can't really stop them because they would threaten him or maybe beat him up. So he just reads the newspaper. But it's bad for me because I really want to learn."

According to extensive figures provided by the National Center for Education Statistics[3] 1.5 million acts of violence were perpetrated in public schools in the calendar years 1999–2000 alone. These astonishing numbers include bodily assault, violent robbery, and rape. A full seventy-seven percent of city and sixty-seven percent of "urban fringe" schools reported incidents of violence. Surveys and studies conducted over a five-year period (1998–2002) revealed that 234,000 teachers had been the victims of non-fatal crimes at school, 90,000 of which were of a violent nature.

Many of the country's little darlings are not only armed to the teeth but trigger-happy as well. Seventeen percent of the adolescent respondents to questions tabulated by the Youth Risk Behavior Survey in 2003 admitted to carrying weapons, and six percent acknowledged having done so on school premises.

When teachers are constantly forced to think about the very real possibility that little Johnny or Jose just might "pull out a .32 Magnum and blow my brains out if I cross him," social promotion and an "anything-you-say-honey" attitude become the safest path out. *You say "6 x 4 = 30"? I say "That sounds right to me too!"* No need for a bad report card here, not when the alternative is a nighttime drive-by.

Among the affluent, well-educated parents of suburbia, the quest to find the best education possible for mommy's dearest has begun to resemble the Japanese "escalator" system. To get into the top universities in the country, students need to have completed advanced placement courses at the most challenging, prestigious high schools. But that presupposes the best preparation possible during middle school, which in turn reflects mastery of all the solid fundamentals taught at elementary school. And to make sure their loved ones get a head start over the rest of the pack, parents cull the environs for the best possible preschools or kindergartens. Private schools and magnet schools compete with public facilities for the dollars of the best and brightest. But money doesn't guarantee acceptance in the most sought-after programs. Like elsewhere in life, connections are a big plus.

In major American urban centers, demographic statistics often dictate the options. With large concentrations of poorer Hispanic families, many of whom may even be undocumented, the number of students with very limited English proficiency has been rising dramatically. Native English-speaking children from more affluent "professional" households already enjoy a huge educational advantage over kids whose parents with a sixth-grade education possibly can't even read themselves and remain their entire lives lacking in social capital. With over thirty-six million residents, California has large numbers of inner-city schools with eighty to ninety percent immigrant children of limited English proficiency.

These schools routinely rank very low on the state's "Academic Performance Index" (API), which in turn is decisive in setting real estate prices. In 1999, California passed the Public Schools Accountability Act requiring the Department of Education to tabulate the indexed assessment of all public and charter schools statewide. The resulting Academic Performance Index ranks the state's schools on an assigned point system ranging from 200 to 1000. In general there is a direct correlation between the API of a region's schools and the median prices of homes located within that region. In a poorly performing area whose schools score only a paltry 300 on the API, the average home price would accordingly be a "mere" $300,000 (with eternal sunshine and roses and tulips in bloom year-round, a small price to pay perhaps). Logically, higher achieving schools at the upper end of the spectrum weigh in in the $1 million-plus tier.

Across the board nationwide, poverty is the clearest indicator of troubled youth who fail to complete high school, commit violent crimes, or end up in prison. The flight of money, education, and social capital away from the inner cities and impoverished neighborhoods into the safely secluded glens and dales of tree-lined suburban cul-de-sacs only exacerbates the problem by taking with it the much-needed funds for community development. The resulting economic-educational apartheid reflects the growing income disparity in the nation as a whole. Poverty breeds ignorance. Poverty breeds violence. Poverty breeds poverty.

Those left behind pin their hopes on the hoops or football. Talented youngsters from the neighborhood basketball courts have little left but dreams of one day making it into college on a generous athletic scholarship. To solve the problem of getting a talented basketballer (who perhaps can barely read and write) into a top-notch NCAA team, various fly-by-night bargain basement "prep schools" and "academies" have been established all around the country. Many offer "genuine" high school diplomas for "courses" (taught by the basketball coach himself) in spelling and math from the convenience of the neighborhood garage. A few high-tech versions even dole out online diplomas for athletes eager to get into the big leagues, with virtually no requirements. American colleges and universities do their part to perpetuate the scam by grabbing up the future Michaels and Kobes and offering the best conditions imaginable. There's money in them thar heels.[4]

Volumes can be and have been written about the long-term effects this sizzling potential for violence and overall social degradation have on the "learning environment" as a whole. But educators who have ever had the privilege of teaching in the poorest, remotest regions of Africa or Asia can testify to the ceaseless will to learn common to virtually all the students they encounter. Many will trek barefoot over miles of rocky terrain before the crack of dawn to take their seats on rickety wooden benches in a one-room dirt-floor classroom. Their thirst for learning cannot be stilled; their love of books is boundless. Witnessing the learning experience among the world's poorest children is the greatest reward any teacher can have. Yet it is a true rarity in American schools where kids have far more important and interesting things to do—checking out the latest video game, trying out the newest designer drugs, sporting the latest Nikes, pimpin' the hot new car. *Reading is like so not cool!*

In the days before NBA superstar Kobe Bryant let his testosterone get the better of him in a Las Vegas hotel, the young gazillionaire was more widely recognized by fans than any president living or dead could ever dream to be. To rake in a couple of additional millions the young super-hooper starred in a TV soft drink ad that purportedly featured some of his old teachers way back in his uncool school days. The Plain Jane Hasbeens from his math and science classes lauded his talent at learning. One teacher remarked that as a young kid Kobe even had what it took to become a scientist if he had wanted to. The camera swept back into the cooler world of the NBA locker room crowd to Kobe swallowing a load of his chosen soft drink, segued by a *Yeah, whatever* look. The message was clear: the great Kobe Bryant is rich beyond all get-out and this brood of book-wormy dorks and dweebs are a bunch of pathetic losers who even have to buy a car on an installment plan.

As it stands today, the United States now imports forty-eight percent of all its doctoral engineers from other countries, primarily from Asia. Once the home turf of the majority of the world's patent applicants, Nobel Prize winners, and research scientists in every conceivable field, the U.S. has lost its stranglehold on knowledge and technological expertise. Does this "culture of narcissism" realize it is no longer the envy of the rest of the planet? With the governments of China and India committed to leading the world into a new millennium dominated by new names and faces, the Americans have suddenly found themselves on the losing end of a long-term global strategy in which RBIs and touchdowns are relegated to the kids' corner. When Asians and Europeans have introduced the newest round of quantum computers and RNAi therapies, Americans will find themselves in perhaps an entirely new role in what they do best—entertaining the world. From sea to shining sea, one giant Disney World, with never-ending golf courses, football fields, and basketball courts, complete with cute entertainers of the highest self-esteem. *An entire country that loves to see you smile.*

Mucho Macho

Ignorance alone does not suffice to make the "all-American male" the most hated representative of the human species. Arrogance has done that. Thanks to self-fulfilling stereotypes perpetuated in dozens of Hollywood clichés, Chuck "Lethal" Macho is forever taking on everything from the common thug to invading armies of alien life forms and whipping them all. He's there to save the day and kick some ass. Irrespective of racial profile, his chiseled jaws of stone, muscles of steel, boundless courage, and alpha gorilla walk (NB: there are plenty of female reps of this ilk out there as well) never fail to set the rest of the world straight on who's "talking the talk and walking the walk."

In all likelihood the world would have been far less repulsed had the Abu Ghraib perpetrators looked more like Dick Cheney with an *iz-it-säfe* dentist drill. Instead, the global community was treated yet again to another *damned-yankee* pose of smirking schoolyard bullies beating the shit out of the "bad guys," for fun!

These were, after all, the faces and gestures familiar to every weaker sissy in schoolyard after schoolyard all across the United States. For all the red-blooded Americans out there in Bush country, boys had damned well better grow up to be kick-ass hard-hearted men and not some self-reflecting nanny-pansies. Better to have them totin' their guns[5] into kindergarten than gettin' all mushy over girl's stuff like empathy and concern for others.

Perhaps that explains "the fun" those two marines had as they marched out into the hills of Nevada and slaughtered thirty-seven wild horses including several pregnant mares—*just to watch 'em die*—"for the fun of it." Or the teenage boys who broke into a midwest animal shelter and beat the cats and kittens to death with baseball bats—"for the fun of it." Nope, no accusations of empathy there.

Or the three Florida teenage boys caught on video beating a homeless man to death—"for the fun of it." The National Coalition for the Homeless documented eighty-four hate crimes and acts of violence in 2005 alone. The organization also reported the fatal attack on a forty-nine-year-old ninety-pound homeless woman in Berkeley, California. The woman had worked as a legal writer and was known for her generosity to others, giving local kids her last cookies when she had any. Witnesses reported that the two eighteen-year-old perpetrators—it's always boys—had mercilessly attacked the woman, kicking her all over her body. Once she was down on the ground and no longer moving, they walked away. One then turned back and realized there might be one last thrill waiting to be had, so he took a running start and vaulted on top of the dying body with both feet. In Holly

Hill, Florida, five teenage boys sought relief from boredom by attacking Michael Roberts, a fifty-three year-old homeless man. After repeatedly beating the man with everything in sight, the teens left the man to bleed to death internally. The NCH emphasizes that many of the violent acts committed against society's defenseless go unreported, thereby impeding an accurate count of how many people fall victim to teenage "fun-and-games." The numbers are no doubt staggering.

Abu Ghraib was not a one-off aberration but the extension of sadistic domination consciously cultured by the most violent society in the industrialized world —real kick-ass potential enjoying a field day under just the right circumstances. America's frat-house humor has already begun to reap the whirlwind of global hatred. And if the intensity of world resentment is any reliable indicator, there's much more to come. By extension, as Chalmers Johnson[6] has demonstrated, America's self-ascribed role of global super-bully has laid the groundwork for many varied forms of retribution from friend and foe alike. From the rape of Japanese schoolgirls by U.S. enlisted men (*and the Pentagon insisted on keeping gays and lesbians out of the military?*), the invasion of islands and occupation of foreign lands, to the country's intransigence and deception on global issues that concern us all, America's "imperial hubris" has won it few friends, but an endless stream of enemies.

Last Curtain Call

There is a serious price to pay for the conscious decision to leave millions of people to their own devices. Organizational entities that have attained the complexity of advanced multi-ethnic nation-states linked in an array of globalized economic and monetary co-dependence require internal political-economic stability and goal-oriented predictability in order to function as viable partners. The IMF and the World Bank have long regarded such internal stability as an important prerequisite for a country's credit-worthiness. But societal stability and political integrity are predicated on an equally complex infrastructure developed over considerable time with long-term planning. It requires furthermore the coordination of interdisciplinary knowledge-based analyses and the cooperation of experts and human resources committed to a future vision. Among vast segments of the U.S. populace today, the only vision of any importance is that in the full-length mirror.

Throughout the Cold War Americans pictured their demise in a carpet of mushroom clouds seeding the landscape. Far more likely is a very "un-Hollywood" happy end—simply fading into mediocrity, as evidence everywhere suggests. Michel Albert lamented at the conclusion of the Reagan-Bush I era—a period that many hoped would mark the final curtain on the insanity of supply-side econom-ics—that America increasingly resembled not the self-described "world's only su-perpower" or the number one destination for brain-drain, nor the paragon model of technological expertise. Instead, Albert saw clear indications that the world's great *We're number one!* was beginning to resemble the developing world, with a select elite hermetically secured at the top, a dwindling middle class struggling to eke out an existence with few if any rewards, and a breathtaking array of abject poverty and ignorance. In a political system rigged to benefit the wealthy, all decisions in Wash-ington are determined by money. Both parties feed at the trough of key financial in-terests, and the people pay the price. And suffer.

As corporations abolish their pension plans in favor of temporary workers, millions of men and women are just a few lost paychecks away from homeless-ness, as a result of debts that cannot be repaid, chronic/acute illness, or trendy corporate downsizing. Subject to the whims of the giants of the drug industry, the working poor are often forced to choose between death by starvation or paying for acute medical emergencies.[7] Duped by their own small domains of provincial trivia, many of those most affected by public policies *According to Big Business* are too preoccupied with image betterment and car or body wax to pay much atten-tion to the fact that "income and wealth are piling up at the very top. More and more jobs are keeping people in poverty instead of out of poverty."[8]

A young USC student from provincial China openly explained how shocked he was when he took his first walk around the university campus near downtown Los Angeles. His image of America as the wealthiest and most technologically ad-vanced country on earth was immediately shattered as he gazed at the filthy houses and broken water mains; streets in a perpetual state of "closed for repair" thanks to more than 350,000 potholes deep enough to breed goldfish in; hand-scribbled "We're open" signs marred by swirls of ominous graffiti; and many beneficiaries of "trickle-down" economic policy rummaging through garbage cans for anything of value. Abject poverty. It reminded him, he said, "of the poorest parts of China." The result, as policy analyst Adam Hughes of OMB Watch put it, of

> ...years of federal budgets with severely misplaced priorities. Invest-ments in communities, people and infrastructure have been cut or scaled back each year under Bush. The average American family has more debt, less income, higher expenses, fewer government services and supports and less opportunity...Yet huge tax cuts for the wealthy continue and have resulted in a government in debt up to its eyeballs.[9]

The days of the United States as the dominant superpower are now in the past. In the best-case scenario of the country's fate, the business community's insatiable greed for cheap labor will permanently change the character of the American Empire. Impoverished migrants seeking to better themselves and their loved ones will inexorably replace the coldly efficient, rational-bureaucratic superstructure that dominated the latter half of the twentieth century. The country will slowly acquire a less imperialistically ambitious, less belligerent, and perhaps even more humane face as Spanish chips away at the hegemony of American dominance in English-based science and technology. The country will discover new interests rooted in different sounds, spicier flavors, traditions, and complexions. At the same time, those hardest hit by the downward spiral of wages will no doubt have wished congressional salaries could have been reduced to $12,000 per year so that both partisan blocs might then have been replaced with immigrants willing to "take the legislative jobs Americans don't want."

At the same time, the world has witnessed a momentous shift in wealth and financial prowess with a noticeable decline in American influence and buying power. The result has been what Maureen Dowd of the *New York Times* called a "red, white and blue tag sale" of the United States, as foreign sovereign wealth funds have stepped in to buy up all the cheap property *made in USA*, including, large stakes in the country's most prized financial power houses. When Harvard, Stanford, MIT, and Cal Tech have become the crown jewels of Beijing and/or Dubai, the people will perhaps realize what they have allowed to happen to their country. *Sic transit potentia.*

Alas, a much bleaker forecast is equally likely. For all its talk about the dangers posed by Al Qaeda in its "relentless war" against "Western ideals," the Bush administration was remarkably lax about the comings and goings across U.S. borders. (It was almost as if those in charge secretly knew there was no "real" danger lurking in the background. Had they truly believed in the boogey-men they publicly hung out to dry, they would have gained control of those borders.) Experts have repeatedly testified that it would require nothing but a little careful preparation for any sworn enemy to bring in a number of various types of weapons of mass destruction via container ships, trucks or small vans. Even the explosion of a conventional bomb laced with potent radioactive isotopes smuggled in in a backpack would suffice to force the indefinite evacuation of sixty blocks in a city like Manhattan. The clean-up costs alone would total in the trillions, bankrupting an already bankrupt regime. The same scenario repeated in Los Angeles,

Chicago, Houston, Dallas, Seattle, San Francisco, and Boston, would reduce the giant among giants to nothing more than a squeaking mouse. Perhaps the Republican butch boys would then decide to invade Australia, preferring once again to "fight them there so that we don't have to do so here." With Pandora's release of suicide squads sworn to exact revenge on the West's supermacho, means and motive combine in deadly combination. As Susan Neiman aptly put it, "If combined with the deliberate reproduction of nature's worst elements, like plague, terrorism's blend of moral and natural evil is so appalling that we seem doomed to despair."[10] But the Bush administration countered the threat with a smirking swagger and grossly misplaced priorities. Luckily for Al-Qaeda, the country is as vulnerable as it ever was. One can only wonder why.

The triumph of ignorance and bliss has brought the last vestiges of American "democracy" dangerously close to an altogether new form of society and government. The usurpation of power by corporate interests has succeeded so effortlessly that one could easily be led to believe that a cabal of political masterminds colluded to effect this silent coup d'état. Present policies seem to suggest that this is so. As many recent trends in voting patterns confirm, abstinence from the electoral process is also an indicator of hopeless helplessness.

On the one hand, voters know full well that hordes of GOP zealots and corporate lobbyists have a strangle hold on government, hence the growing popularity of grassroots initiatives and ballot measures that seek a direct form of government without the intermediaries of "elected" "representatives." The right-wing/centrist political establishment of the McCain ilk unerringly pontificates on the wonders of Reaganomics and free-market capitalism as a natural panacea for the human species. In truth, the Rhine and Scandinavian models of social market economies have put northern Europeans in much better positions when compared to the United States, with "healthier economies and longer healthy life expectancies, greater math and science literacy, free or affordable education from preschool through college, universal health care, less poverty and inequality and more corporations combining social responsibility with world-class innovation."[11] And they are still able to afford a minimum of four full weeks paid vacation, sick leave, two to three months of paid maternity leave, child day-care programs, all while achieving higher worker productivity.

At the other extreme are America's masses of nameless losers, victims ripe for the reaping by any party that should ever fearlessly put life above profit. But unable to read, doped up on crack and meth, dying from exposure to the elements and malnutrition, can these potential voters remember who they are? Are they registered to vote? Do they know what voting is? Are they even able to care?

Somewhere in between these two income extremes, radical individualism has created the appropriate climate in which the do-your-own-thing theme dominates, loosening the networks of inter-connectedness among people and robbing potential opposition of a common social reality. Across the board, knowledge is highly context-specific and provincial, resulting in further de-cohesion. No longer dependent on society as such, the omni-wireless individual has begun to deconstruct the political and to replace it with *myplace, myworld* as whatever I want it to be. A sanitized construct replete with imminent bliss—forever emptied of boredom and the efforts of concepts (or *Anstrengung des Begriffs* as Hegel called it). Highly idiosyncratic and cohort-based interests coupled with ignorance of the world outside the individual's specific framework of reference (one need only think of the video game industry's capacity to achieve total occupancy rates in the minds and daily schedules of teenage boys) have linked in a *fait accompli* fatal to the prerequisites of a functioning non-totalitarian form of government. The potentiality of group-targeted Internet-based entertainment systems signals one further step in allowing individuals and their perceived cohorts to rearrange "reality" with a focus on apolitical personal concepts of fun to the exclusion of all the ugly sides that reality offers on a daily basis. Cell phones and iPods with dozens of channels allowing the like-minded to share a ceaseless menu of entertainment offerings will form the sole content of what's left of a mental apparatus. A world of created ignorance becomes synonymous with apolitical bliss based on the exclusive dominance of a surrogate reality. So effective is the perpetual party-on machine that those occupying the frontline trenches in today's class warfare are not even aware of the battles they're losing.

The remnants of the political process seek to salvage what's left of the Republic following years of gutting by free-market Republicans at the helm. The situation was indeed so dire at the end of the George W Bush administration that all but the most hardened *Flip-Flop!* Stalwarts realized that they just might be looking at the bitter end of the American experiment and at an irredeemably distraught planet. If given the choice, many would likely have cast their votes for a Donald Duck/Dr. Dre ticket in lieu of anything resembling a continuation of the Bush & Co. regime. But the electorate continued to place too much emphasis on the image and personality of its presidential candidates at the expense of hardcore economic analyses and measures to correct the moribund status quo.

For millions of (finally) left-leaning younger voters, the great anything-but-Bush moment of hope arrived in the person of Barack Obama, Oprah protégé. But the persona was a construct based largely on a projected abstraction of youth, skin color, a counter-culture image, and an urgent need for post-incumbent *CHANGE!* Progressive-liberal Americans are eager to overcome barriers of race, gender, creed, and sexual orientation; Obama's progress in politics attested to the much-welcomed strides made in this direction. But his feel-good message rang hollow: *We are a nation that has grown apart*, he repeatedly lamented, with millions of media-savvy voters joining in on the refrain's promise of *bringing us together again as one people. We are all Americans!*

A classic instance of missing the mark by diverting attention away from core ills to more telegenic pep-rally symptoms. The problems visible everywhere in major U.S. cities and in failing global policies are not based on a schoolyard *He-said…She said…Did so!* spat, but on deeply rooted socioeconomic disparities and hopelessly outdated ideologies that cannot ever be overcome without *real conflicts* carried out in ways that would likely get far more vicious than a simple bedroom/boardroom huff. The forces that determine American policies will be quite happy to get along with such a nice, non-confrontational sunny boy—a nationally loved symbol of audaciously impotent hope and harmony that can continue to perpetuate the American illusion.

Many of the problems touched upon in these pages are rooted in the "American Way of Life" itself. Accompanying the pathogenesis of modernity were forces at odds with our collective survival. The adamant insistence that individual liberty, free of the dictates of any external authority, is the highest goal of democracy, leaves vital collective concerns in an ideological no-man's land. At the same time, the democratic process has been replaced by a show-and-tell version of different faces of sameness made up and typecast just like this fall's new TV lineup. All that life ever was, is, or will be is right here before your eyes. Innovations in technology merely bring us one step closer to the inevitable dissolution of social action networks of critical, politically conscious opponents to the existing corporate plutocracy. As Robert Kuttner correctly surmised, "mass media, focus groups, TV advertising, and the treatment of politics as just another form of marketing and mass entertainment have served to further distance citizens from democracy."[12]

With a population content to kick back after work with a downloaded music video or movie and to leave the thinking to others, the most diabolical *schmoozers* and *machers*, plotters and schemers can have free hand at redesigning reality and changing the rules of the game. *Does Enron ring a bell?* If market forces are allowed to dictate what the content of the media message should be as well as how and when that content is delivered, the future of the public as an informed body politic is indeed bleak.

The ostensibly cyclical re-emergence of GOP attitudes, norms, and policies should be seen as historically mediated manifestations of the underlying ideology mentioned in the opening pages of Chapter 4. Just as quantitative thinking has been a fundamental element of Western thought from the time of the Roman Empire, so too is the ideology of individual freedom and the correlate capitalist economic system an identifying characteristic of Classical Liberalism. Both are defining elements in modern Anglo-Saxon history. It is rather the cyclical occurrence of opposing forms of progressive communitarian movements that should be seen as welcome exceptions. This explains in part perhaps why it has proven difficult for the Democratic Party to clearly distinguish itself from the dominant political trend and policies, except in instances of internal conflict, dramatic economic downturns, or in war. The Great Society projects of the Johnson era coincided with the dramatic re-emergence of racism and poverty as sources of societal instability and conflict. "Obama-ism" (as Cass Sunstein dubbed the syndrome) now confirms the rule as America loses its financial and technological hegemony.

Central to the ideology defining the Republican Party is a belief system predicated on the power of "healthy greed" to shape reality in ways believed beneficial to all. Reality has proved the premise wrong. When the going gets tough, the sick, the aged, and the poor fall by the wayside or are cast into oblivion. The conscious decision to permit policies promoting sickness, famine, homelessness, and widespread ecological destruction is despicable in any legitimate ethical system that values life. In the long term, such policies entrap society in a spiral of self-destruction.

The *modus operandi* of corporate capitalism dictates that the competition for profit pull all stops to extract the most from its servants, while giving the least possible in return. The existing Republican model of globalization has in effect resurrected the basic architecture of feudalism as human labor is forced into take-it-or-leave-it, live or-die alternatives between "the Man" and poverty. Absent a larger state-enforced social safety net, the actual monetary reward for hours of minimum wage labor cannot guarantee survival as promised in the post-war baby-boom years.

The American economic system is predicated on individual self-reliance and the concomitant quest for freedom and independence. The premises of such a system make no provisions for those who for whatever reason don't make it. But instead of calling a general theoretical time-out in order to question the moral and societal foundations of this self-perpetuating system, the internalized mechanisms of self-preservation dispel all concerns for the human tragedy of others and the dire outlook for our planet, allowing and even encouraging the successful to turn a blind eye to all negative outcomes of the struggle for economic survival.

Modernity's emancipation culminated in the American declaration sanctifying life, liberty, and the pursuit of individual happiness; the muted voice of its conscience still rings out in the *Universal Declaration of Human Rights*. Instrumental reason culminated in globalization with an essentially American character. From Beijing and Bangalore to the hyper-modern hotels of Dubai, the resultant radical overhaul of traditional modes of contact, interaction, and commerce are defined by the quest to have, and to be, the biggest, tallest, fastest, strongest. The promising emancipative potential introduced by the leveling of archaic power structures has failed to rid itself of that destructive counterpart rooted in the pathogenesis of modernity itself. Progress is thus reduced once again to the reversed formula of haphazard irrational goals as the bastard offspring of privatization schemes. Philosophy's failure to legitimize those overarching cosmopolitan concerns affecting us all has left us wanting for an effective counterweight to the status quo.

Not all Americans have fallen equally for the identity scheme defined by wealth and the accumulation of consumer items. Many of the discontented have abandoned the political realm altogether, preferring instead to create their own personal, communal versions of a safer, more just world. Such an approach suffers ultimately from the inefficacy created by a closed system of influence. The problems we face are so massive and threatening that nothing short of a radical reorientation of our collective goals and actions on a planetary scale can even hope to reverse the course of destruction we find ourselves on. Even without the worst-case scenarios of rising ocean levels, melting polar ice, and storms and droughts of unprecedented magnitude, changes in rainfall patterns and crop cycles alone could force mass displacements of millions of people and animals, with accompanying military conflicts brought on through desperate attempts to avert starvation.

Causes higher than petty individual concerns or ethnic/national interests demand that we cease and desist industrial practices that inflict lasting harm on our planet. Legislative lip-service will do little to help. Luckily, there are still many individual Americans who are ready and willing to join forces with other equally concerned citizens from all continents, creeds, and walks of life in a united purpose to protect our planetary future. Their voices are still largely unheard, their actions still largely impotent.

The damage already inflicted on this planet may be irreversible. But the political bodies and industrial interests that continue to unleash many of capitalism's most destructive forces are not themselves invulnerable. Progressive thinkers around the world must relearn and master the instruments of organized dissent and revolt. Recent trends among the more politicized elements of civil society reveal a vast potential for internet-connected movements of truly global dimensions. Raising the awareness of citizens around the world to the impact industry-government policies are having is merely the first step in any organized countermovement. Concerned citizens, scientists, and sympathetic politicians should use the phenomenal power of international boycotts, organized through vast networks in constant communication with each other, to teach those who would willingly sacrifice our planet for the sake of profit, that there is a heavy price to pay for callous decisions. When tens of millions of people worldwide join forces to punish the culprits, their helpers and helpers' helpers by refusing to buy their products or patronize their services, the message will hit hard and fast. Such concerted action should have been the defining response to America's coup d'état in 2000—and the people's response should have been relentless.

There should be serious retribution for crimes against the planet; the potential annihilation of millions of forms of life cannot allow statutes to place limits on crimes of a global nature. In an ideal world, an International Court for Planetary Protection and Justice along the lines of the trials at Nürnberg would convict and punish the Bush administration as well as its international industrial partners in environmental crime.

Had concerned and outraged citizens around the world acted as one—*for the common good of life itself*—by refusing to buy anything *Made in USA*, the powers that continue to put the credo of profit over life into the highest offices would have heard the message loud and clear.

The potential power of the people does not stop there. Changes in lifestyle and consumption habits; choices about who to do business with and what charities to give to; forms of civil disobedience and uncivil disruption can challenge the existing system to the breaking point. Many different courses of action are necessary if we are to save our planet from the malignant forces of greed.

There is no guarantee of success, as our efforts may very well fail. But inaction is not a morally acceptable alternative. All who hope—*and hope we must*—for a better world and a future blessed with the magnificence of life itself should once again muster the courage and storm the Bastille.

Notes

1 The survey results can be downloaded as a pdf file from http://www.nationalgeographic. com/geosurvey/download/RoperSurvey.pdf.

2 Source: Press release 99-113, September 30 1999, NASA Jet Propulsion Laboratory. Text available at: http://mars.jpl.nasa.gov/msp98/news/mco990930.html.

3 The yearly NCES reports are available as pdf files from http://nces.ed.gov.

4 See Pete Thamel, "The Quick Fix. Schools Where the Only Real Test Is Basketball," *New York Times*, 25 February 2006, A1.

5 Just days after the fatal ambush at a local Jonesboro, Arkansas, school in March of 1998 in which four middle school girls and a teacher were killed and eleven others wounded, "concerned parents" were emphasizing the necessity of teaching their children of the dangers that lurk in our evil world and that children must learn to resist these "dark forces." What they had in mind, *mutatis mutandis*, was of course gay men and sexual predators, along with an added dose of secular liberals no doubt. The boys themselves, Mitchell Johnson (13) and Andrew Golden (11) had been armed with no less than: 1 universal .30-caliber carbine; 1 Davis Ind. .38 special 2-shot; 1 .380 rifle; 1 Ruger Security Six .357 caliber revolver; 1 Remington 722, .30-06 caliber; 1 Smith & Wesson .38-caliber pistol; 1 Double Deuce Buddie 2-shot derringer; 1 Charter Arms .38 special pistol; 1 Star .380-caliber semiautomatic; 3 pocketknives; 19 .44-caliber shells; 60 .38-caliber shells; 67 .357-caliber shells; 13 .30-06 shells; 49 .380-caliber shells; 2 .30-06 clips; 2 speed loaders (loaded with .38 shells); 6 .22-caliber shells; 10 .38-caliber "Rat Sot"; 16 .38 special shells; 6 .30-caliber shells. (Source: *Los Angeles Times*, 28 March 1998).

6 See in particular the trilogy: *Blowback: The Costs and Consequences of American Empire* (New York: Henry Holt & Co., Inc.) 2003; *The Sorrows of Empire: Militarism, Secrecy, and the End of the Republic* (New York, Holt Paperbacks, 2004); *Nemesis: The Last Days of the American Republic* (New York, Holt Paperbacks, 2008).

7 In contrast to most other industrialized nations, the USA allows its drug corporations to set their own prices, free of government control. Governments in other leading industrialized nations set price controls over pharmaceuticals, not to mention making health care available for all. America's drug industry argues that the profits it gains yearly from those desperate to live are necessary for further research and development. Still, profits achieved by pharmaceutical giants have been rising exponentially on a yearly basis, with many increasing the prices of their leading medications by hundreds of percent in just weeks.

8 Holly Sklar, "Wanted: A High-Road Economy," TomPaine.com, 17 March 2006.

9 Adam Hughes, "Bankrupt Nation," Tompaine.com, 4 April 2006.

10 Susan Neiman, *Evil in Modern Thought: An Alternative History of Philosophy* (Princeton: Princeton University Press, 2002) 287.

11 Holly Sklar, *supra* n. 8.

12 Robert Kuttner, *The Squandering of America. How the Failure of Our Politics Undermines Our Prosperity* (New York: Alfred A. Knopf, 2007) 268.

Index

THE NEW LEFT: Legacy and Continuity
Dimitrios Roussopoulos, editor

The greatest contribution of the New Left of the 1960s was its determination to build a culture and politics of popular participation at every level of society. A radical conception of democracy, called participatory democracy, inspired the movements for civil rights, for world peace and human solidarity, and which evolved in the following decade into a larger movement for gender and sexual equality. It framed the social and political debate, in terms of community-centered democratic theory, that continues to guide, and inspire, well into the 21st century.

As the contributors to this anthology revisit the sixties to identify its ongoing impact on North American politics and culture, it becomes evident how this legacy has blended with, and has influenced today's world-wide social movements. Apart from evoking memories of past peace and freedom struggles from those who worked on the social movements of the 1960s, this work also includes a number of essays from a rising generation of intellectual and activists, too young to have experienced the 1960s firsthand, whose perspective enables them to offer fresh insights and analyses.

> "An eclectic mix of memoir and commentary that accents the legacies of the 60s rebellious youth, and the continuities of the political dissent and oppositional challenges of that decade." —*Canadian Dimension*

Contributors include: Dimitrios Roussopoulos, Andrea Levy, Anthony Hyde, Jacques Martin, Mark Rudd, Katherina Haris, Gregory Nevala Calvert, Natasha Kapoor, and Tom Hayden.

DIMITRIOS ROUSSOPOULOS was a prominent New Left activist in the 1960s, locally and internationally. He continues to write and edit on major issues while being a committed activist testing theory with practice. He is the author and/or editor of some eighteen books, the most recent being *Faith in Faithlessness: An Anthology of Atheism* (2008).

2007: 224 pages
Paperback ISBN: 978-1-55164-298-7 $19.99
Hardcover ISBN:978-1-55164-299-4 $48.99

AFTER PATRICK HENRY: A Second American Revolution
Neal Q. Herrick

Author Neal Herrick considers government corruption to be the predominant problem facing the world today. Although bribery and influence peddling are the most visible aspect of this corruption, they are not, in Herrick's opinion, the most serious. For Herrick, the more serious aspect of government corruption is the laws that bribery and influence peddling produce—laws that favor the corporations—resulting in, what he calls, a kind of delusional corruption that leads to unjust and unnecessary wars. *After Patrick Henry* is a book about both kinds of corruption, as they are inseparable and arise from the same structural 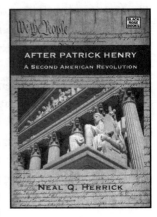 failing: the failure to make the interests of government coincident with the interests of the people.

> "What a great book! A powerful indictment ... well researched and grounded!" —A. Robert Smith, *The Tiger in the Senate*

> "Herrick ... knows not just politics, but government from the inside. A good critical read." —Dick Howard, *The Specter of Democracy*

> "Rigorous and disarmingly honest." —Rev. Dr. Howard E. Friend, Jr., *Voice from the Edge*

> "A profoundly insightful analysis of the historical journey leading to the circumstances in which we now find ourselves, that proposes a clear and compelling way forward." —Terry Mazany, President and CEO of the Chicago Community Trust

Author and editor of three books on constitutional theory, NEAL Q. HERRICK is a retired University of Michigan academic in industrial relations who headed the HEW/Labor task force that drafted the Occupational Safety and Health Act submitted to Congress in 1968.

2008: 475 pages
Paperback ISBN: 978-1-55164-320-5 $24.99
Hardcover ISBN: 978-1-55164-321-2 $44.99

SCRAMBLE FOR AFRICA: Darfur—Intervention and the USA
Steven Fake and Kevin Funk

The Scramble for Africa analyzes the current humanitarian crisis in Darfur and the activist movements surrounding it, thereby taking on both the U.S. Government and the Save Darfur coalition alike. The authors present the basic information on the political and military aspects of the conflict, examine the options, and suggest ways forward, always with a concern for the broader international implications and for the hundreds of thousands of victims.

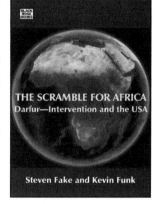

"This extremely well-documented work ... combines deep compassion with a keen critical analysis to show how we might best support the suffering people of Darfur." —Stephen R. Shalom, *Imperial Alibis: Rationalizing U.S. Intervention After the Cold War*

"One of the few works to tackle honestly the vexing question of what is to be done about Darfur." —Rahul Mahajan, *Full Spectrum Dominance: U.S. Power in Iraq and Beyond*

"Offers a fresh analysis of Darfur in its larger geopolitical context. It belongs on every Darfur activist's bookshelf." —David Morse, activist and journalist

"This excellent book is exactly what is needed and I hope it is very widely read. I will recommend it to everyone." —Justin Podur, writer and activist

STEVEN FAKE is an activist and political commentator. He is a graduate of the University of Pittsburgh, and a member of the Lucy Parson Center. KEVIN FUNK earned degrees in Journalism, Political Science, and Latin American Studies from the University of Pittsburgh. An activist himself, Funk writes frequently on U.S. foreign policy.

2008: 208 pages
Paperback ISBN: 978-1-55164-322-9 $19.99
Hardcover ISBN: 978-1-55164-323-6 $39.99

Also Available from BLACK ROSE BOOKS

ADVENTURES ALONG BORDERS: Personal Reminiscences
Graeme S. Mount

For decades as a History Professor at Laurentian University, Graeme Mount taught a course on global history during the 20th century. Lesson preparation and research took him to all continents except Antarctica, and he pursued a lifelong interest in international borders. Most border crossings were uneventful, others highly memorable, as were the occasions when he approached, but did not actually cross, borders. These pages recount his most noteworthy adventures at, and along, international borders.

Borders in question include the one between Canada and the United States; borders of the former Yugoslavia in 1989 with Albania and Romania; certain Latin American borders; the inter-German border three months before the opening of the Berlin Wall; the border between Austria and Hungary in August 1989, between the removal of the physical Iron Curtain between those two countries and the opening of the border so that East Germans could circumvent the Berlin Wall and drive to West Germany; the Inter-Irish border during the IRA campaign against British rule; Zimbabwe's border with Mozambique in 1990, after Zimbabwean forces intervened in Mozambique's civil war; North Korea's borders with South Korea (1999) and China (2006); and the maritime boundaries of Trinidad and Tobago, Venezuela and Barbados.

> "From a prism of internal and international borders, Mount's study allows a personal yet timely and fascinating examination of some of the suspicions and barriers which we, as humans, have created over time."
> —Aubrey A. Thompson, Morgan State University, Maryland

> "Drawing from a wealth of knowledge and personal experiences coupled with vivid pictures, Mount's lucid and lively writing proves to be an interesting read." —Clint MacNeil, St. Charles College, Ontario

GRAEME S. MOUNT, PhD, is the author of some thirteen books. His most recent is *895 Days That Changed the World: The Presidency of Gerald R. Ford* (2005).

2008: 208 pages, 32-page photo essay
Paperback ISBN: 978-1-55164-324-3 $19.99
Hardcover ISBN: 978-1-55164-325-0 $39.99

PARTICIPATORY DEMOCRACY: Prospects for Democratizing Democracy

Dimitrios Roussopoulos, with C.George Benello

A completely revised edition of the classic and widely consulted 1970 version

First published as a testament to the legacy of the concept made popular by the New Left of the 1960s, and
with the perspective of the intervening decades, this
book opens up the way for re-examining just what is
involved in democratizing democracy. With its emphasis on citizen participation, here, presented in one
volume are the best arguments for participatory democracy written by some of the most relevant contributors to the debate, both in an historic, and in a
contemporary, sense.

This wide-ranging collection probes the historical
roots of participatory democracy in our political culture, analyzes its application to
the problems of modern society, and explores the possible forms it might take on
every level of society from the work place, to the community, to the nation at large.
Part II, "The Politics of Participatory Democracy," covers Porto Alegre, Montreal,
the new Urban ecology, and direct democracy.

> "The book is, by all odds, the most encompassing one so far in revealing
> the practical actual subversions that the New Left wishes to visit upon us."
> —*Washington Post*

Apart from the editors, contributors include: George Woodcock, Murray
Bookchin, Don Calhoun, Stewart Perry, Rosabeth Moss Kanter, James Gillespie,
Gerry Hunnius, John McEwan, Arthur Chickering, Christian Bay, Martin
Oppenheimer, Colin Ward, Sergio Baierle, Anne Latendresse, Bartha Rodin, and
C.L.R. James.

DIMITRIOS ROUSSOPOULOS was a prominent New Left activist in the 1960s,
locally and internationally. He continues to write and edit on major issues while
being a committed activist testing theory with practice. He is the author and/or
editor of some eighteen books, the most recent being *Faith in Faithlessness: An Anthology of Atheism* (2008).

2004: 380 pages
Paperback ISBN: 1-55164-224-7 $24.99
Hardcover ISBN: 1-55164-225-5 $53.99

THORSTEIN VEBLEN AND THE AMERICAN WAY OF LIFE
Louis Patsouras

Thorstein Veblen (1857-1929) was an unrelenting critic of the American way of life. In his first and best-known work, *The Theory of the Leisure Class*, Veblen defined the social attitudes and values that condoned the misuse of wealth and the variety of ways in which the resources of modern society were wasted. Though most famous for the term "conspicuous consumption"—a pattern of consumerism that more than survives to the present day—he also attacked other American institutions and traditions, but his ideas on society were often dismissed because of his reputation as an eccentric. Unsuccessful in his university career and his two marriages, and in his private life described as strange, bitter, and detached, in his books, Veblen shone.

Thorstein Veblen remains a baffling figure in American intellectual history, and this important work, undertaken by Louis Patsouras, attempts both to unravel the riddles that surround his reputation and to assess his varied and important contributions to modern social theory.

By setting Veblen's work in its social and intellectual context, and by considering Veblen not just as an economist or a sociologist—as has been the case up to now—Patsouras also examines Veblen's politics, in particular the early manifestations of American socialism and anarchism, as well as his support of labor unions. Veblen's views are then compared and contrasted with other well-known historical and contemporary thinkers.

In this process, Patsouras makes clear just how vital Veblen was and remains to our cultural and political landscape and why it is that through an understanding of Veblen we can move toward an understanding of modern America.

LOUIS PATSOURAS is Professor of History at Kent State University. His other published works include *Simone Weil and the Socialist Tradition, The Crucible of Socialism, Debating Marx, Essays on Socialism, Continuity and Change in Marxism* and *The Anarchism of Jean Grave*.

2004: 296 pages
Paperback ISBN: 1-55164-228-X $26.99
Hardcover ISBN: 1-55164-229-8 $55.99

CONCISE GUIDE TO GLOBAL HUMAN RIGHTS

Daniel Fischlin, Martha Nandorfy
Prologue by Vandana Shiva

Much more than a simple 'guide to global human rights,' this book is an urgently needed and sophisticated reflection on the vital nature of human rights in the 21st century. Daniel Fischlin and Martha Nandorfy argue that, when the environment, health, water, and food are more at risk than ever before, human rights must become the tangible expression of an 'all-encompassing respect for life.'

"In a world facing the growing challenges of globalized apartheid and pandemic poverty, human rights will determine the future of every one of us and our sustainability as a species. This book allows us at least to reclaim our hope in that future." —Roger Clark, former Secretary General of Amnesty International

"*The Concise Guide to Global Human Rights* is an excellent road map for navigating the labyrinthian challenges posed by globalization. It should be used by human rights activists and students alike." —Micheline Ishay, *The History of Human Rights: From Ancient Times to the Era of Globalization*

"This concise guide to global human rights...reminds us, with Mahatma Gandhi, that only the power of emotional intelligence embodied in heroic...resistance may help transform the law from being the convenience of the powerful into a platform and portal for collective human action for global justice...This eloquent call for the future of human rights and a just world order is a must read." —Dr. Upendra Baxi, University of Warwick

DANIEL FISCHLIN and MARTHA NANDORFY are co-authors of the groundbreaking book *Eduardo Galeano: Through the Looking Glass* (2000). Fischlin is, as well, co-editor with Ajay Heble of *Rebel Musics: Human Rights, Resistant Sounds, and the Politics of Music Making* (2003), in which Nandorfy is a contributor. Both teach at the University of Guelph (Ontario, Canada).

2006: 288 pages
Paperback ISBN: 1-55164-294-8 $24.99
Hardcover ISBN: 1-55164-295-6 $53.99